Seraph of the End
—VAMPIRE REIGN—

14

STORY BY **Takaya Kagami**
ART BY **Yamato Yamamoto**
STORYBOARDS BY **Daisuke Furuya**

CHARACTERS

SHIHO KIMIZUKI

Yuichiro's friend. Smart but abrasive. His Cursed Gear is Kiseki-o, twin blades.

YOICHI SAOTOME

Yuichiro's friend. His sister was killed by a vampire. His Cursed Gear is Gekkouin, a bow.

YUICHIRO HYAKUYA

A boy who escaped from the vampire capital, he has both great kindness and a great desire for revenge. Lone wolf. His Cursed Gear is Asuramaru, a katana.

MITSUBA SANGU

An elite soldier who has been part of the Moon Demon Company since age 13. Bossy. Her Cursed Gear is Tenjiryu, a giant axe.

SHINOA HIRAGI

Guren's subordinate and Yuichiro's surveillance officer. Member of the illustrious Hiragi family. Her Cursed Gear is Shikama Doji, a scythe.

MIKAELA HYAKUYA

Yuichiro's best friend. He was supposedly killed but has come back to life as a vampire. Currently working with Shinoa Squad.

KY LUC

A Fifth Progenitor vampire under Second Progenitor Urd Geales. Currently guarding the two vampires undergoing exposure torture.

MAKOTO NARUMI

Former leader of Narumi Squad. After his entire squad died during the battle of Nagoya, he deserted the Demon Army with Shinoa Squad.

KRUL TEPES

Queen of the Vampires and a Third Progenitor. Dethroned by Ferid.

CROWLEY EUSFORD

A Thirteenth Progenitor vampire. Part of Ferid's faction.

FERID BATHORY

A Seventh Progenitor vampire, he killed Mikaela.

SHIGURE YUKIMI
A 2nd Lieutenant and Guren's subordinate along with Sayuri. Very calm and collected.

SAYURI HANAYORI
A 2nd Lieutenant and Guren's subordinate. She's devoted to Guren.

GUREN ICHINOSE
Lieutenant Colonel of the Moon Demon Company, a Vampire Extermination Unit. He recruited Yuichiro into the Japanese Imperial Demon Army. He's been acting strange ever since the battle in Nagoya... His Cursed Gear is Mahiru-no-yo, a katana.

SHINYA HIRAGI
A Major General and an adopted member of the Hiragi family. He was Mahiru Hiragi's fiancé.

NORITO GOSHI
A Colonel and a member of the Goshi family. He has been friends with Guren since high school.

MITO JUJO
A Colonel and a member of the Jujo family. She has been friends with Guren since high school.

STORY

A mysterious virus decimates the human population, and vampires claim dominion over the world. Yuichiro and his adopted family of orphans are kept as vampire fodder in an underground city until the day Mikaela, Yuichiro's best friend, plots an ill-fated escape for the orphans. Only Yuichiro survives and reaches the surface.

Four years later, Yuichiro enters into the Moon Demon Company, a Vampire Extermination Unit in the Japanese Imperial Demon Army, to enact his revenge. There he gains Asuramaru, a demon-possessed weapon capable of killing vampires. Along with his squad mates Yoichi, Shinoa, Kimizuki and Mitsuba, Yuichiro deploys to Shinjuku with orders to thwart a vampire attack.

In a battle against the vampires, Yuichiro discovers that not only is his friend Mikaela alive, but he also has been turned into a vampire. After misunderstandings and near-misses, Yuichiro and Mikaela finally meet each other in Nagoya.

Kureto Hiragi begins an experiment on the Seraph of the End at Nagoya Airport. Caught up in the cruel procedure, the Moon Demon Company suffers extreme losses. Even worse, Guren appears to betray his friends, participating in the experiment and gravely wounding Yuichiro. To further complicate things, vampires appear to stop the experiment and Ferid stages a coup, capturing the Vampire Queen and throwing everything into chaos.

Declaring enough is enough, Shinoa Squad deserts the Demon Army and escapes Nagoya to hide away in a small seaside town. Ferid tracks them down and tells them that Guren was the one who caused the Catastrophe eight years ago, and that all the answers are in Osaka. The group arrives just in time to meet up with Second Progenitor Urd Geales and a horde of vampire nobles. They're all captured, and Ferid and Krul are sentenced to torture by exposure. Watching both vampires burning under the sun's light, Yu makes the decision to rescue them...

Seraph of the End

—VAMPIRE REIGN—

14

CONTENTS

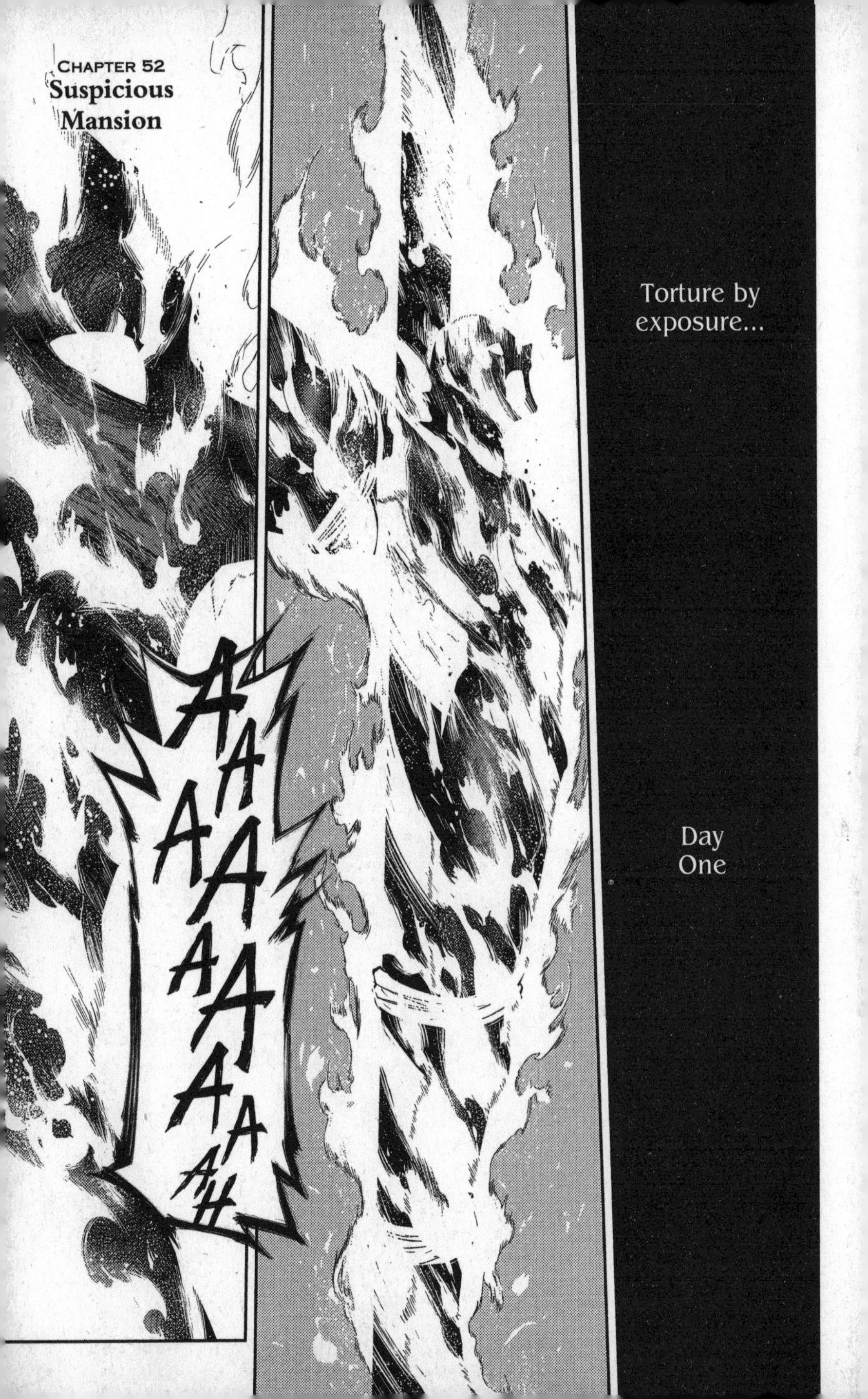
Torture by exposure...
Day One
CHAPTER 52
Suspicious Mansion
AAAAAAAAAAAAH

CHAPTER 52
Suspicious Mansion

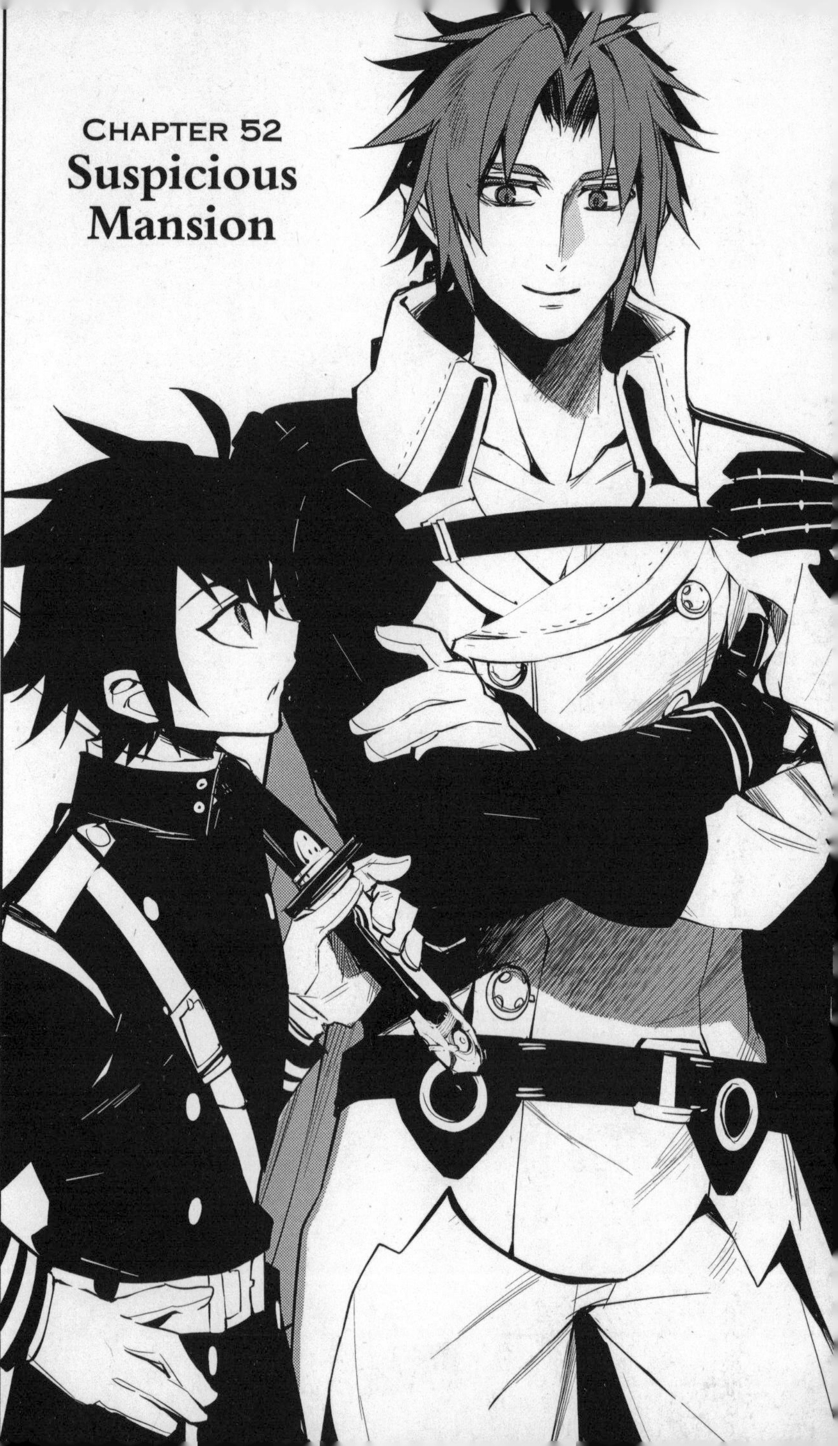

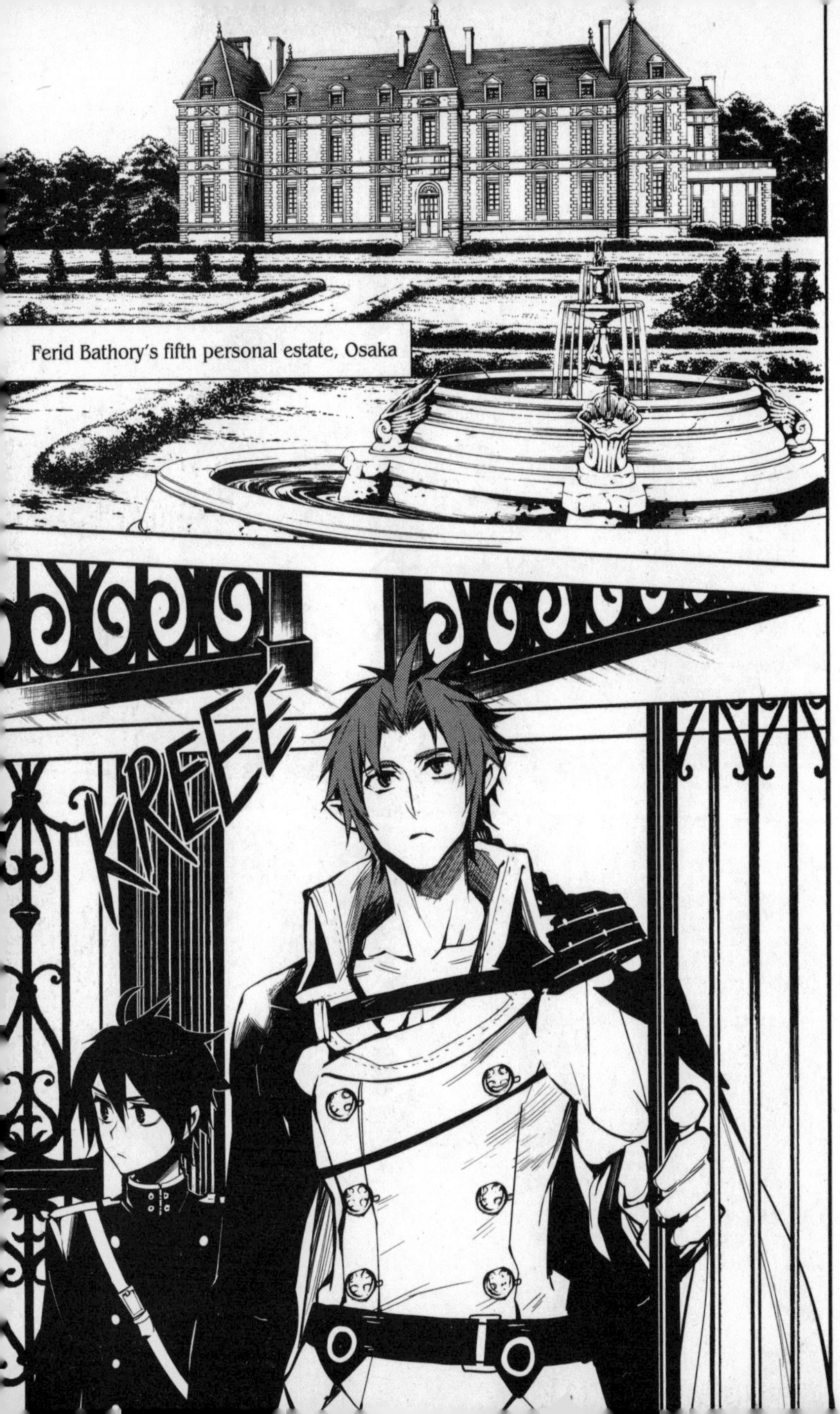
Ferid Bathory's fifth personal estate, Osaka
KREEE

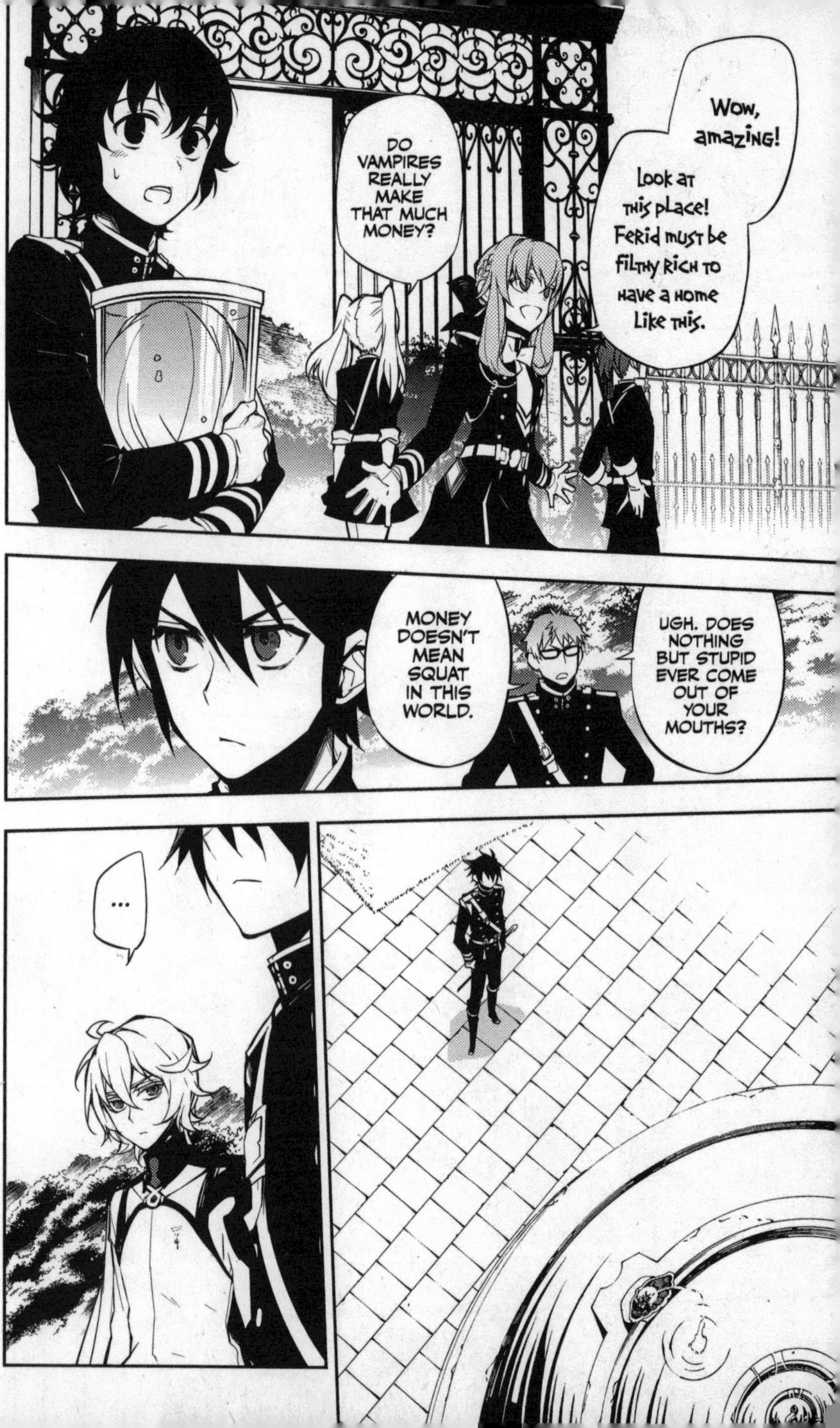
Wow, amazing!
Look at this place! Ferid must be filthy rich to have a home like this.
DO VAMPIRES REALLY MAKE THAT MUCH MONEY?
UGH. DOES NOTHING BUT STUPID EVER COME OUT OF YOUR MOUTHS?
MONEY DOESN'T MEAN SQUAT IN THIS WORLD.
...

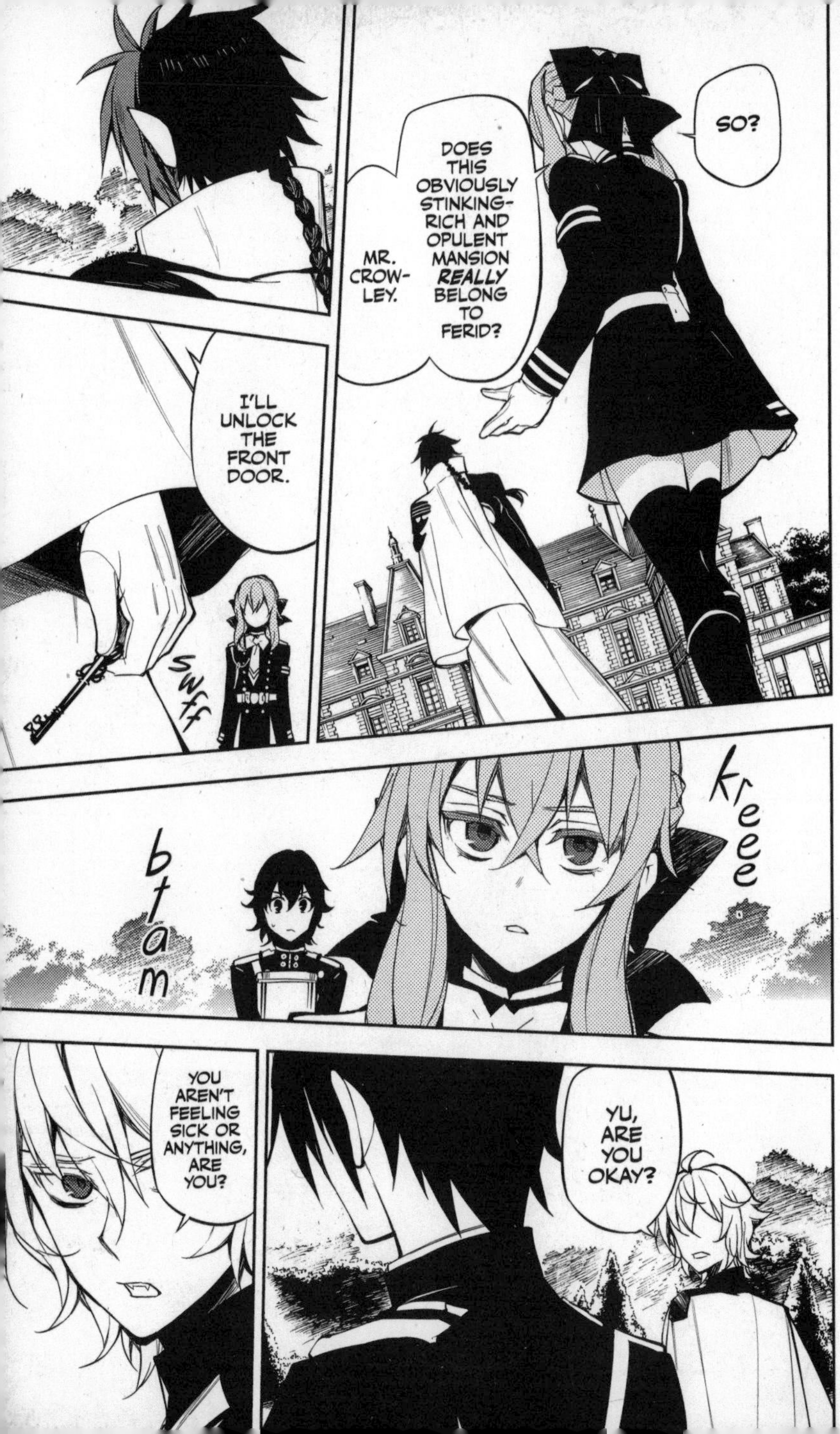
SO?
DOES THIS OBVIOUSLY STINKING-RICH AND OPULENT MANSION *REALLY* BELONG TO FERID?
MR. CROWLEY.
I'LL UNLOCK THE FRONT DOOR.
swff
kreee
btam
YU, ARE YOU OKAY?
YOU AREN'T FEELING SICK OR ANYTHING, ARE YOU?

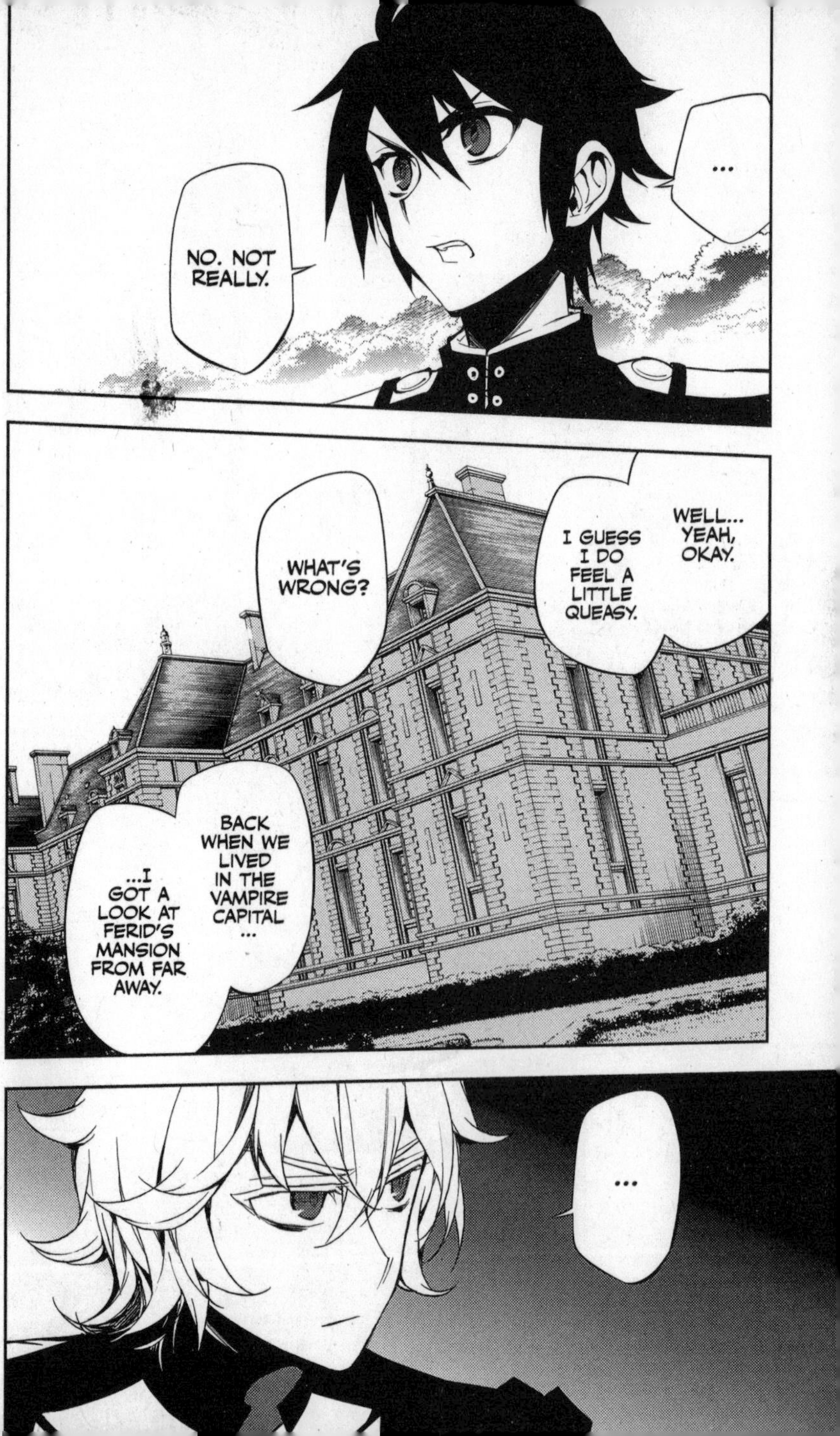
...
NO. NOT REALLY.
WELL... YEAH, OKAY.
I GUESS I DO FEEL A LITTLE QUEASY.
WHAT'S WRONG?
BACK WHEN WE LIVED IN THE VAMPIRE CAPITAL...
...I GOT A LOOK AT FERID'S MANSION FROM FAR AWAY.
...

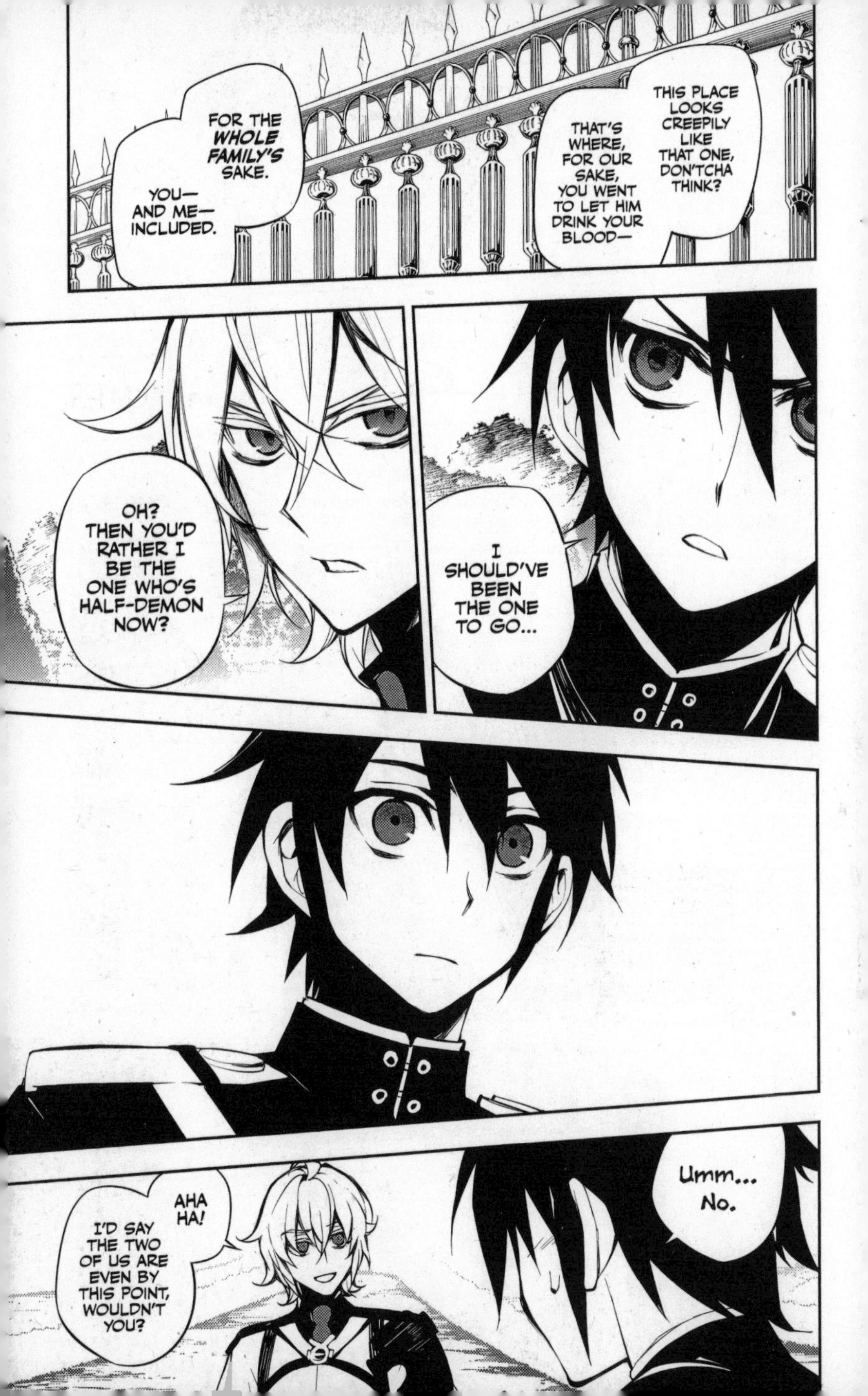
THIS PLACE LOOKS CREEPILY LIKE THAT ONE, DON'TCHA THINK?
THAT'S WHERE, FOR OUR SAKE, YOU WENT TO LET HIM DRINK YOUR BLOOD—
FOR THE *WHOLE FAMILY'S* SAKE.
YOU—AND ME—INCLUDED.
I SHOULD'VE BEEN THE ONE TO GO...
OH? THEN YOU'D RATHER I BE THE ONE WHO'S HALF-DEMON NOW?
Umm... No.
AHA HA!
I'D SAY THE TWO OF US ARE EVEN BY THIS POINT, WOULDN'T YOU?

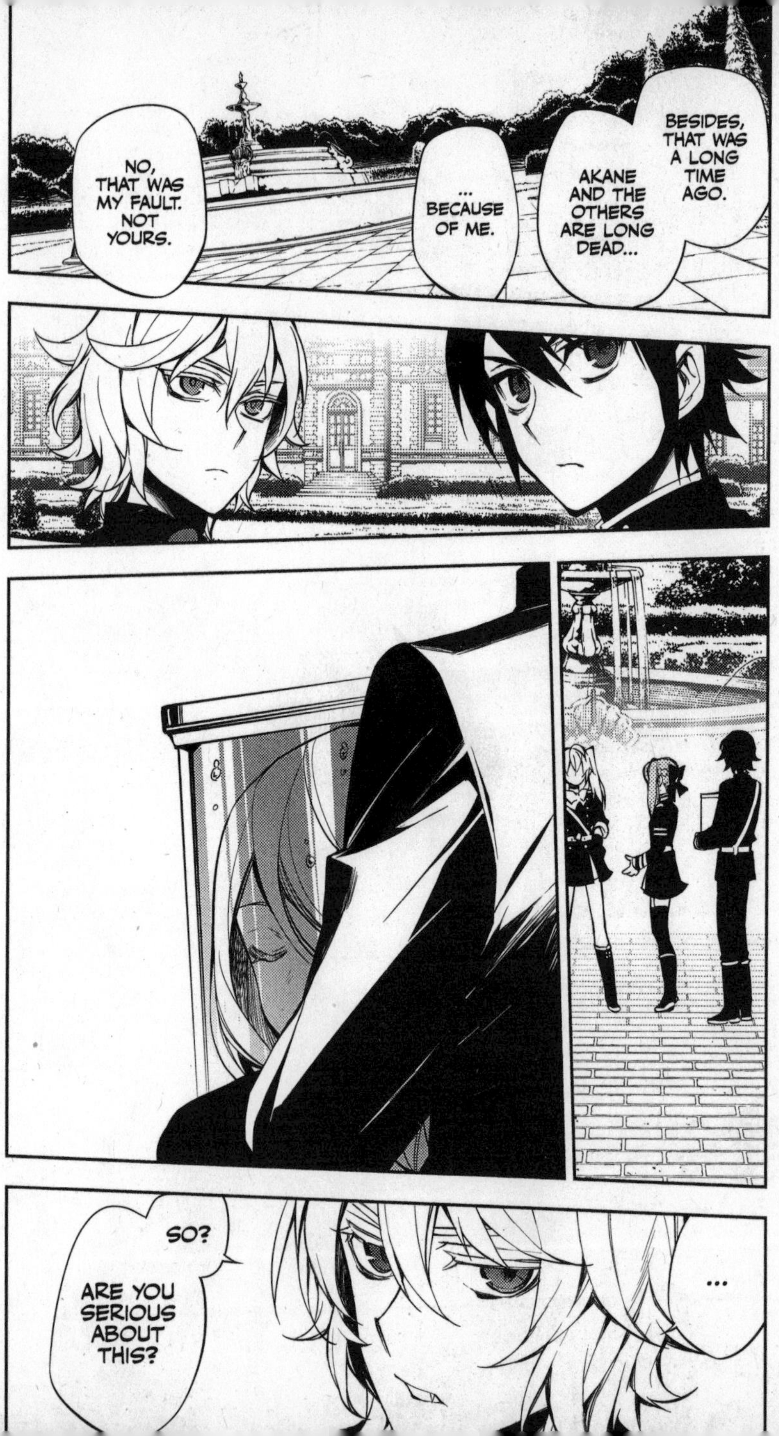
BESIDES, THAT WAS A LONG TIME AGO.
AKANE AND THE OTHERS ARE LONG DEAD...
... BECAUSE OF ME.
NO, THAT WAS MY FAULT. NOT YOURS.
...
SO?
ARE YOU SERIOUS ABOUT THIS?

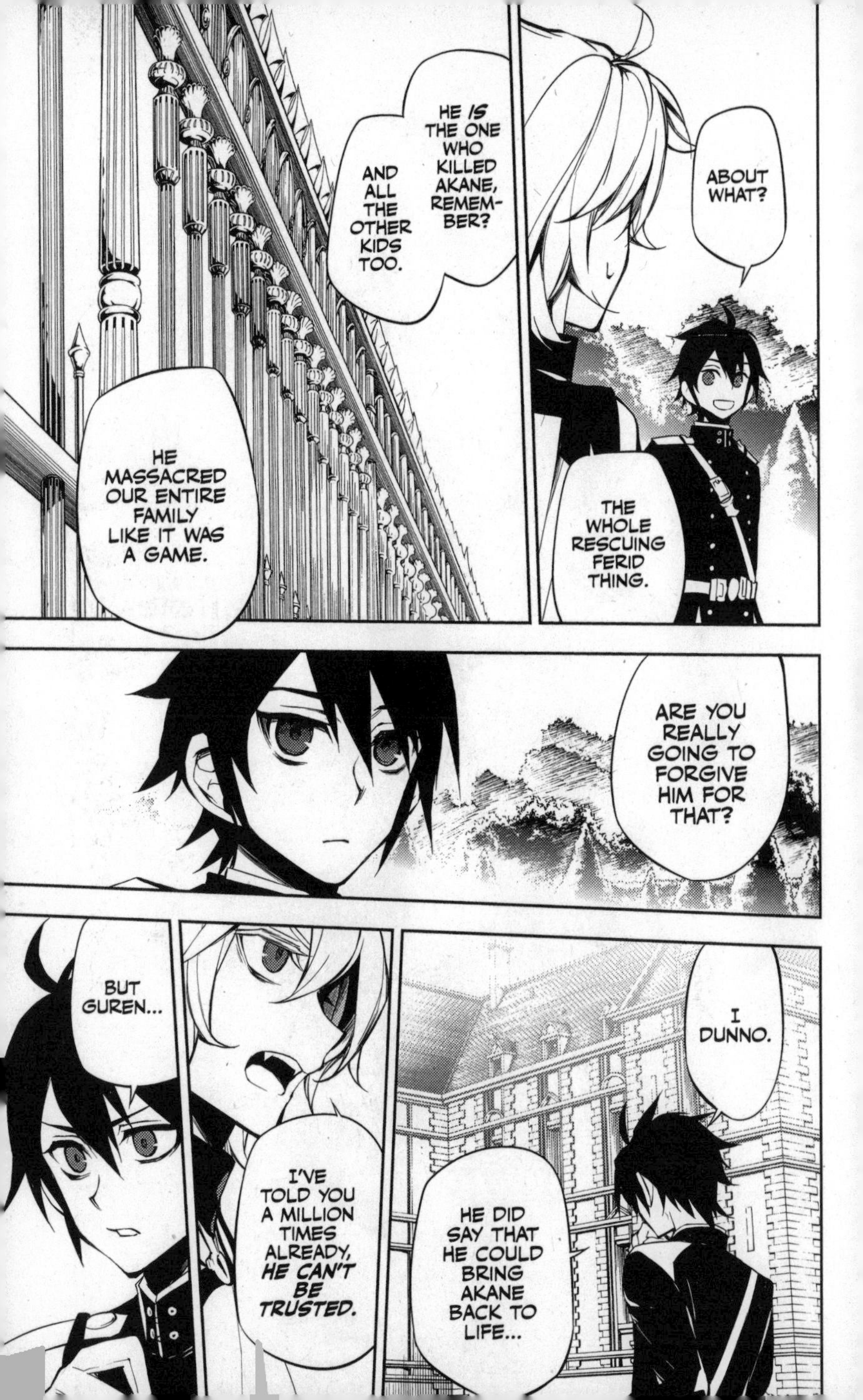
ABOUT WHAT?
THE WHOLE RESCUING FERID THING.
HE *IS* THE ONE WHO KILLED AKANE, REMEMBER?
AND ALL THE OTHER KIDS TOO.
HE MASSACRED OUR ENTIRE FAMILY LIKE IT WAS A GAME.
ARE YOU REALLY GOING TO FORGIVE HIM FOR THAT?
I DUNNO.
HE DID SAY THAT HE COULD BRING AKANE BACK TO LIFE...
I'VE TOLD YOU A MILLION TIMES ALREADY, ***HE CAN'T BE TRUSTED.***
BUT GUREN...

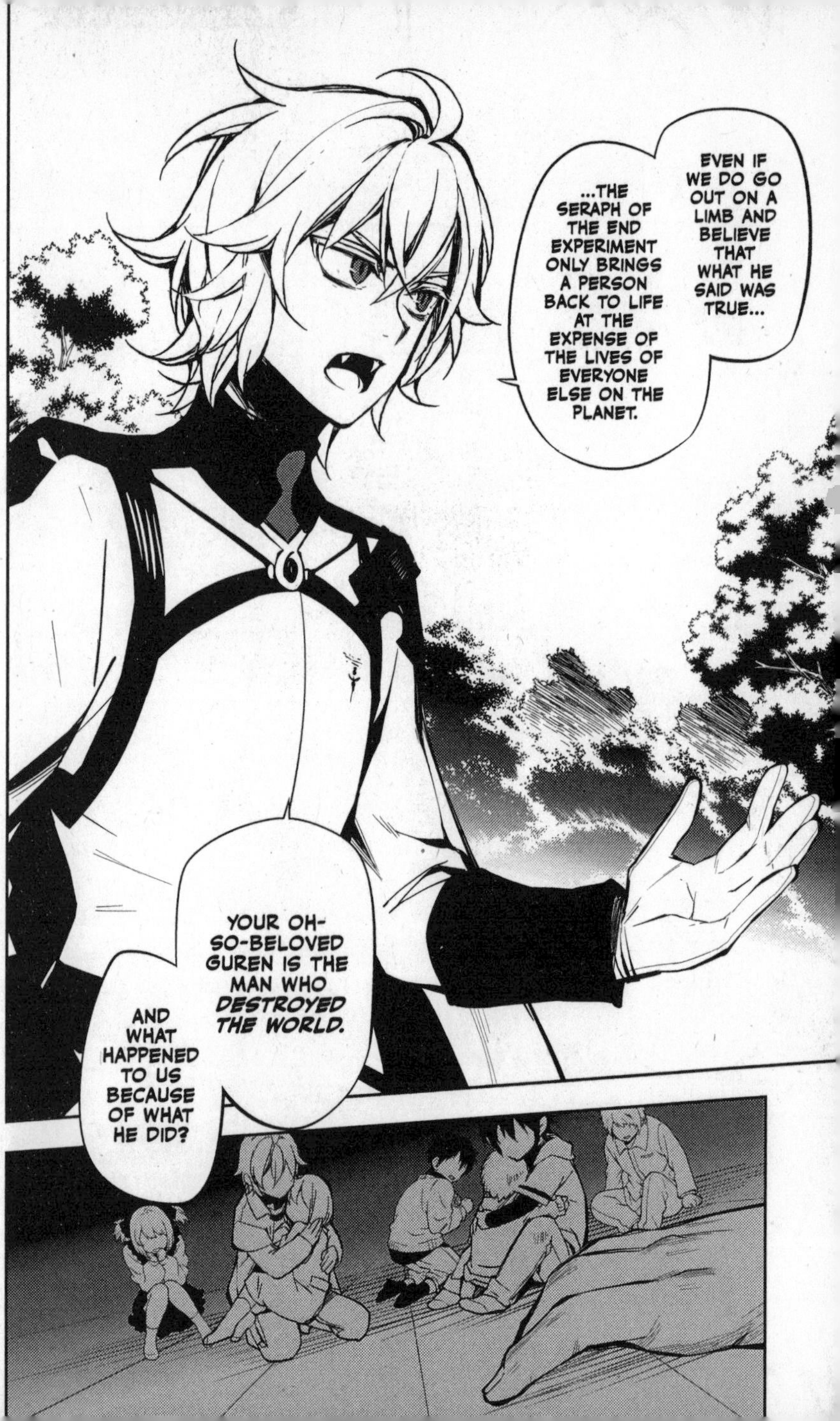
EVEN IF WE DO GO OUT ON A LIMB AND BELIEVE THAT WHAT HE SAID WAS TRUE...
...THE SERAPH OF THE END EXPERIMENT ONLY BRINGS A PERSON BACK TO LIFE AT THE EXPENSE OF THE LIVES OF EVERYONE ELSE ON THE PLANET.
YOUR OH-SO-BELOVED GUREN IS THE MAN WHO *DESTROYED THE WORLD.*
AND WHAT HAPPENED TO US BECAUSE OF WHAT HE DID?

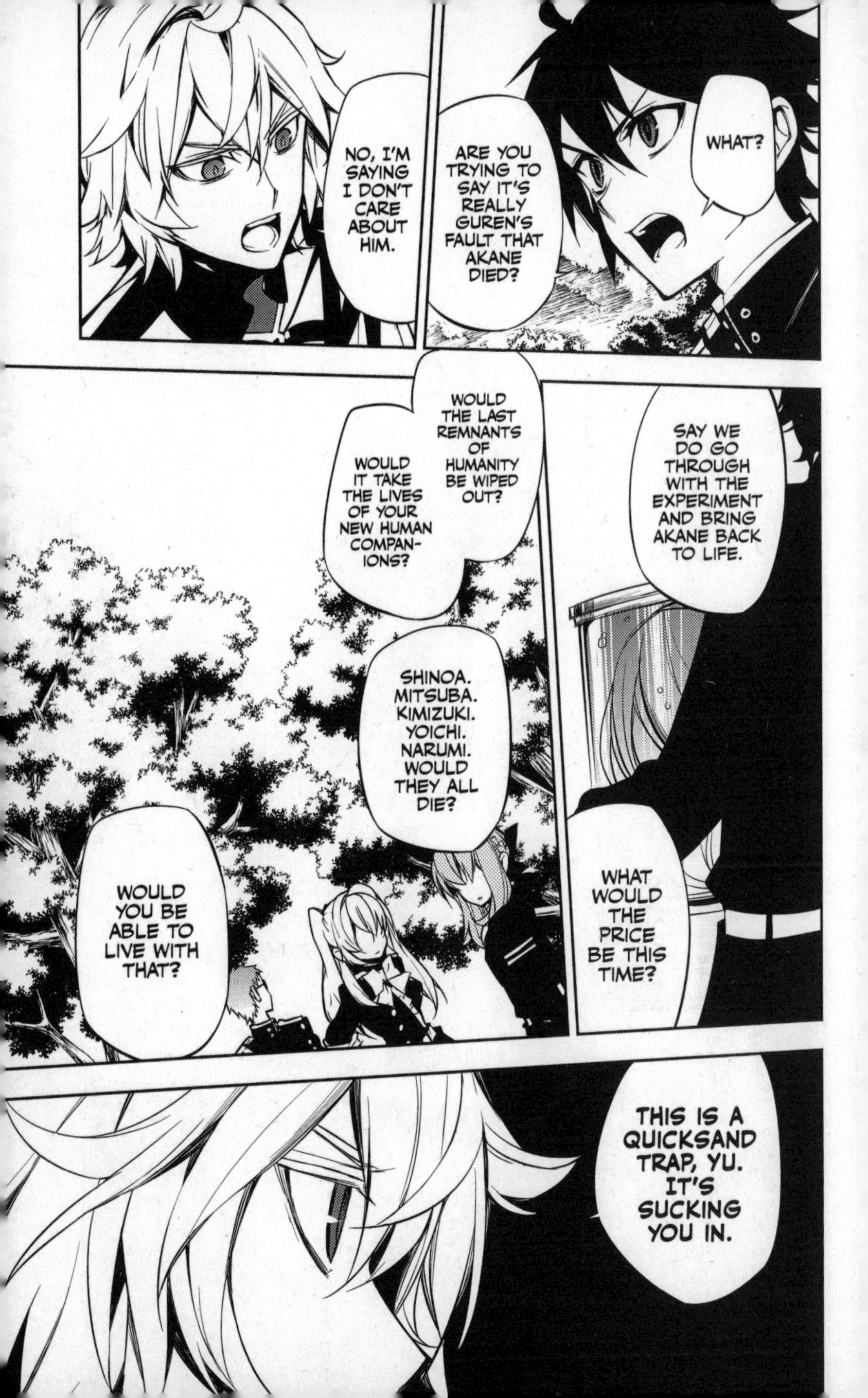
WHAT?
ARE YOU TRYING TO SAY IT'S REALLY GUREN'S FAULT THAT AKANE DIED?
NO, I'M SAYING I DON'T CARE ABOUT HIM.
SAY WE DO GO THROUGH WITH THE EXPERIMENT AND BRING AKANE BACK TO LIFE.
WHAT WOULD THE PRICE BE THIS TIME?
WOULD THE LAST REMNANTS OF HUMANITY BE WIPED OUT?
WOULD IT TAKE THE LIVES OF YOUR NEW HUMAN COMPANIONS?
SHINOA. MITSUBA. KIMIZUKI. YOICHI. NARUMI. WOULD THEY ALL DIE?
WOULD YOU BE ABLE TO LIVE WITH THAT?
THIS IS A QUICKSAND TRAP, YU. IT'S SUCKING YOU IN.

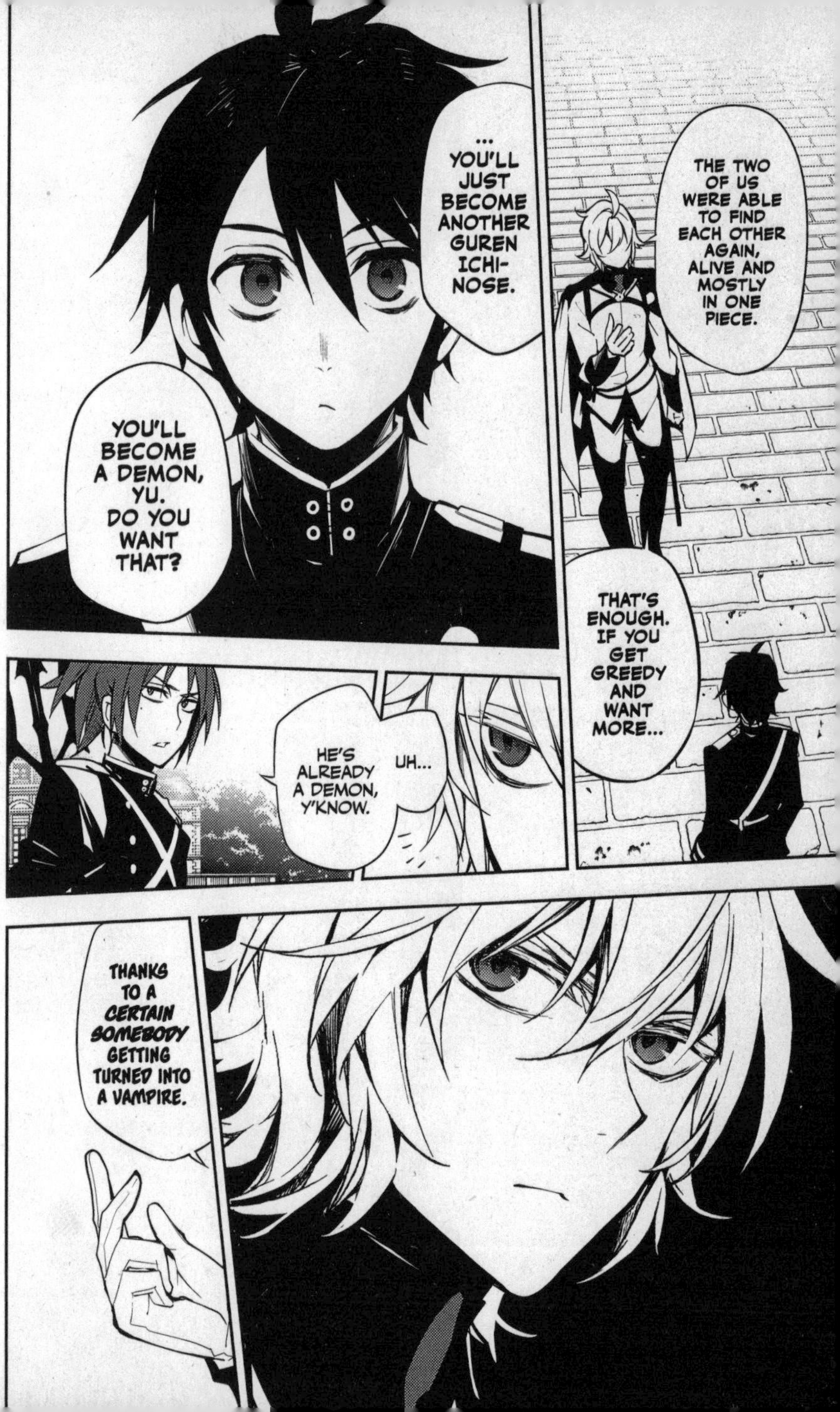
THE TWO OF US WERE ABLE TO FIND EACH OTHER AGAIN, ALIVE AND MOSTLY IN ONE PIECE.
THAT'S ENOUGH. IF YOU GET GREEDY AND WANT MORE...
...YOU'LL JUST BECOME ANOTHER GUREN ICHI-NOSE.
YOU'LL BECOME A DEMON, YU. DO YOU WANT THAT?
UH...
HE'S ALREADY A DEMON, Y'KNOW.
THANKS TO A CERTAIN SOMEBODY GETTING TURNED INTO A VAMPIRE.

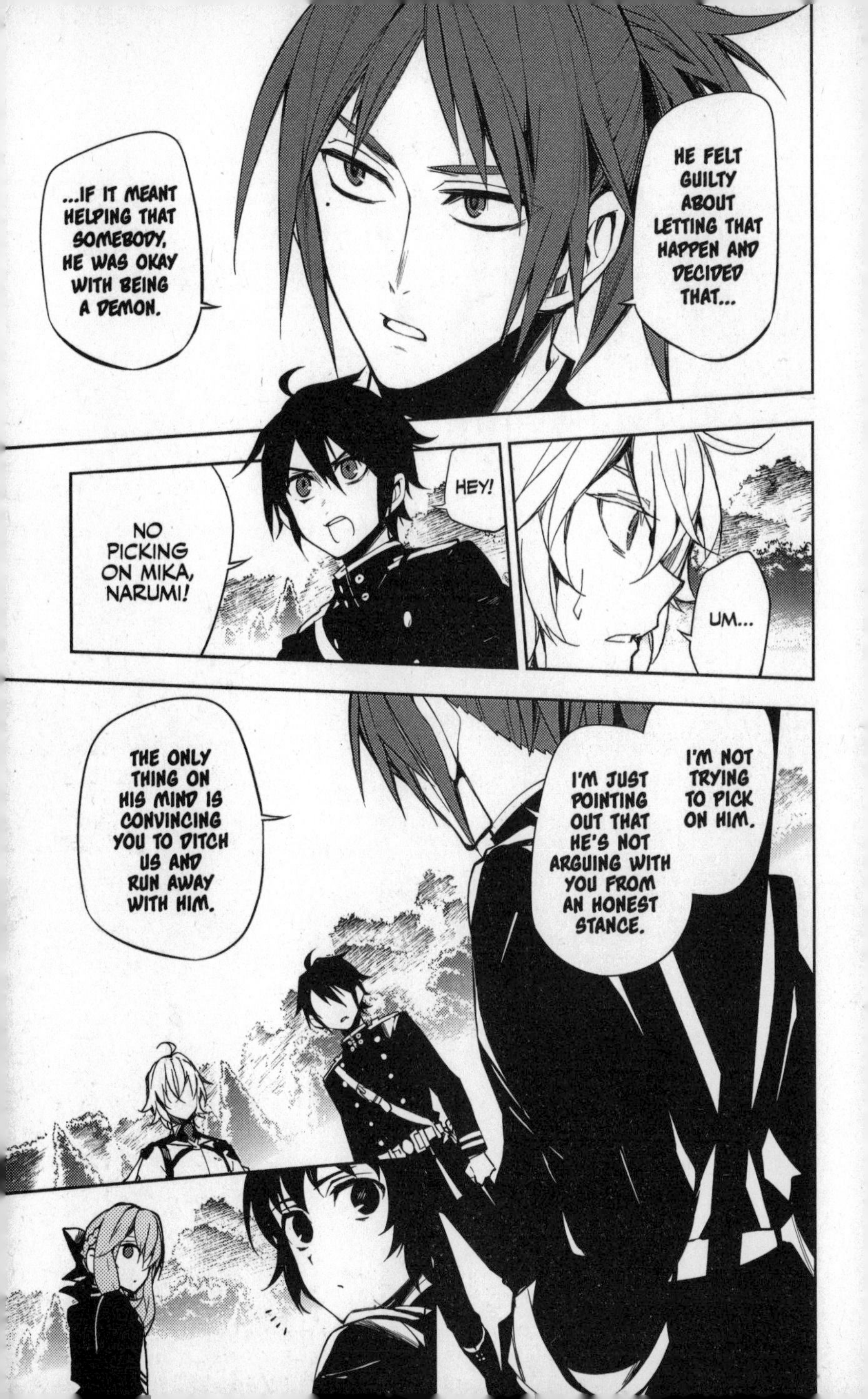
HE FELT GUILTY ABOUT LETTING THAT HAPPEN AND DECIDED THAT...
...IF IT MEANT HELPING THAT SOMEBODY, HE WAS OKAY WITH BEING A DEMON.
UM...
HEY!
NO PICKING ON MIKA, NARUMI!
I'M NOT TRYING TO PICK ON HIM.
I'M JUST POINTING OUT THAT HE'S NOT ARGUING WITH YOU FROM AN HONEST STANCE.
THE ONLY THING ON HIS MIND IS CONVINCING YOU TO DITCH US AND RUN AWAY WITH HIM.

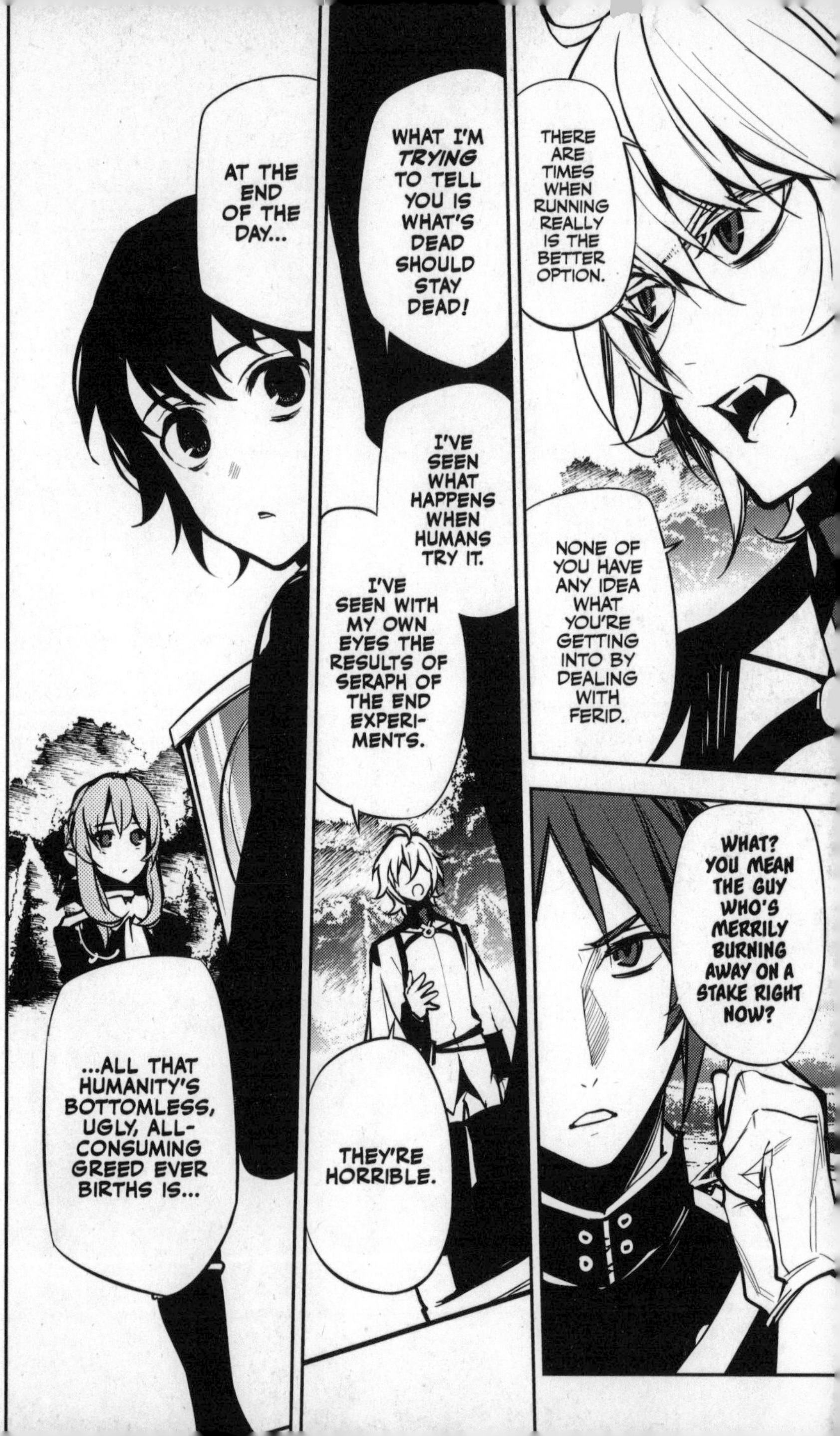
THERE ARE TIMES WHEN RUNNING REALLY IS THE BETTER OPTION.
NONE OF YOU HAVE ANY IDEA WHAT YOU'RE GETTING INTO BY DEALING WITH FERID.
WHAT? YOU MEAN THE GUY WHO'S MERRILY BURNING AWAY ON A STAKE RIGHT NOW?
WHAT I'M *TRYING* TO TELL YOU IS WHAT'S DEAD SHOULD STAY DEAD!
I'VE SEEN WHAT HAPPENS WHEN HUMANS TRY IT.
I'VE SEEN WITH MY OWN EYES THE RESULTS OF SERAPH OF THE END EXPERIMENTS.
THEY'RE HORRIBLE.
AT THE END OF THE DAY...
...ALL THAT HUMANITY'S BOTTOMLESS, UGLY, ALL-CONSUMING GREED EVER BIRTHS IS...

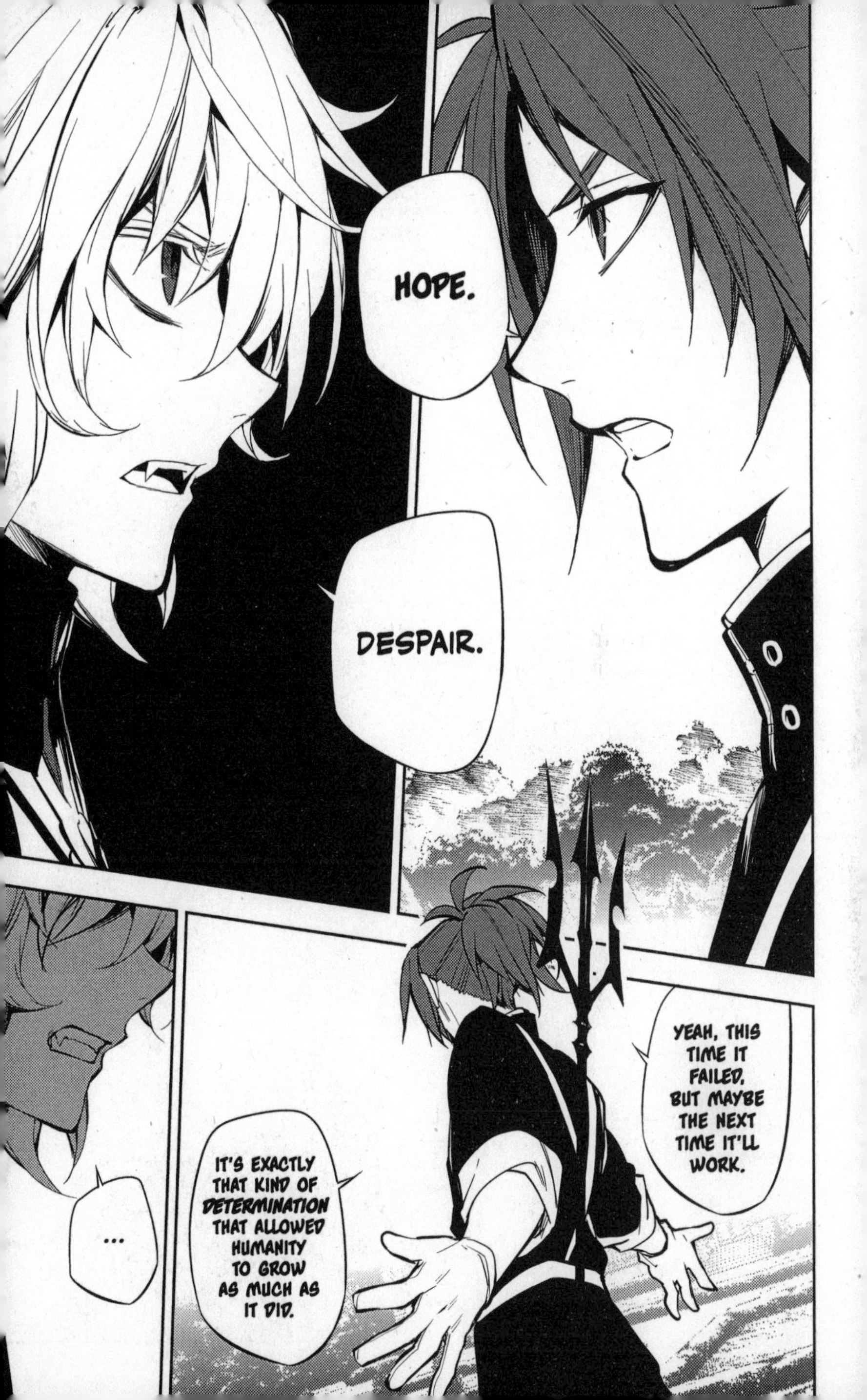
HOPE.
DESPAIR.
YEAH, THIS TIME IT FAILED. BUT MAYBE THE NEXT TIME IT'LL WORK.
IT'S EXACTLY THAT KIND OF DETERMINATION THAT ALLOWED HUMANITY TO GROW AS MUCH AS IT DID.
...

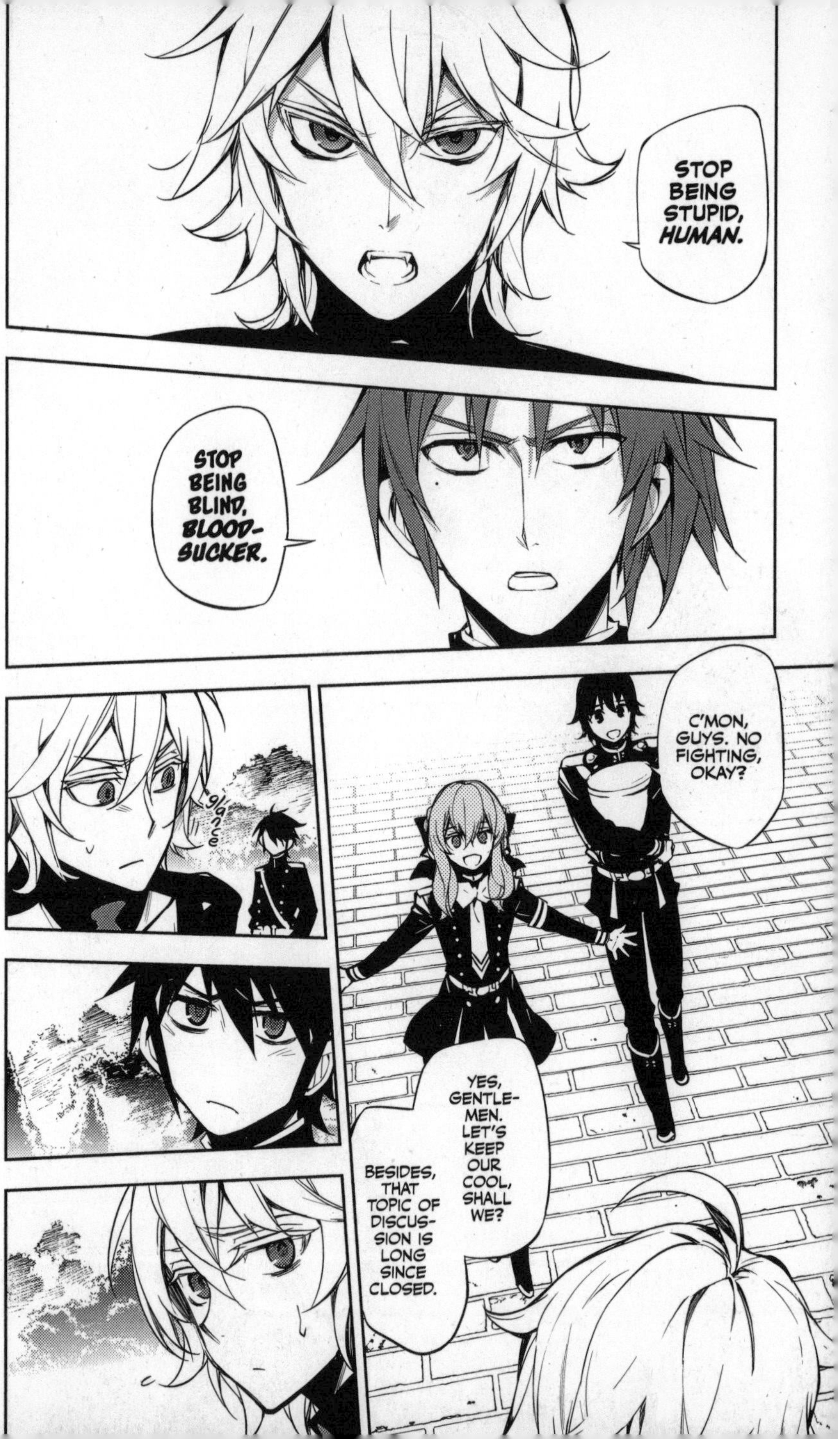
STOP BEING STUPID, HUMAN.
STOP BEING BLIND, BLOOD-SUCKER.
C'MON, GUYS. NO FIGHTING, OKAY?
YES, GENTLE-MEN. LET'S KEEP OUR COOL, SHALL WE?
BESIDES, THAT TOPIC OF DISCUS-SION IS LONG SINCE CLOSED.
glance

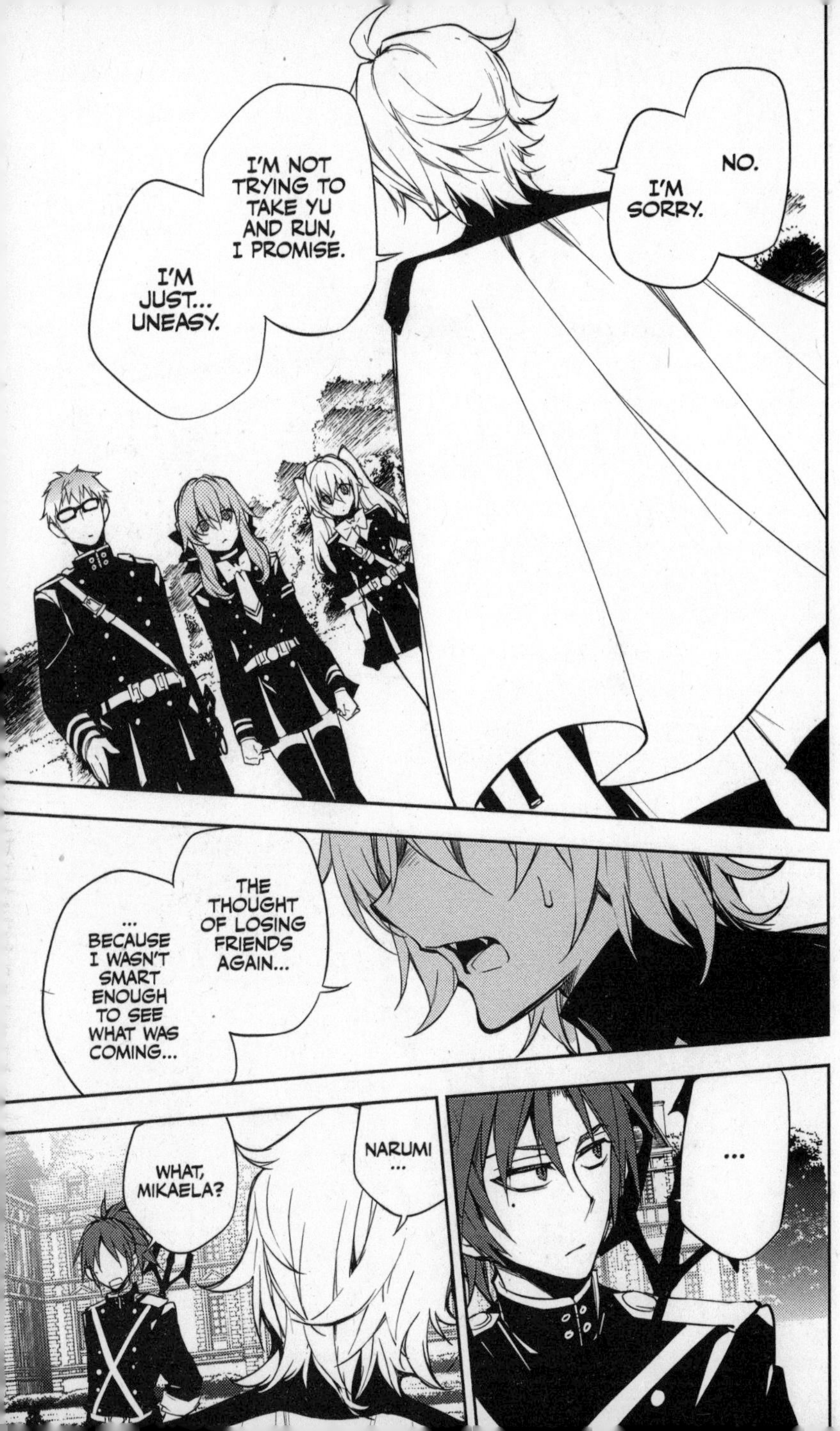
NO.
I'M SORRY.
I'M NOT TRYING TO TAKE YU AND RUN, I PROMISE.
I'M JUST... UNEASY.
THE THOUGHT OF LOSING FRIENDS AGAIN...
...BECAUSE I WASN'T SMART ENOUGH TO SEE WHAT WAS COMING...
...
NARUMI...
WHAT, MIKAELA?

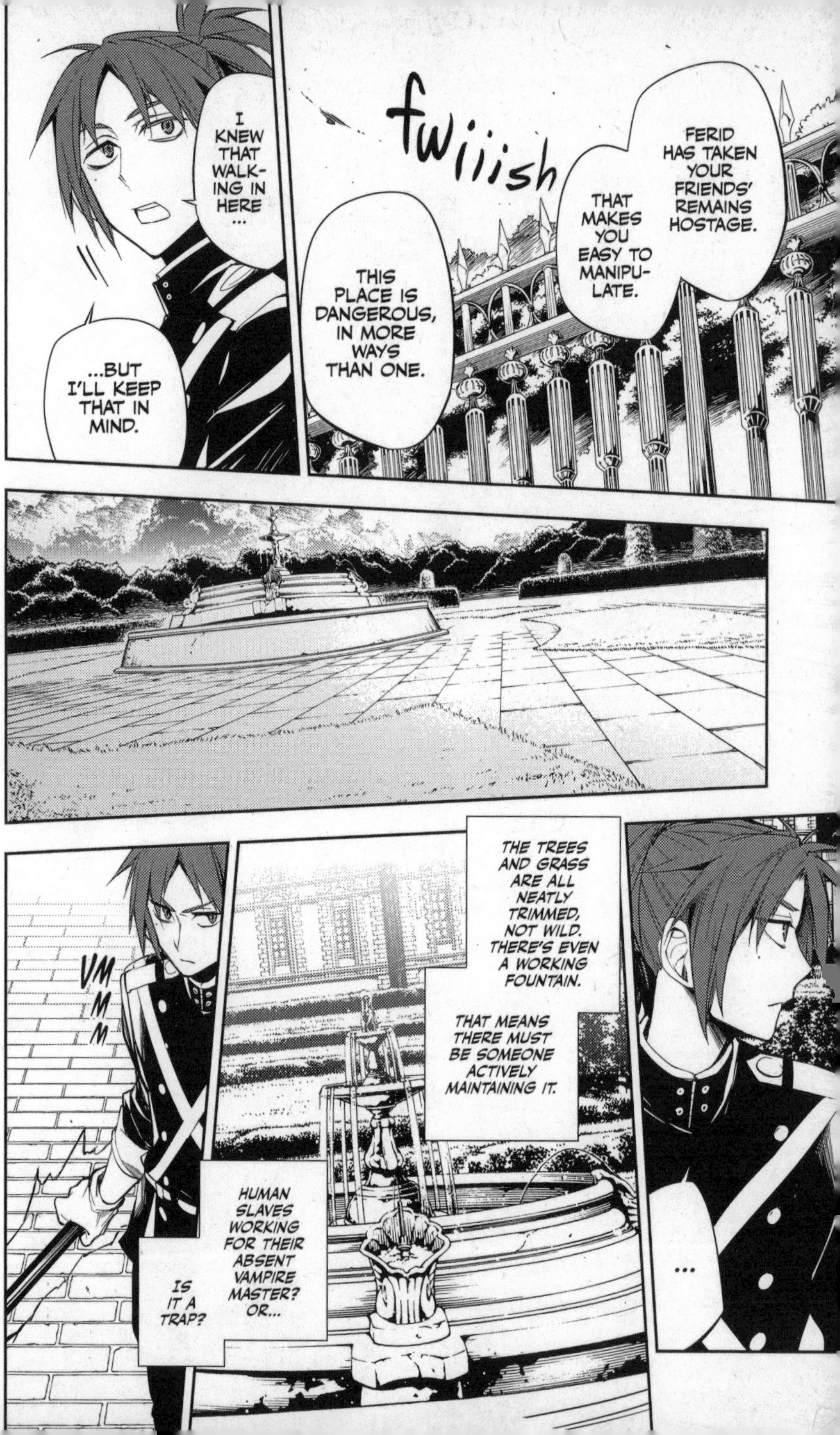
FERID HAS TAKEN YOUR FRIENDS' REMAINS HOSTAGE.
THAT MAKES YOU EASY TO MANIPU-LATE.
fwiiish
THIS PLACE IS DANGEROUS, IN MORE WAYS THAN ONE.
I KNEW THAT WALK-ING IN HERE ...
...BUT I'LL KEEP THAT IN MIND.
...
THE TREES AND GRASS ARE ALL NEATLY TRIMMED, NOT WILD. THERE'S EVEN A WORKING FOUNTAIN.
THAT MEANS THERE MUST BE SOMEONE ACTIVELY MAINTAINING IT.
HUMAN SLAVES WORKING FOR THEIR ABSENT VAMPIRE MASTER? OR...
IS IT A TRAP?
VMMM

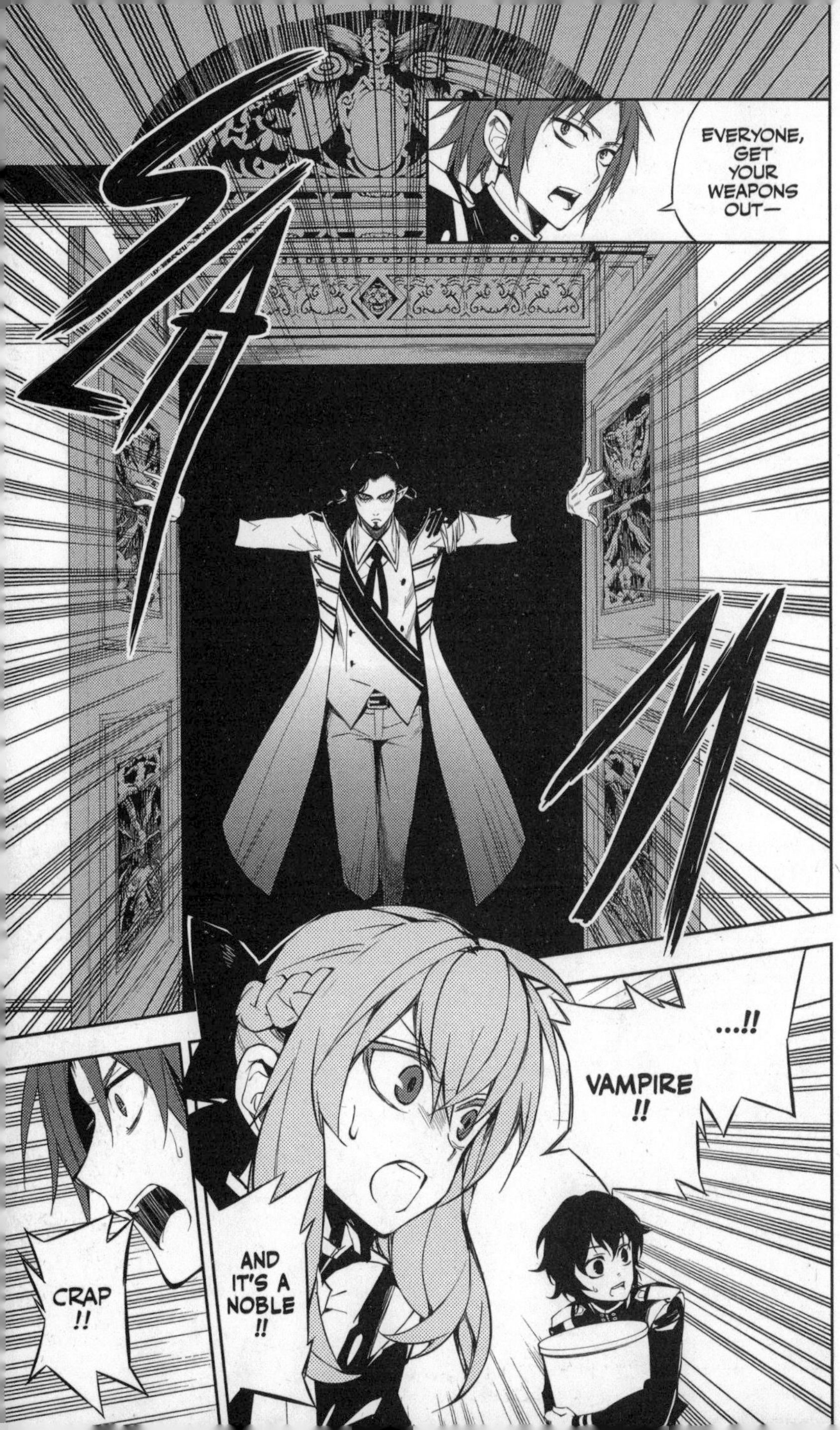
EVERYONE, GET YOUR WEAPONS OUT—
...!!
VAMPIRE !!
AND IT'S A NOBLE !!
CRAP !!

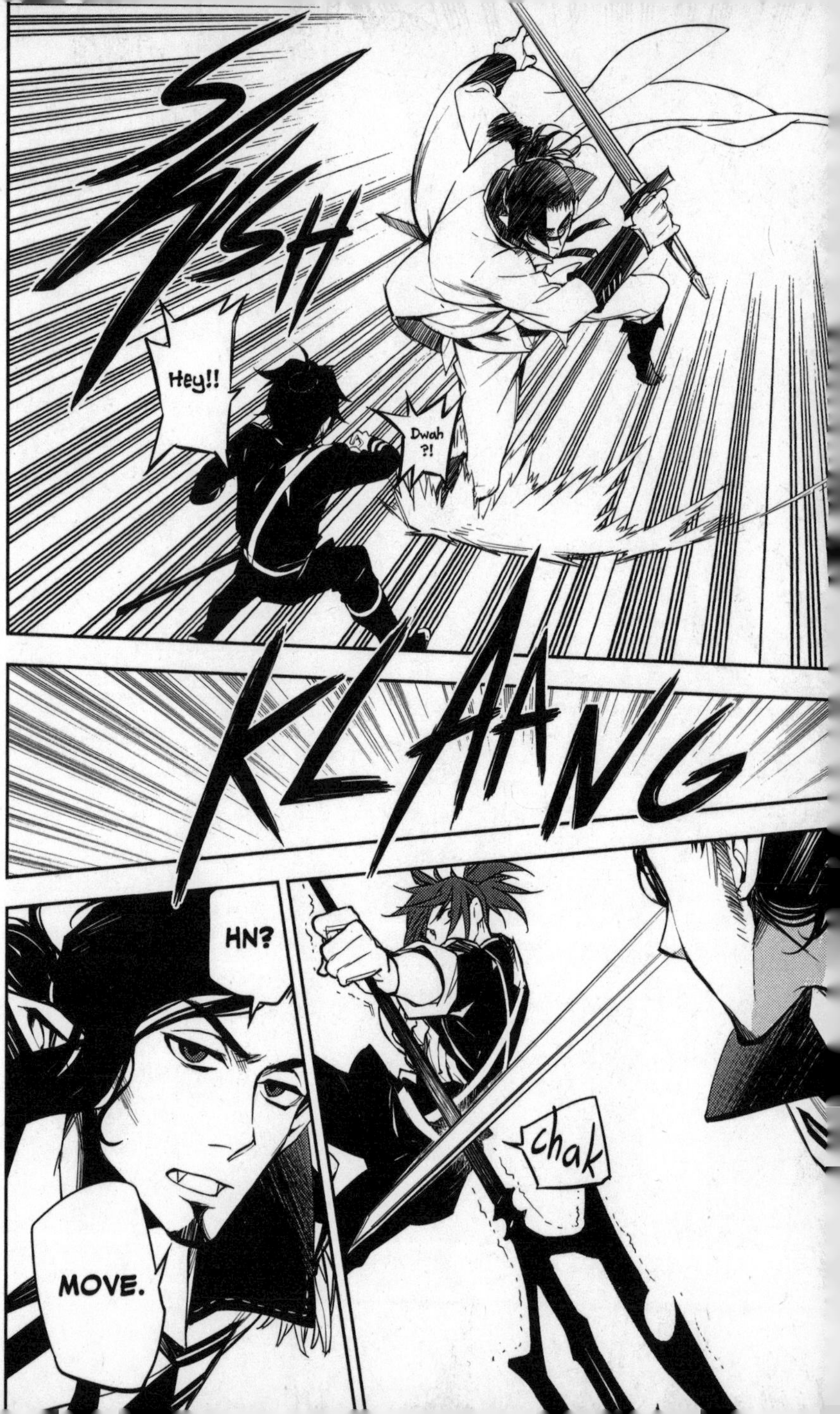

SSH
Dwah ?!
Hey!!
KLAANG
chak
HN?
MOVE.

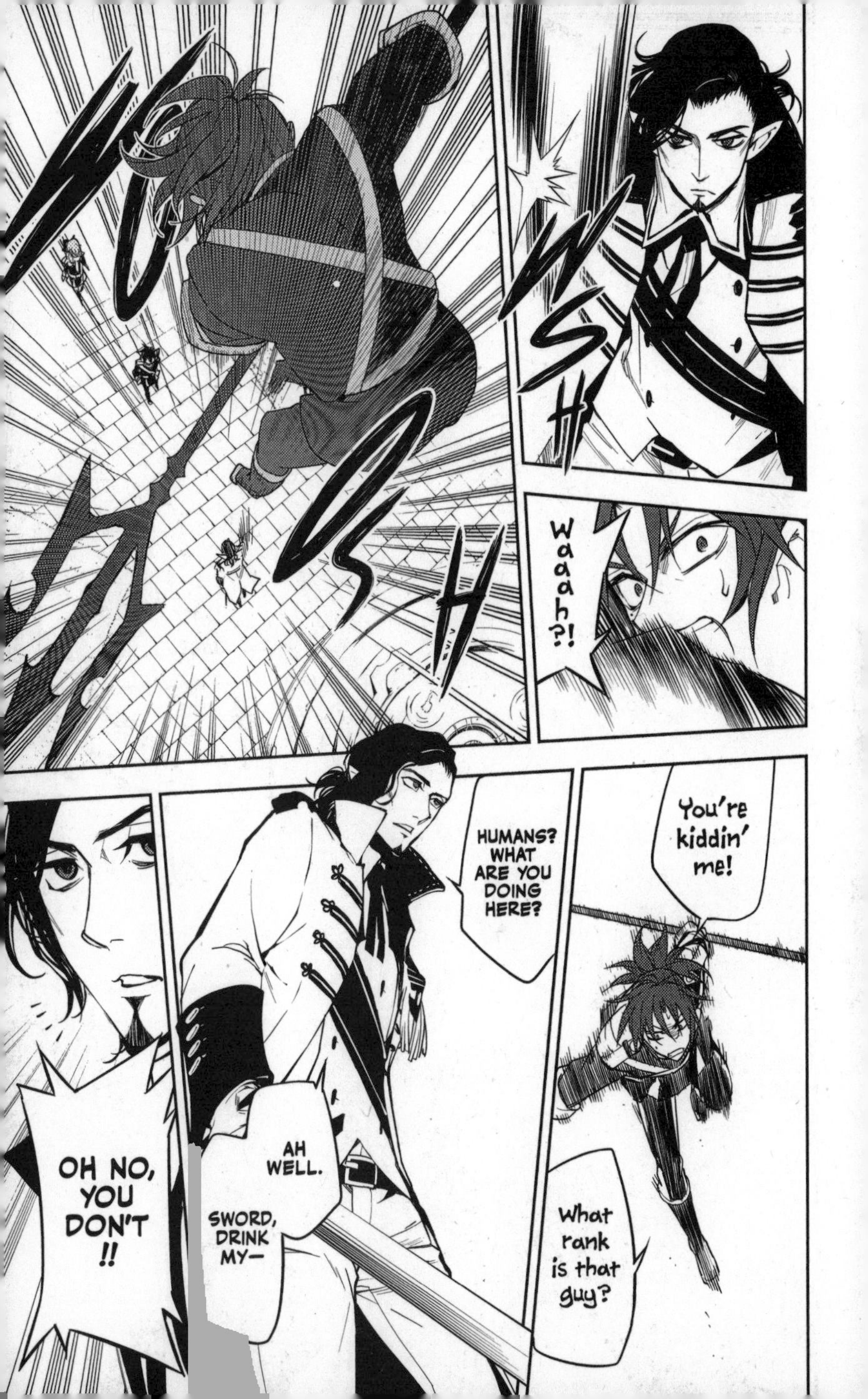
Waaah?!
WHOOSH
You're kiddin' me!
What rank is that guy?
HUMANS? WHAT ARE YOU DOING HERE?
AH WELL.
SWORD, DRINK MY—
OH NO, YOU DON'T!!

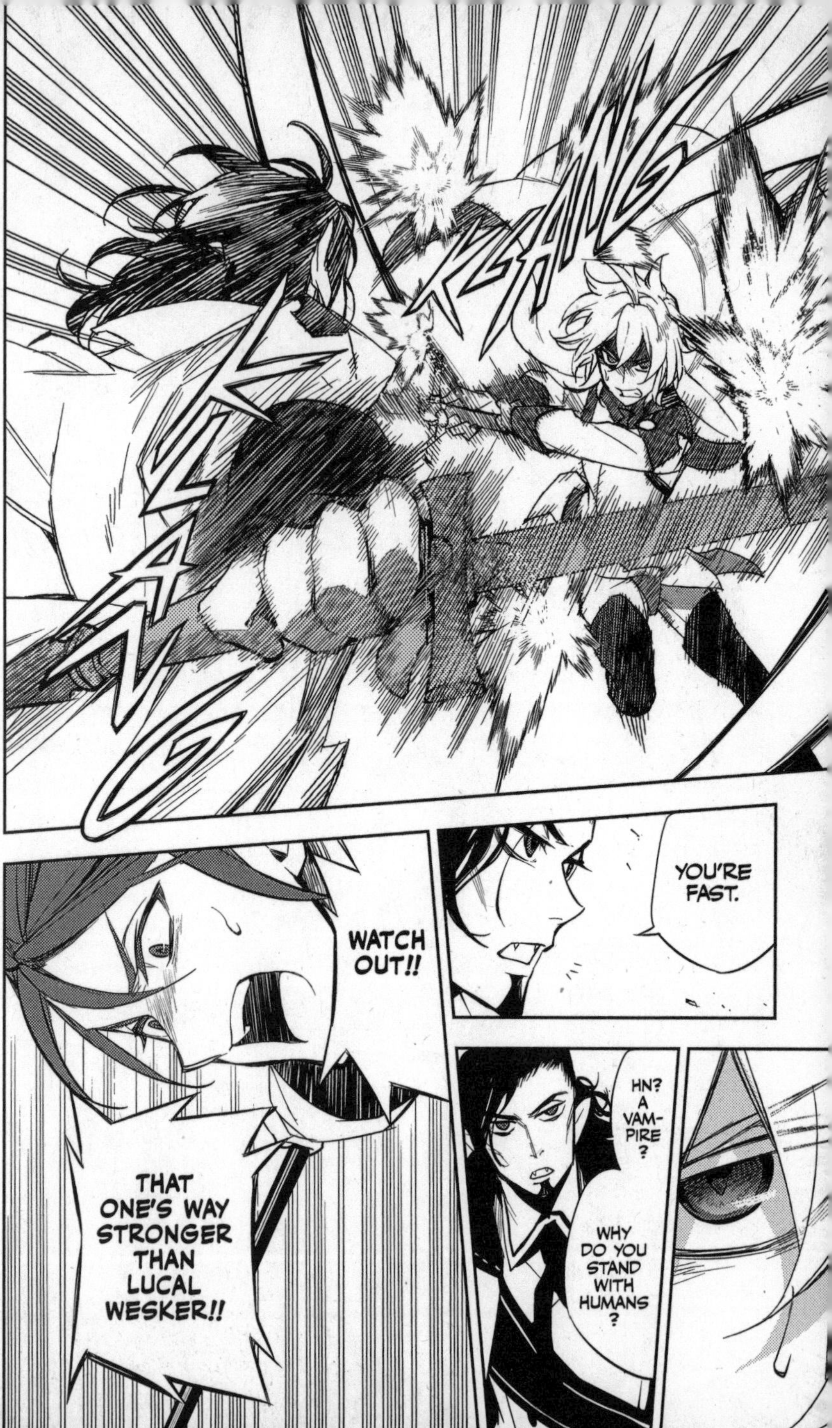
KSHANG
KLANG
YOU'RE FAST.
HN? A VAMPIRE?
WHY DO YOU STAND WITH HUMANS?
WATCH OUT!!
THAT ONE'S WAY STRONGER THAN LUCAL WESKER!!

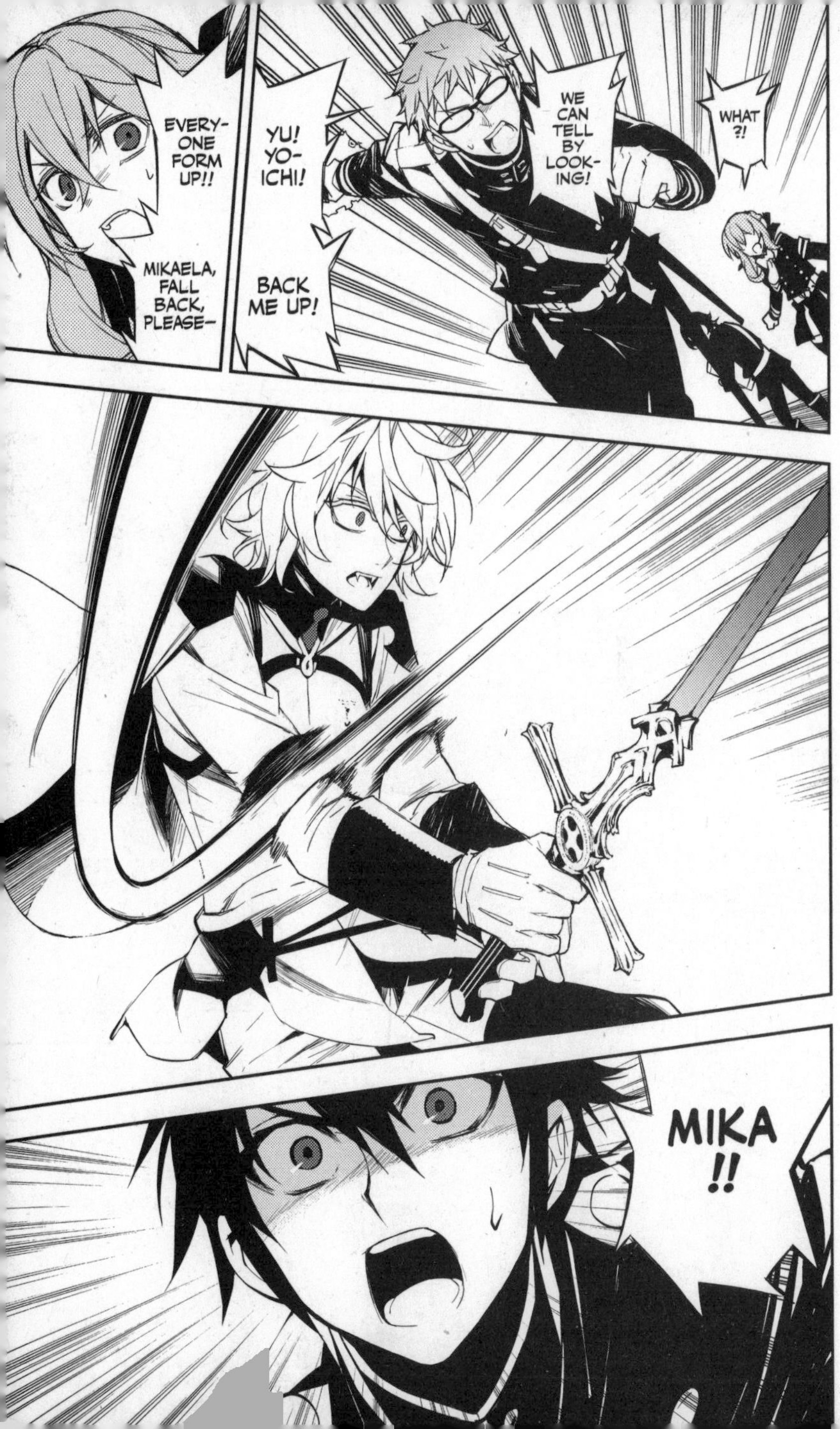
WHAT?!
WE CAN TELL BY LOOKING!
YU! YO-ICHI!
BACK ME UP!
EVERY-ONE FORM UP!!
MIKAELA, FALL BACK, PLEASE—
MIKA!!

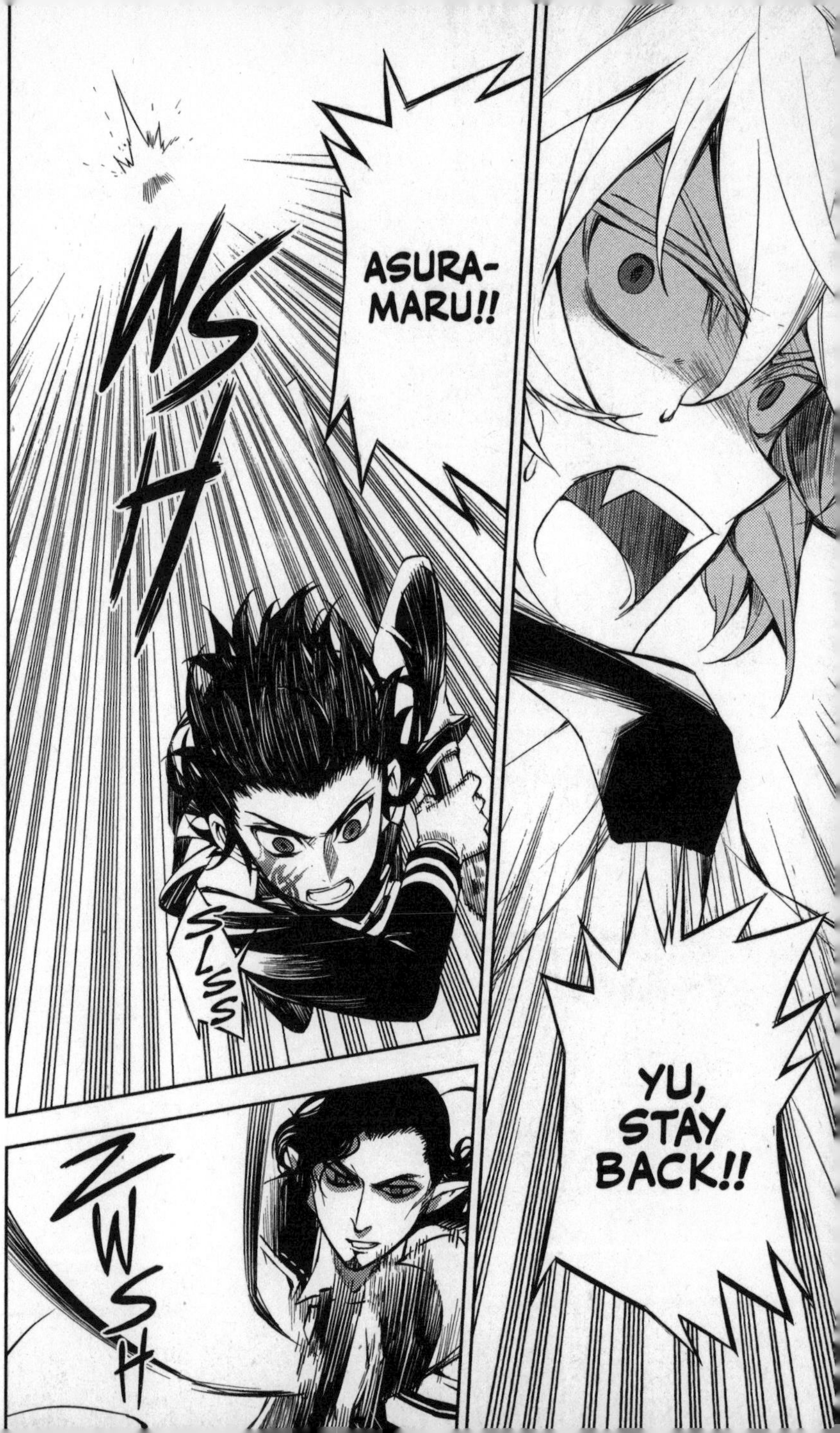
YU, STAY BACK!!
ASURA-MARU!!
WSH
SLSS
ZWSH

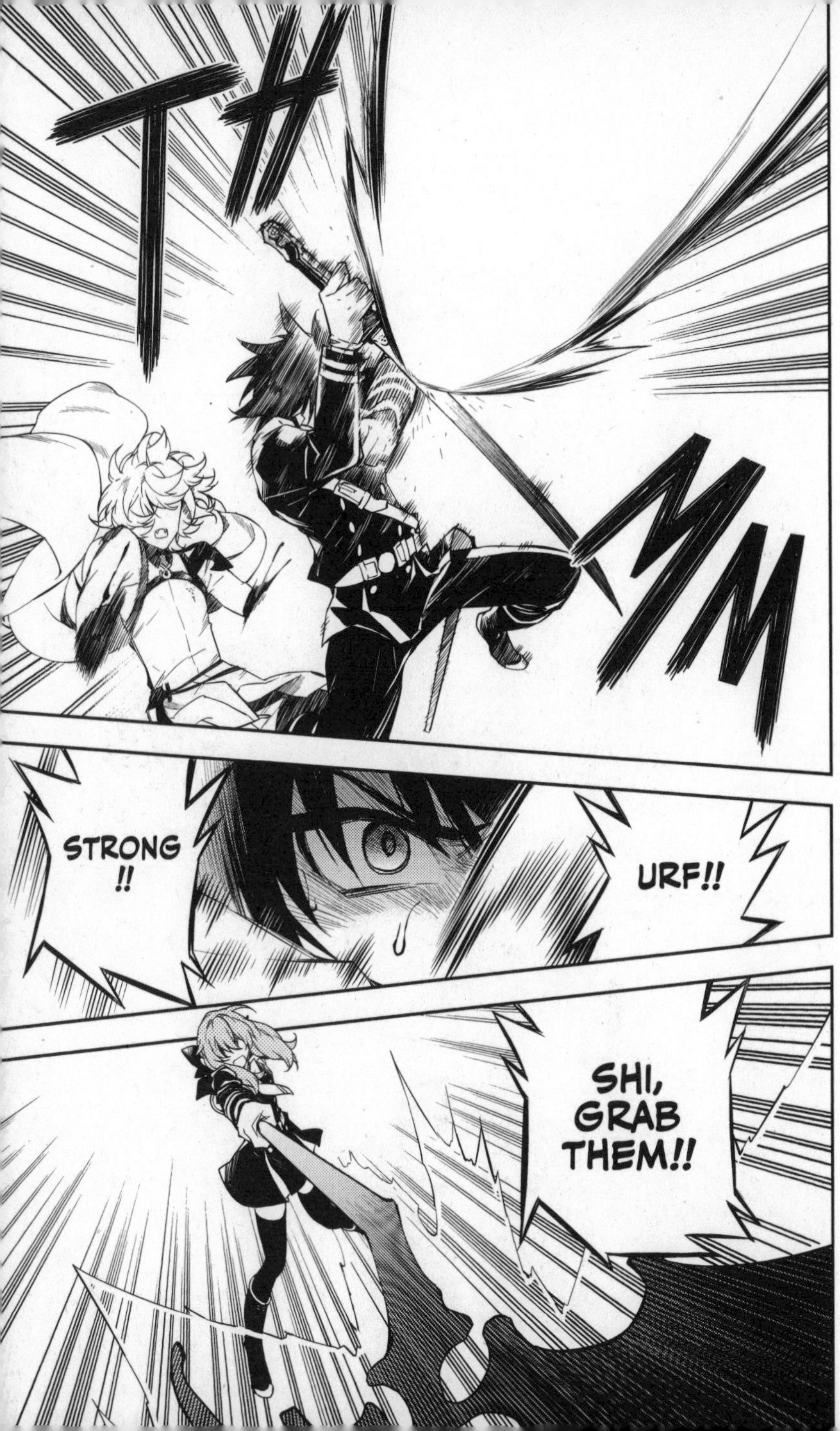
THMM
URF!!
STRONG !!
SHI, GRAB THEM!!

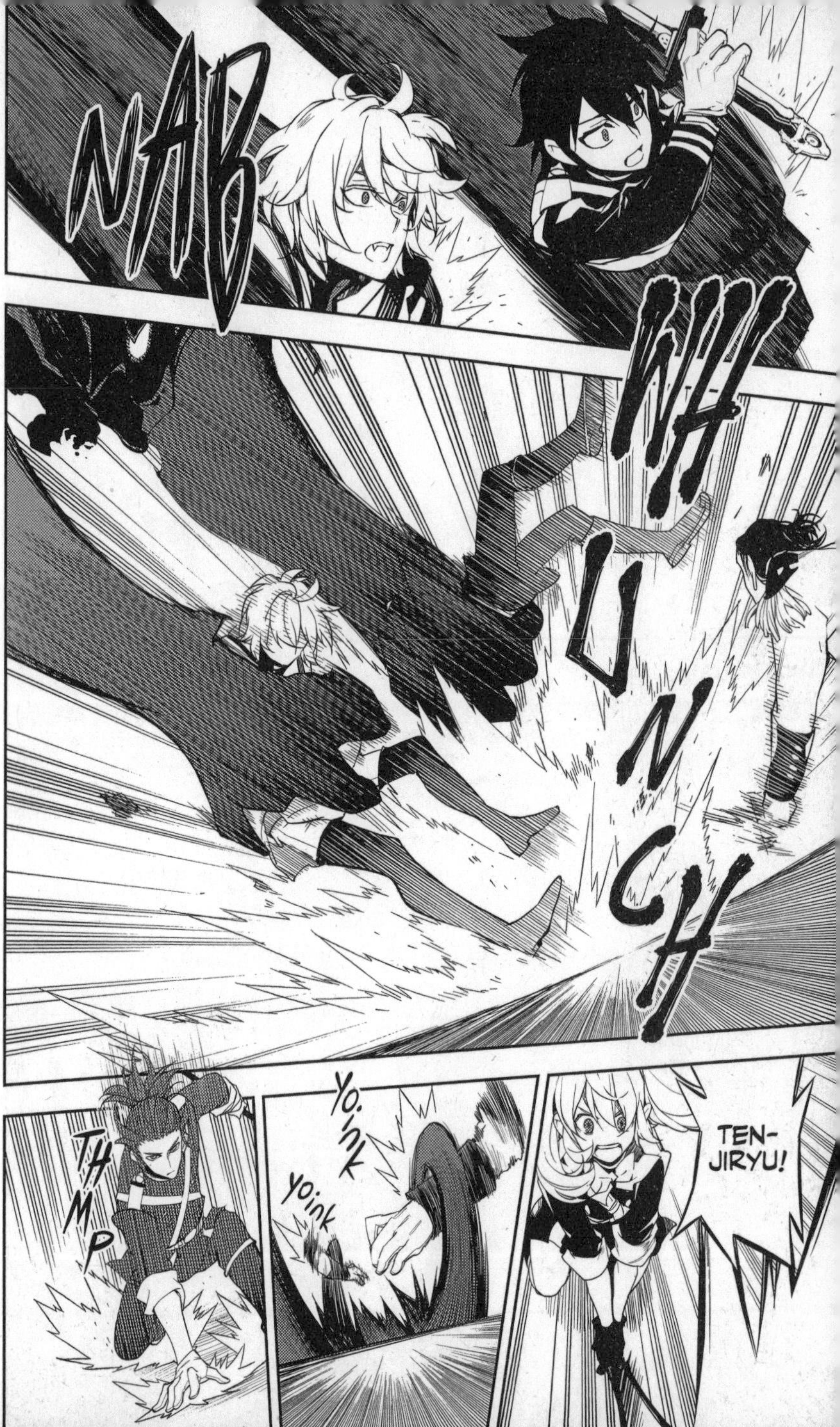
NAB
WHUNCH
TEN-JIRYU!
YOink
yoink
THMP

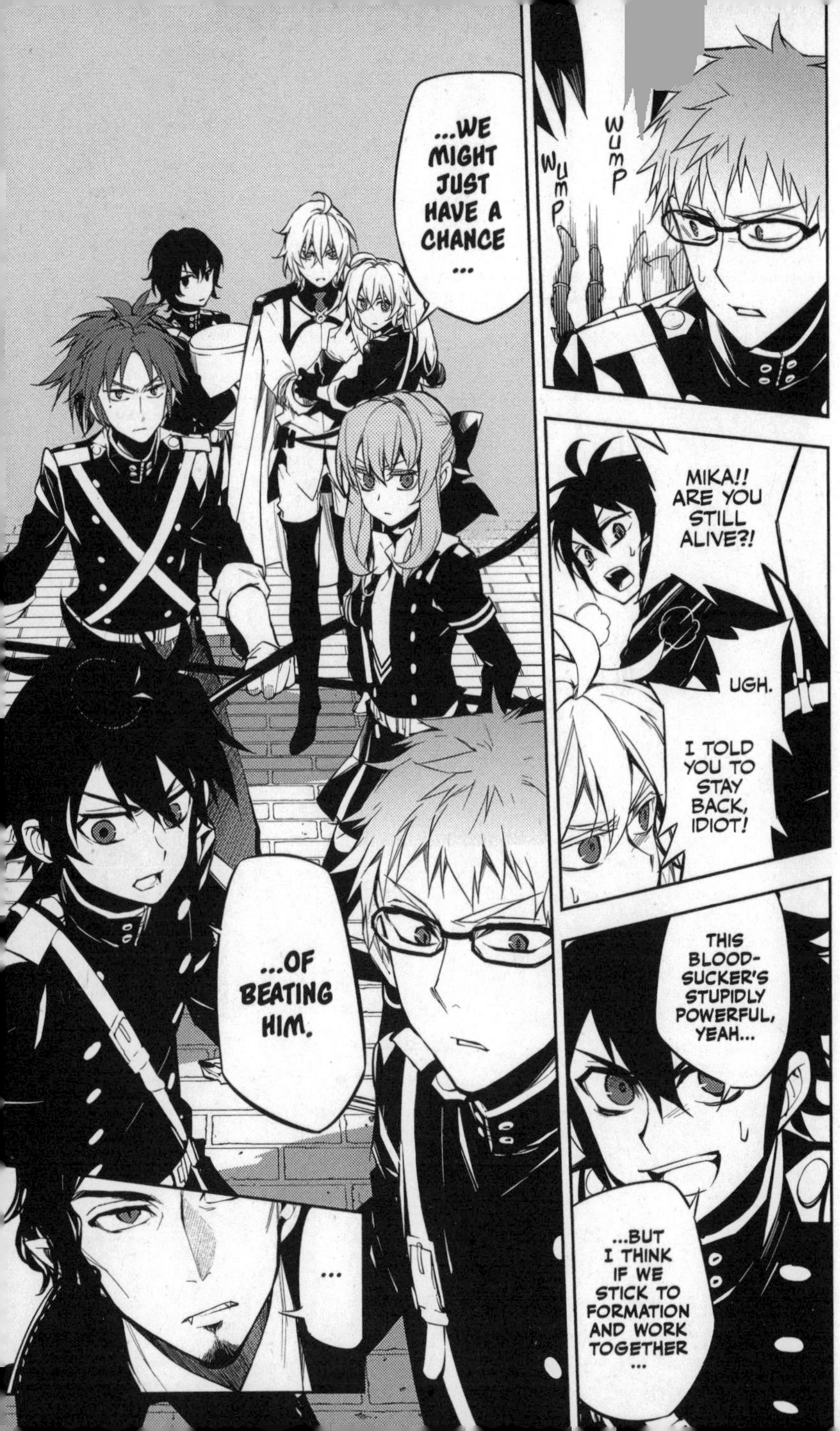
WUMP
WUMP
MIKA!! ARE YOU STILL ALIVE?!
UGH.
I TOLD YOU TO STAY BACK, IDIOT!
THIS BLOOD-SUCKER'S STUPIDLY POWERFUL, YEAH...
...BUT I THINK IF WE STICK TO FORMATION AND WORK TOGETHER...
...WE MIGHT JUST HAVE A CHANCE...
...OF BEATING HIM.
...

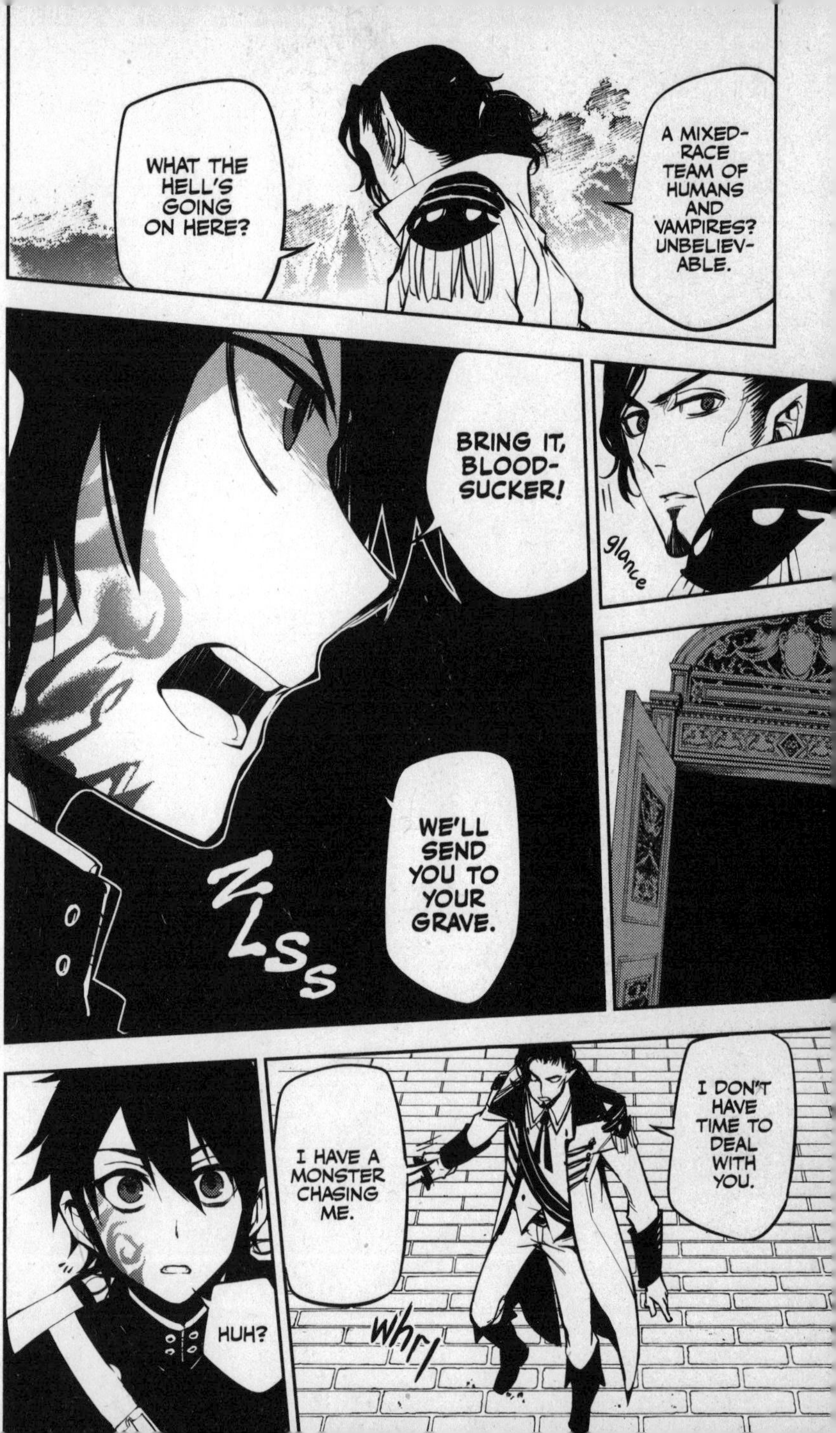
A MIXED-RACE TEAM OF HUMANS AND VAMPIRES? UNBELIEVABLE.
WHAT THE HELL'S GOING ON HERE?
glance
BRING IT, BLOODSUCKER!
WE'LL SEND YOU TO YOUR GRAVE.
ZLSS
I DON'T HAVE TIME TO DEAL WITH YOU.
I HAVE A MONSTER CHASING ME.
whrl
HUH?

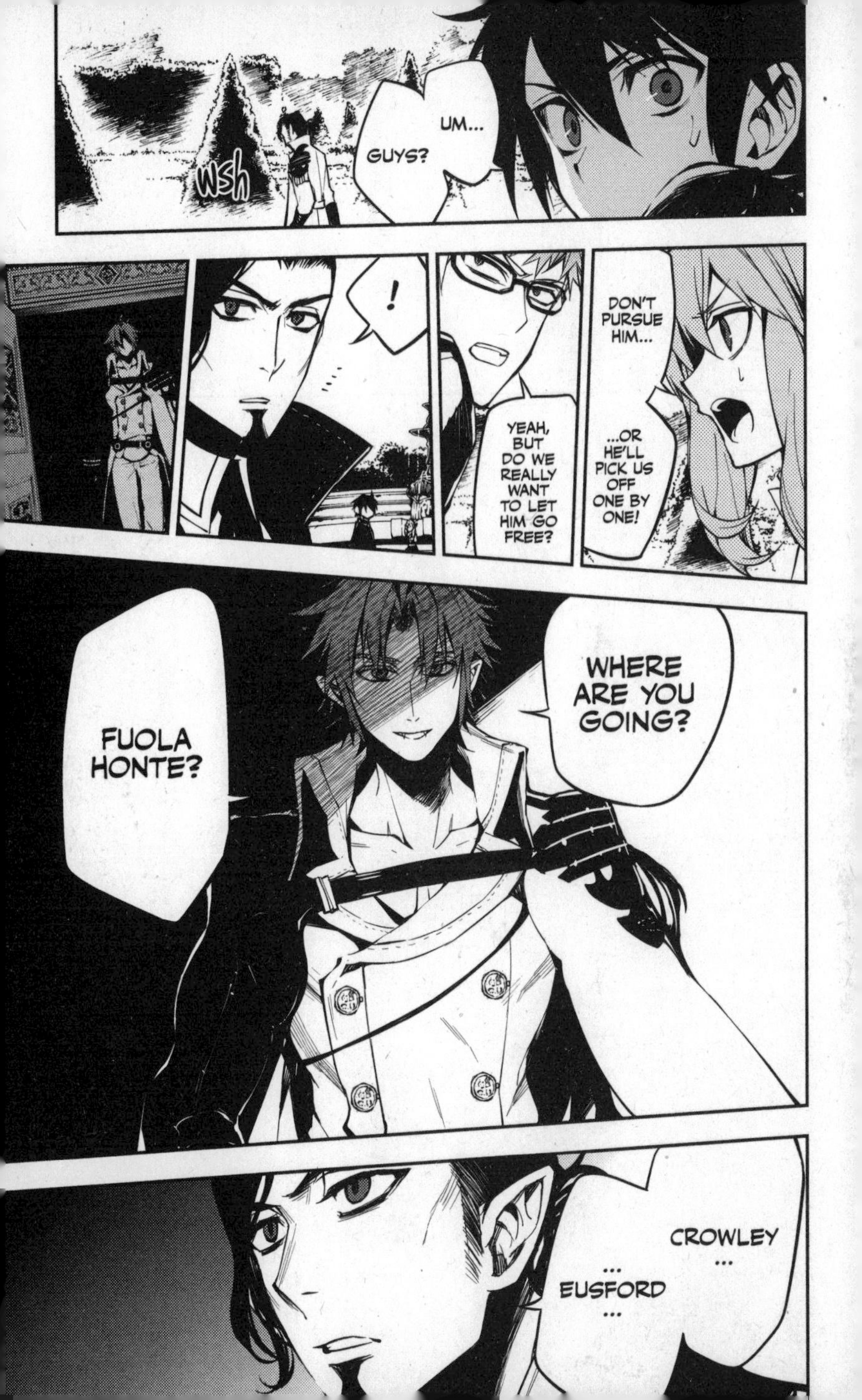
UM... GUYS?
WSH
DON'T PURSUE HIM...
...OR HE'LL PICK US OFF ONE BY ONE!
YEAH, BUT DO WE REALLY WANT TO LET HIM GO FREE?
!
...
WHERE ARE YOU GOING?
FUOLA HONTE?
CROWLEY ...
... EUSFORD ...

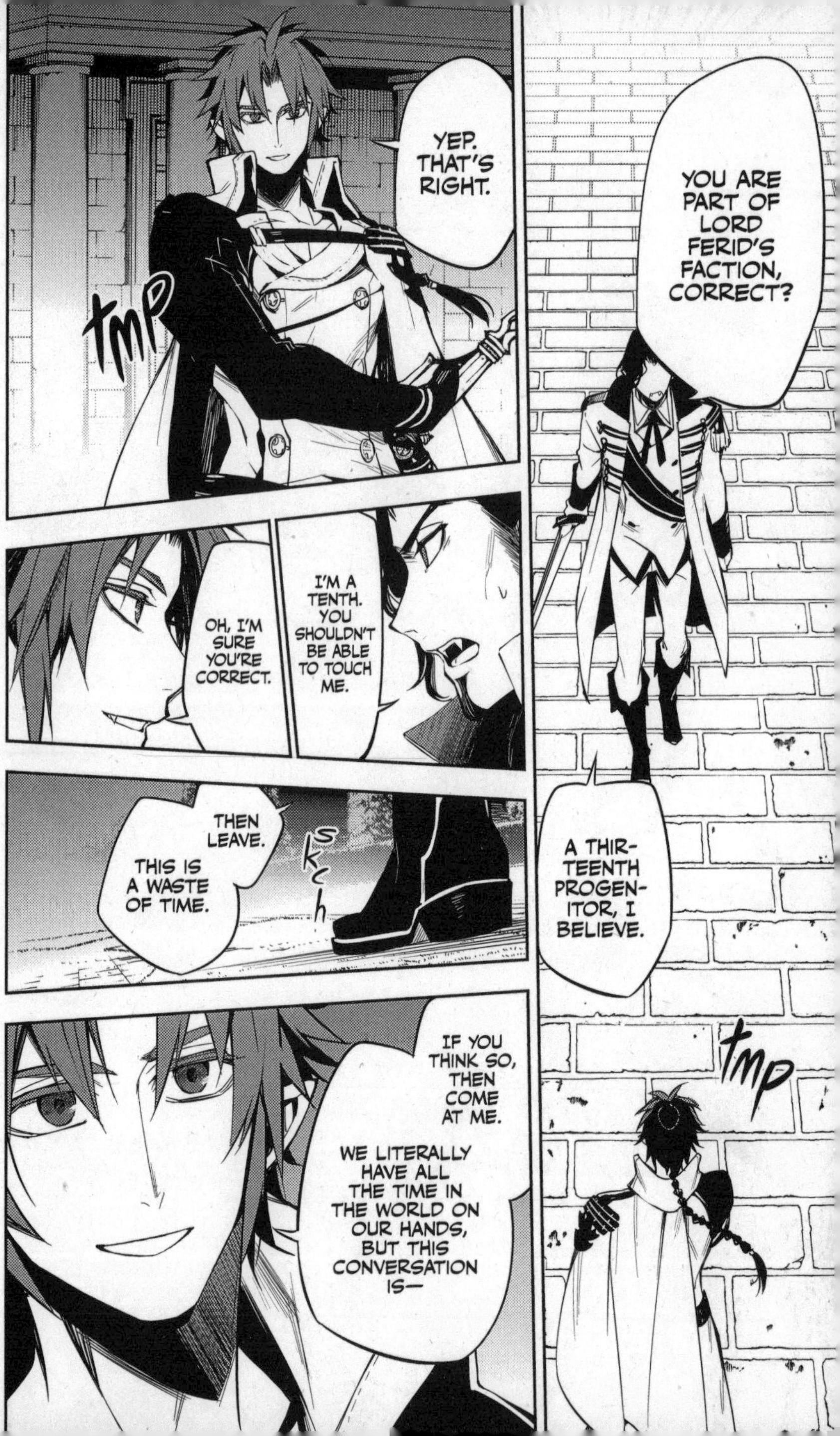
YOU ARE PART OF LORD FERID'S FACTION, CORRECT?
A THIRTEENTH PROGENITOR, I BELIEVE.
tmp
YEP. THAT'S RIGHT.
tmp
I'M A TENTH. YOU SHOULDN'T BE ABLE TO TOUCH ME.
OH, I'M SURE YOU'RE CORRECT.
THEN LEAVE.
THIS IS A WASTE OF TIME.
skch
IF YOU THINK SO, THEN COME AT ME.
WE LITERALLY HAVE ALL THE TIME IN THE WORLD ON OUR HANDS, BUT THIS CONVERSATION IS—

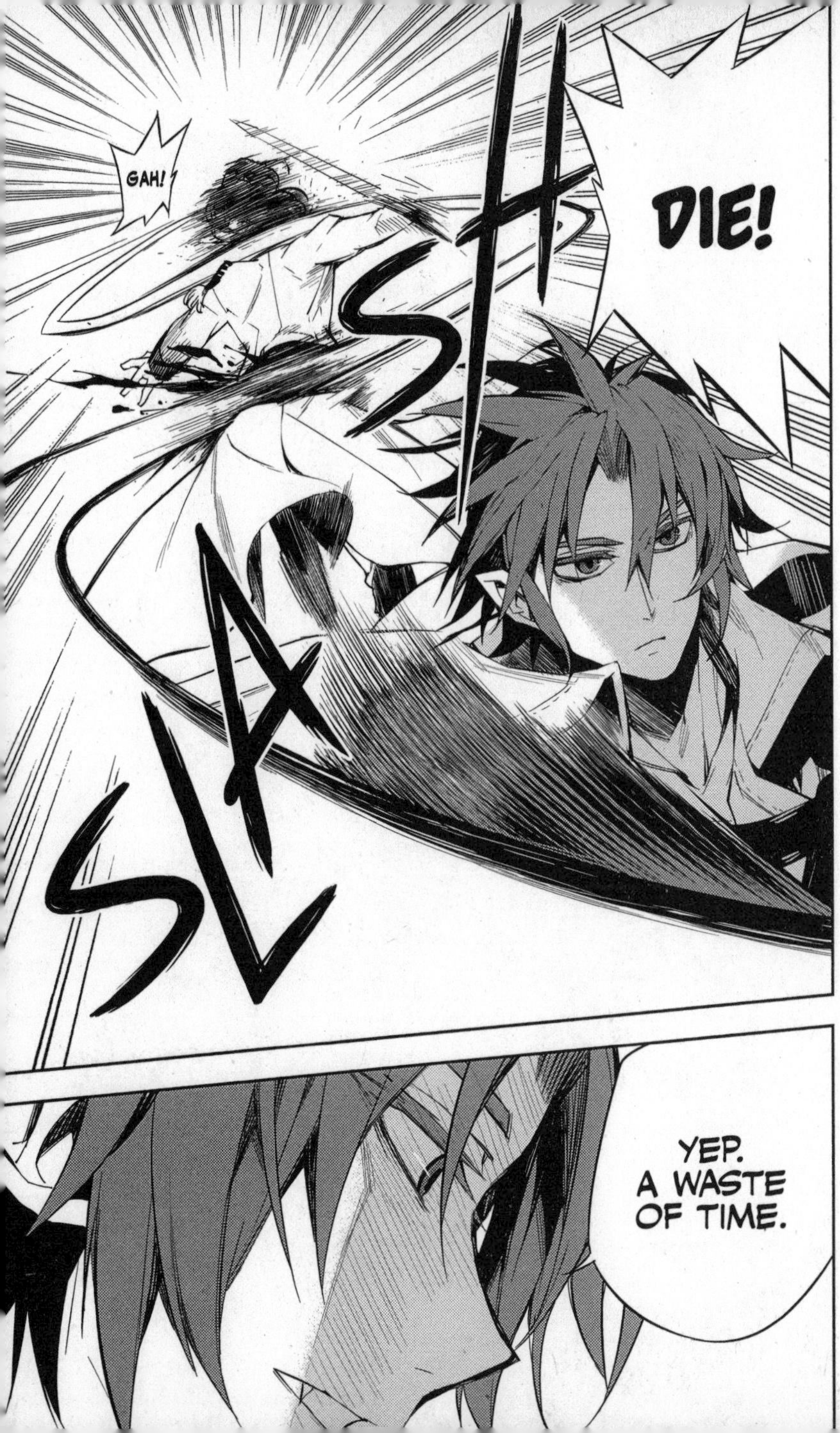
DIE!
GAH!
SLASH
YEP. A WASTE OF TIME.

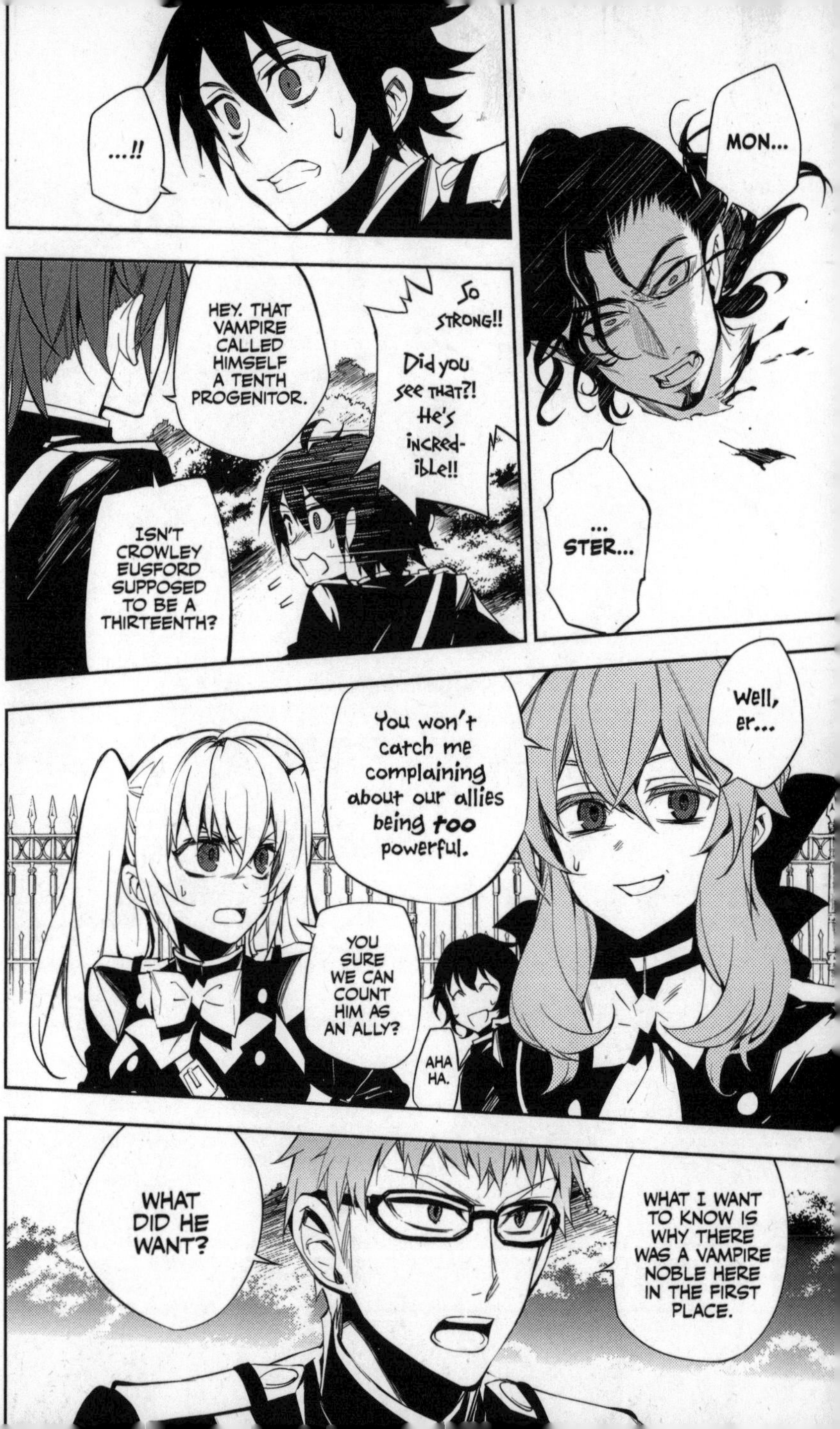
MON...
...STER...
...!!
SO STRONG!!
Did you see that?! He's incred-ible!!
HEY. THAT VAMPIRE CALLED HIMSELF A TENTH PROGENITOR.
ISN'T CROWLEY EUSFORD SUPPOSED TO BE A THIRTEENTH?
Well, er...
You won't catch me complaining about our allies being *too* powerful.
YOU SURE WE CAN COUNT HIM AS AN ALLY?
AHA HA.
WHAT I WANT TO KNOW IS WHY THERE WAS A VAMPIRE NOBLE HERE IN THE FIRST PLACE.
WHAT DID HE WANT?

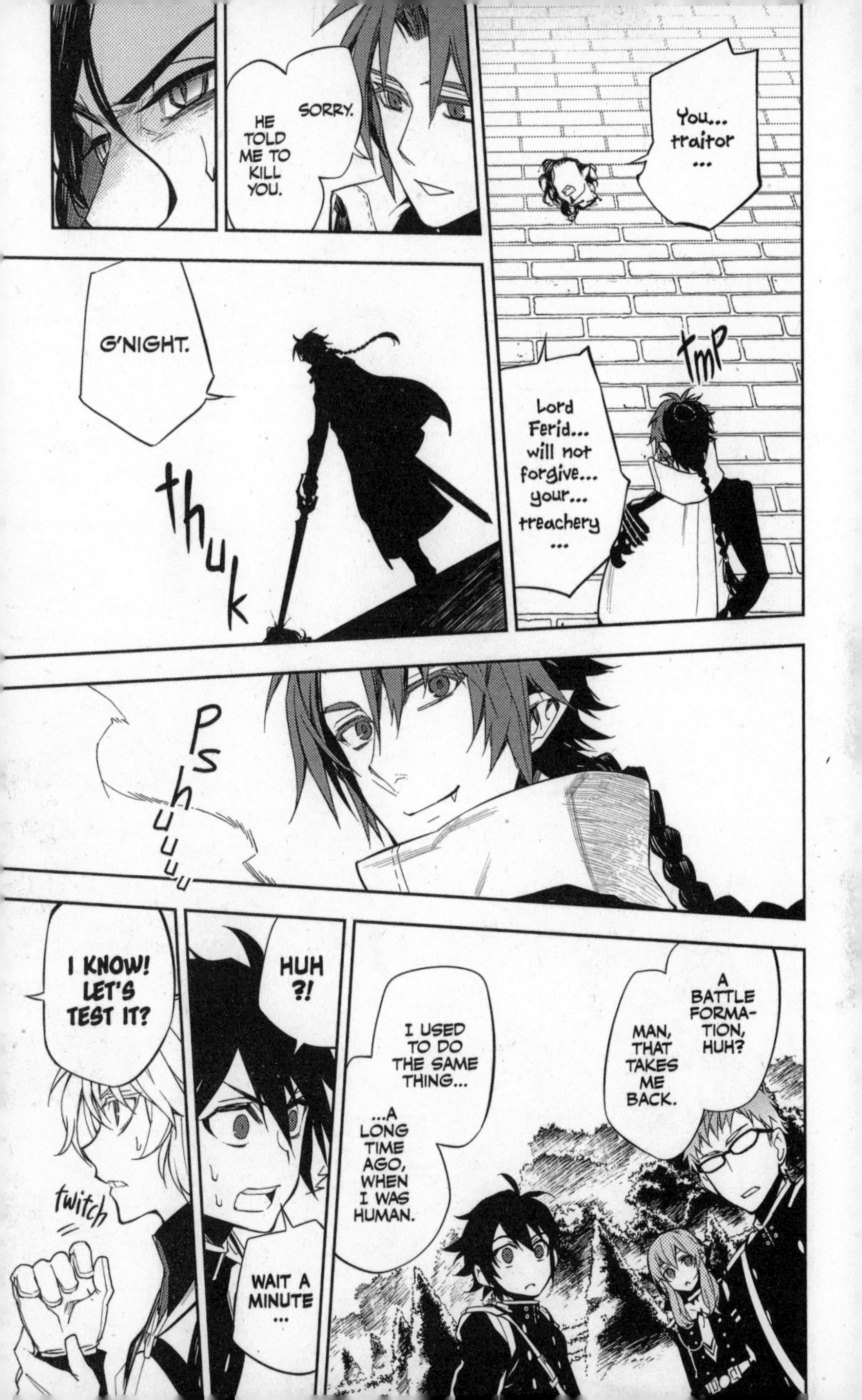
You... traitor ...
SORRY. HE TOLD ME TO KILL YOU.
tmP
Lord Ferid... will not forgive... your... treachery ...
G'NIGHT.
thuk
Pshuuuuu
A BATTLE FORMATION, HUH?
MAN, THAT TAKES ME BACK.
I USED TO DO THE SAME THING...
...A LONG TIME AGO, WHEN I WAS HUMAN.
HUH ?!
WAIT A MINUTE ...
I KNOW! LET'S TEST IT?
twitch

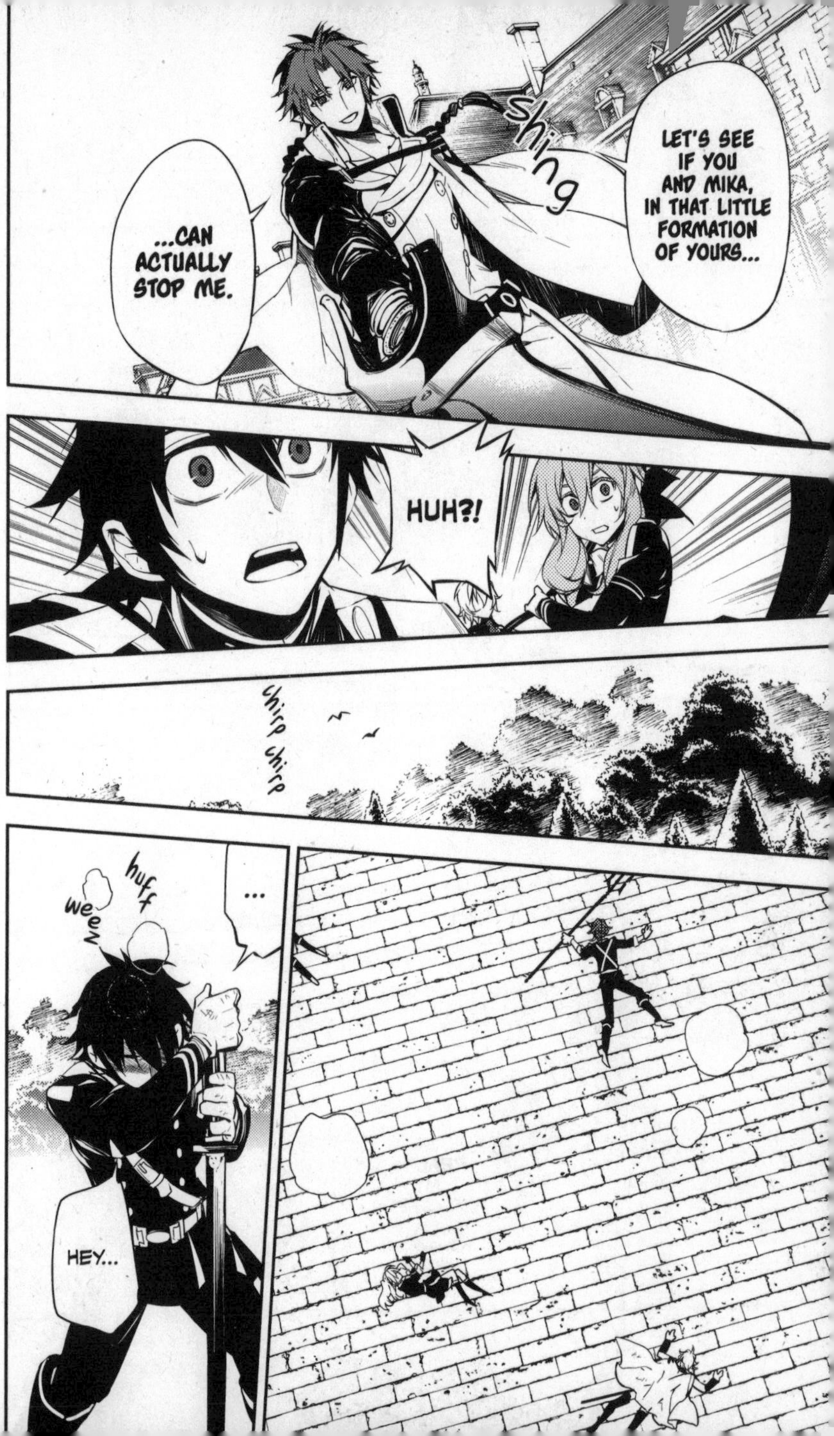
LET'S SEE IF YOU AND MIKA, IN THAT LITTLE FORMATION OF YOURS...
shing
...CAN ACTUALLY STOP ME.
HUH?!
chirp chirp
...
huff
weez
HEY...

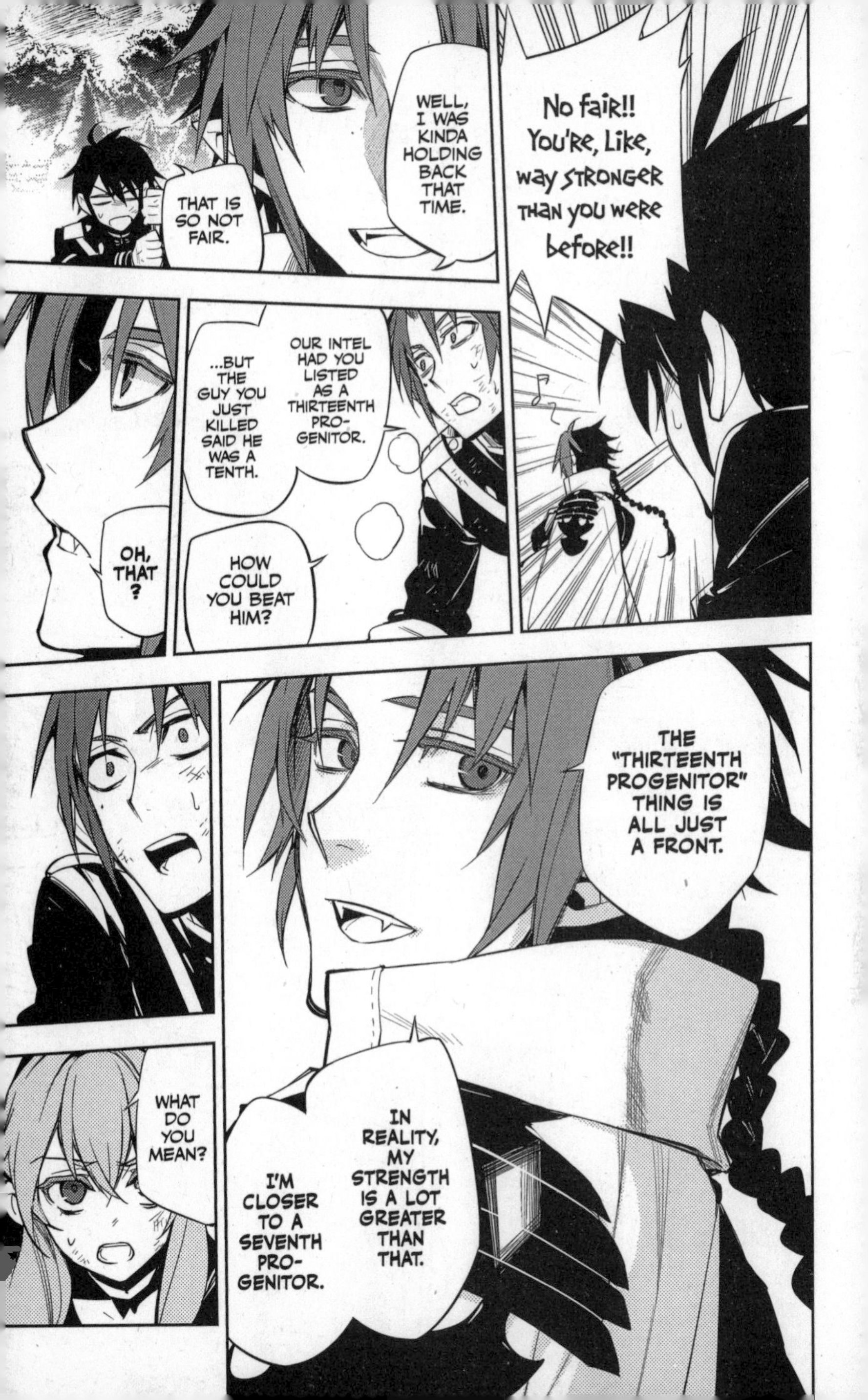
No fair!! You're, Like, way stronger than you were before!!
WELL, I WAS KINDA HOLDING BACK THAT TIME.
THAT IS SO NOT FAIR.
OUR INTEL HAD YOU LISTED AS A THIRTEENTH PRO-GENITOR.
...BUT THE GUY YOU JUST KILLED SAID HE WAS A TENTH.
HOW COULD YOU BEAT HIM?
OH, THAT?
THE "THIRTEENTH PROGENITOR" THING IS ALL JUST A FRONT.
IN REALITY, MY STRENGTH IS A LOT GREATER THAN THAT.
I'M CLOSER TO A SEVENTH PRO-GENITOR.
WHAT DO YOU MEAN?

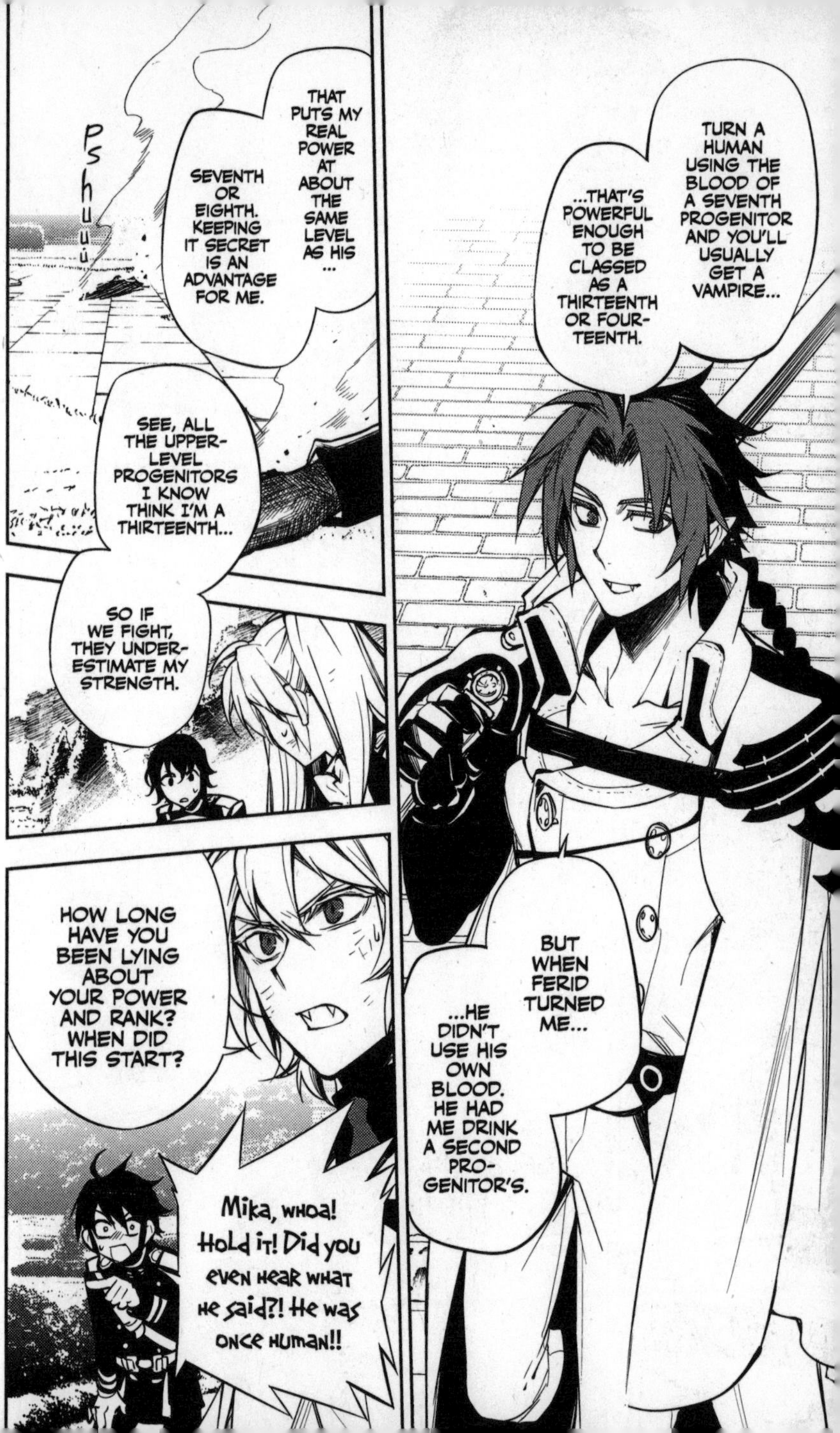
TURN A HUMAN USING THE BLOOD OF A SEVENTH PROGENITOR AND YOU'LL USUALLY GET A VAMPIRE...
...THAT'S POWERFUL ENOUGH TO BE CLASSED AS A THIRTEENTH OR FOUR-TEENTH.
BUT WHEN FERID TURNED ME...
...HE DIDN'T USE HIS OWN BLOOD. HE HAD ME DRINK A SECOND PRO-GENITOR'S.
THAT PUTS MY REAL POWER AT ABOUT THE SAME LEVEL AS HIS...
SEVENTH OR EIGHTH. KEEPING IT SECRET IS AN ADVANTAGE FOR ME.
Pshuuu
SEE, ALL THE UPPER-LEVEL PROGENITORS I KNOW THINK I'M A THIRTEENTH...
SO IF WE FIGHT, THEY UNDER-ESTIMATE MY STRENGTH.
HOW LONG HAVE YOU BEEN LYING ABOUT YOUR POWER AND RANK? WHEN DID THIS START?
Mika, whoa! Hold it! Did you even hear what he said?! He was once human!!

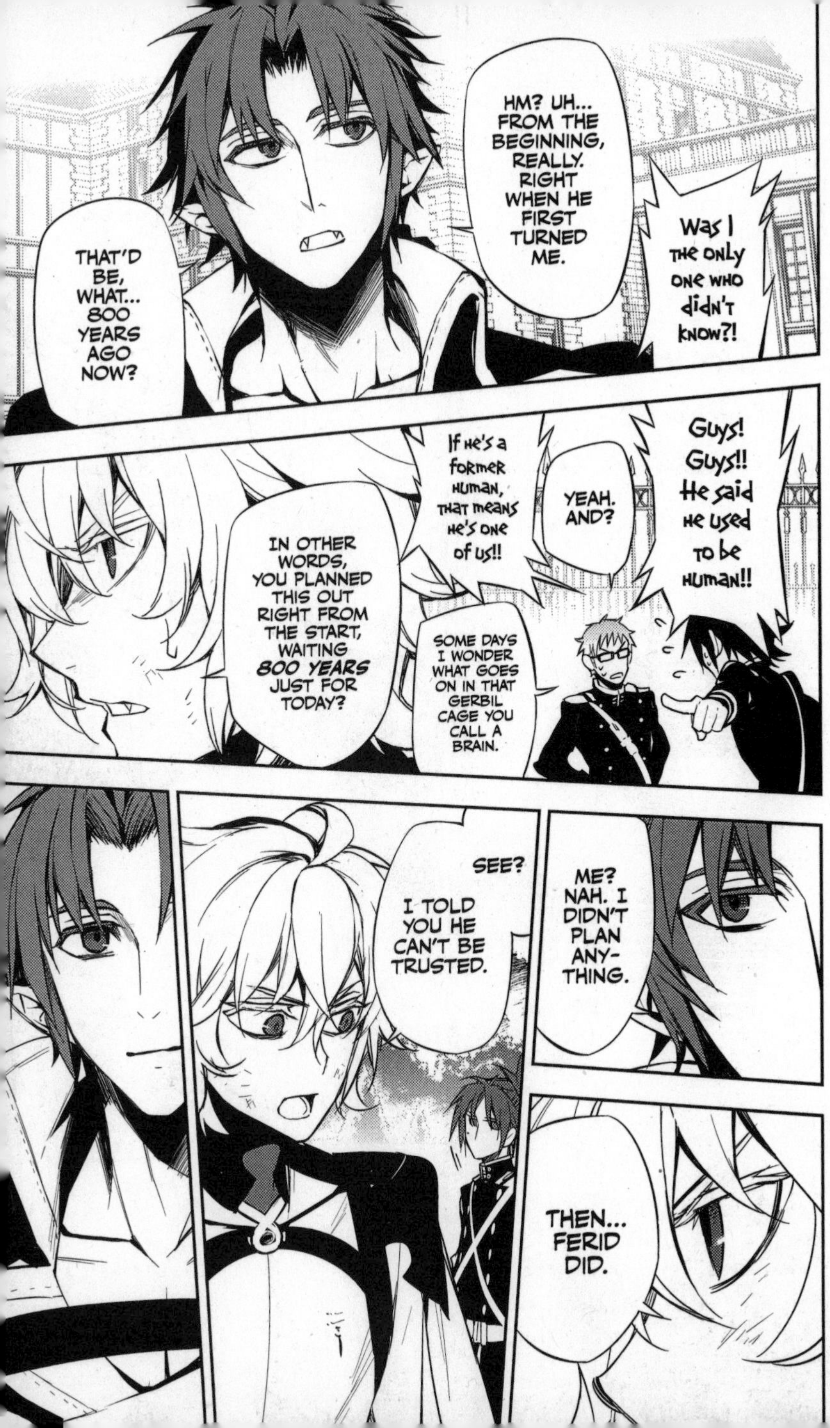
Was I the only one who didn't know?!
HM? UH... FROM THE BEGINNING, REALLY. RIGHT WHEN HE FIRST TURNED ME.
THAT'D BE, WHAT... 800 YEARS AGO NOW?
Guys! Guys!! He said he used to be human!!
YEAH. AND?
If he's a former human, that means he's one of us!!
SOME DAYS I WONDER WHAT GOES ON IN THAT GERBIL CAGE YOU CALL A BRAIN.
IN OTHER WORDS, YOU PLANNED THIS OUT RIGHT FROM THE START, WAITING 800 YEARS JUST FOR TODAY?
ME? NAH. I DIDN'T PLAN ANY-THING.
THEN... FERID DID.
SEE?
I TOLD YOU HE CAN'T BE TRUSTED.

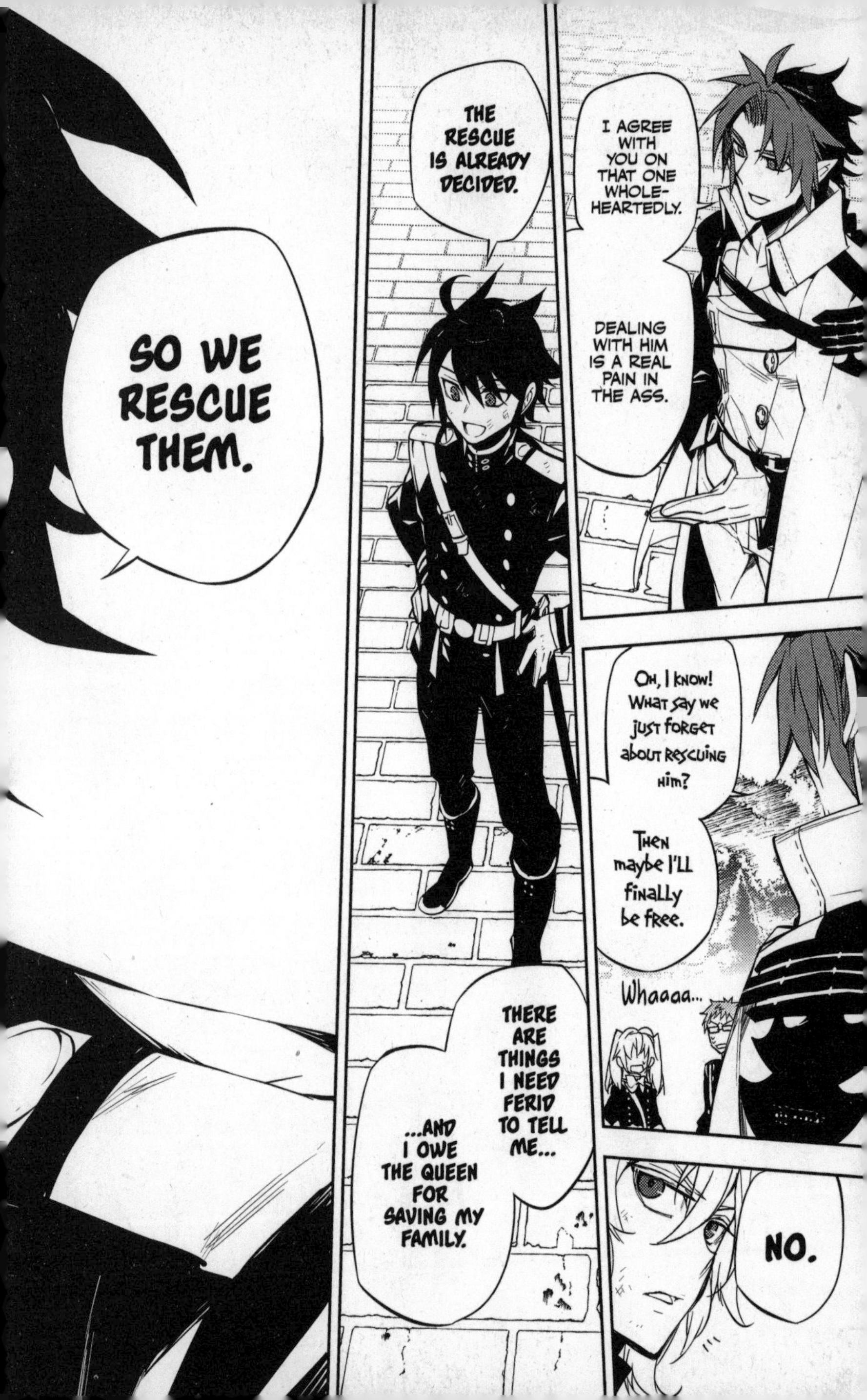
I AGREE WITH YOU ON THAT ONE WHOLE-HEARTEDLY.
DEALING WITH HIM IS A REAL PAIN IN THE ASS.
Oh, I know! What say we just forget about rescuing him?
Then maybe I'll finally be free.
Whaaaa...
NO.
THE RESCUE IS ALREADY DECIDED.
THERE ARE THINGS I NEED FERID TO TELL ME...
...AND I OWE THE QUEEN FOR SAVING MY FAMILY.
SO WE RESCUE THEM.

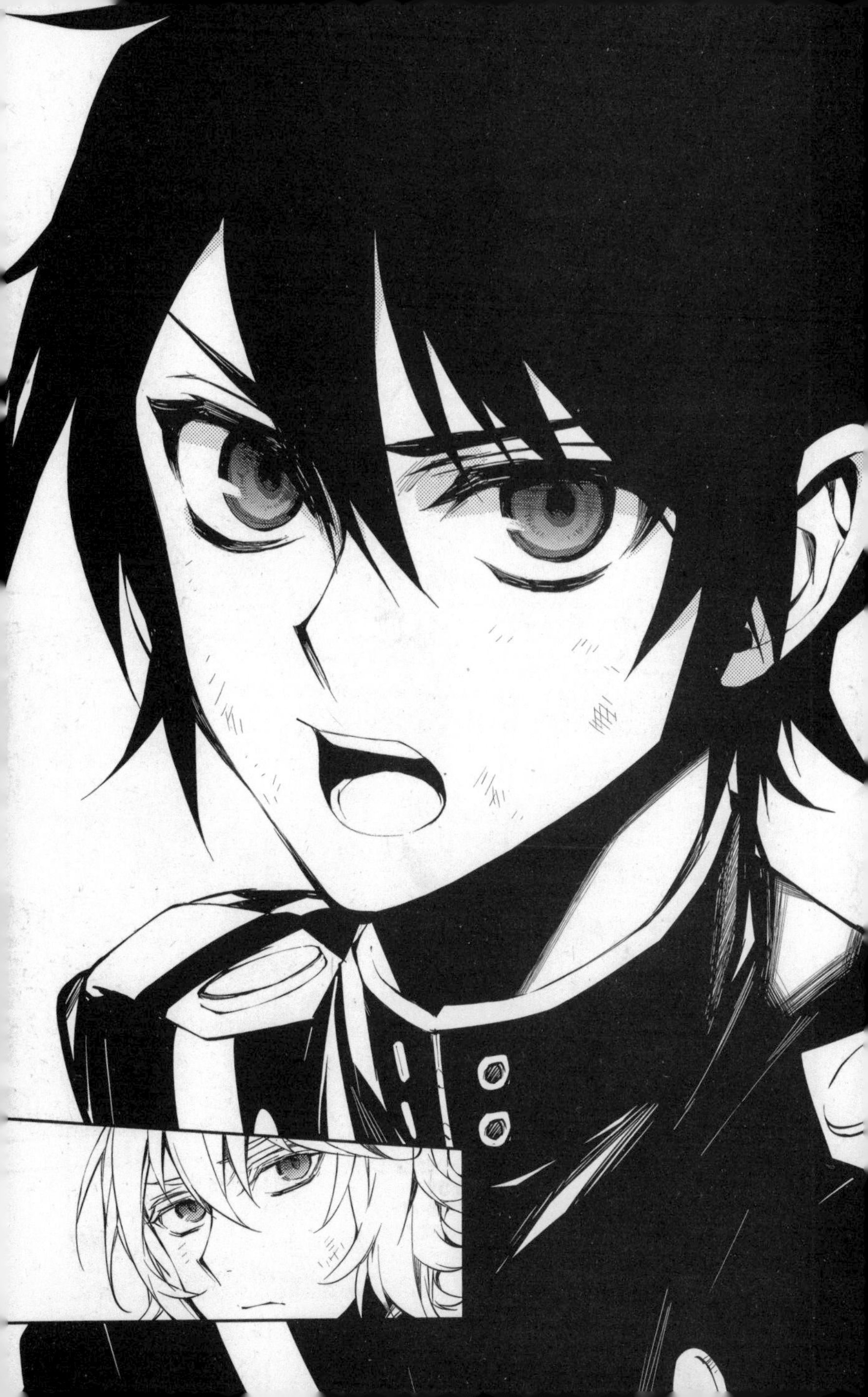

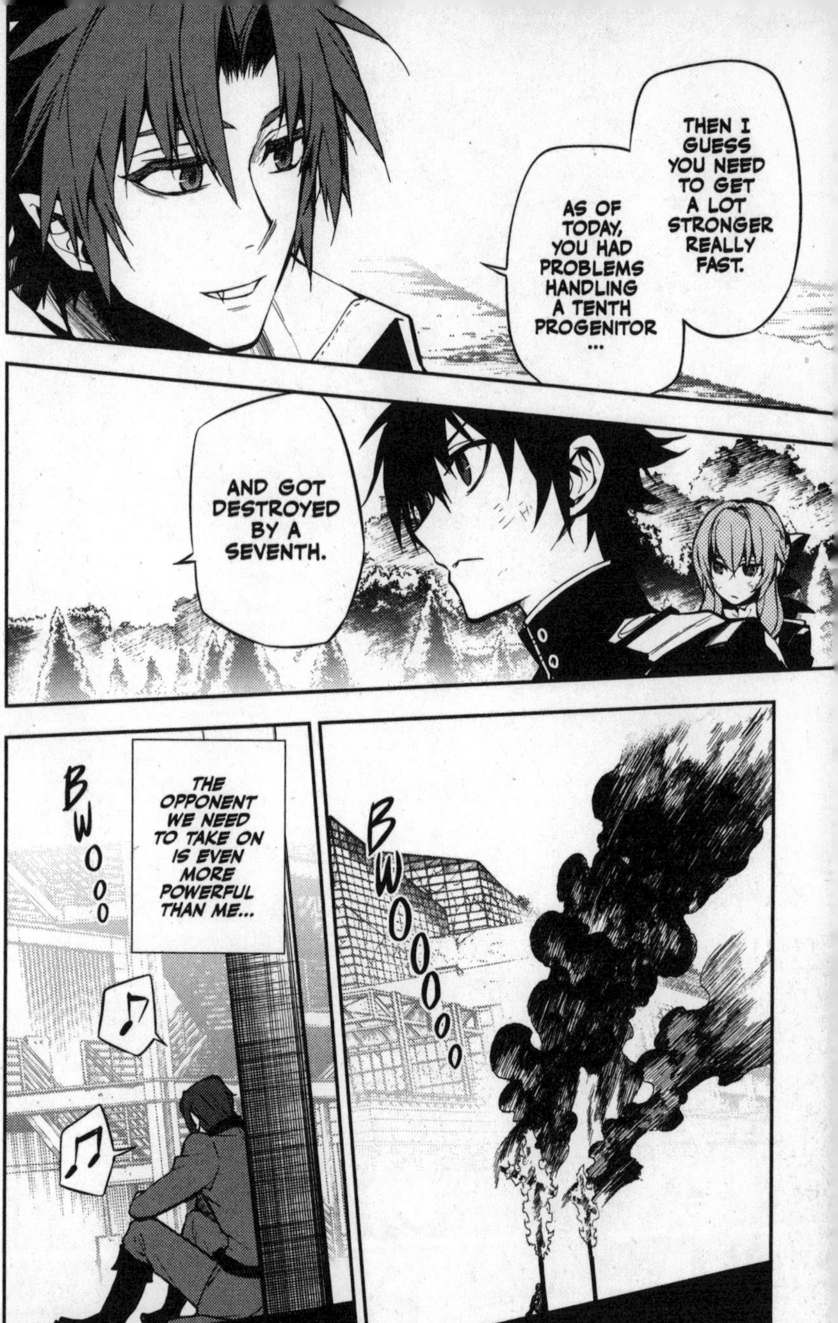
THEN I GUESS YOU NEED TO GET A LOT STRONGER REALLY FAST.
AS OF TODAY, YOU HAD PROBLEMS HANDLING A TENTH PROGENITOR...
AND GOT DESTROYED BY A SEVENTH.
BWOOOOOOO
THE OPPONENT WE NEED TO TAKE ON IS EVEN MORE POWERFUL THAN ME...
BWOOO
♪
♫

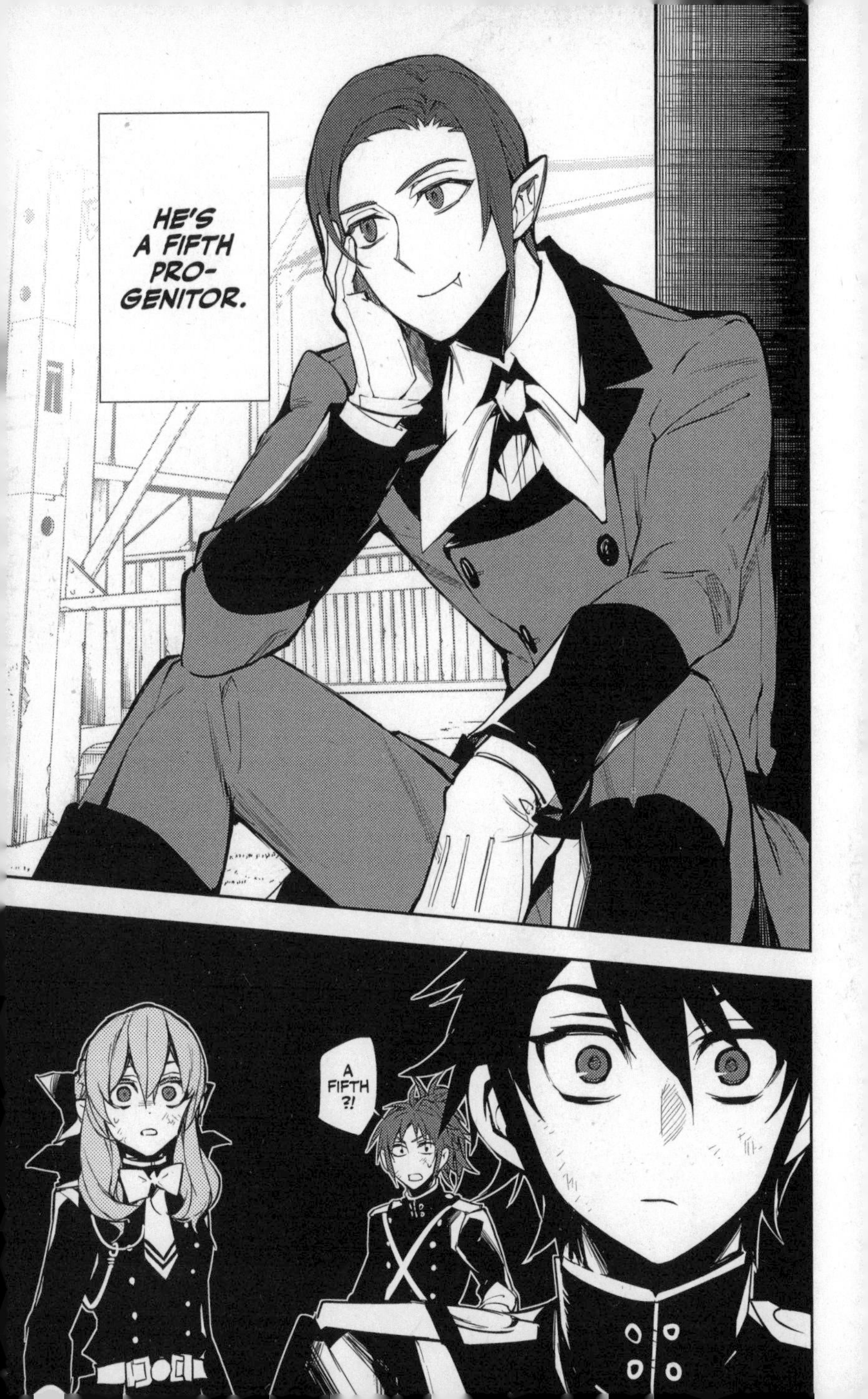
HE'S A FIFTH PRO-GENITOR.
A FIFTH ?!

Seraph of the End

—VAMPIRE REIGN—

Chapter 53
Holy Knight's Secret

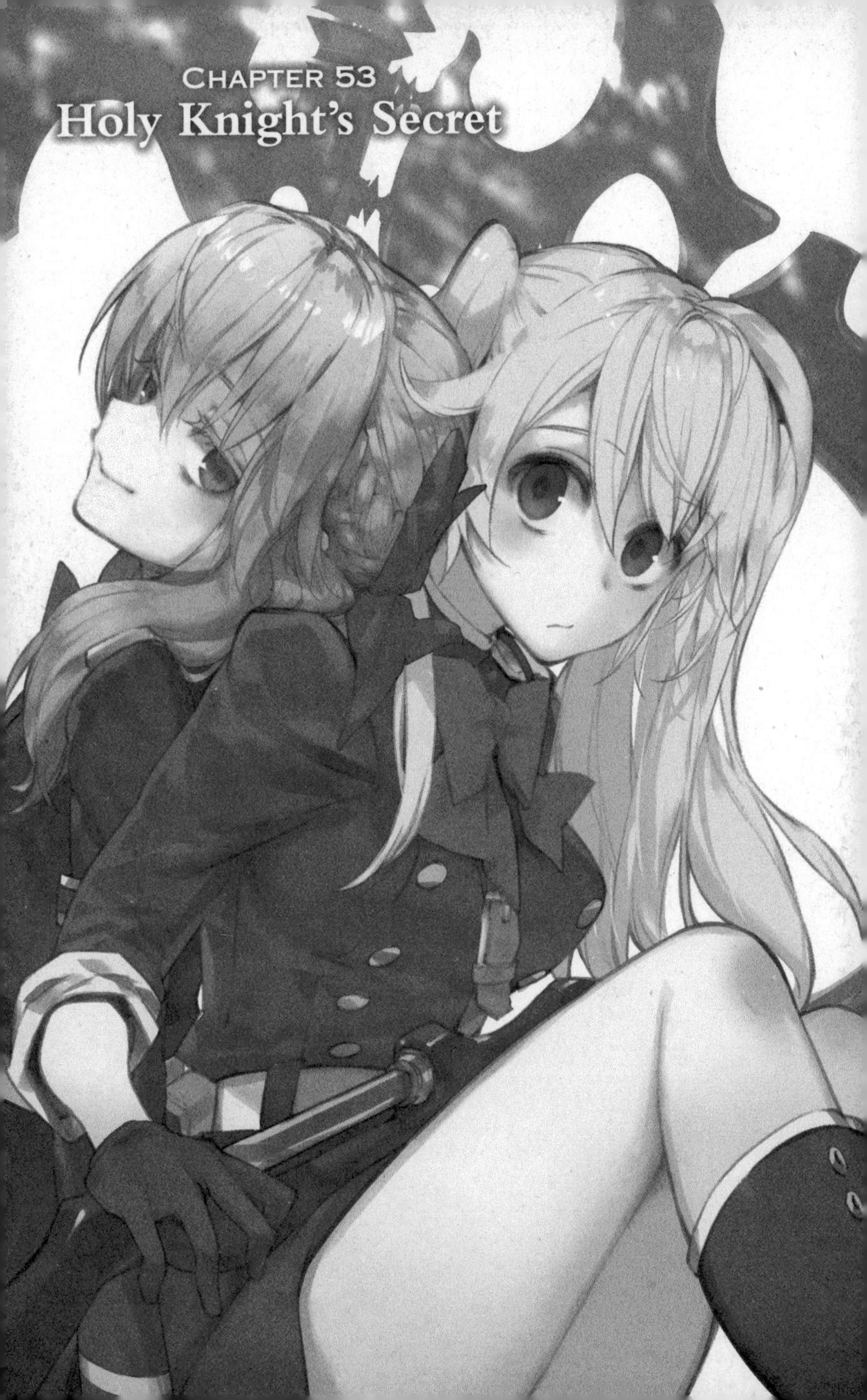

Seraph of the End

—VAMPIRE REIGN—

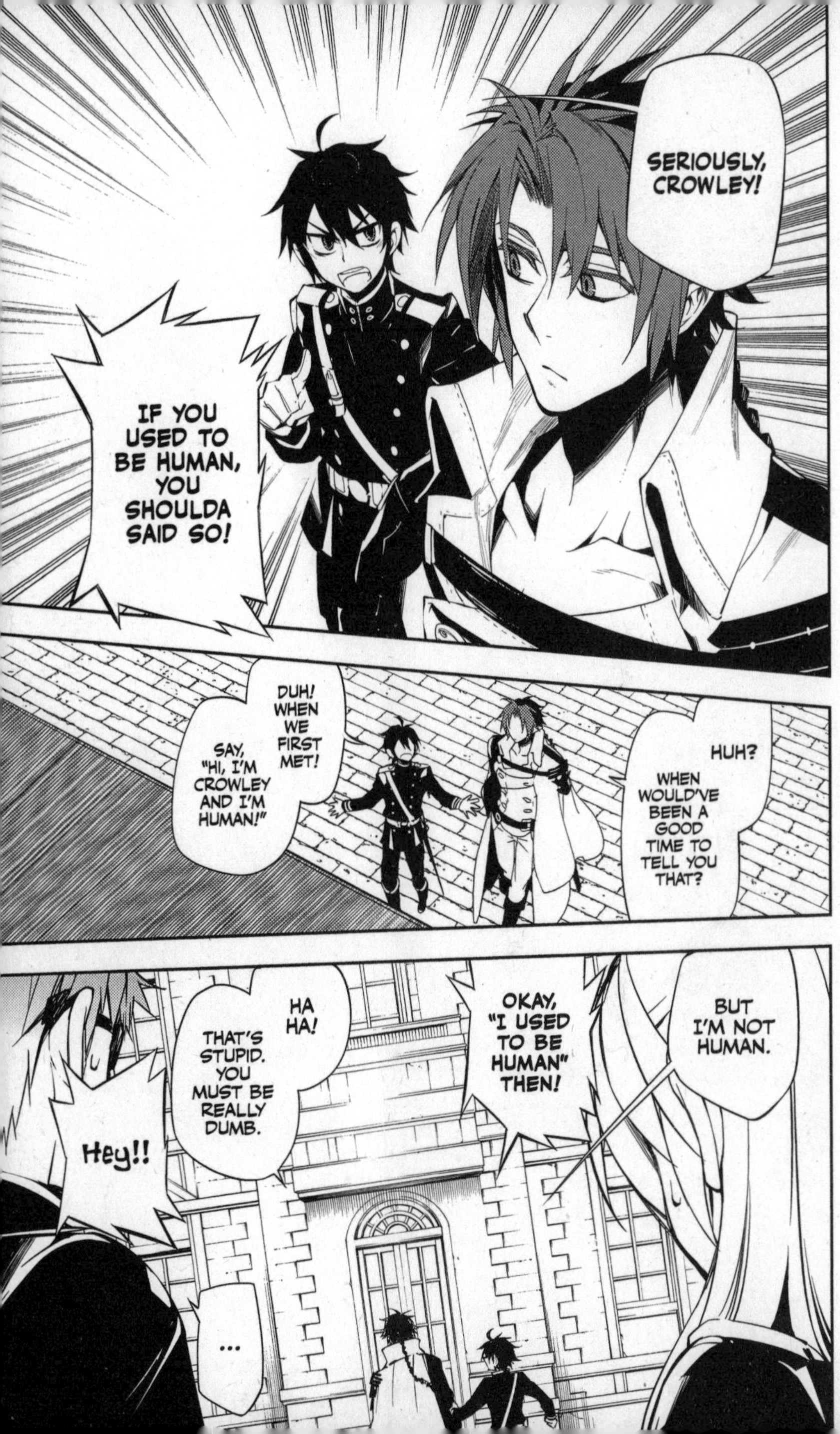
SERIOUSLY, CROWLEY!
IF YOU USED TO BE HUMAN, YOU SHOULDA SAID SO!
HUH?
WHEN WOULD'VE BEEN A GOOD TIME TO TELL YOU THAT?
DUH! WHEN WE FIRST MET!
SAY, "HI, I'M CROWLEY AND I'M HUMAN!"
BUT I'M NOT HUMAN.
OKAY, "I USED TO BE HUMAN" THEN!
HA HA!
THAT'S STUPID. YOU MUST BE REALLY DUMB.
Hey!!
...

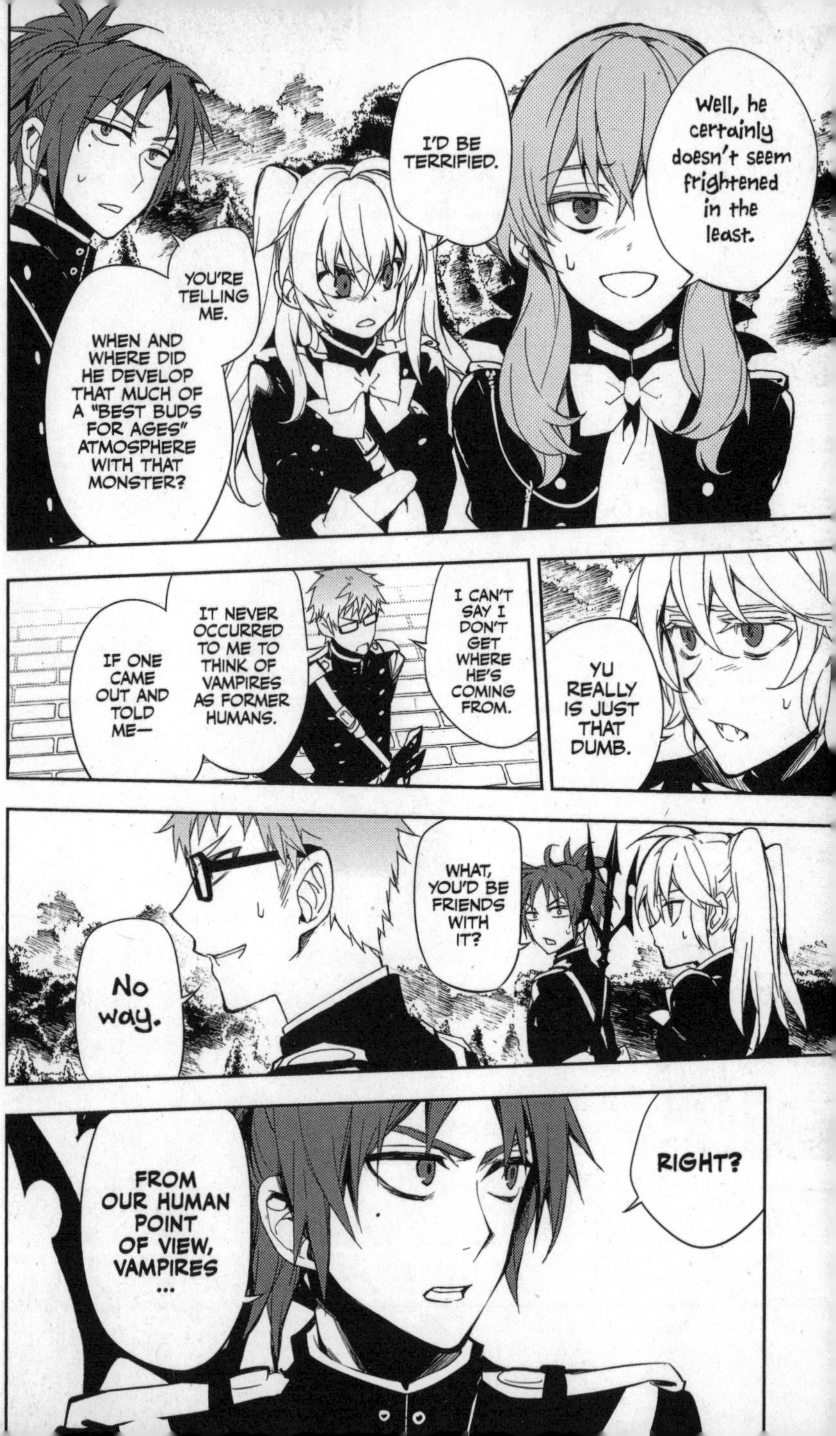
Well, he certainly doesn't seem frightened in the least.
I'D BE TERRIFIED.
YOU'RE TELLING ME.
WHEN AND WHERE DID HE DEVELOP THAT MUCH OF A "BEST BUDS FOR AGES" ATMOSPHERE WITH THAT MONSTER?
YU REALLY IS JUST THAT DUMB.
I CAN'T SAY I DON'T GET WHERE HE'S COMING FROM.
IT NEVER OCCURRED TO ME TO THINK OF VAMPIRES AS FORMER HUMANS.
IF ONE CAME OUT AND TOLD ME—
WHAT, YOU'D BE FRIENDS WITH IT?
No way.
RIGHT?
FROM OUR HUMAN POINT OF VIEW, VAMPIRES ...

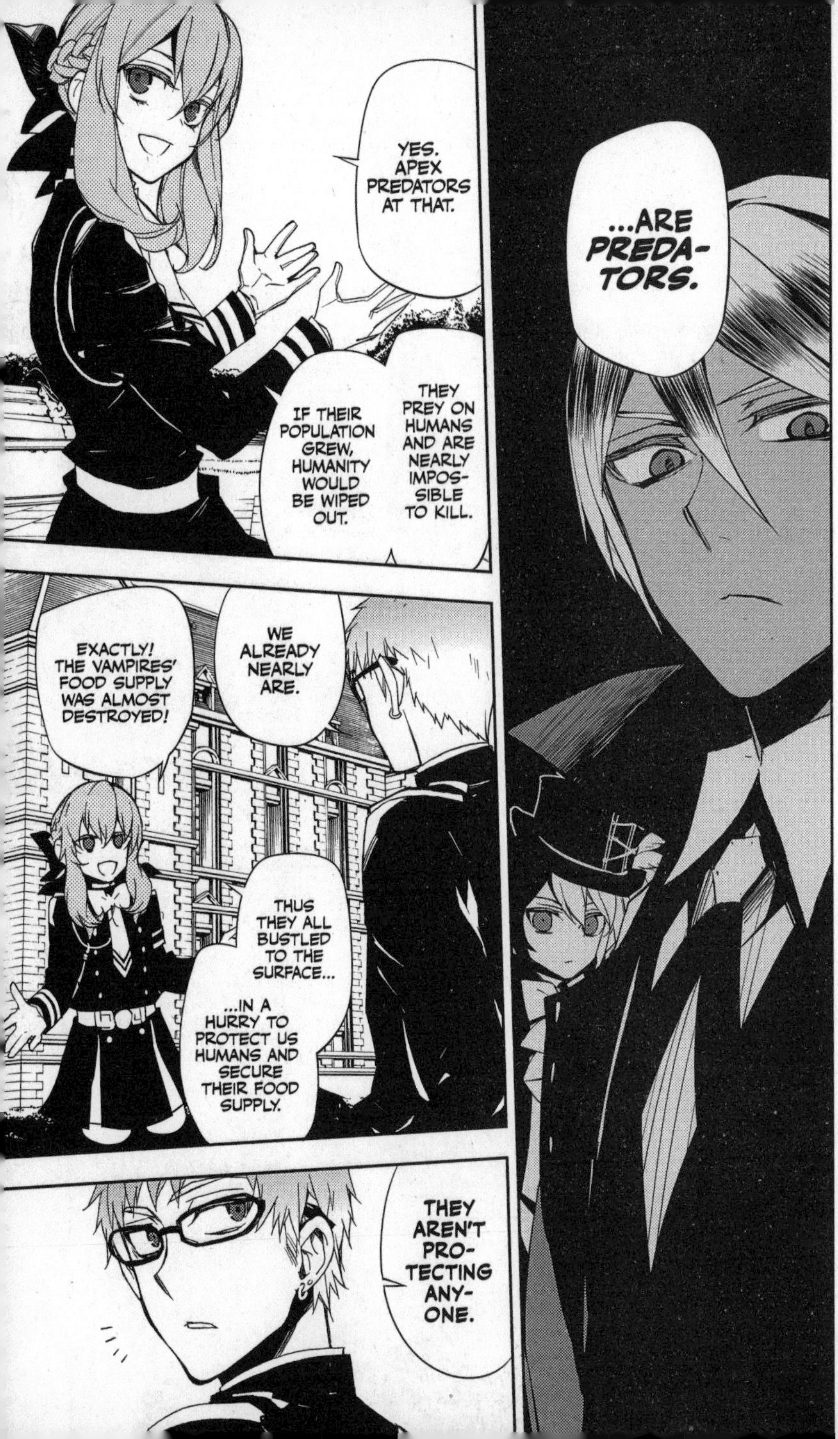
...ARE PREDATORS.
YES. APEX PREDATORS AT THAT.
THEY PREY ON HUMANS AND ARE NEARLY IMPOSSIBLE TO KILL.
IF THEIR POPULATION GREW, HUMANITY WOULD BE WIPED OUT.
WE ALREADY NEARLY ARE.
EXACTLY! THE VAMPIRES' FOOD SUPPLY WAS ALMOST DESTROYED!
THUS THEY ALL BUSTLED TO THE SURFACE...
...IN A HURRY TO PROTECT US HUMANS AND SECURE THEIR FOOD SUPPLY.
THEY AREN'T PROTECTING ANYONE.

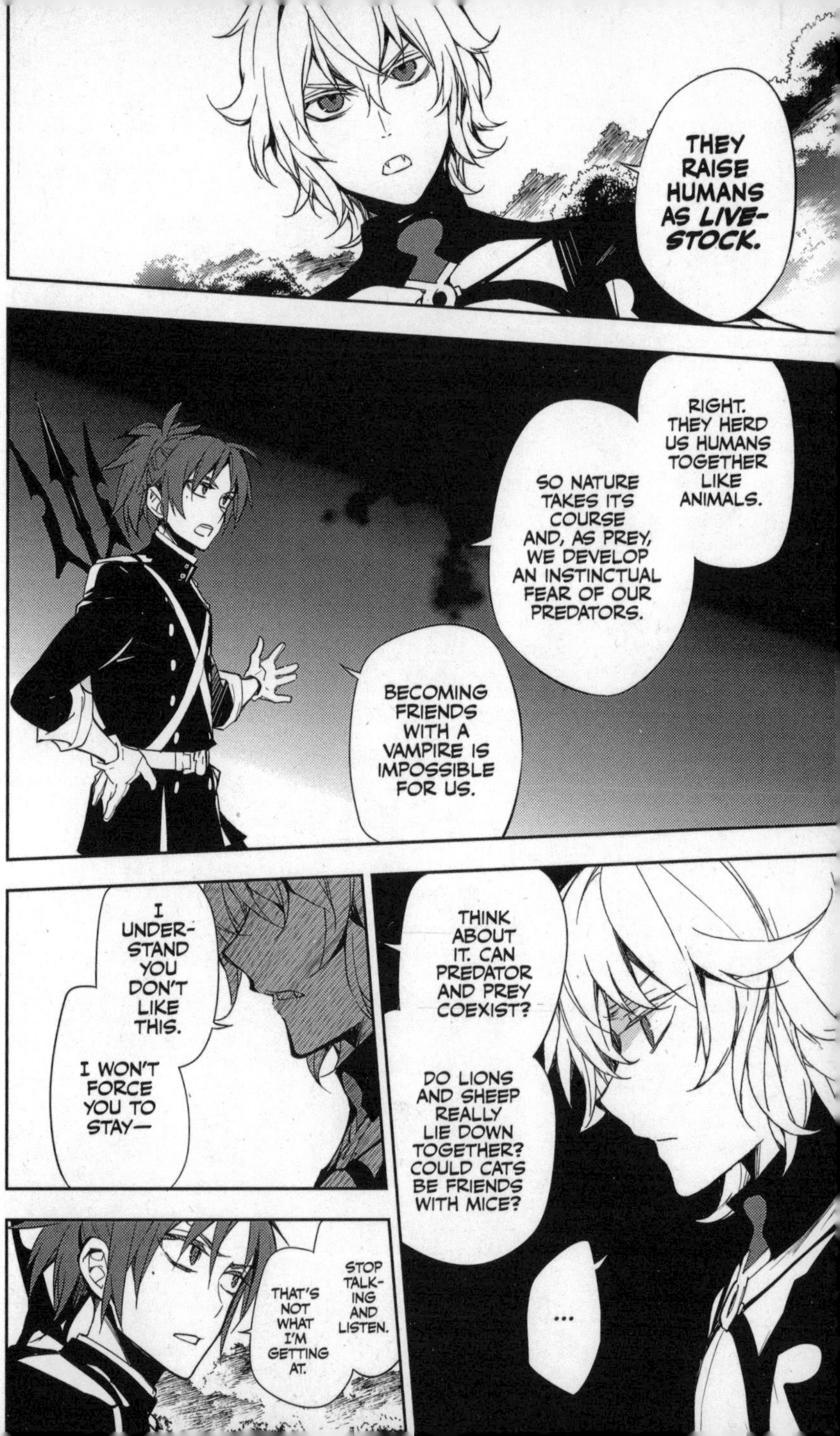
THEY RAISE HUMANS AS LIVE-STOCK.
RIGHT. THEY HERD US HUMANS TOGETHER LIKE ANIMALS.
SO NATURE TAKES ITS COURSE AND, AS PREY, WE DEVELOP AN INSTINCTUAL FEAR OF OUR PREDATORS.
BECOMING FRIENDS WITH A VAMPIRE IS IMPOSSIBLE FOR US.
THINK ABOUT IT. CAN PREDATOR AND PREY COEXIST?
DO LIONS AND SHEEP REALLY LIE DOWN TOGETHER? COULD CATS BE FRIENDS WITH MICE?
I UNDER-STAND YOU DON'T LIKE THIS.
I WON'T FORCE YOU TO STAY—
...
STOP TALK-ING AND LISTEN.
THAT'S NOT WHAT I'M GETTING AT.

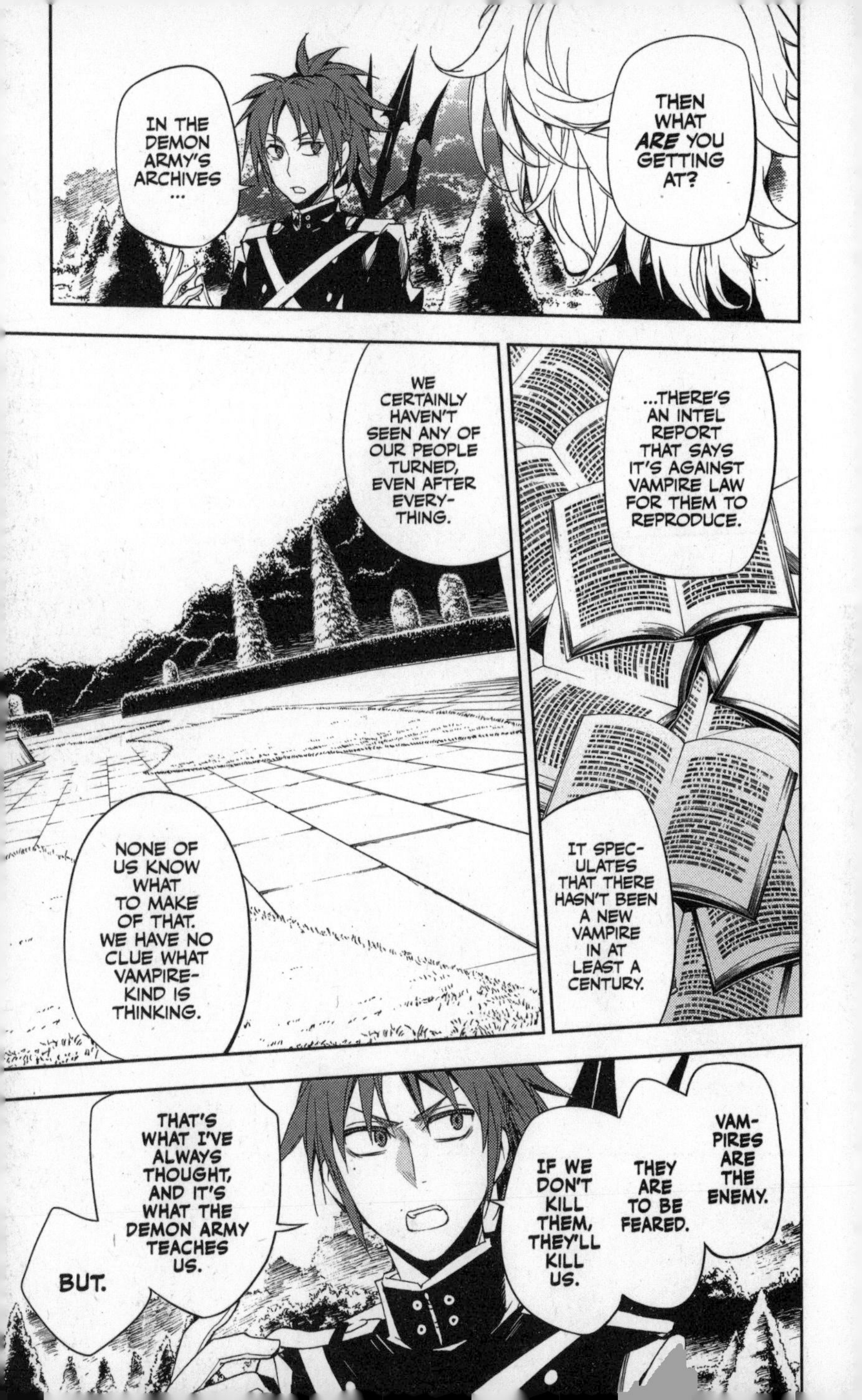
THEN WHAT *ARE* YOU GETTING AT?
IN THE DEMON ARMY'S ARCHIVES...
...THERE'S AN INTEL REPORT THAT SAYS IT'S AGAINST VAMPIRE LAW FOR THEM TO REPRODUCE.
IT SPECULATES THAT THERE HASN'T BEEN A NEW VAMPIRE IN AT LEAST A CENTURY.
WE CERTAINLY HAVEN'T SEEN ANY OF OUR PEOPLE TURNED, EVEN AFTER EVERY-THING.
NONE OF US KNOW WHAT TO MAKE OF THAT. WE HAVE NO CLUE WHAT VAMPIRE-KIND IS THINKING.
VAM-PIRES ARE THE ENEMY.
THEY ARE TO BE FEARED.
IF WE DON'T KILL THEM, THEY'LL KILL US.
THAT'S WHAT I'VE ALWAYS THOUGHT, AND IT'S WHAT THE DEMON ARMY TEACHES US.
BUT.

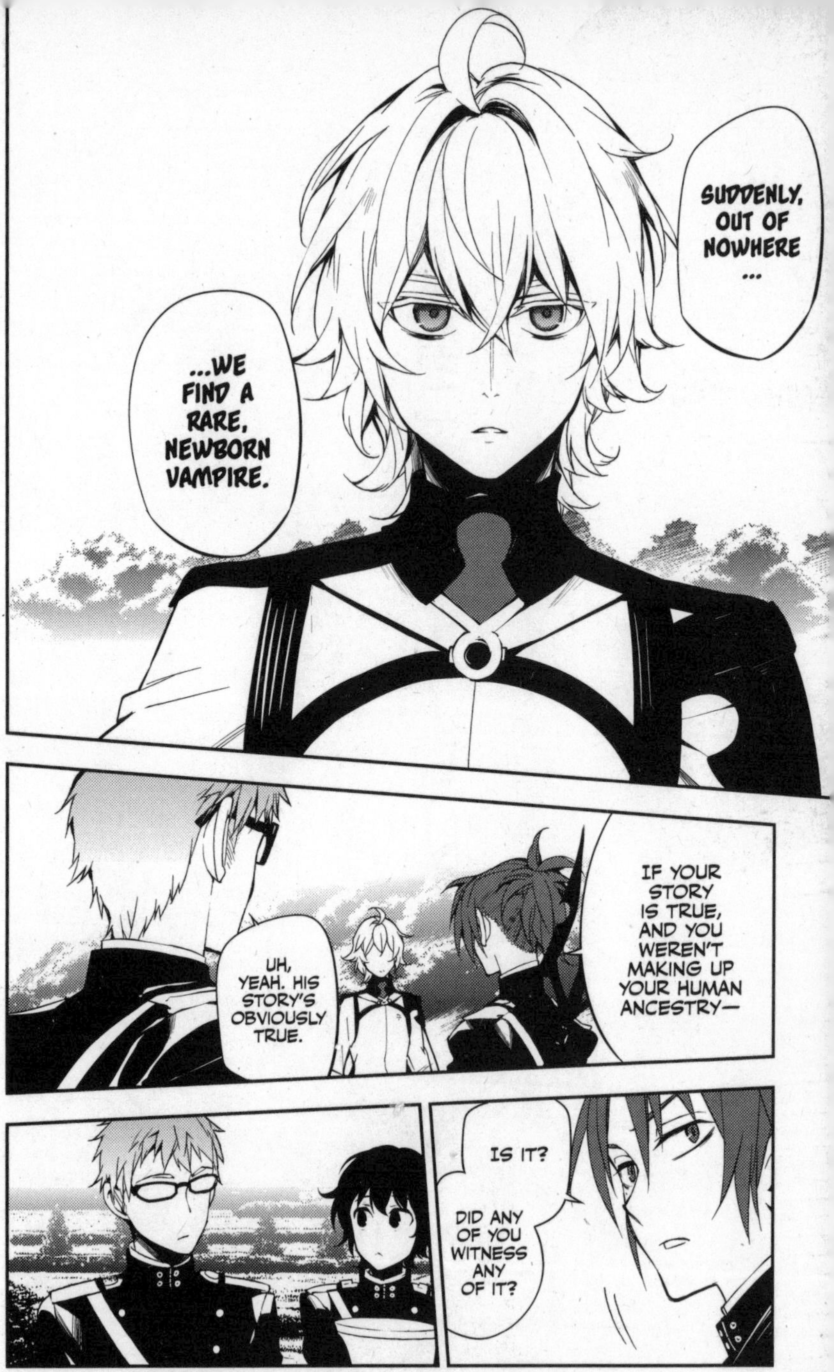
SUDDENLY, OUT OF NOWHERE...
...WE FIND A RARE, NEWBORN VAMPIRE.
IF YOUR STORY IS TRUE, AND YOU WEREN'T MAKING UP YOUR HUMAN ANCESTRY—
UH, YEAH. HIS STORY'S OBVIOUSLY TRUE.
IS IT?
DID ANY OF YOU WITNESS ANY OF IT?

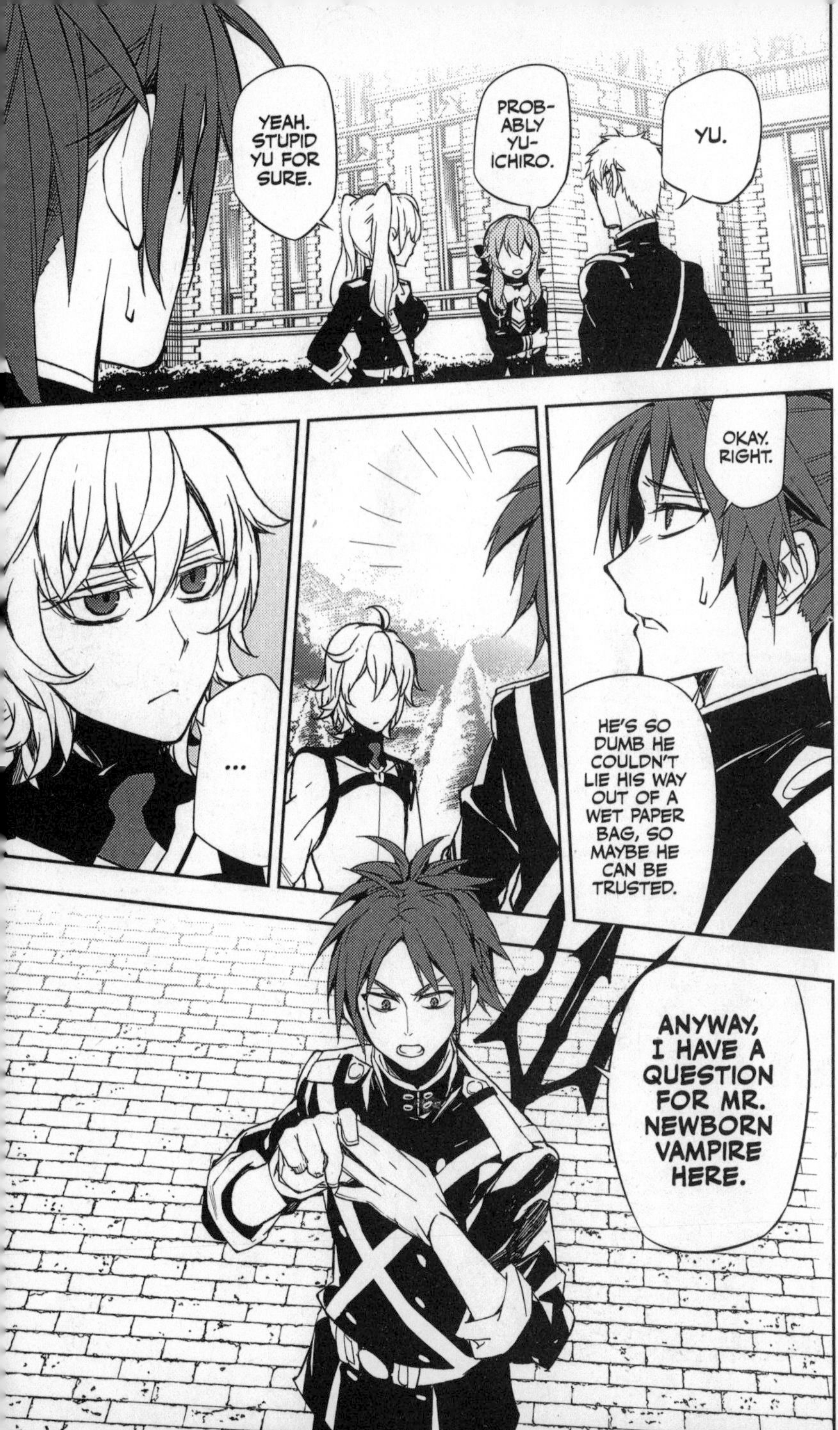
YU.
PROB-ABLY YU-ICHIRO.
YEAH. STUPID YU FOR SURE.
OKAY. RIGHT.
HE'S SO DUMB HE COULDN'T LIE HIS WAY OUT OF A WET PAPER BAG, SO MAYBE HE CAN BE TRUSTED.
...
ANYWAY, I HAVE A QUESTION FOR MR. NEWBORN VAMPIRE HERE.

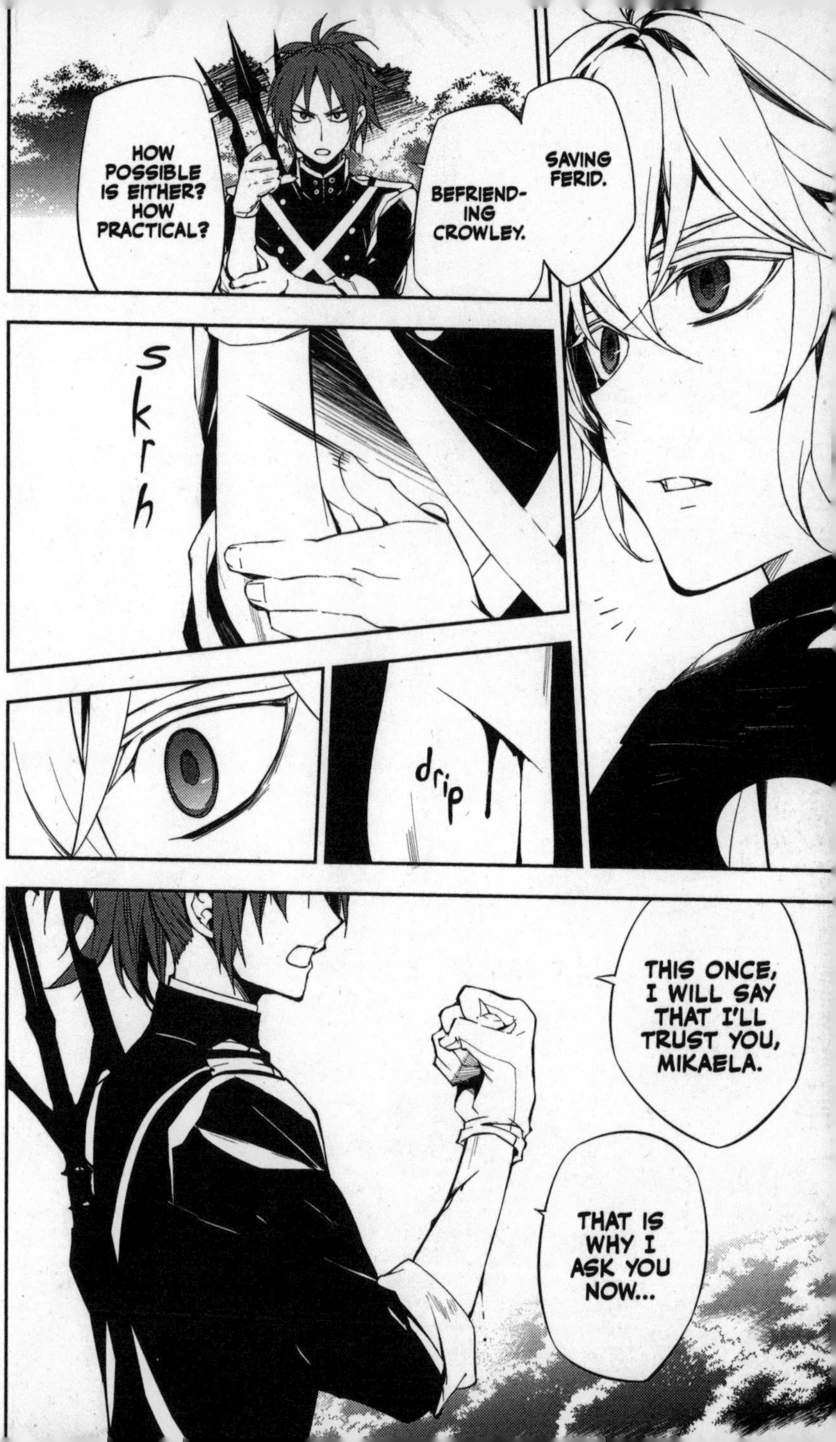
SAVING FERID.
BEFRIEND-ING CROWLEY.
HOW POSSIBLE IS EITHER? HOW PRACTICAL?
skrh
drip
THIS ONCE, I WILL SAY THAT I'LL TRUST YOU, MIKAELA.
THAT IS WHY I ASK YOU NOW...

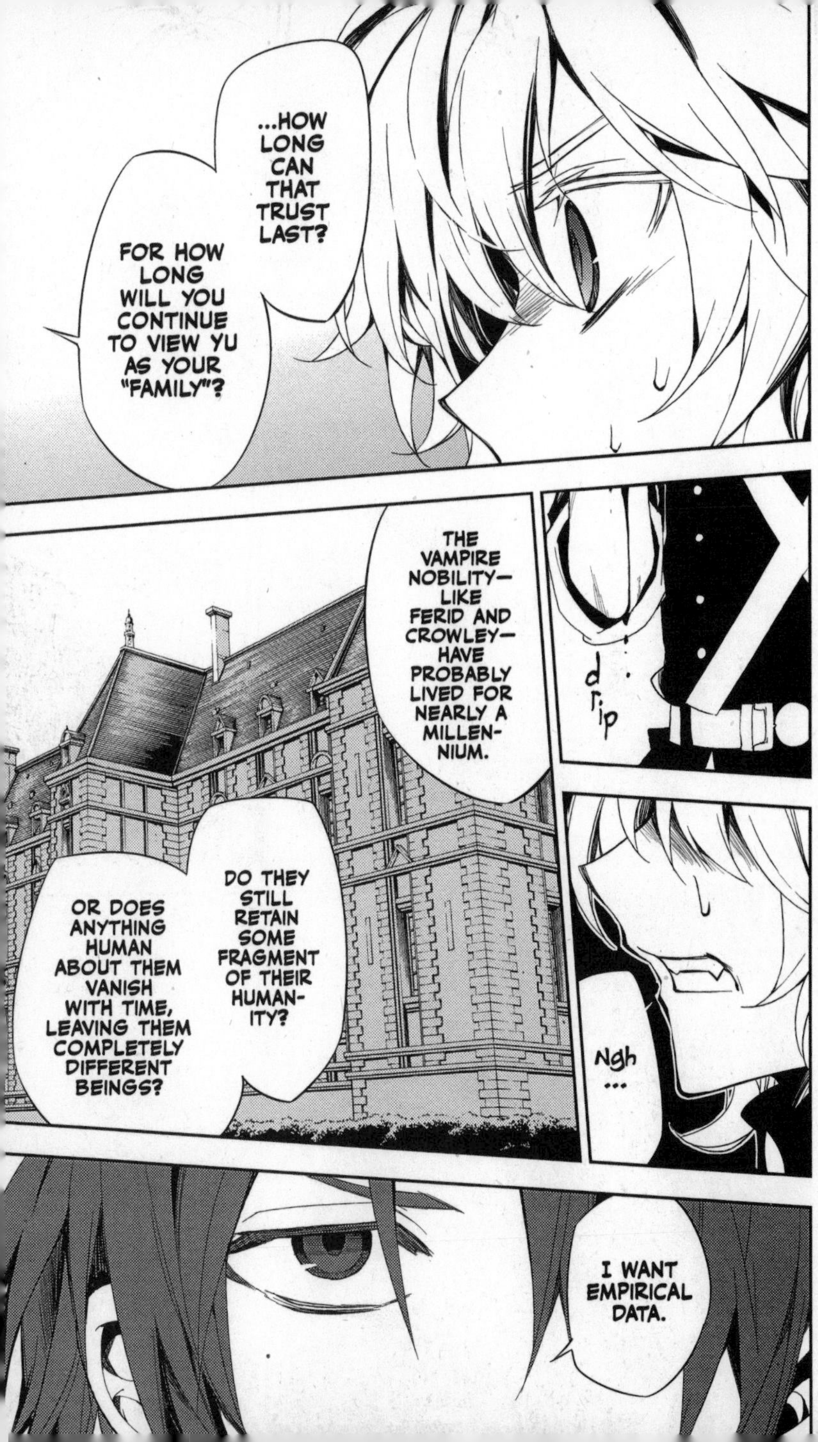
...HOW LONG CAN THAT TRUST LAST?
FOR HOW LONG WILL YOU CONTINUE TO VIEW YU AS YOUR "FAMILY"?
drip
Ngh...
THE VAMPIRE NOBILITY—LIKE FERID AND CROWLEY—HAVE PROBABLY LIVED FOR NEARLY A MILLENNIUM.
DO THEY STILL RETAIN SOME FRAGMENT OF THEIR HUMANITY?
OR DOES ANYTHING HUMAN ABOUT THEM VANISH WITH TIME, LEAVING THEM COMPLETELY DIFFERENT BEINGS?
I WANT EMPIRICAL DATA.

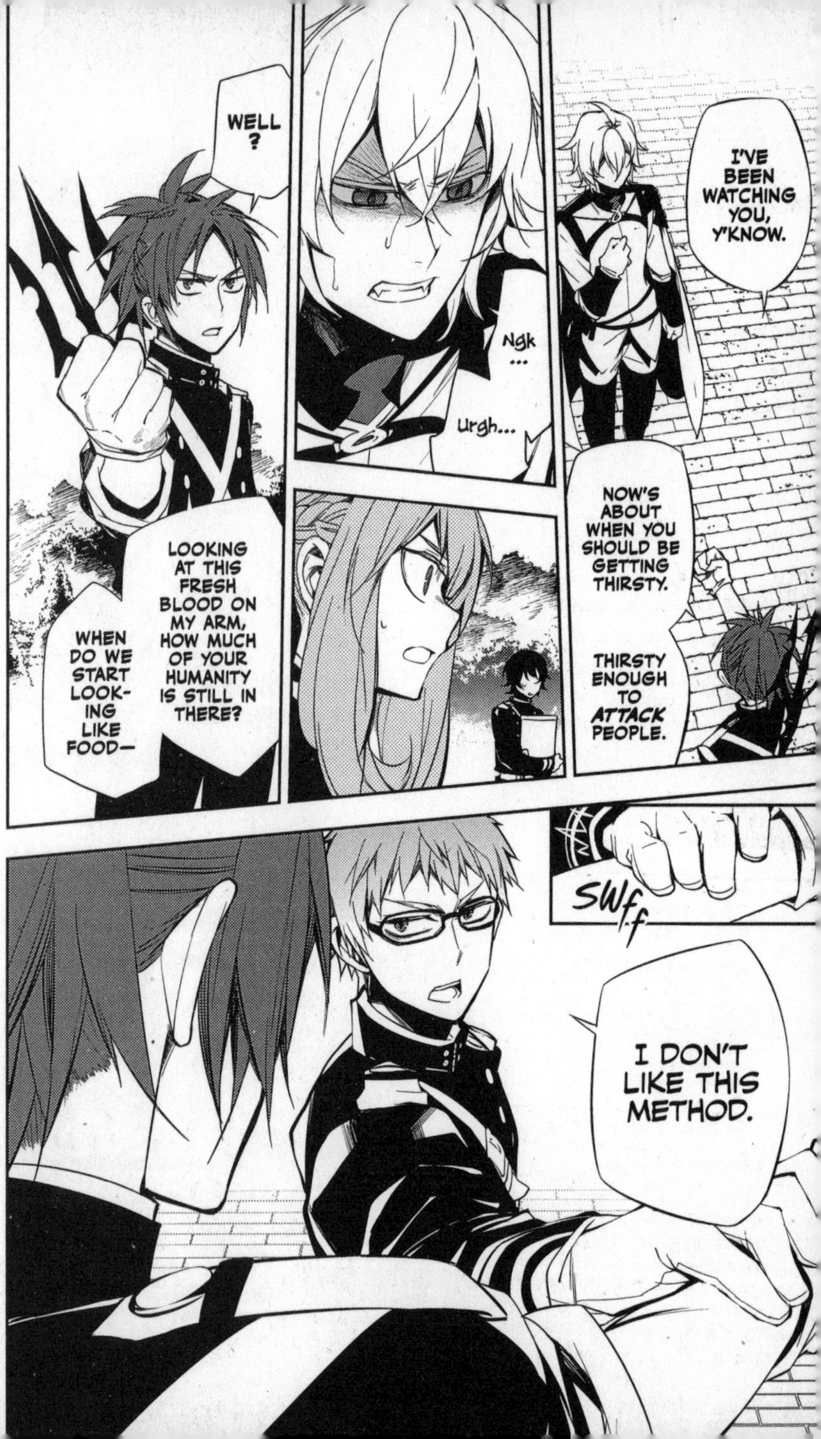

I'VE BEEN WATCHING YOU, Y'KNOW.
Ngk...
Urgh...
NOW'S ABOUT WHEN YOU SHOULD BE GETTING THIRSTY.
THIRSTY ENOUGH TO *ATTACK* PEOPLE.
WELL?
LOOKING AT THIS FRESH BLOOD ON MY ARM, HOW MUCH OF YOUR HUMANITY IS STILL IN THERE?
WHEN DO WE START LOOKING LIKE FOOD—
SWff
I DON'T LIKE THIS METHOD.

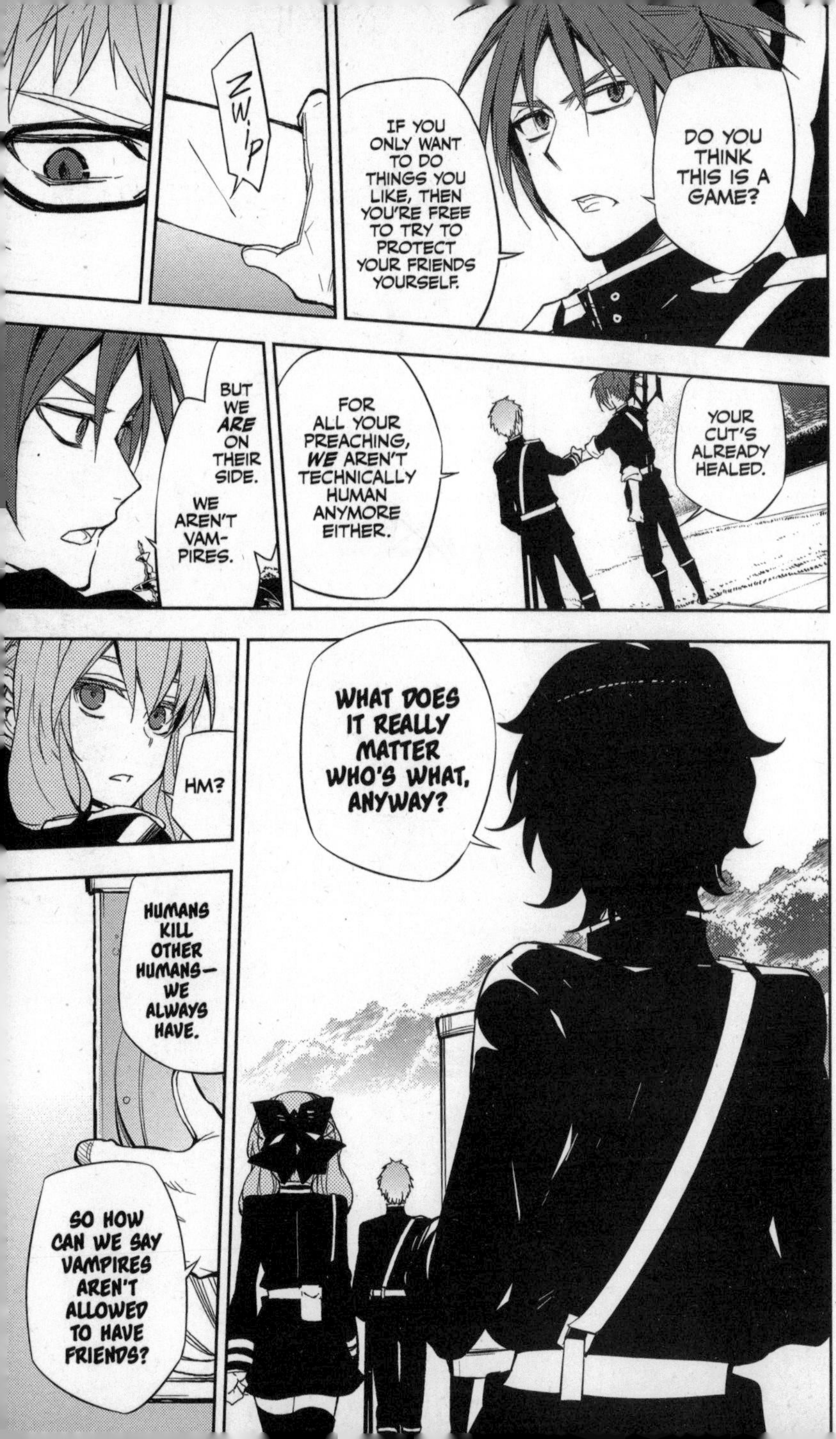
DO YOU THINK THIS IS A GAME?
IF YOU ONLY WANT TO DO THINGS YOU LIKE, THEN YOU'RE FREE TO TRY TO PROTECT YOUR FRIENDS YOURSELF.
ZWIP
YOUR CUT'S ALREADY HEALED.
FOR ALL YOUR PREACHING, *WE* AREN'T TECHNICALLY HUMAN ANYMORE EITHER.
BUT WE *ARE* ON THEIR SIDE.
WE AREN'T VAM-PIRES.
WHAT DOES IT REALLY MATTER WHO'S WHAT, ANYWAY?
HM?
HUMANS KILL OTHER HUMANS— WE ALWAYS HAVE.
SO HOW CAN WE SAY VAMPIRES AREN'T ALLOWED TO HAVE FRIENDS?

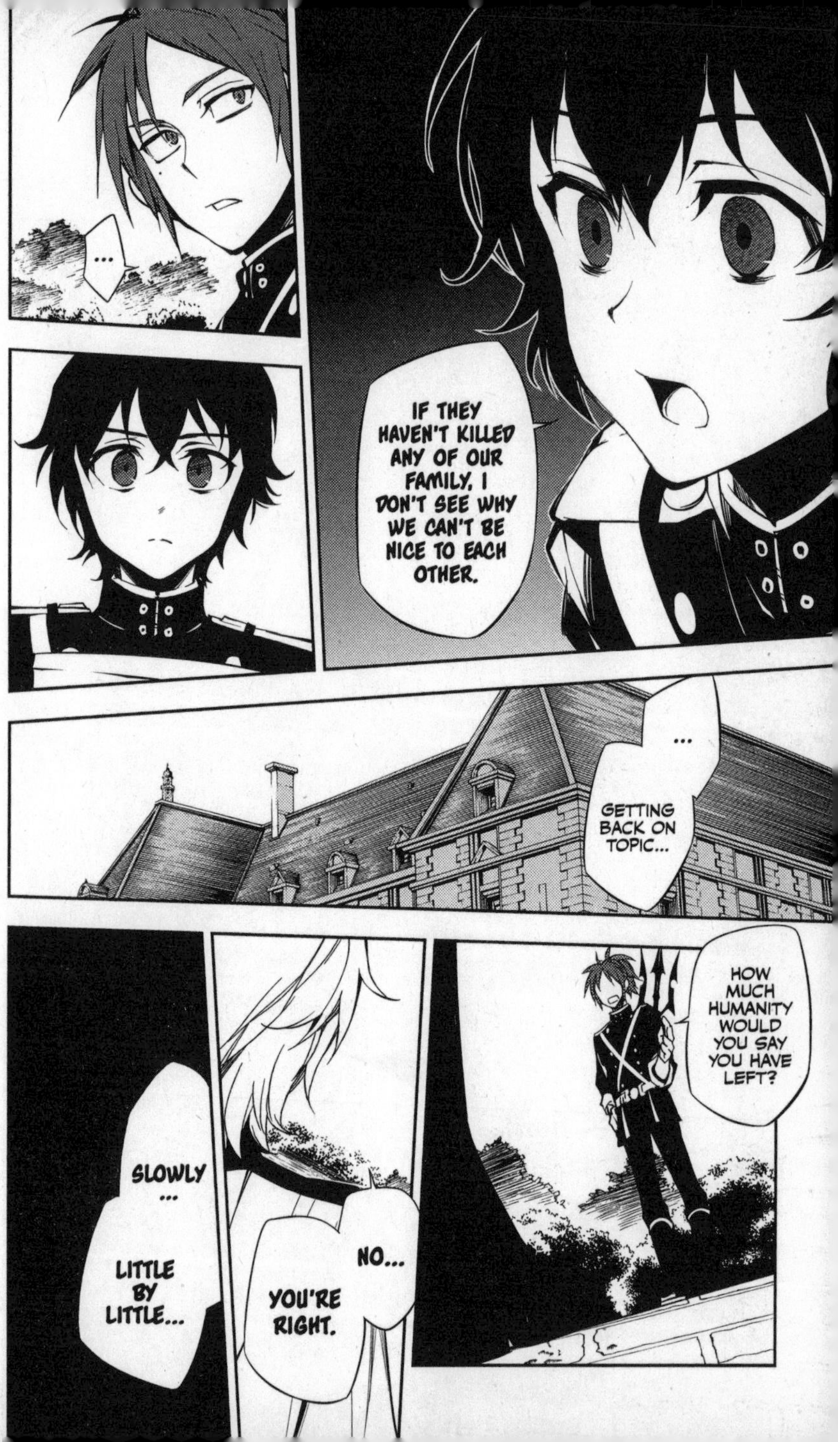
IF THEY HAVEN'T KILLED ANY OF OUR FAMILY, I DON'T SEE WHY WE CAN'T BE NICE TO EACH OTHER.
...
...
GETTING BACK ON TOPIC...
HOW MUCH HUMANITY WOULD YOU SAY YOU HAVE LEFT?
NO...
YOU'RE RIGHT.
SLOWLY...
LITTLE BY LITTLE...

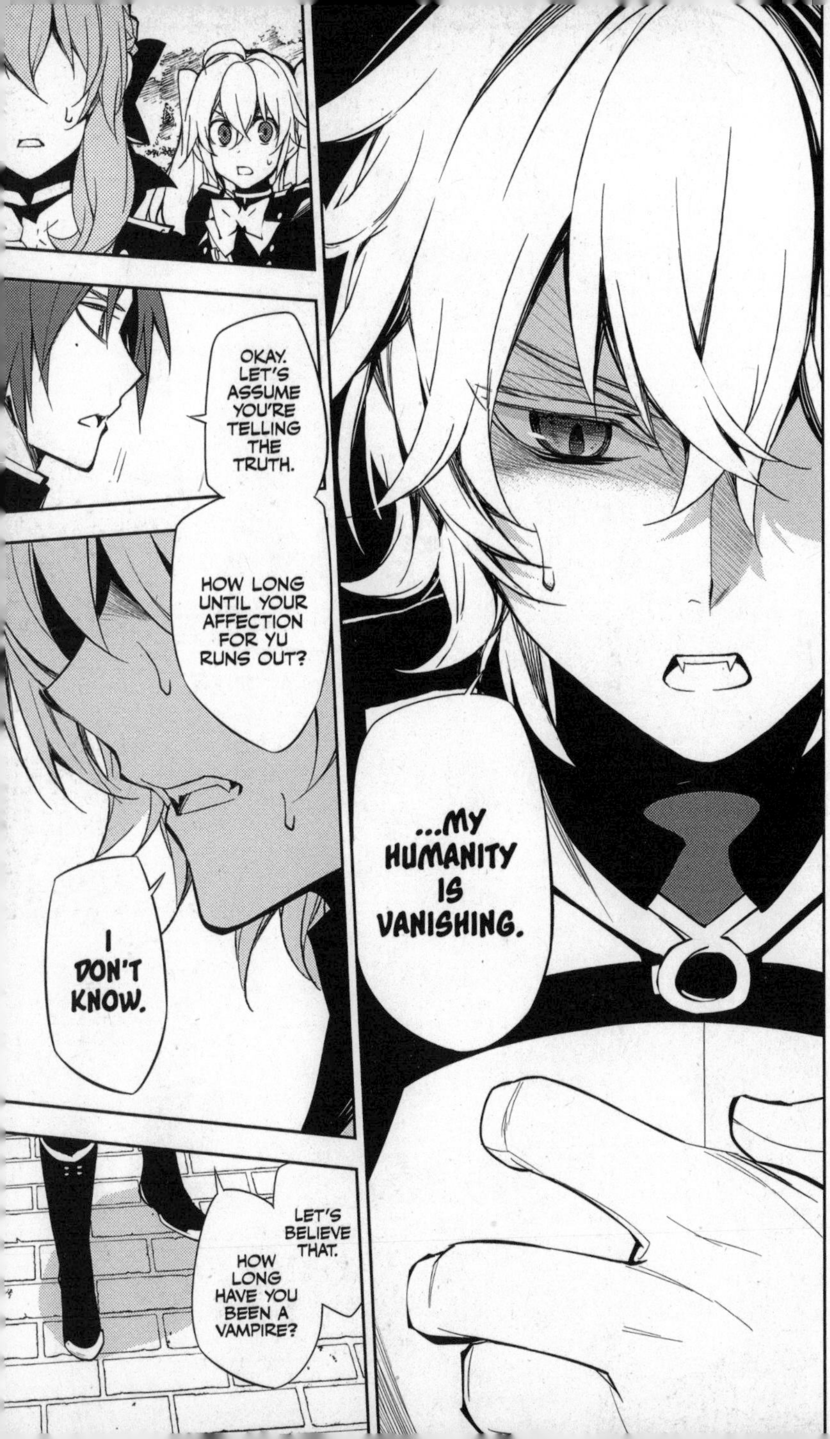
...MY HUMANITY IS VANISHING.
OKAY. LET'S ASSUME YOU'RE TELLING THE TRUTH.
HOW LONG UNTIL YOUR AFFECTION FOR YU RUNS OUT?
I DON'T KNOW.
LET'S BELIEVE THAT.
HOW LONG HAVE YOU BEEN A VAMPIRE?

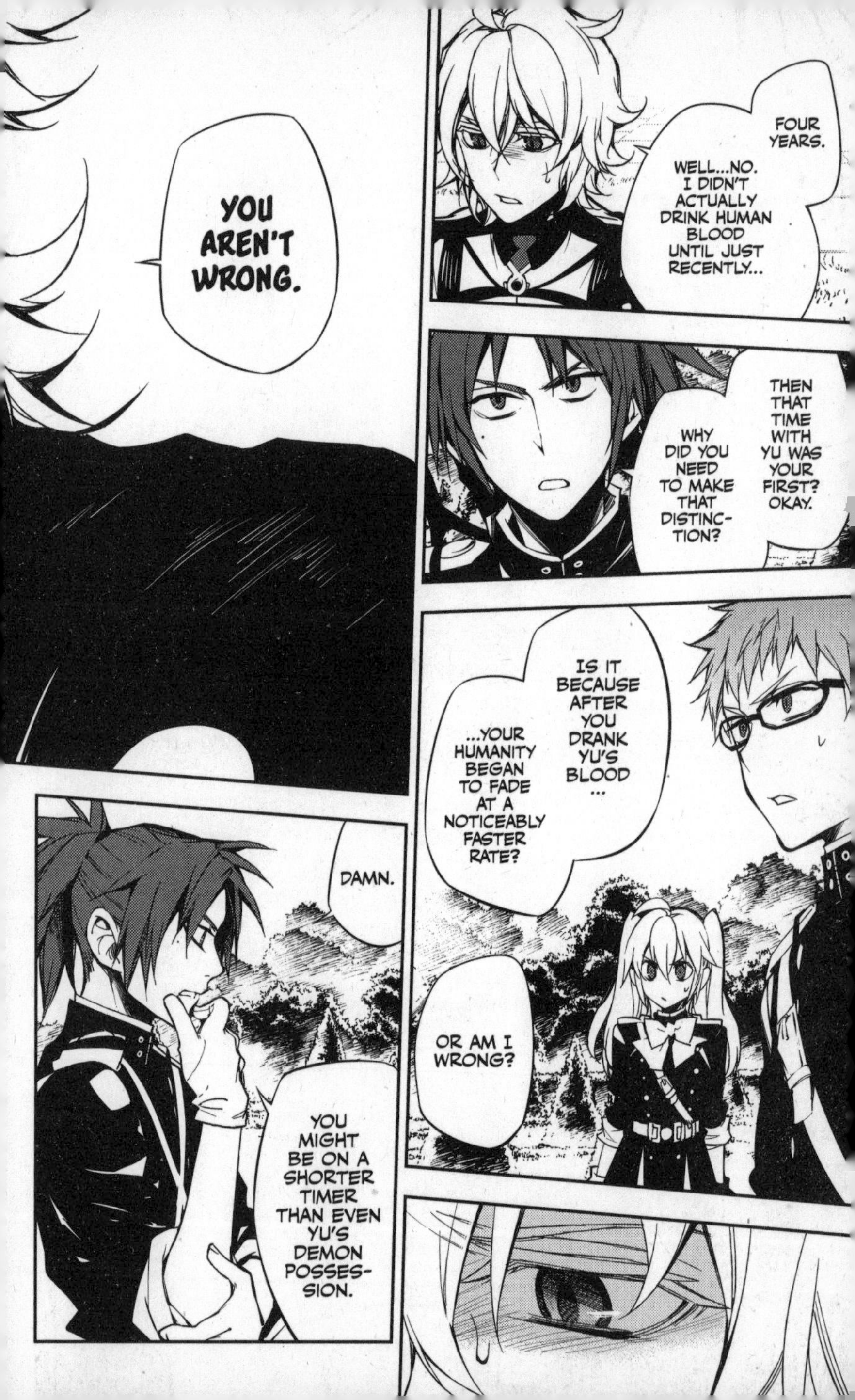
FOUR YEARS.
WELL...NO. I DIDN'T ACTUALLY DRINK HUMAN BLOOD UNTIL JUST RECENTLY...
THEN THAT TIME WITH YU WAS YOUR FIRST? OKAY.
WHY DID YOU NEED TO MAKE THAT DISTINCTION?
IS IT BECAUSE AFTER YOU DRANK YU'S BLOOD...
...YOUR HUMANITY BEGAN TO FADE AT A NOTICEABLY FASTER RATE?
OR AM I WRONG?
YOU AREN'T WRONG.
DAMN.
YOU MIGHT BE ON A SHORTER TIMER THAN EVEN YU'S DEMON POSSESSION.

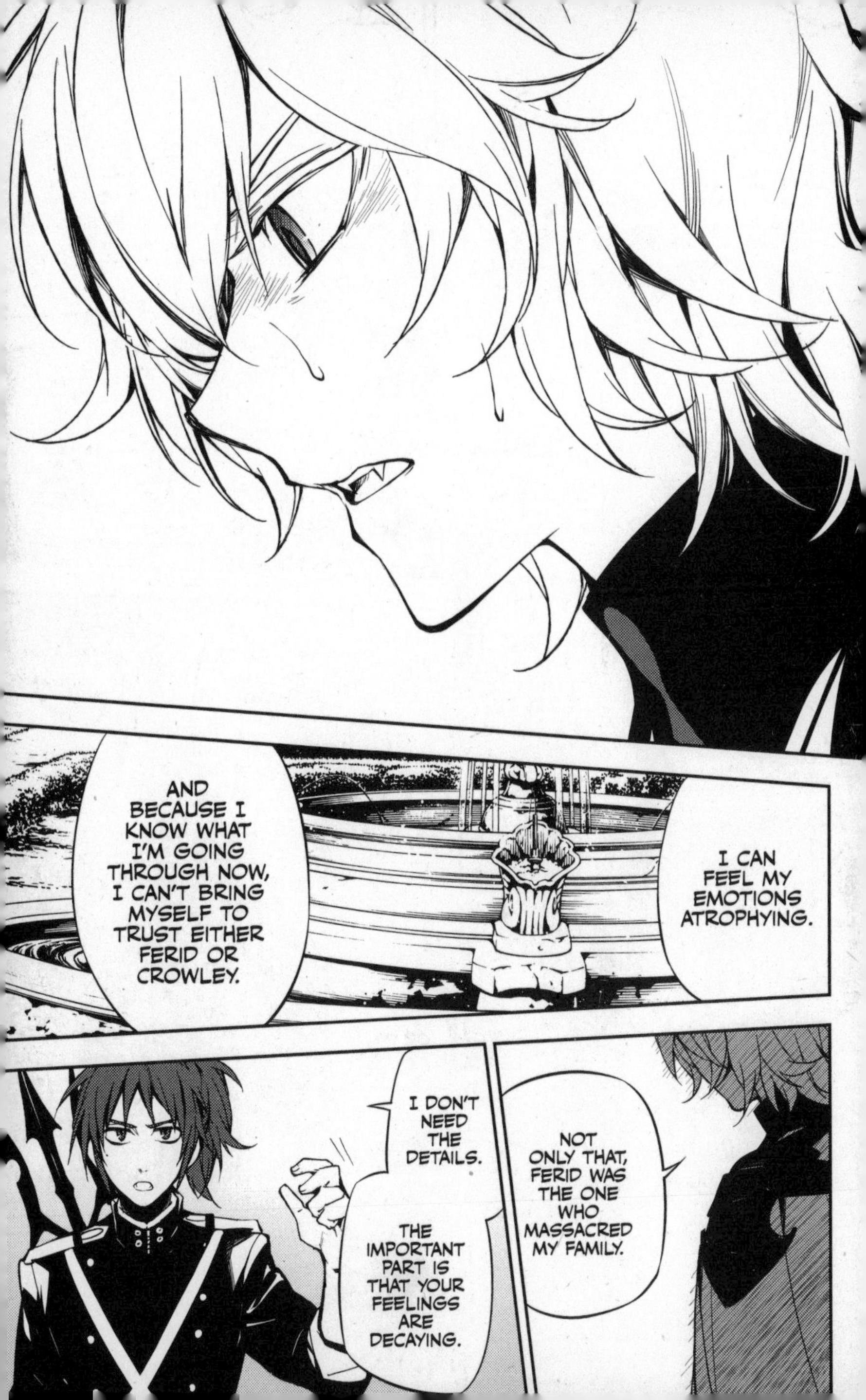
I CAN FEEL MY EMOTIONS ATROPHYING.
AND BECAUSE I KNOW WHAT I'M GOING THROUGH NOW, I CAN'T BRING MYSELF TO TRUST EITHER FERID OR CROWLEY.
NOT ONLY THAT, FERID WAS THE ONE WHO MASSACRED MY FAMILY.
I DON'T NEED THE DETAILS.
THE IMPORTANT PART IS THAT YOUR FEELINGS ARE DECAYING.

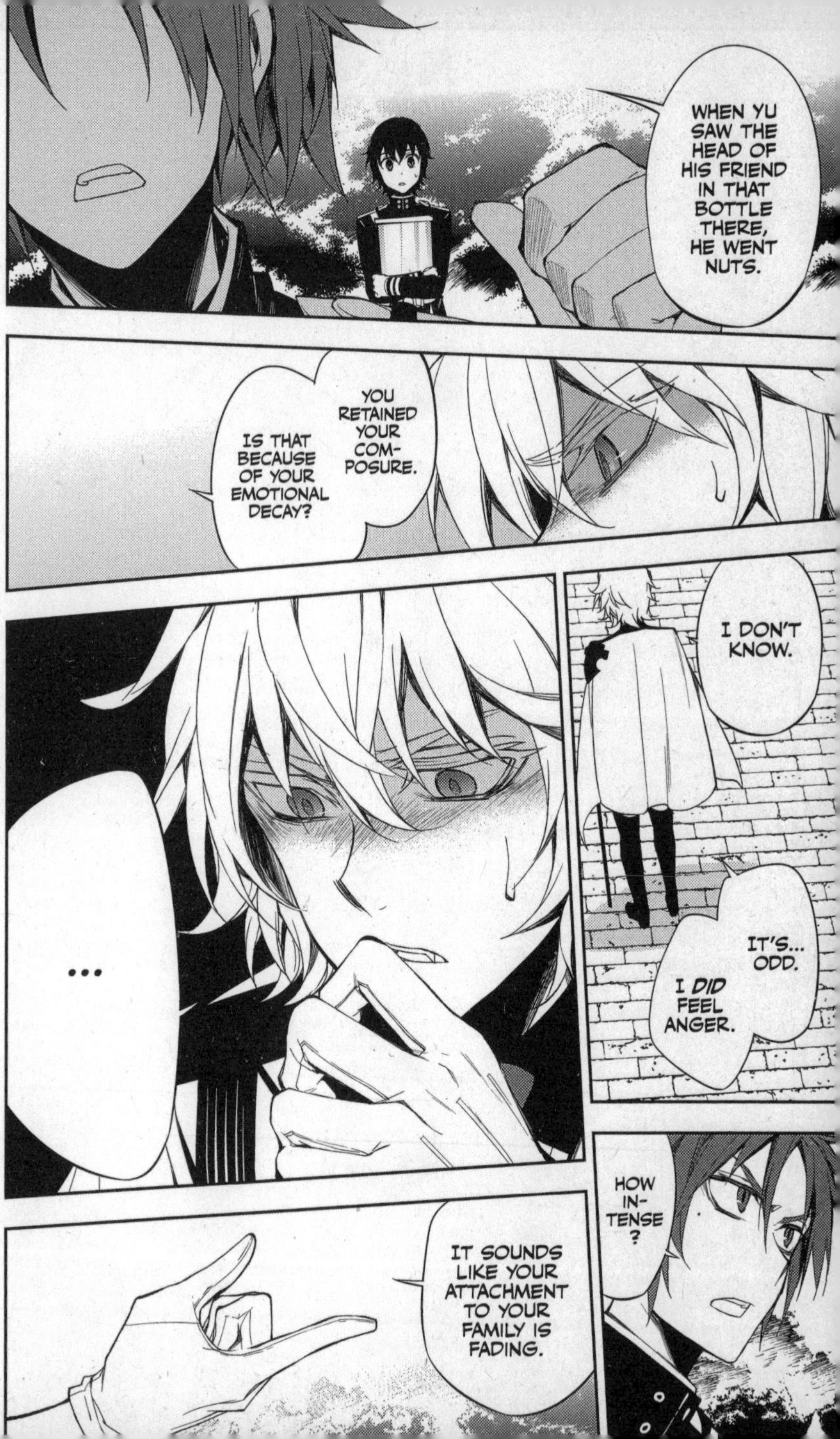
WHEN YU SAW THE HEAD OF HIS FRIEND IN THAT BOTTLE THERE, HE WENT NUTS.
YOU RETAINED YOUR COM-POSURE.
IS THAT BECAUSE OF YOUR EMOTIONAL DECAY?
I DON'T KNOW.
IT'S... ODD.
I *DID* FEEL ANGER.
...
HOW IN-TENSE?
IT SOUNDS LIKE YOUR ATTACHMENT TO YOUR FAMILY IS FADING.

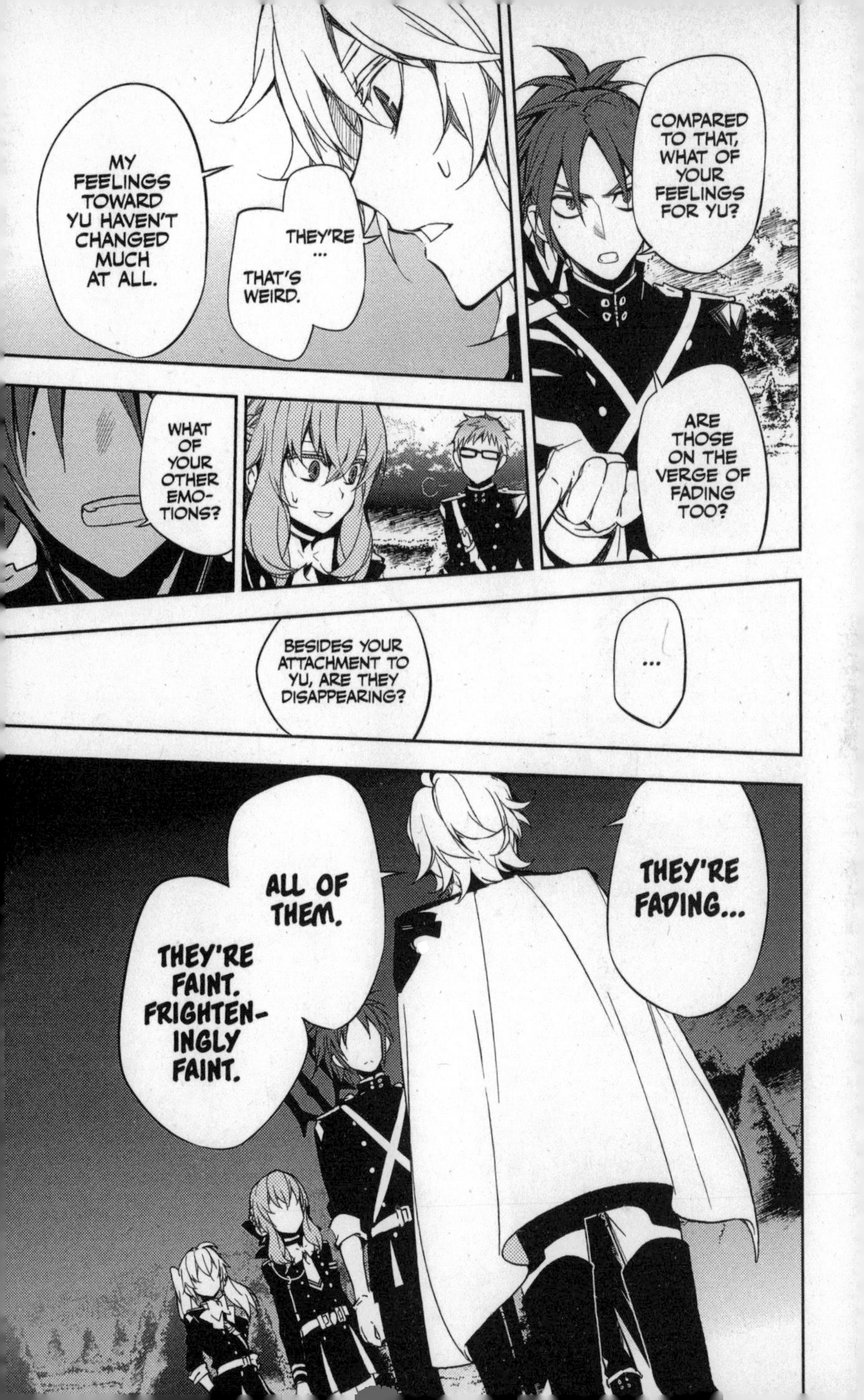
COMPARED TO THAT, WHAT OF YOUR FEELINGS FOR YU?
ARE THOSE ON THE VERGE OF FADING TOO?
THEY'RE ... THAT'S WEIRD.
MY FEELINGS TOWARD YU HAVEN'T CHANGED MUCH AT ALL.
WHAT OF YOUR OTHER EMO-TIONS?
...
BESIDES YOUR ATTACHMENT TO YU, ARE THEY DISAPPEARING?
THEY'RE FADING...
ALL OF THEM.
THEY'RE FAINT. FRIGHTEN-INGLY FAINT.

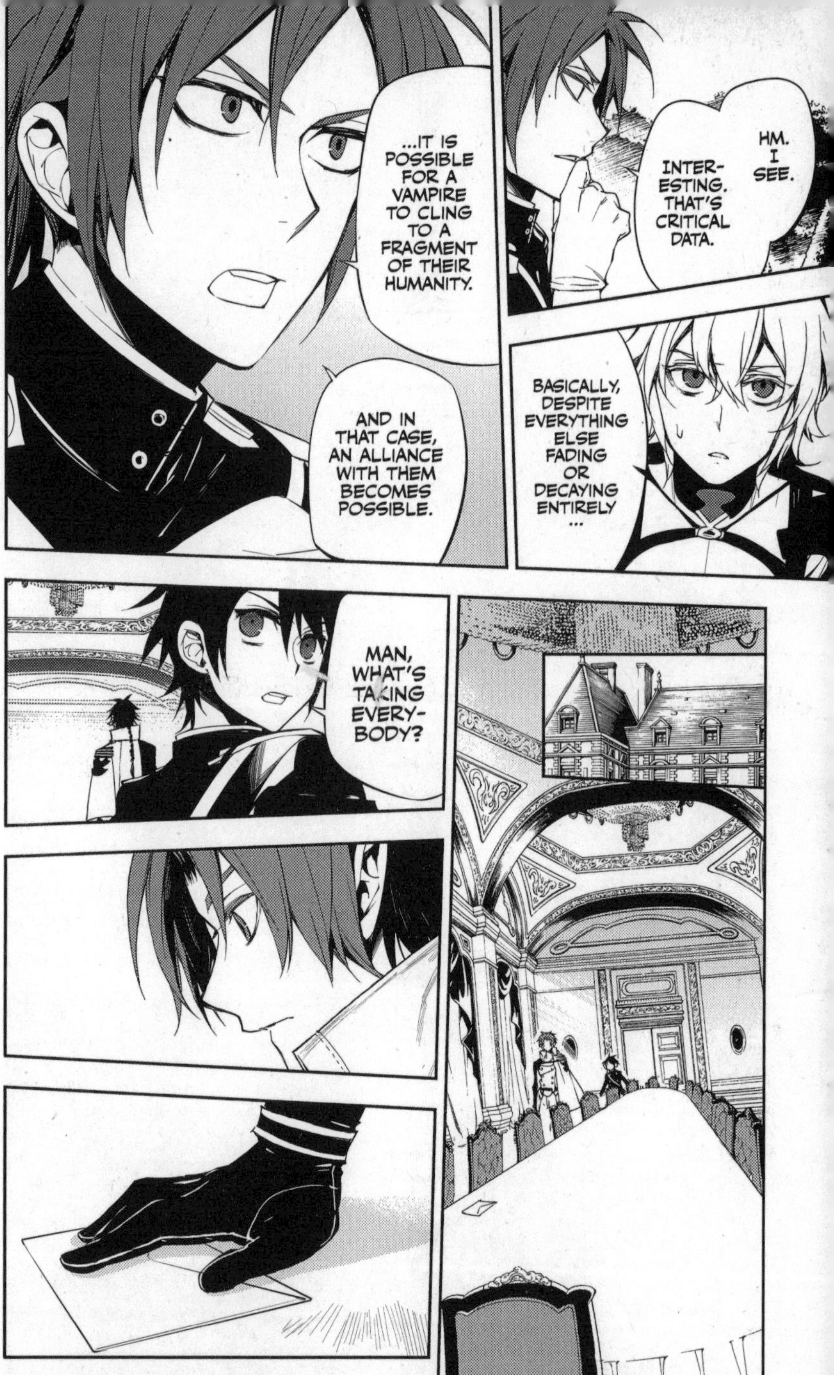
HM. I SEE.
INTER-ESTING. THAT'S CRITICAL DATA.
BASICALLY, DESPITE EVERYTHING ELSE FADING OR DECAYING ENTIRELY...
...IT IS POSSIBLE FOR A VAMPIRE TO CLING TO A FRAGMENT OF THEIR HUMANITY.
AND IN THAT CASE, AN ALLIANCE WITH THEM BECOMES POSSIBLE.
MAN, WHAT'S TAKING EVERY-BODY?

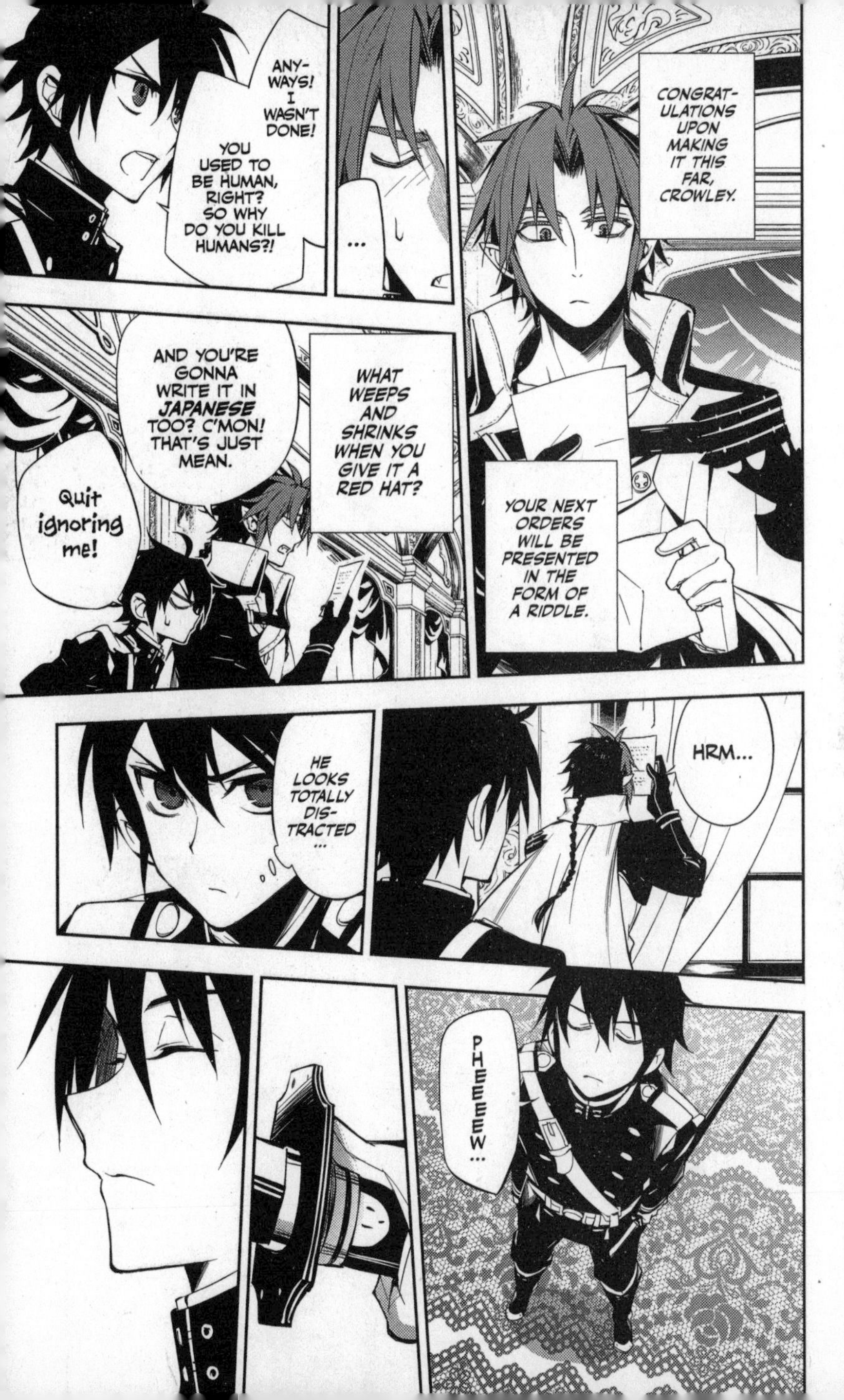
CONGRATULATIONS UPON MAKING IT THIS FAR, CROWLEY.
YOUR NEXT ORDERS WILL BE PRESENTED IN THE FORM OF A RIDDLE.
...
ANYWAYS! I WASN'T DONE!
YOU USED TO BE HUMAN, RIGHT? SO WHY DO YOU KILL HUMANS?!
WHAT WEEPS AND SHRINKS WHEN YOU GIVE IT A RED HAT?
AND YOU'RE GONNA WRITE IT IN *JAPANESE* TOO? C'MON! THAT'S JUST MEAN.
Quit ignoring me!
HRM...
HE LOOKS TOTALLY DISTRACTED...
PHEEEEW...

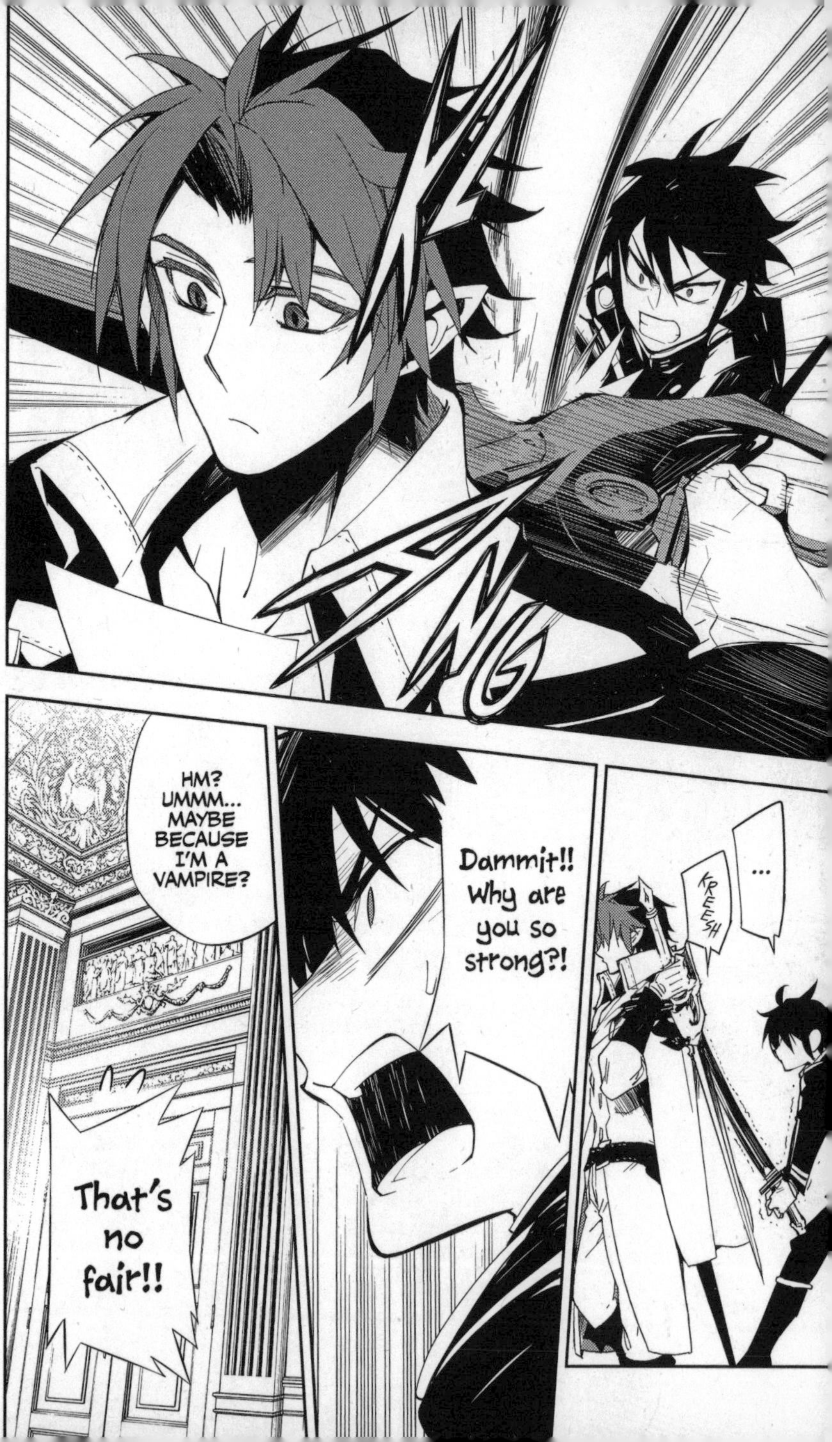
KREEESH
...
Dammit!! Why are you so strong?!
HM? UMMM... MAYBE BECAUSE I'M A VAMPIRE?
That's no fair!!

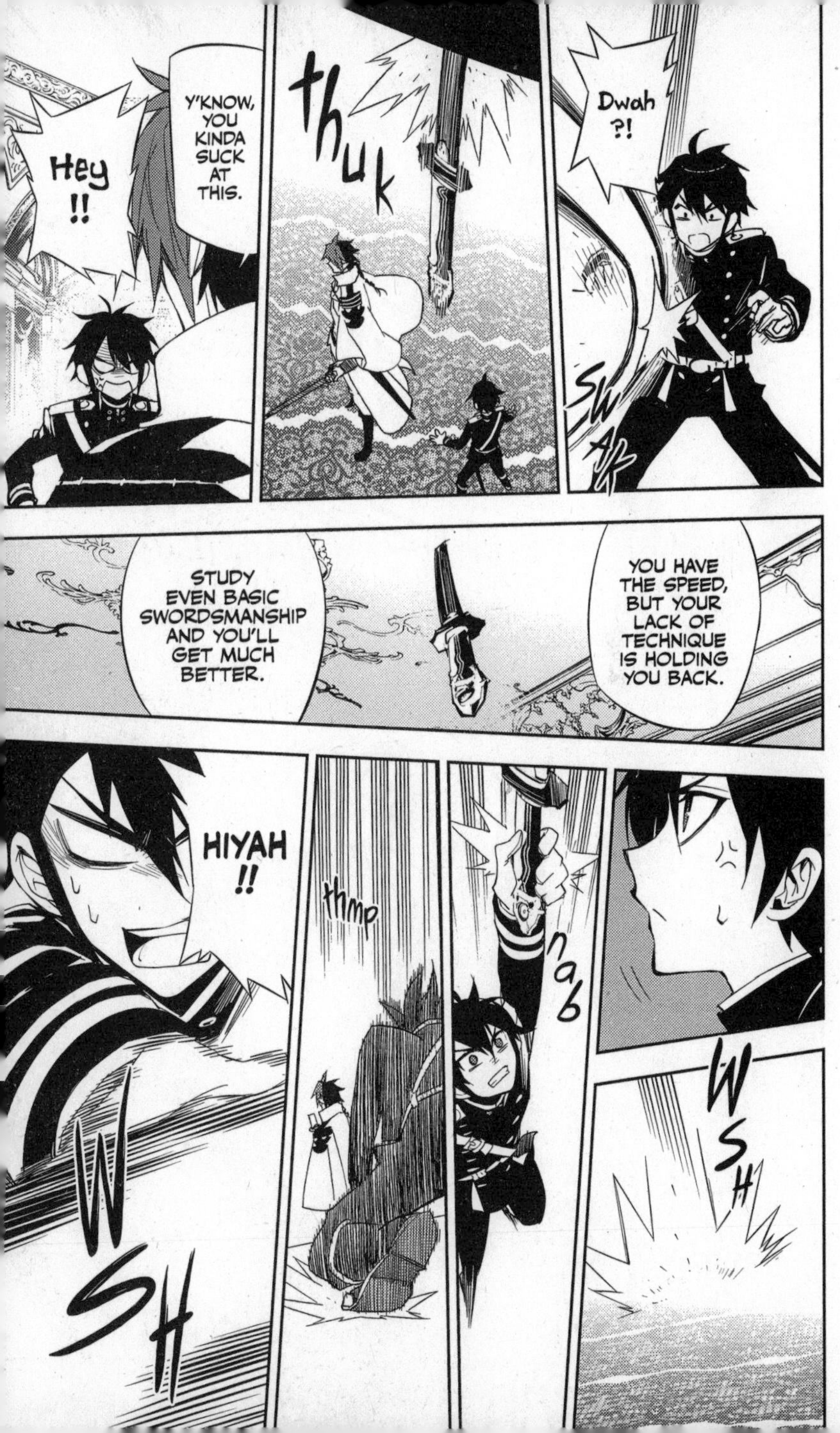
Dwah ?!
SWAK
thuk
Y'KNOW, YOU KINDA SUCK AT THIS.
Hey !!
YOU HAVE THE SPEED, BUT YOUR LACK OF TECHNIQUE IS HOLDING YOU BACK.
STUDY EVEN BASIC SWORDSMANSHIP AND YOU'LL GET MUCH BETTER.
WSH
nab
thmp
HIYAH !!
WSH

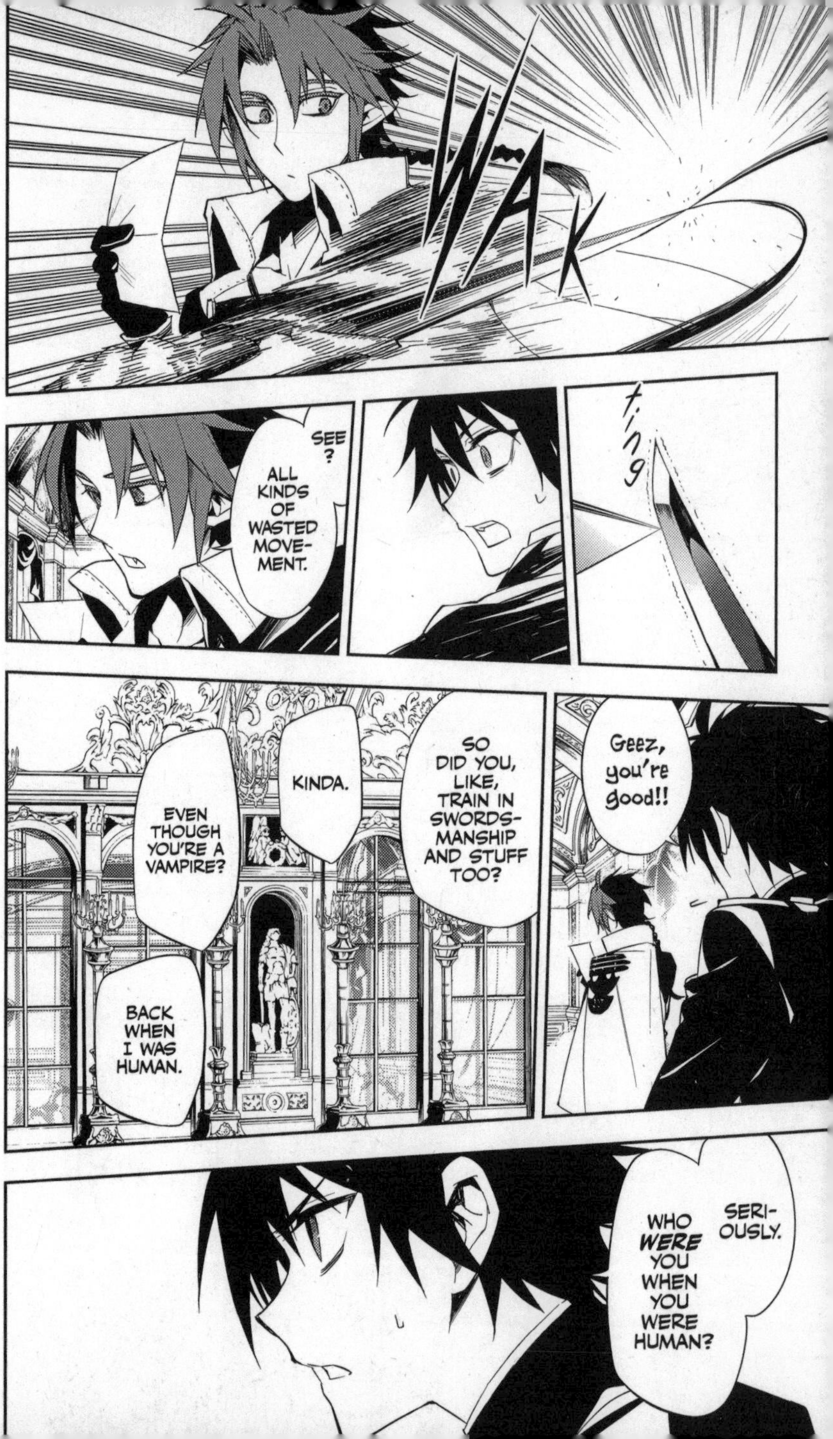
WAK
ting
SEE? ALL KINDS OF WASTED MOVEMENT.
Geez, you're good!!
SO DID YOU, LIKE, TRAIN IN SWORDSMANSHIP AND STUFF TOO?
KINDA.
EVEN THOUGH YOU'RE A VAMPIRE?
BACK WHEN I WAS HUMAN.
SERIOUSLY.
WHO *WERE* YOU WHEN YOU WERE HUMAN?

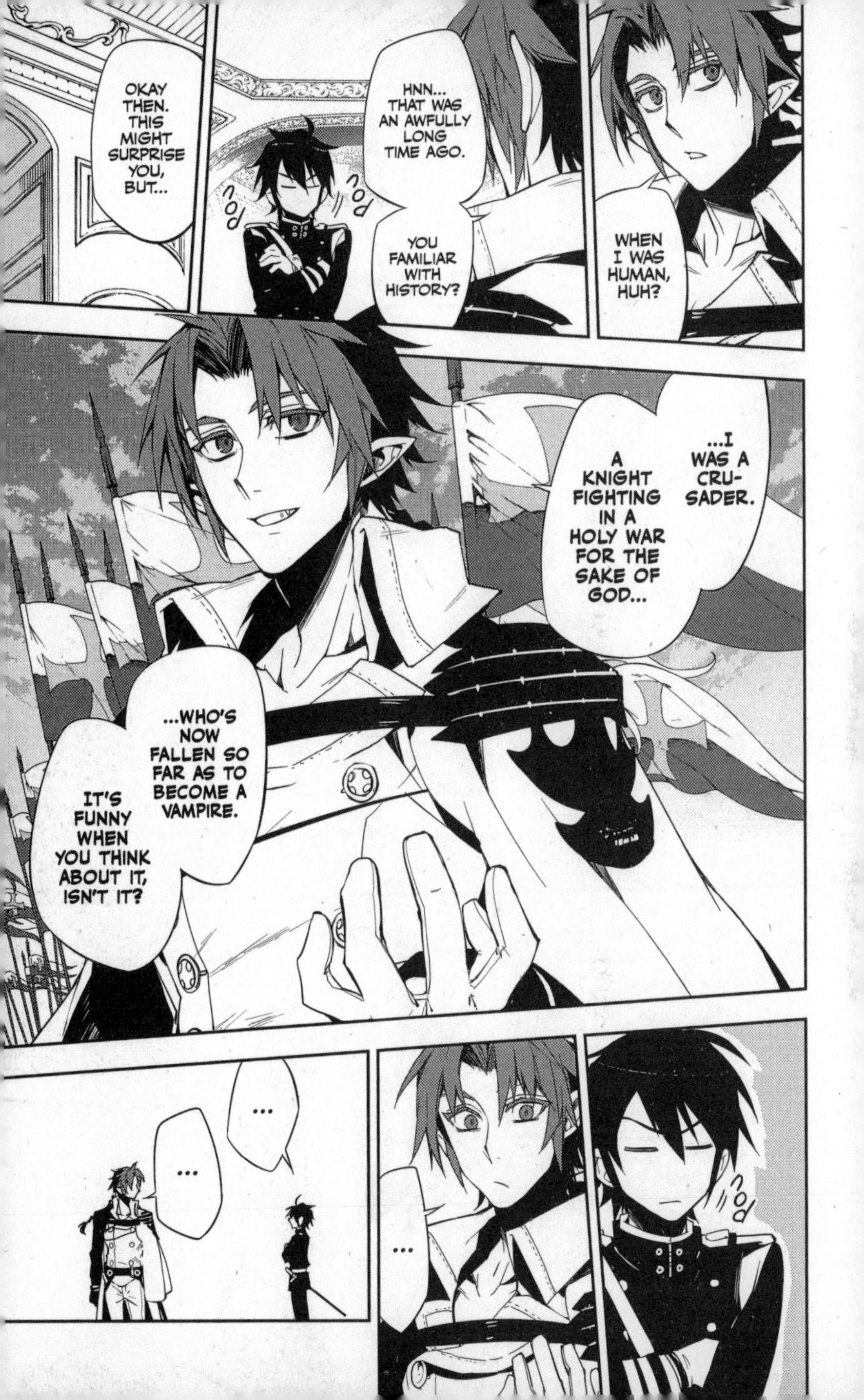
WHEN I WAS HUMAN, HUH?
HNN... THAT WAS AN AWFULLY LONG TIME AGO.
YOU FAMILIAR WITH HISTORY?
nod nod
OKAY THEN. THIS MIGHT SURPRISE YOU, BUT...
...I WAS A CRUSADER.
A KNIGHT FIGHTING IN A HOLY WAR FOR THE SAKE OF GOD...
...WHO'S NOW FALLEN SO FAR AS TO BECOME A VAMPIRE.
IT'S FUNNY WHEN YOU THINK ABOUT IT, ISN'T IT?
nod
...
...
...

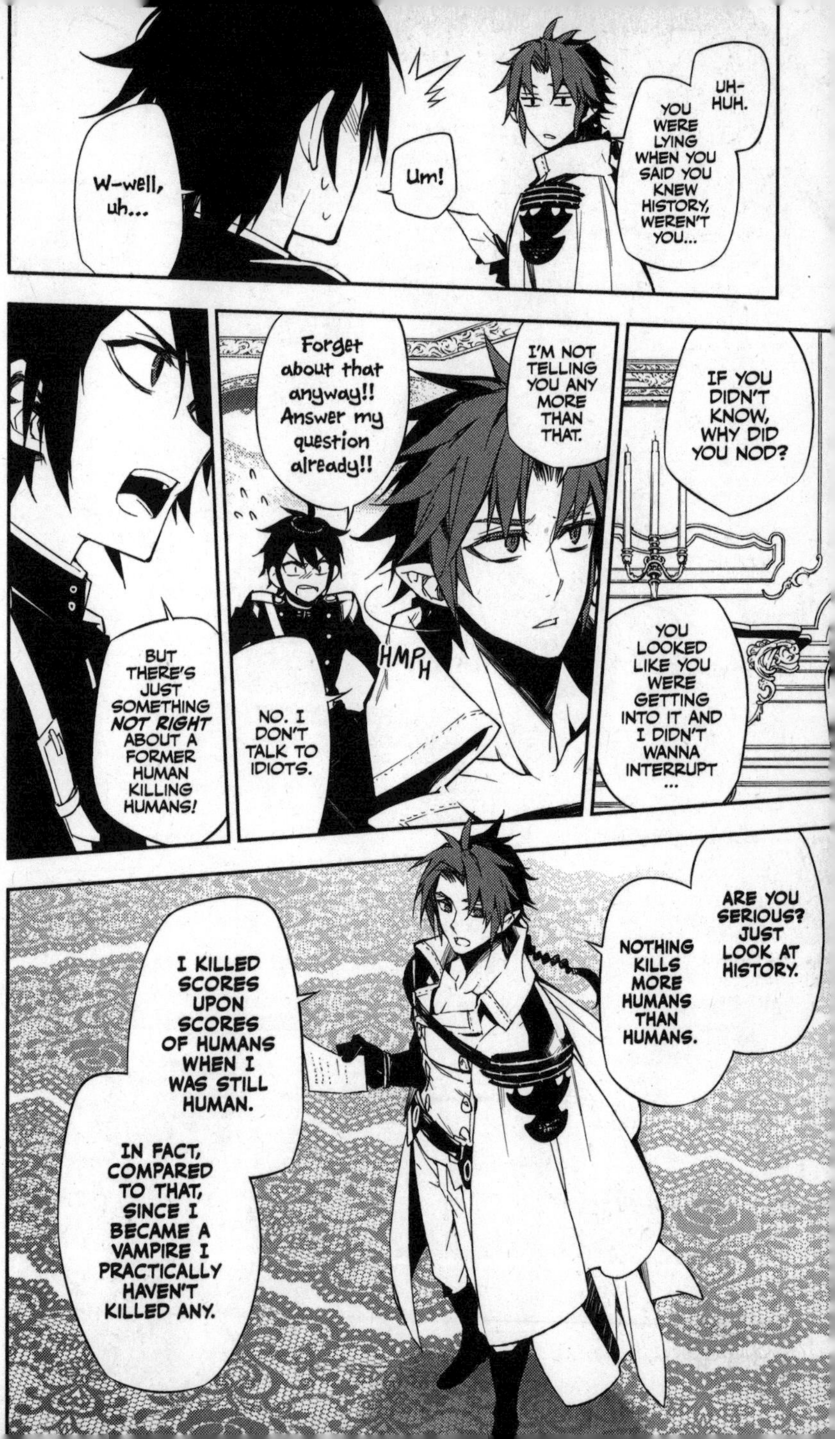
UH-HUH.
YOU WERE LYING WHEN YOU SAID YOU KNEW HISTORY, WEREN'T YOU...
Um!
W-well, uh...
IF YOU DIDN'T KNOW, WHY DID YOU NOD?
YOU LOOKED LIKE YOU WERE GETTING INTO IT AND I DIDN'T WANNA INTERRUPT...
I'M NOT TELLING YOU ANY MORE THAN THAT.
Forget about that anyway!! Answer my question already!!
HMPH
NO. I DON'T TALK TO IDIOTS.
BUT THERE'S JUST SOMETHING *NOT RIGHT* ABOUT A FORMER HUMAN KILLING HUMANS!
ARE YOU SERIOUS? JUST LOOK AT HISTORY.
NOTHING KILLS MORE HUMANS THAN HUMANS.
I KILLED SCORES UPON SCORES OF HUMANS WHEN I WAS STILL HUMAN.
IN FACT, COMPARED TO THAT, SINCE I BECAME A VAMPIRE I PRACTICALLY HAVEN'T KILLED ANY.

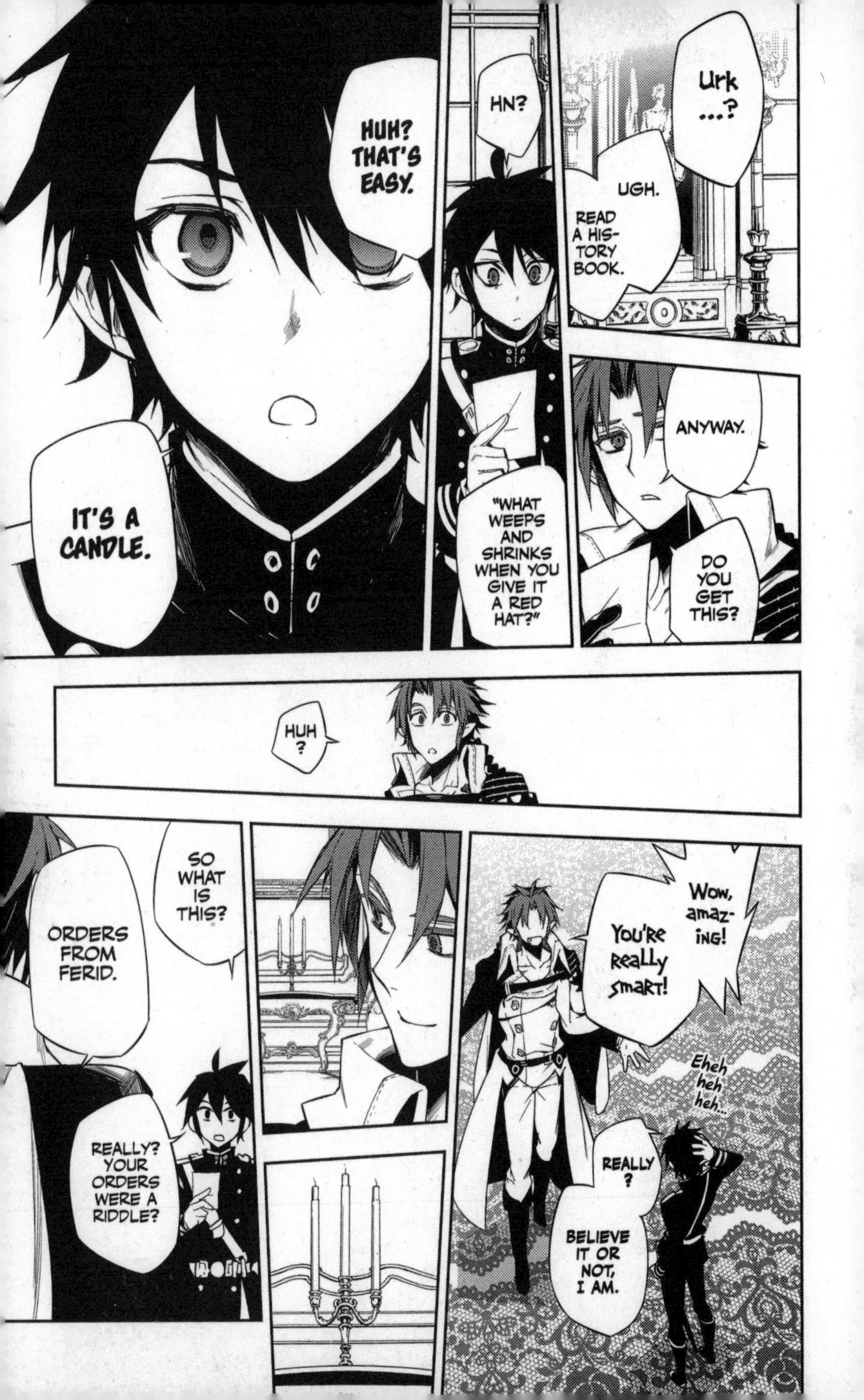
Urk ...?
UGH. READ A HISTORY BOOK.
ANYWAY.
DO YOU GET THIS?
HN?
"WHAT WEEPS AND SHRINKS WHEN YOU GIVE IT A RED HAT?"
HUH? THAT'S EASY.
IT'S A CANDLE.
HUH?
Wow, amazing!
You're really smart!
Eheh heh heh...
REALLY?
BELIEVE IT OR NOT, I AM.
SO WHAT IS THIS?
ORDERS FROM FERID.
REALLY? YOUR ORDERS WERE A RIDDLE?

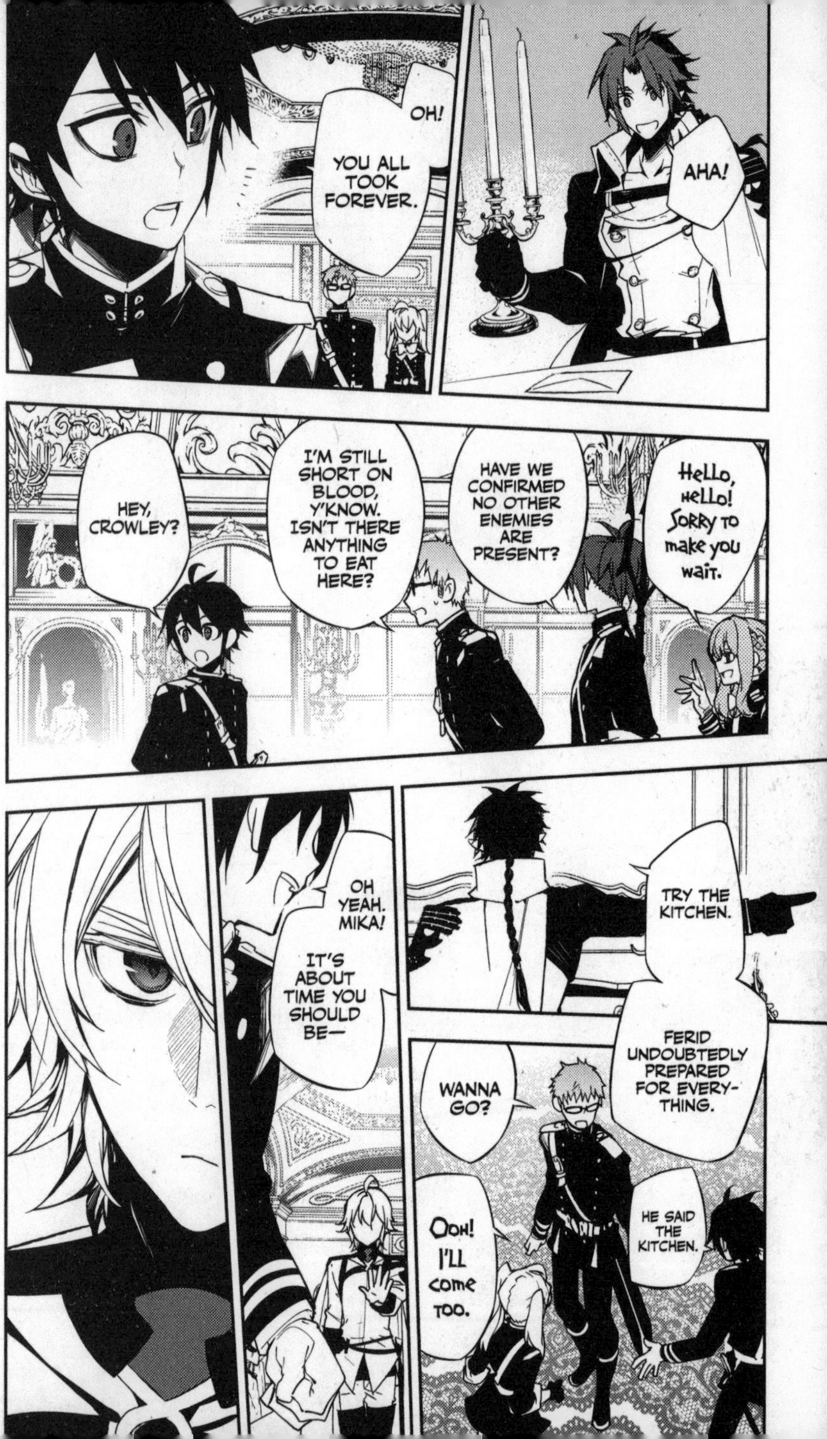
AHA!
OH!
YOU ALL TOOK FOREVER.
Hello, hello! Sorry to make you wait.
HAVE WE CONFIRMED NO OTHER ENEMIES ARE PRESENT?
I'M STILL SHORT ON BLOOD, Y'KNOW. ISN'T THERE ANYTHING TO EAT HERE?
HEY, CROWLEY?
TRY THE KITCHEN.
FERID UNDOUBTEDLY PREPARED FOR EVERY-THING.
WANNA GO?
HE SAID THE KITCHEN.
Ooh! I'LL come TOO.
OH YEAH. MIKA!
IT'S ABOUT TIME YOU SHOULD BE—

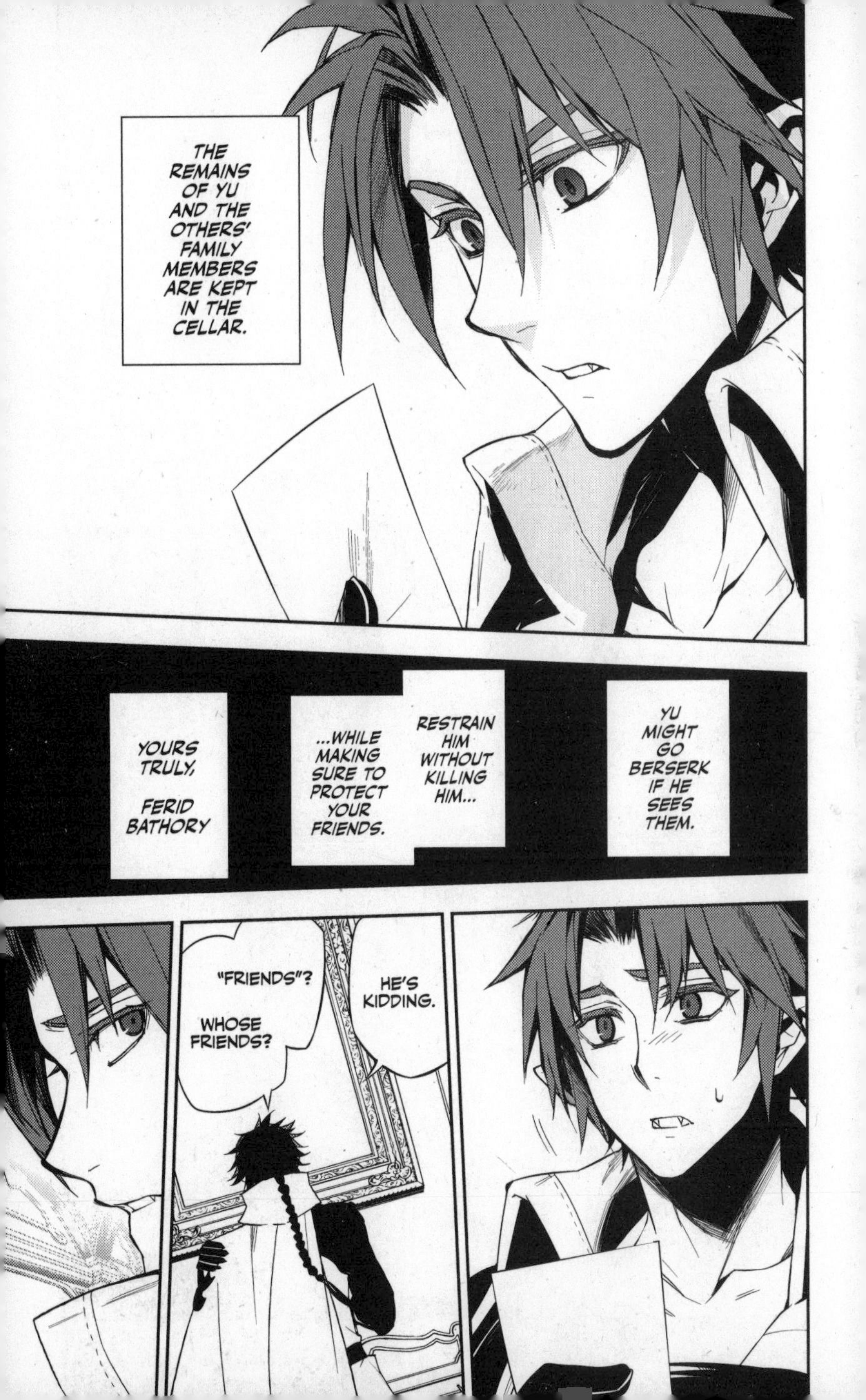
THE REMAINS OF YU AND THE OTHERS' FAMILY MEMBERS ARE KEPT IN THE CELLAR.
YU MIGHT GO BERSERK IF HE SEES THEM.
RESTRAIN HIM WITHOUT KILLING HIM...
...WHILE MAKING SURE TO PROTECT YOUR FRIENDS.
YOURS TRULY,
FERID BATHORY
HE'S KIDDING.
"FRIENDS"?
WHOSE FRIENDS?

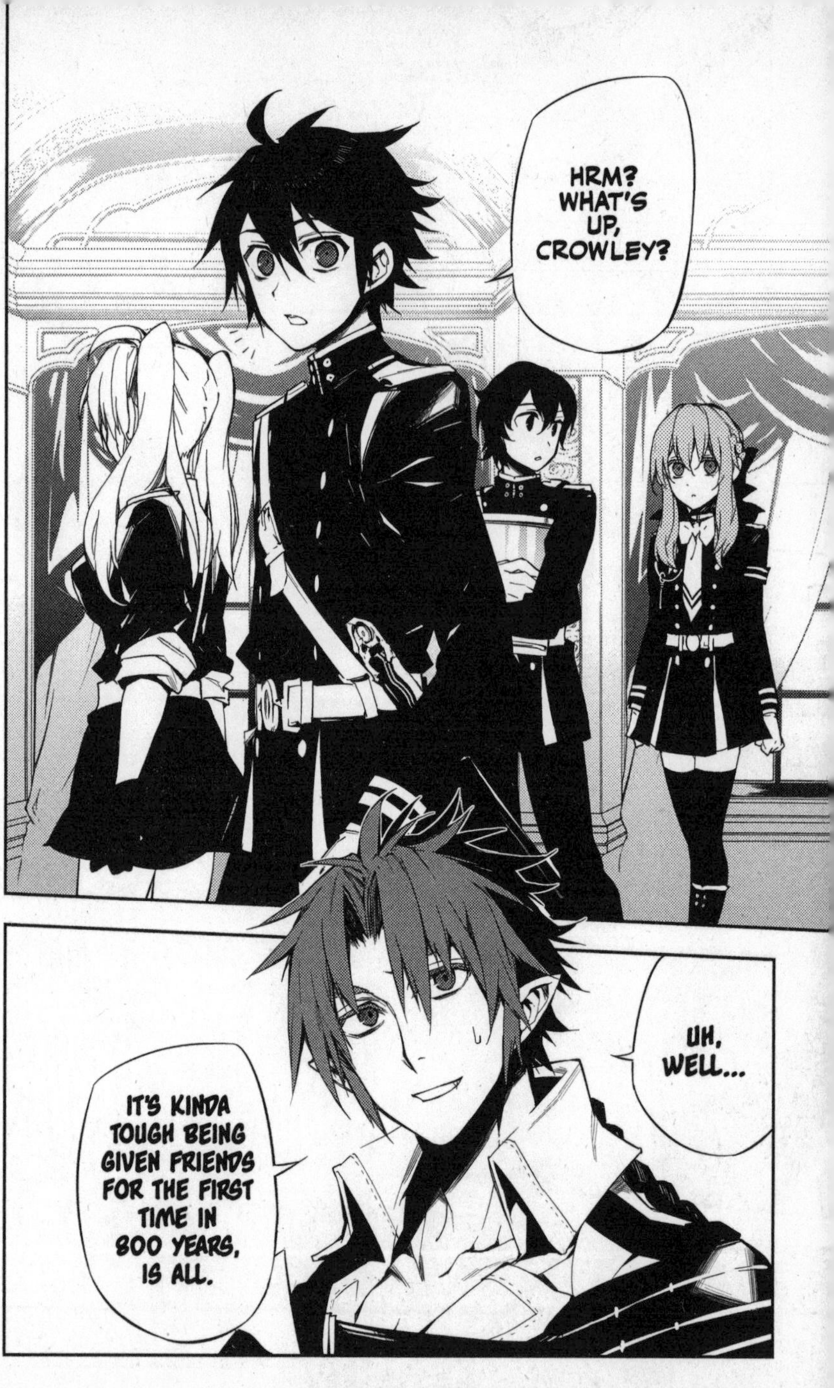
HRM? WHAT'S UP, CROWLEY?
UH, WELL...
IT'S KINDA TOUGH BEING GIVEN FRIENDS FOR THE FIRST TIME IN 800 YEARS, IS ALL.

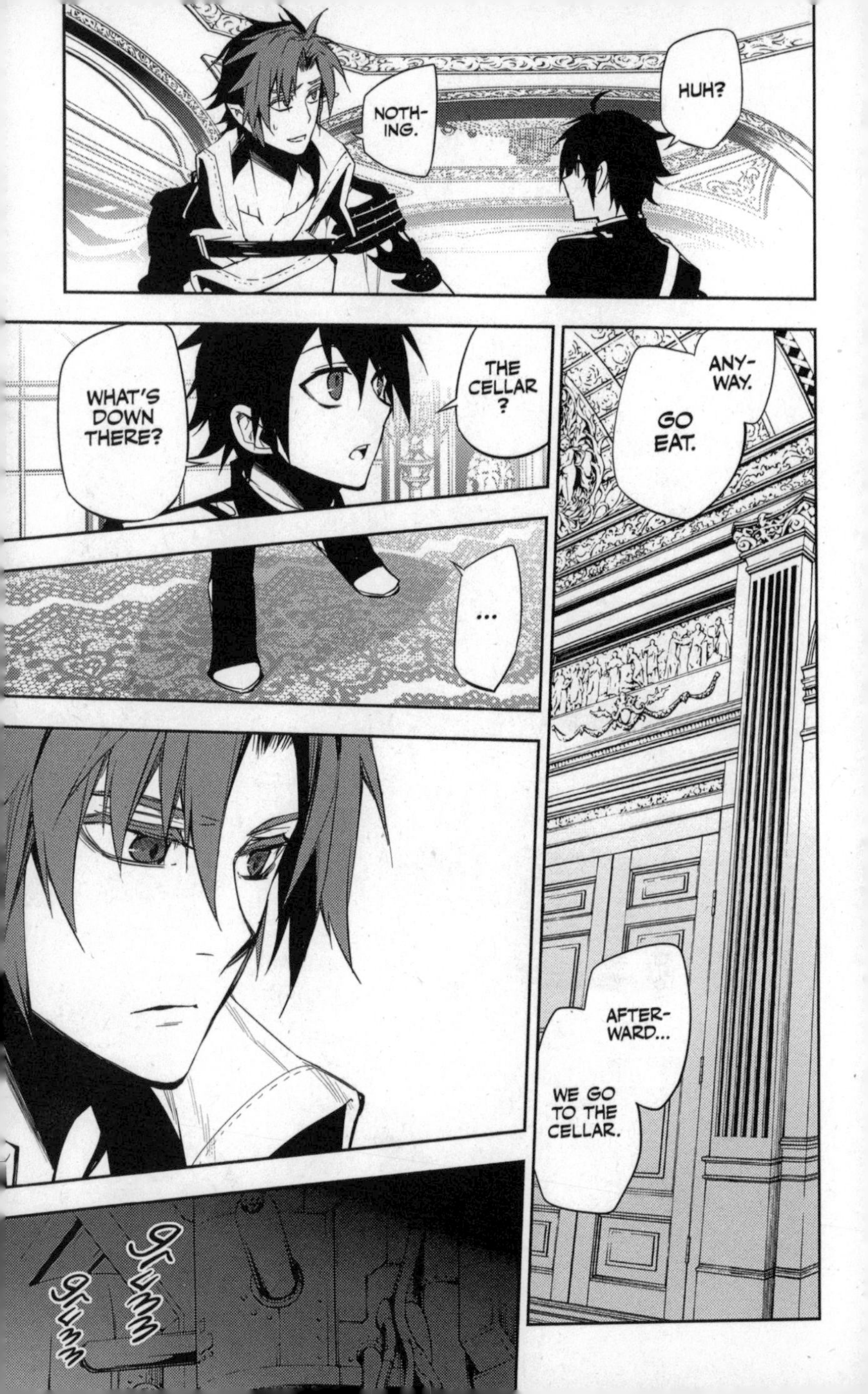
HUH?
NOTH-ING.
ANY-WAY. GO EAT.
THE CELLAR?
WHAT'S DOWN THERE?
...
AFTER-WARD... WE GO TO THE CELLAR.
grumm grumm

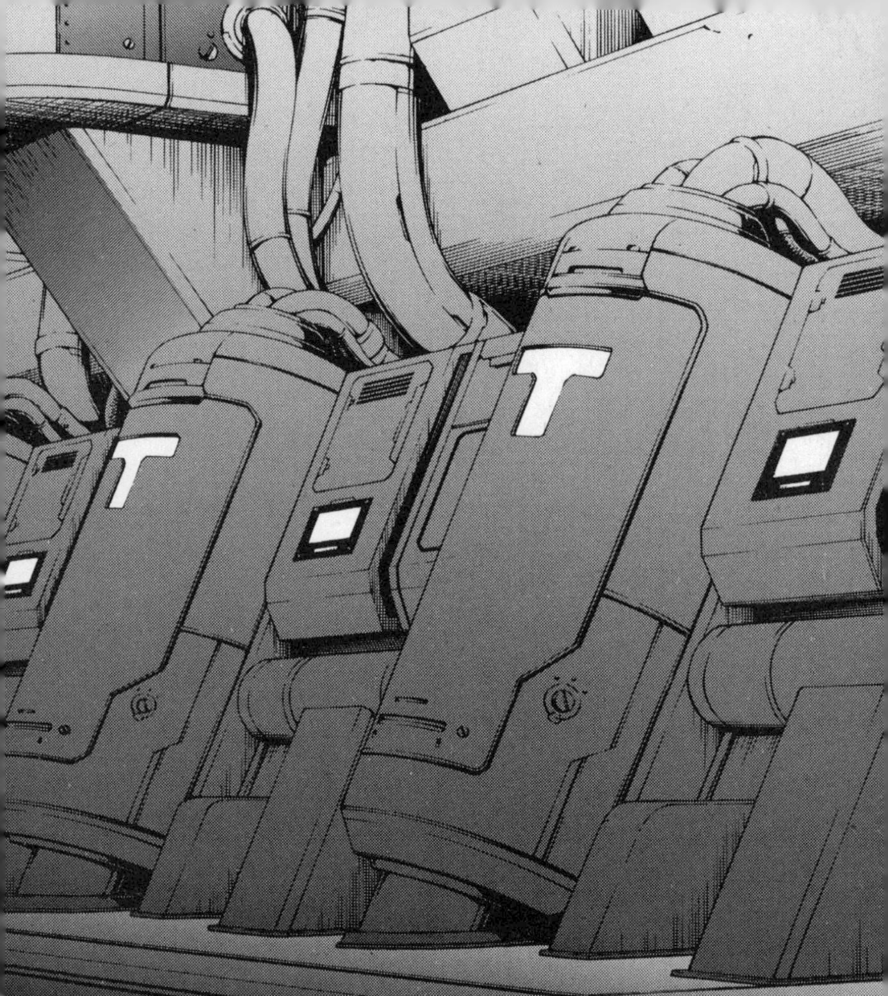

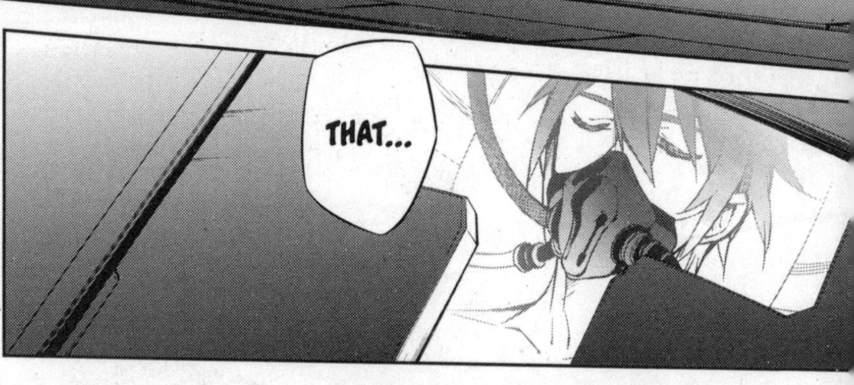
THAT...

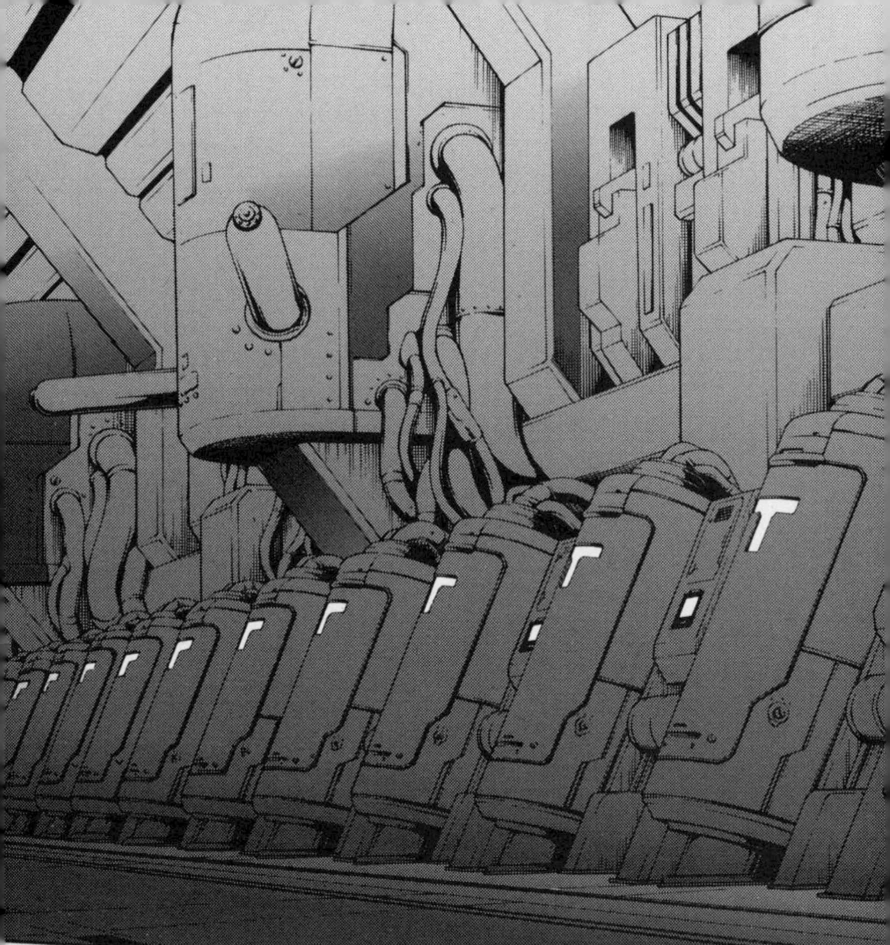
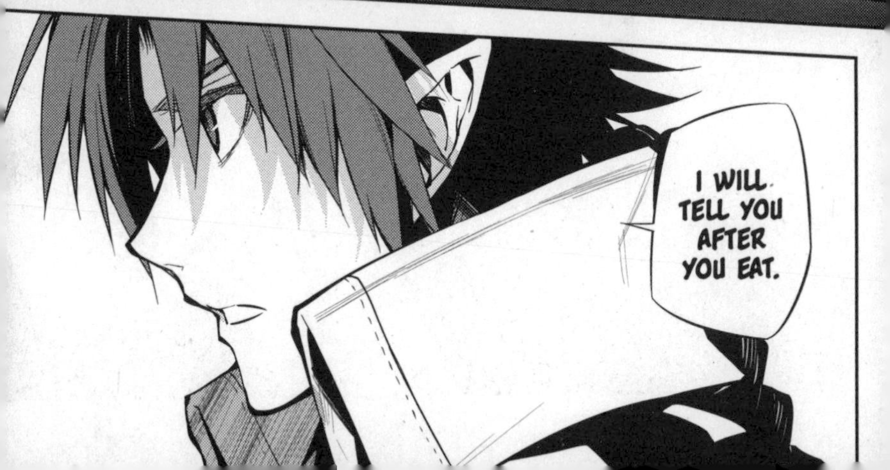
I WILL TELL YOU AFTER YOU EAT.

Seraph of the End

VAMPIRE REIGN

Chapter 54 Sinner's Christmas

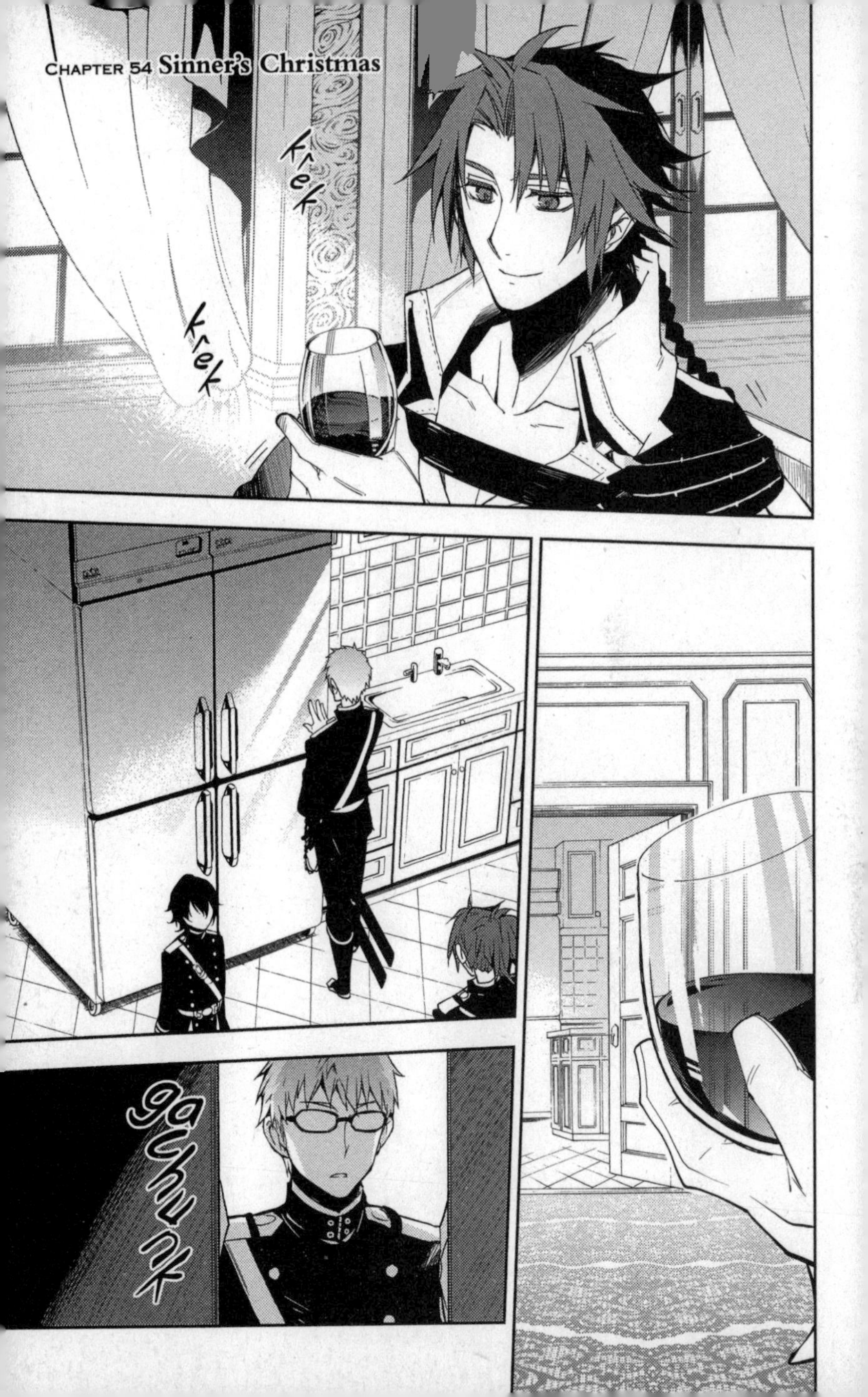
krek
krek
gachunk

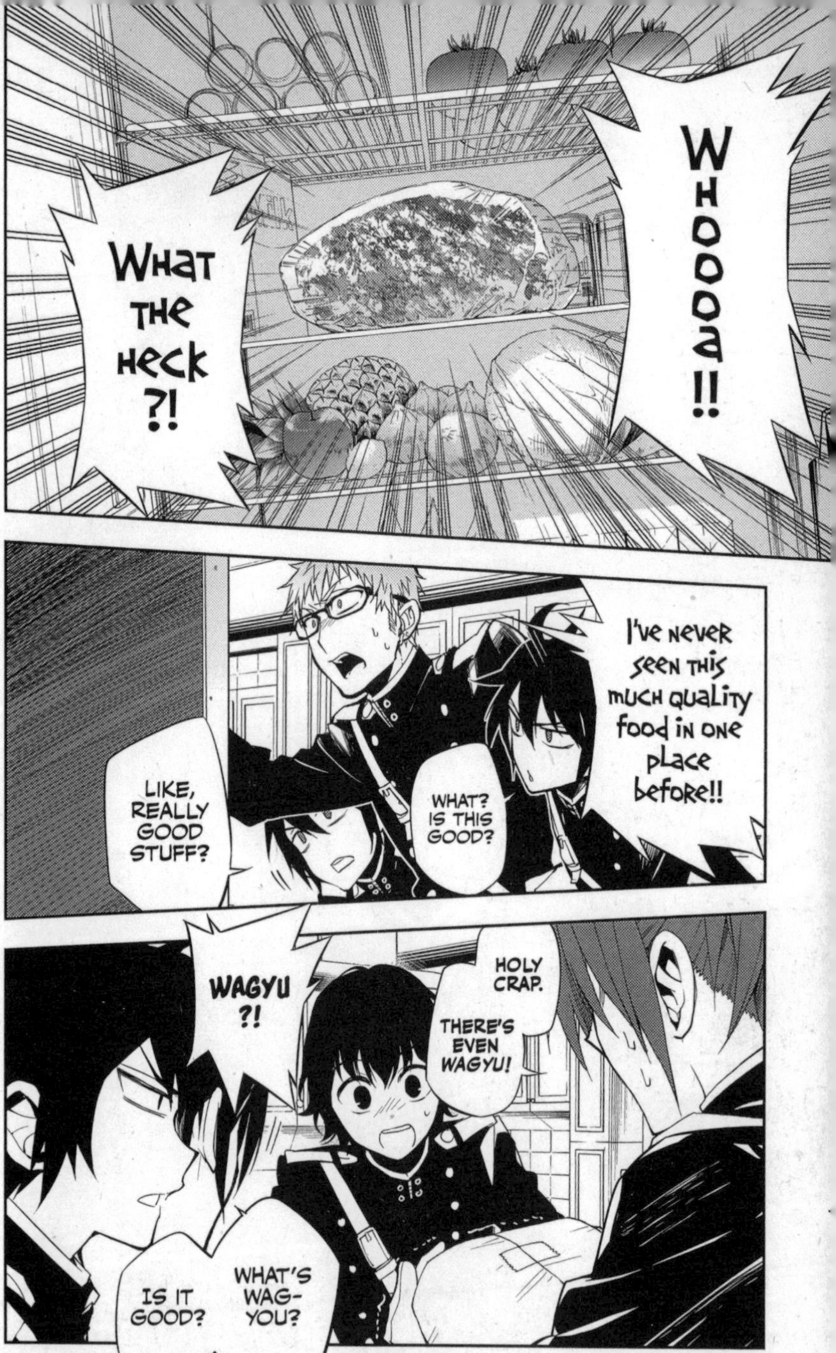
WHOOOA!!
WHAT THE HECK?!
I've never seen this much quality food in one place before!!
WHAT? IS THIS GOOD?
LIKE, REALLY GOOD STUFF?
HOLY CRAP.
THERE'S EVEN WAGYU!
WAGYU?!
WHAT'S WAG-YOU?
IS IT GOOD?

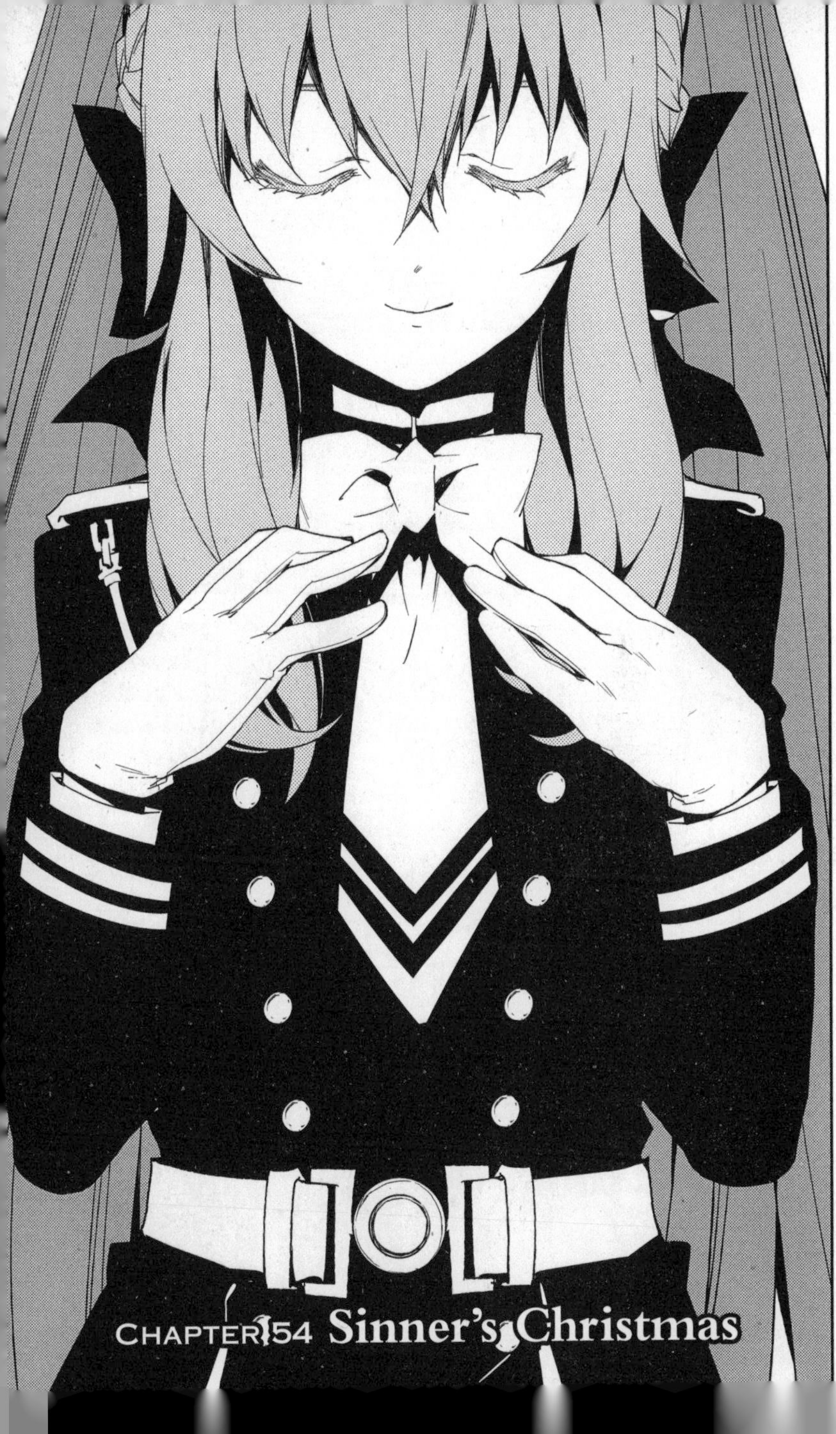
CHAPTER 54 Sinner's Christmas

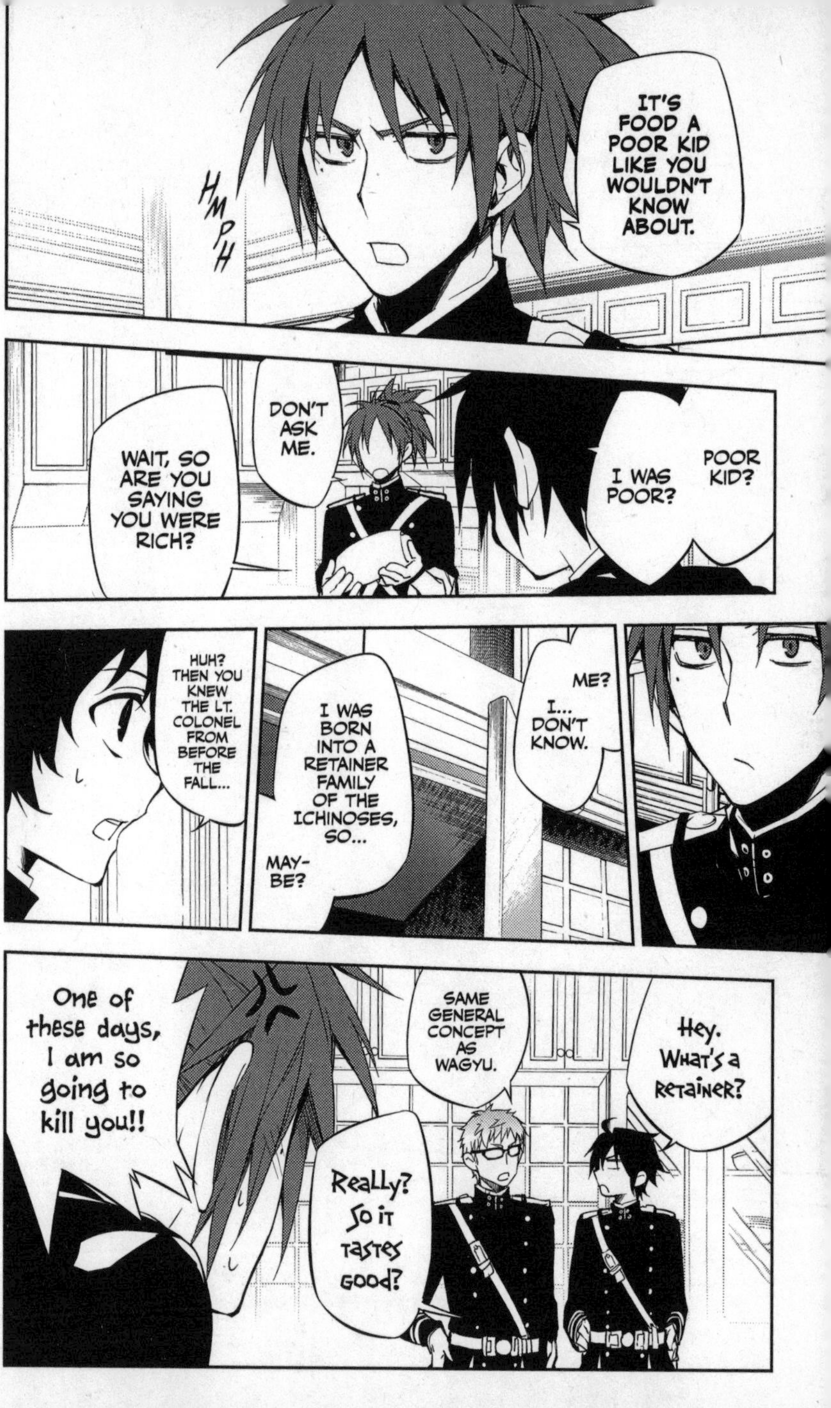
IT'S FOOD A POOR KID LIKE YOU WOULDN'T KNOW ABOUT.
HMPH
POOR KID?
I WAS POOR?
DON'T ASK ME.
WAIT, SO ARE YOU SAYING YOU WERE RICH?
ME?
I... DON'T KNOW.
I WAS BORN INTO A RETAINER FAMILY OF THE ICHINOSES, SO...
MAY-BE?
HUH? THEN YOU KNEW THE LT. COLONEL FROM BEFORE THE FALL...
Hey. What's a retainer?
SAME GENERAL CONCEPT AS WAGYU.
Really? So it tastes good?
One of these days, I am so going to kill you!!

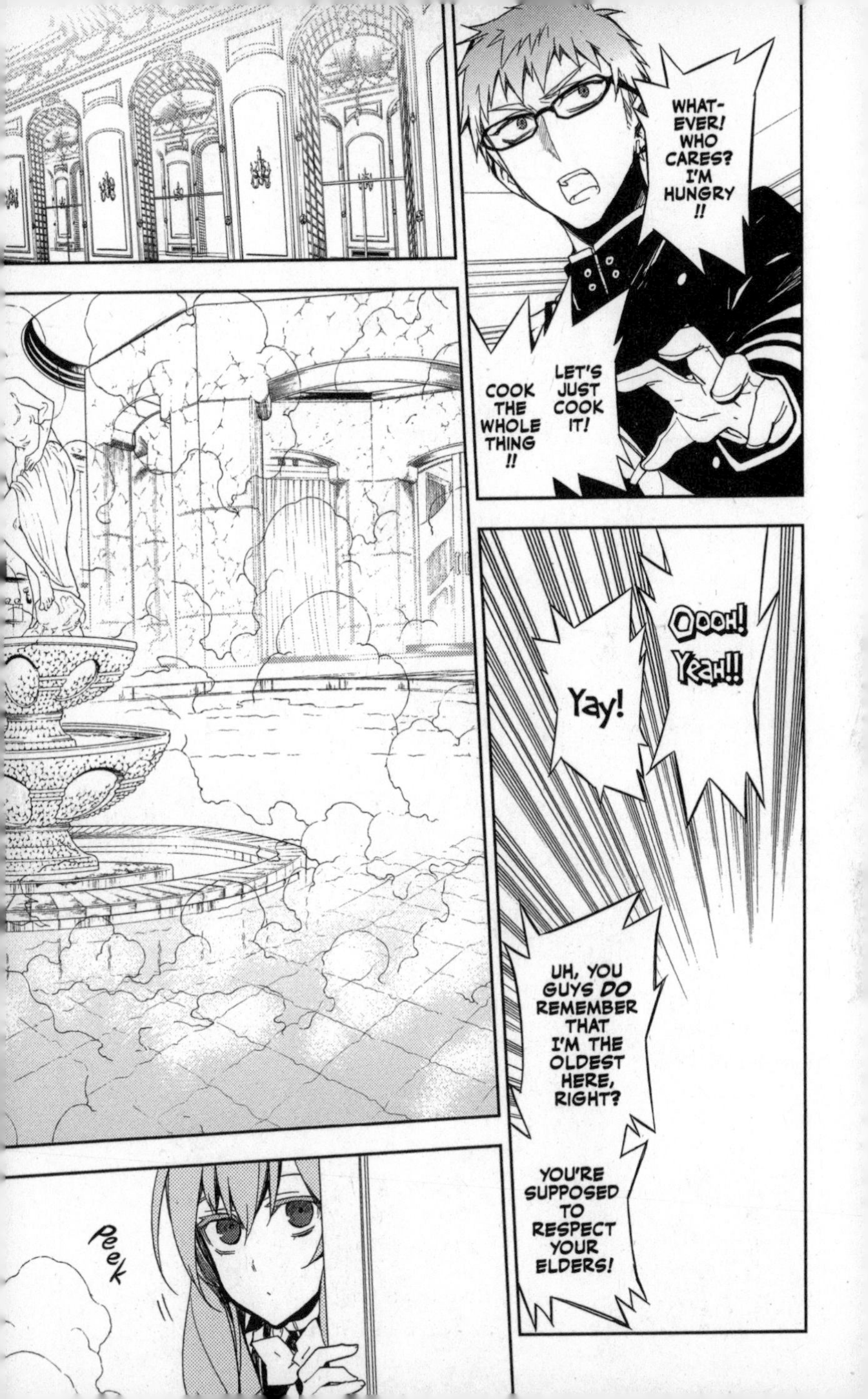
WHAT-EVER! WHO CARES? I'M HUNGRY!!
LET'S JUST COOK IT!
COOK THE WHOLE THING!!
Oooh! Yeah!!
Yay!
UH, YOU GUYS DO REMEMBER THAT I'M THE OLDEST HERE, RIGHT?
YOU'RE SUPPOSED TO RESPECT YOUR ELDERS!
Peek

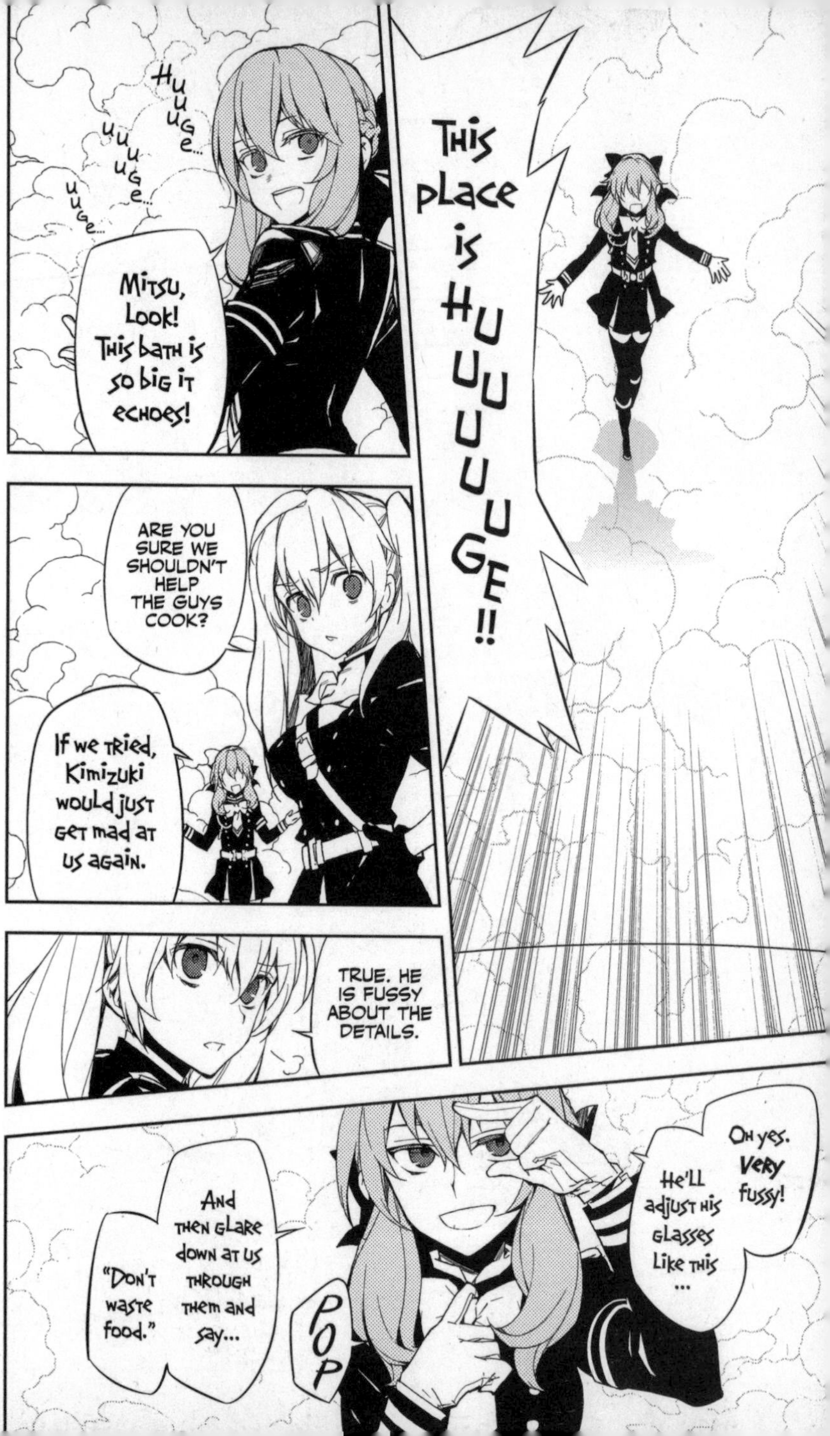
THIS PLACE IS HUUUUUUGE!!
Huuuge... uuuuge... uuge...
Mitsu, look! This bath is so big it echoes!
ARE YOU SURE WE SHOULDN'T HELP THE GUYS COOK?
If we tried, Kimizuki would just get mad at us again.
TRUE. HE IS FUSSY ABOUT THE DETAILS.
Oh yes. Very fussy!
He'll adjust his glasses like this ...
And then glare down at us through them and say...
"Don't waste food."
POP

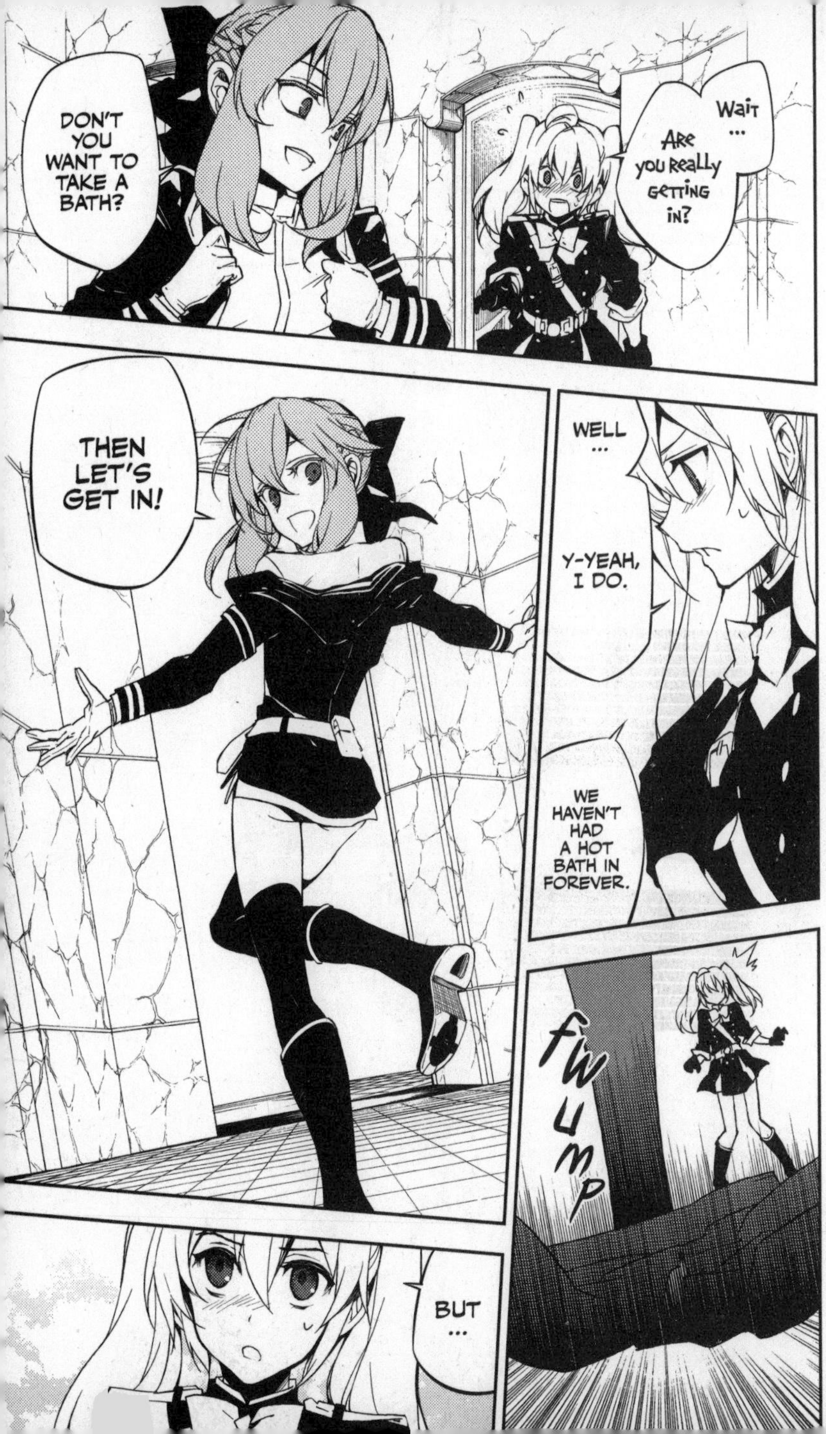
Wait ...
Are you really getting in?
DON'T YOU WANT TO TAKE A BATH?
WELL ...
Y-YEAH, I DO.
WE HAVEN'T HAD A HOT BATH IN FOREVER.
FWUMP
THEN LET'S GET IN!
BUT ...

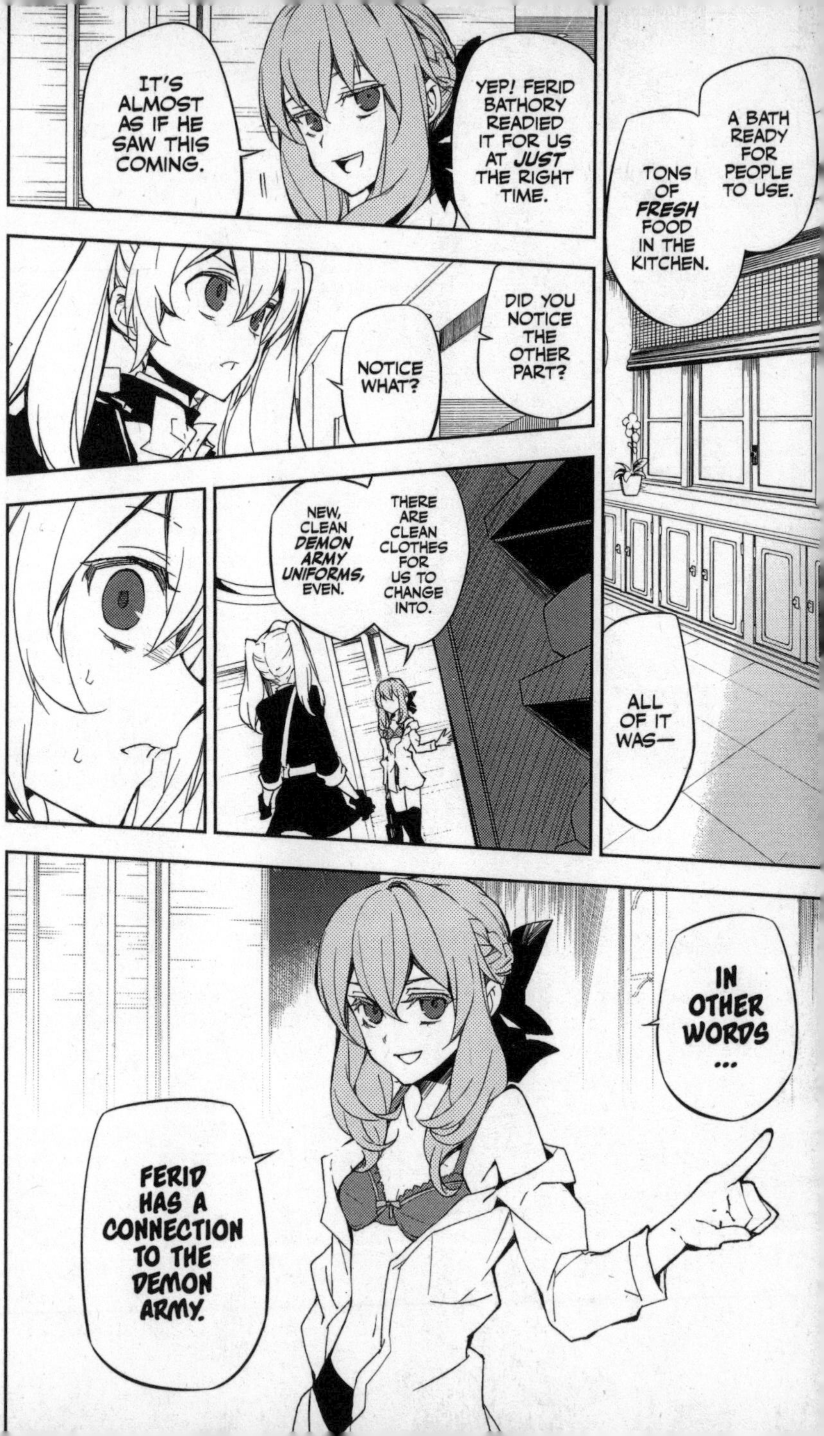
A BATH READY FOR PEOPLE TO USE.
TONS OF FRESH FOOD IN THE KITCHEN.
ALL OF IT WAS—
YEP! FERID BATHORY READIED IT FOR US AT JUST THE RIGHT TIME.
IT'S ALMOST AS IF HE SAW THIS COMING.
DID YOU NOTICE THE OTHER PART?
NOTICE WHAT?
THERE ARE CLEAN CLOTHES FOR US TO CHANGE INTO.
NEW, CLEAN DEMON ARMY UNIFORMS, EVEN.
IN OTHER WORDS...
FERID HAS A CONNECTION TO THE DEMON ARMY.

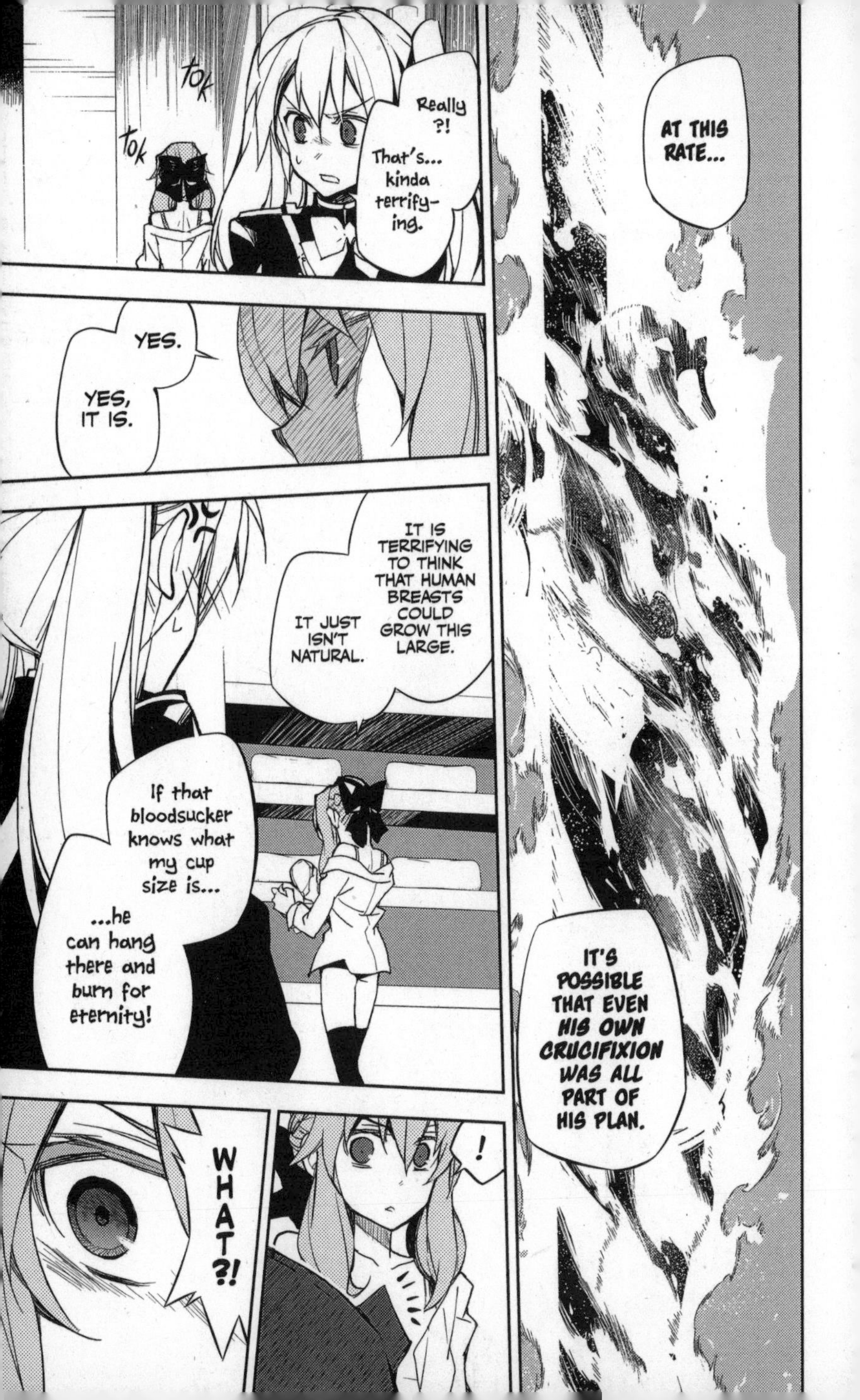
AT THIS RATE...
IT'S POSSIBLE THAT EVEN HIS OWN CRUCIFIXION WAS ALL PART OF HIS PLAN.
TOK
TOK
Really?!
That's... kinda terrifying.
YES.
YES, IT IS.
IT IS TERRIFYING TO THINK THAT HUMAN BREASTS COULD GROW THIS LARGE.
IT JUST ISN'T NATURAL.
If that bloodsucker knows what my cup size is...
...he can hang there and burn for eternity!
!
WHAT?!

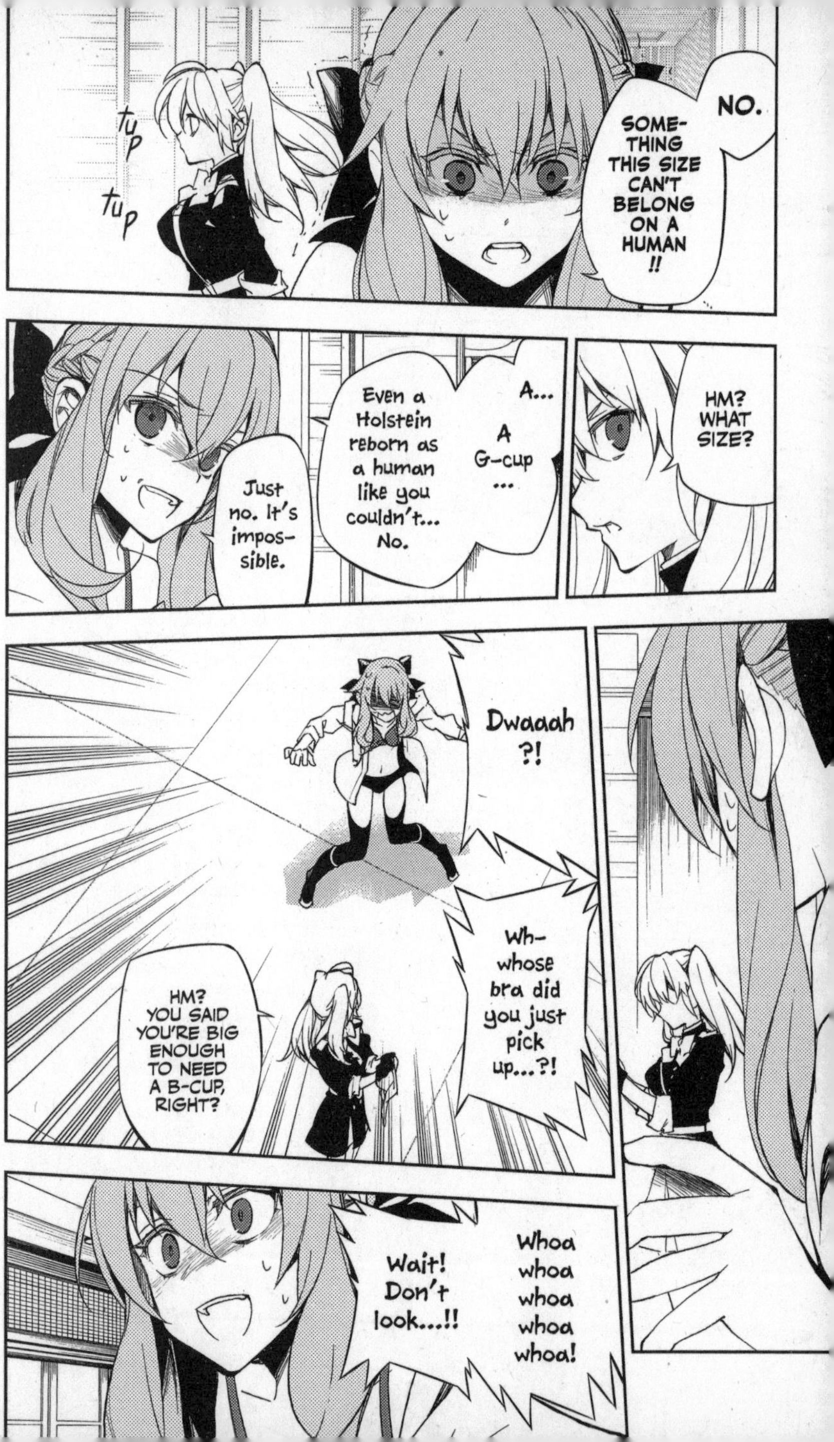
NO.
SOME-THING THIS SIZE CAN'T BELONG ON A HUMAN!!
tup tup
HM? WHAT SIZE?
A... A G-cup...
Even a Holstein reborn as a human like you couldn't... No.
Just no. It's impos-sible.
Dwaaah?!
Wh-whose bra did you just pick up...?!
HM? YOU SAID YOU'RE BIG ENOUGH TO NEED A B-CUP, RIGHT?
Whoa whoa whoa whoa whoa!
Wait! Don't look...!!

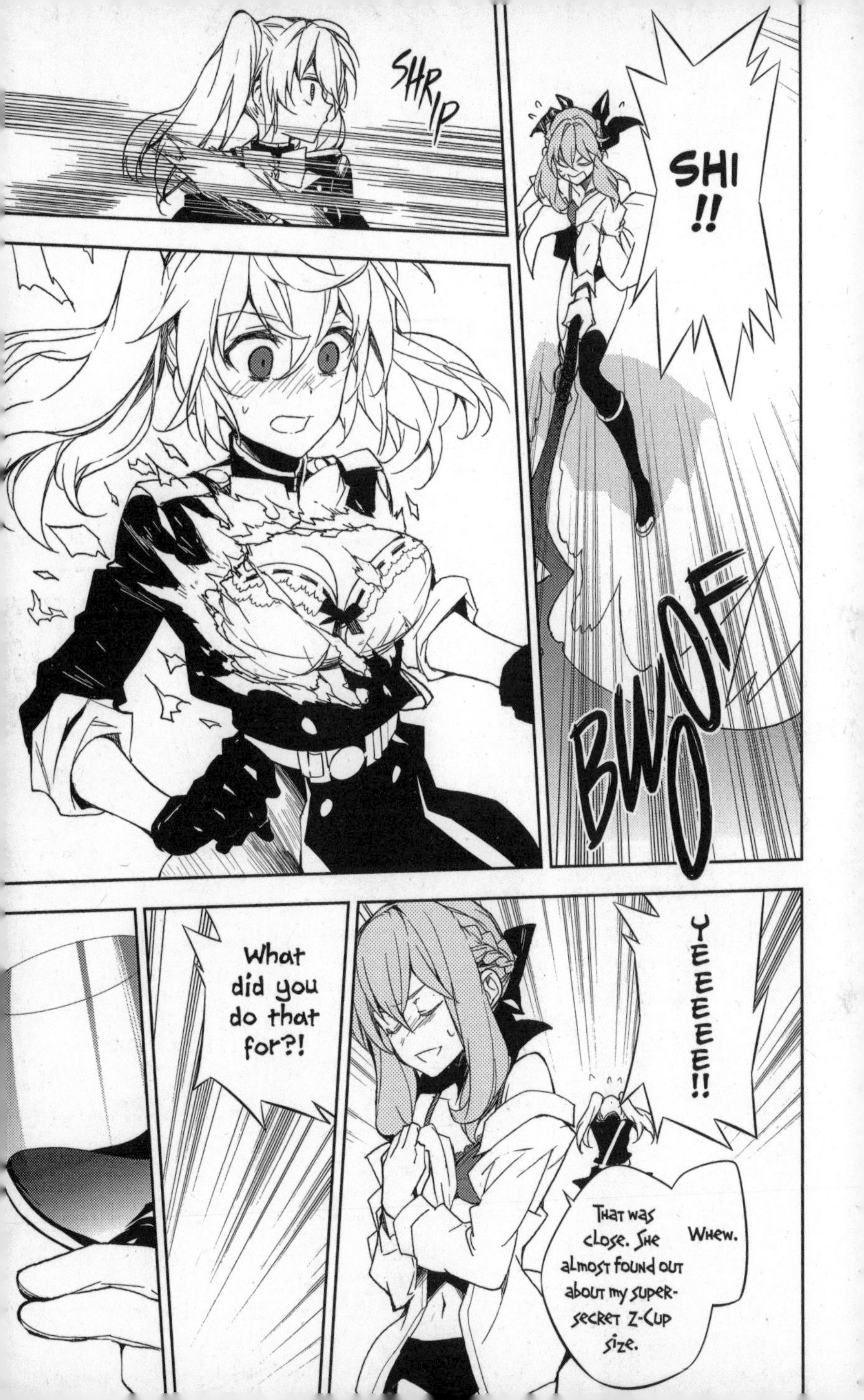
SHI !!
BWOOF
SHRIP
YEEEEEE!!
Whew.
That was close. She almost found out about my super-secret Z-Cup size.
What did you do that for?!

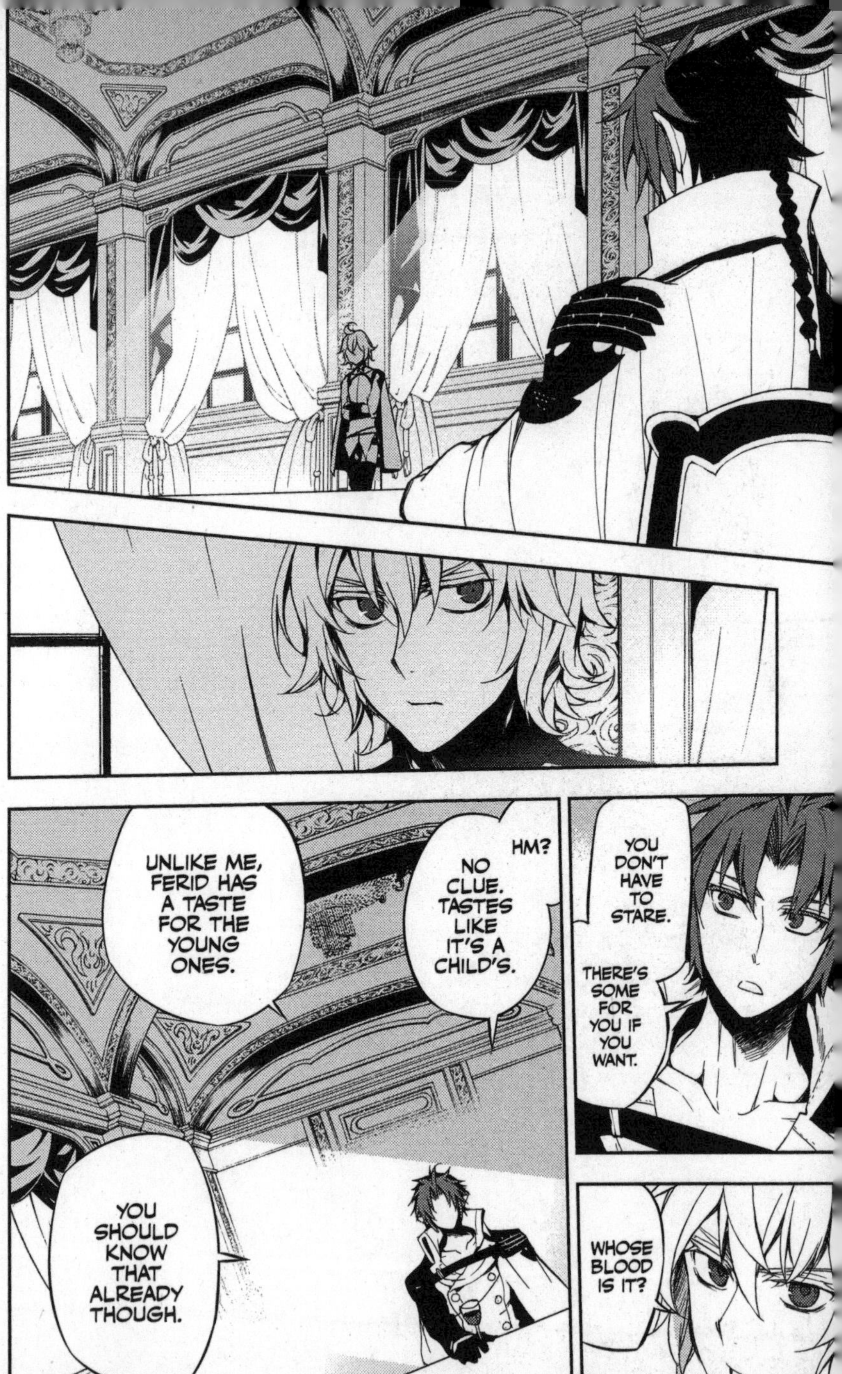
YOU DON'T HAVE TO STARE.
THERE'S SOME FOR YOU IF YOU WANT.
WHOSE BLOOD IS IT?
HM?
NO CLUE. TASTES LIKE IT'S A CHILD'S.
UNLIKE ME, FERID HAS A TASTE FOR THE YOUNG ONES.
YOU SHOULD KNOW THAT ALREADY THOUGH.

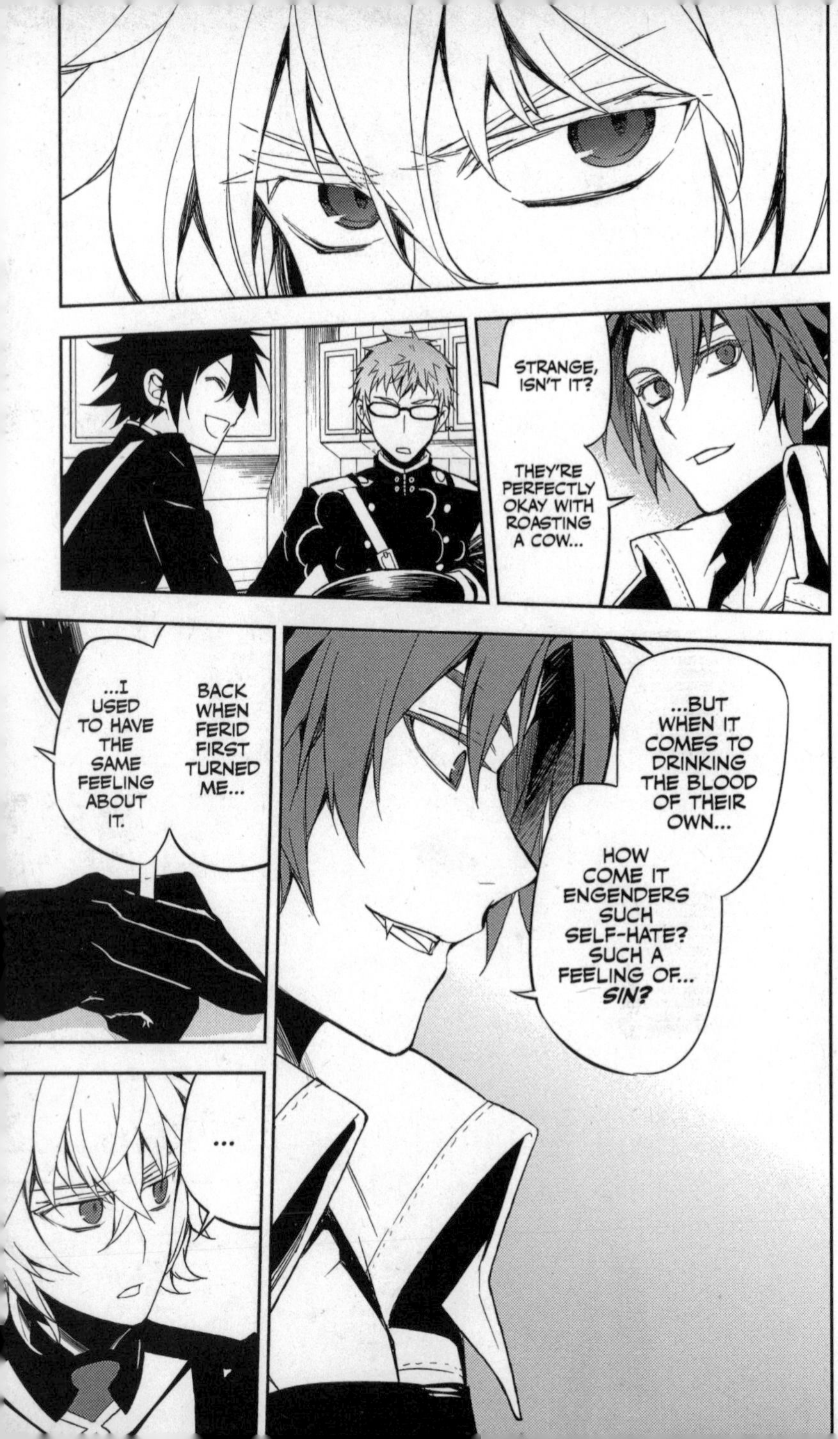
STRANGE, ISN'T IT?
THEY'RE PERFECTLY OKAY WITH ROASTING A COW...
...BUT WHEN IT COMES TO DRINKING THE BLOOD OF THEIR OWN...
HOW COME IT ENGENDERS SUCH SELF-HATE? SUCH A FEELING OF... *SIN?*
BACK WHEN FERID FIRST TURNED ME... ...I USED TO HAVE THE SAME FEELING ABOUT IT.
...

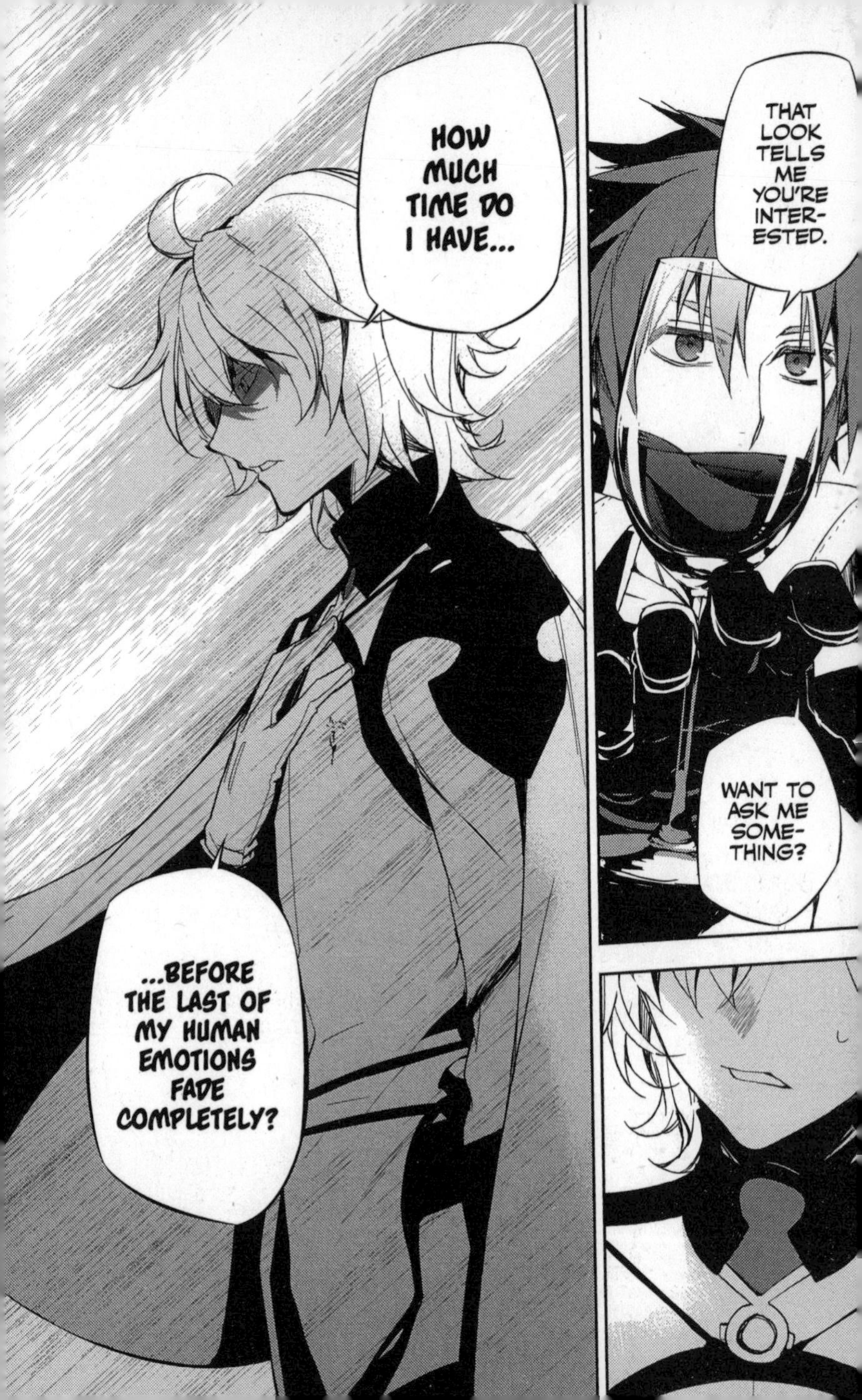
THAT LOOK TELLS ME YOU'RE INTER-ESTED.
WANT TO ASK ME SOME-THING?
HOW MUCH TIME DO I HAVE...
...BEFORE THE LAST OF MY HUMAN EMOTIONS FADE COMPLETELY?

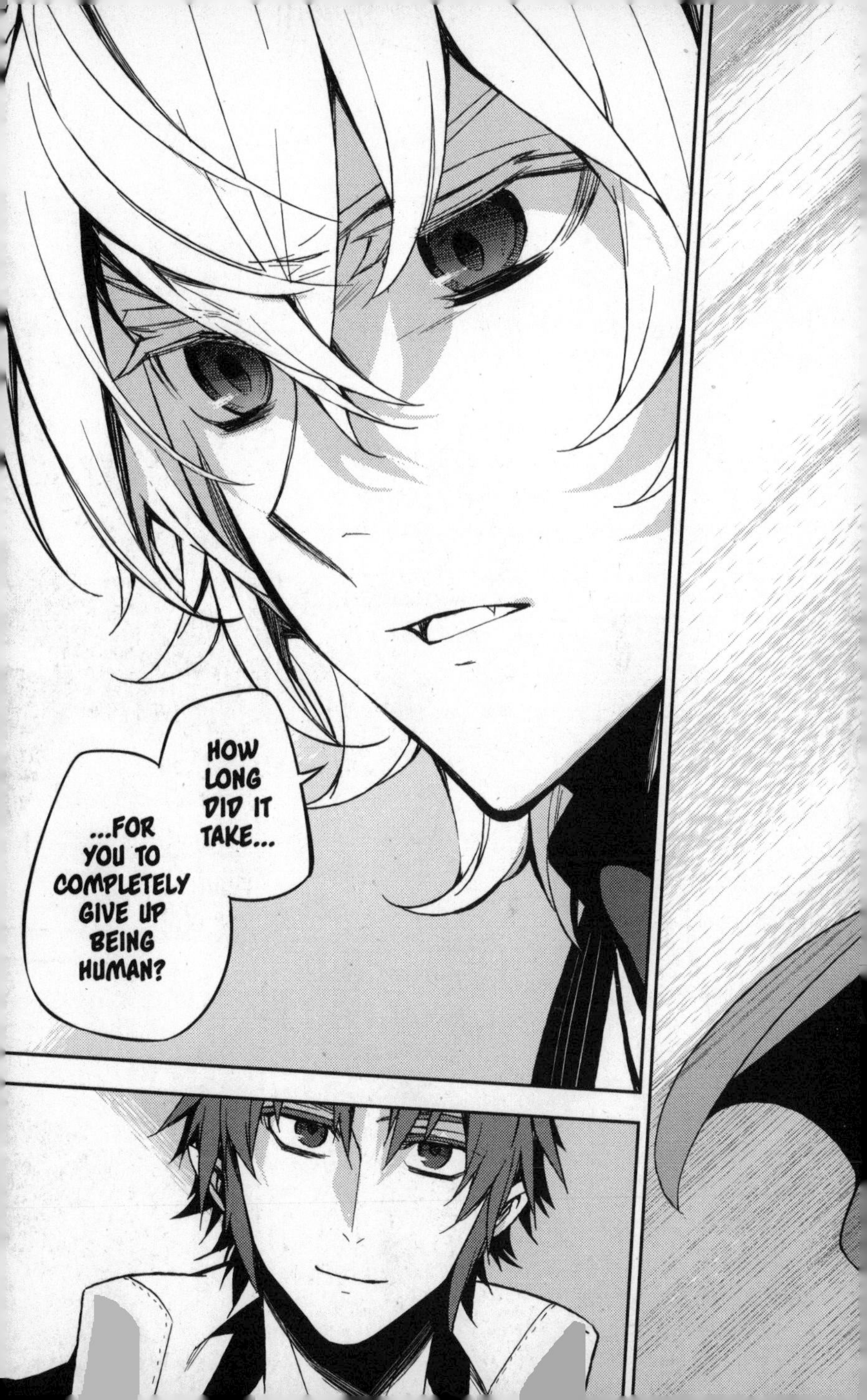
HOW LONG DID IT TAKE... ...FOR YOU TO COMPLETELY GIVE UP BEING HUMAN?

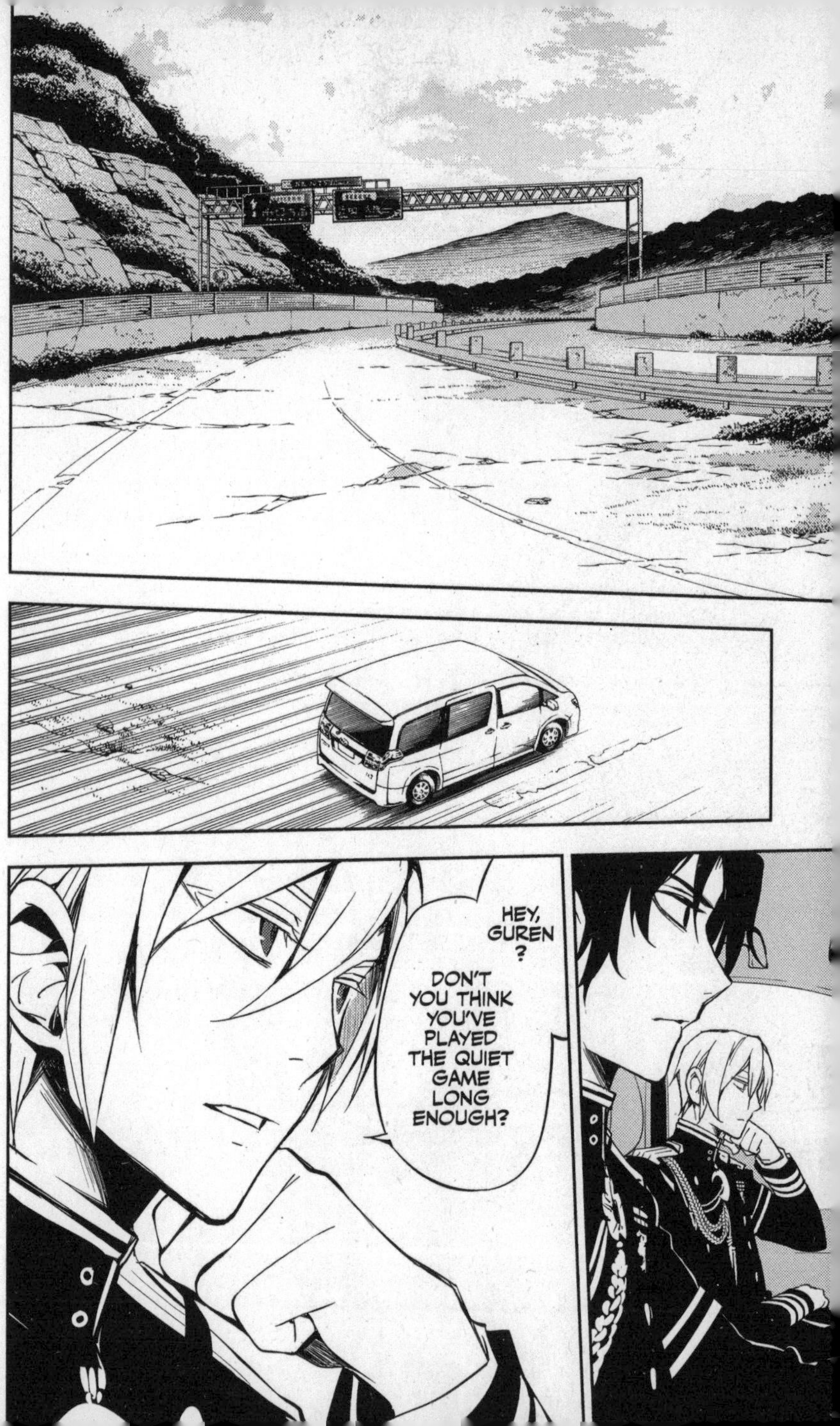
HEY, GUREN?
DON'T YOU THINK YOU'VE PLAYED THE QUIET GAME LONG ENOUGH?

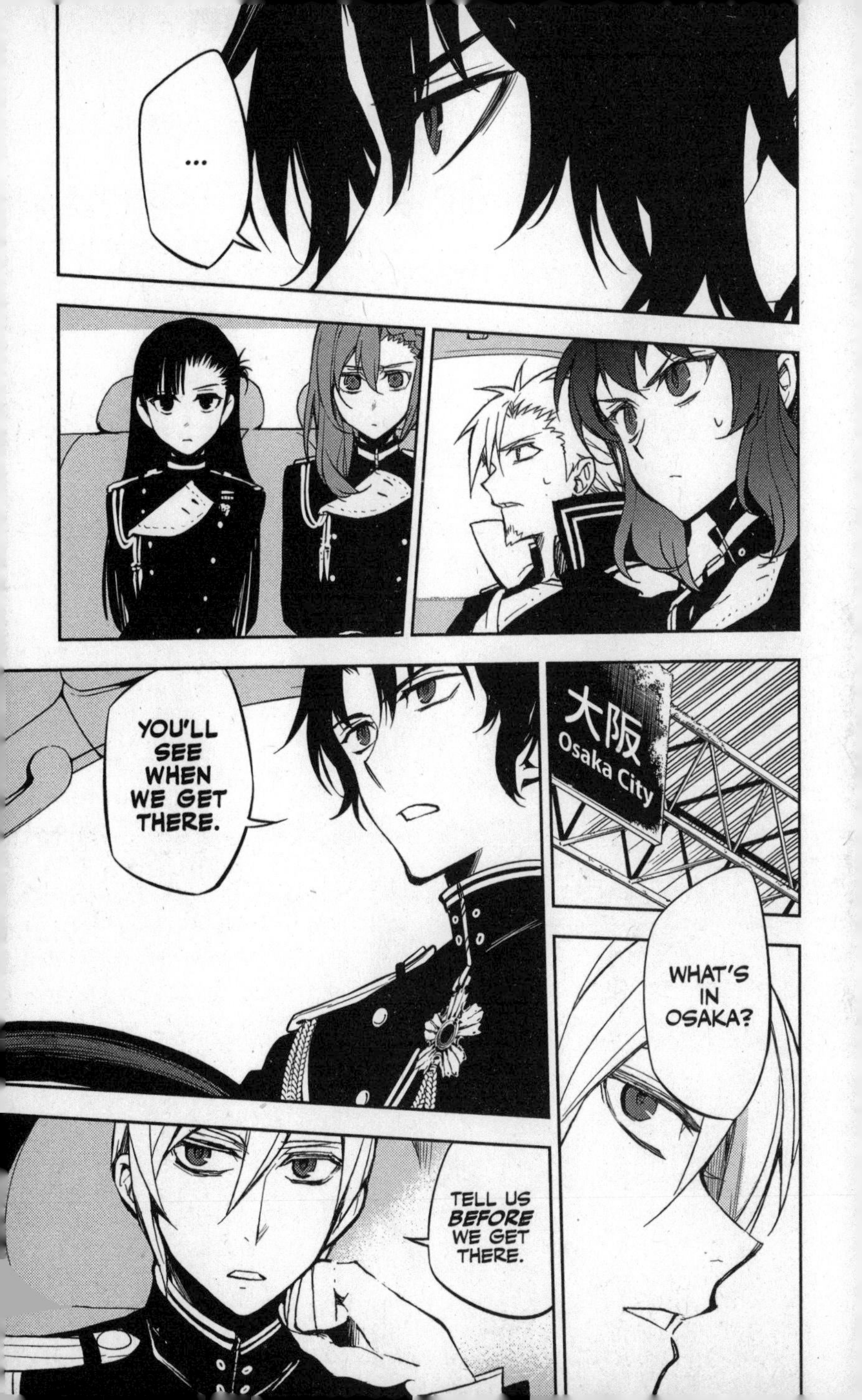
...
大阪
Osaka City
WHAT'S IN OSAKA?
YOU'LL SEE WHEN WE GET THERE.
TELL US *BEFORE* WE GET THERE.

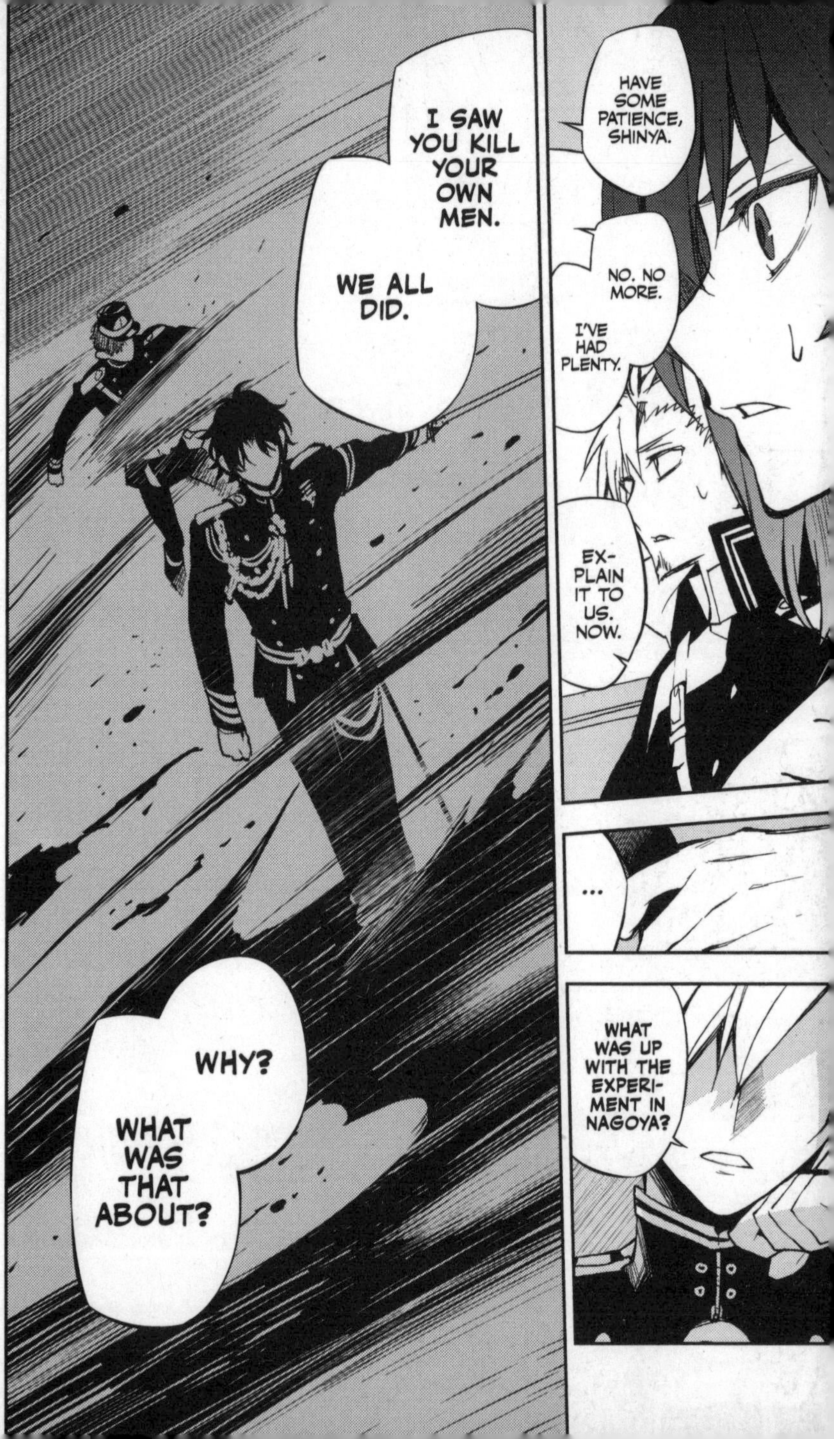
HAVE SOME PATIENCE, SHINYA.
NO. NO MORE.
I'VE HAD PLENTY.
EX-PLAIN IT TO US. NOW.
...
WHAT WAS UP WITH THE EXPERI-MENT IN NAGOYA?
I SAW YOU KILL YOUR OWN MEN.
WE ALL DID.
WHY?
WHAT WAS THAT ABOUT?

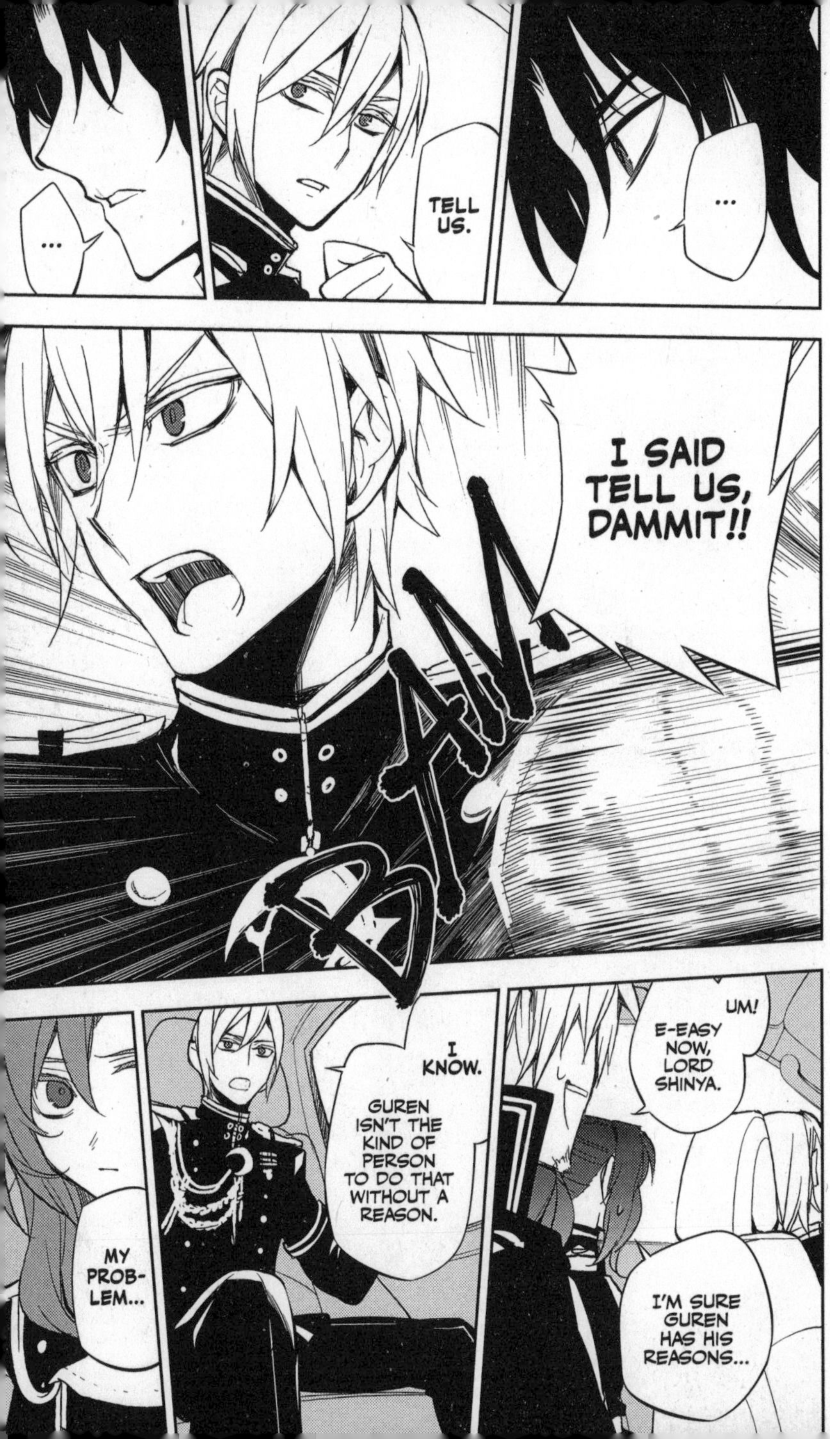
...
TELL US.
...
I SAID TELL US, DAMMIT!!
BAM
UM!
E-EASY NOW, LORD SHINYA.
I'M SURE GUREN HAS HIS REASONS...
I KNOW.
GUREN ISN'T THE KIND OF PERSON TO DO THAT WITHOUT A REASON.
MY PROB-LEM...

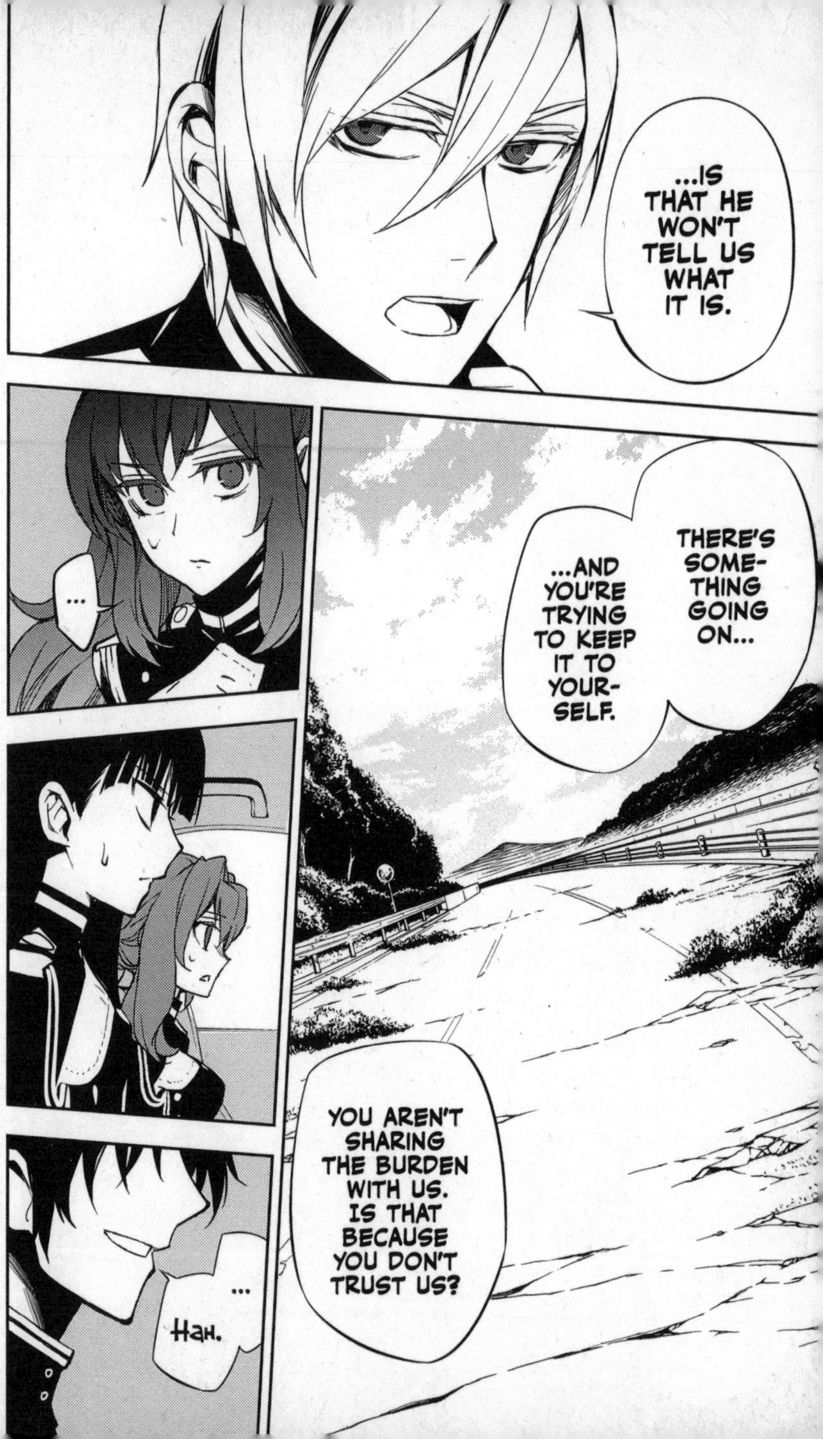
...IS THAT HE WON'T TELL US WHAT IT IS.
THERE'S SOME-THING GOING ON...
...AND YOU'RE TRYING TO KEEP IT TO YOUR-SELF.
YOU AREN'T SHARING THE BURDEN WITH US. IS THAT BECAUSE YOU DON'T TRUST US?
...
...
Hah.

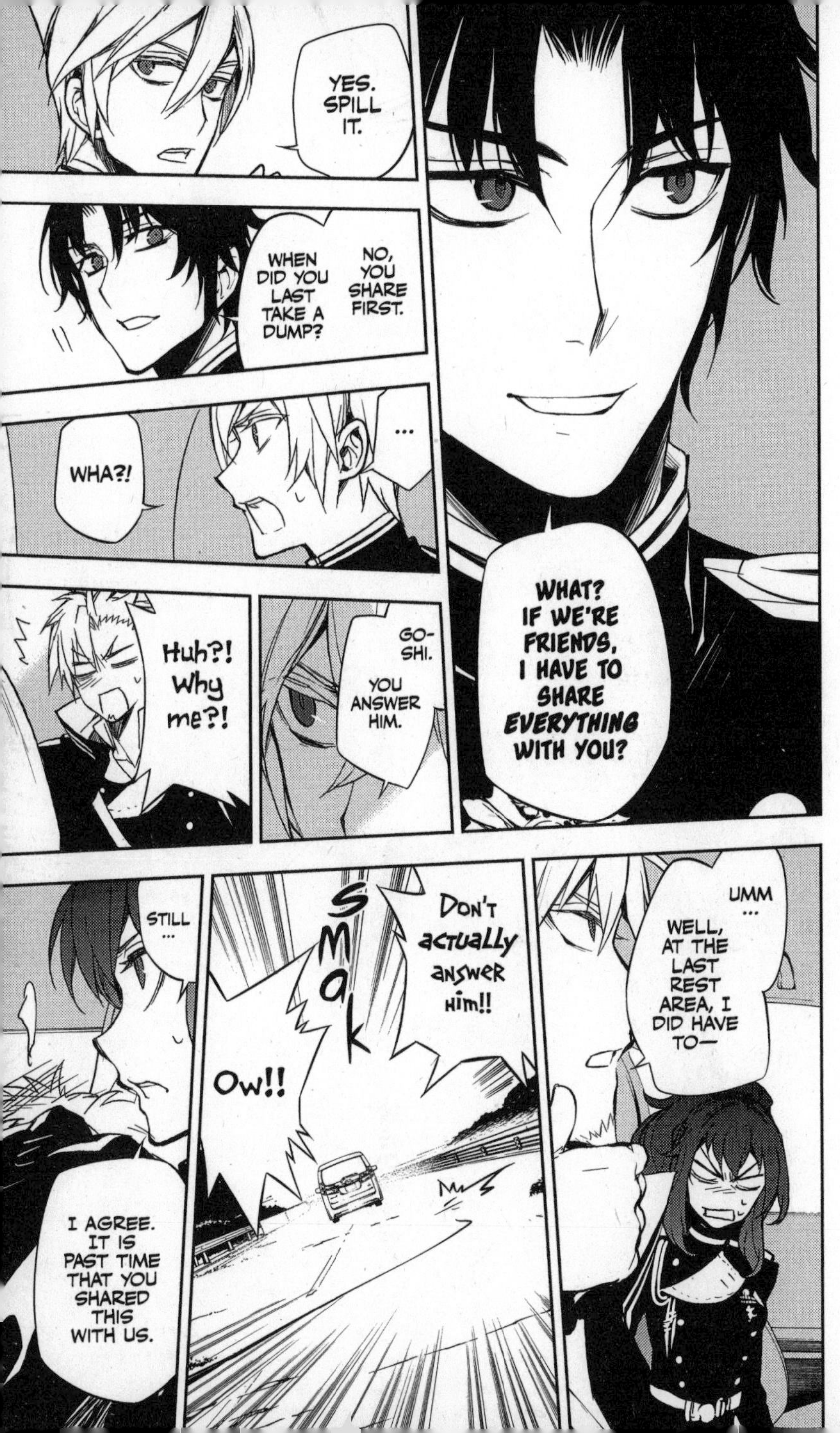
WHAT? IF WE'RE FRIENDS, I HAVE TO SHARE EVERYTHING WITH YOU?
YES. SPILL IT.
NO, YOU SHARE FIRST.
WHEN DID YOU LAST TAKE A DUMP?
...
WHA?!
GO-SHI.
YOU ANSWER HIM.
Huh?! Why me?!
UMM...
WELL, AT THE LAST REST AREA, I DID HAVE TO—
Don't actually answer him!!
SMAK
Ow!!
STILL...
I AGREE. IT IS PAST TIME THAT YOU SHARED THIS WITH US.

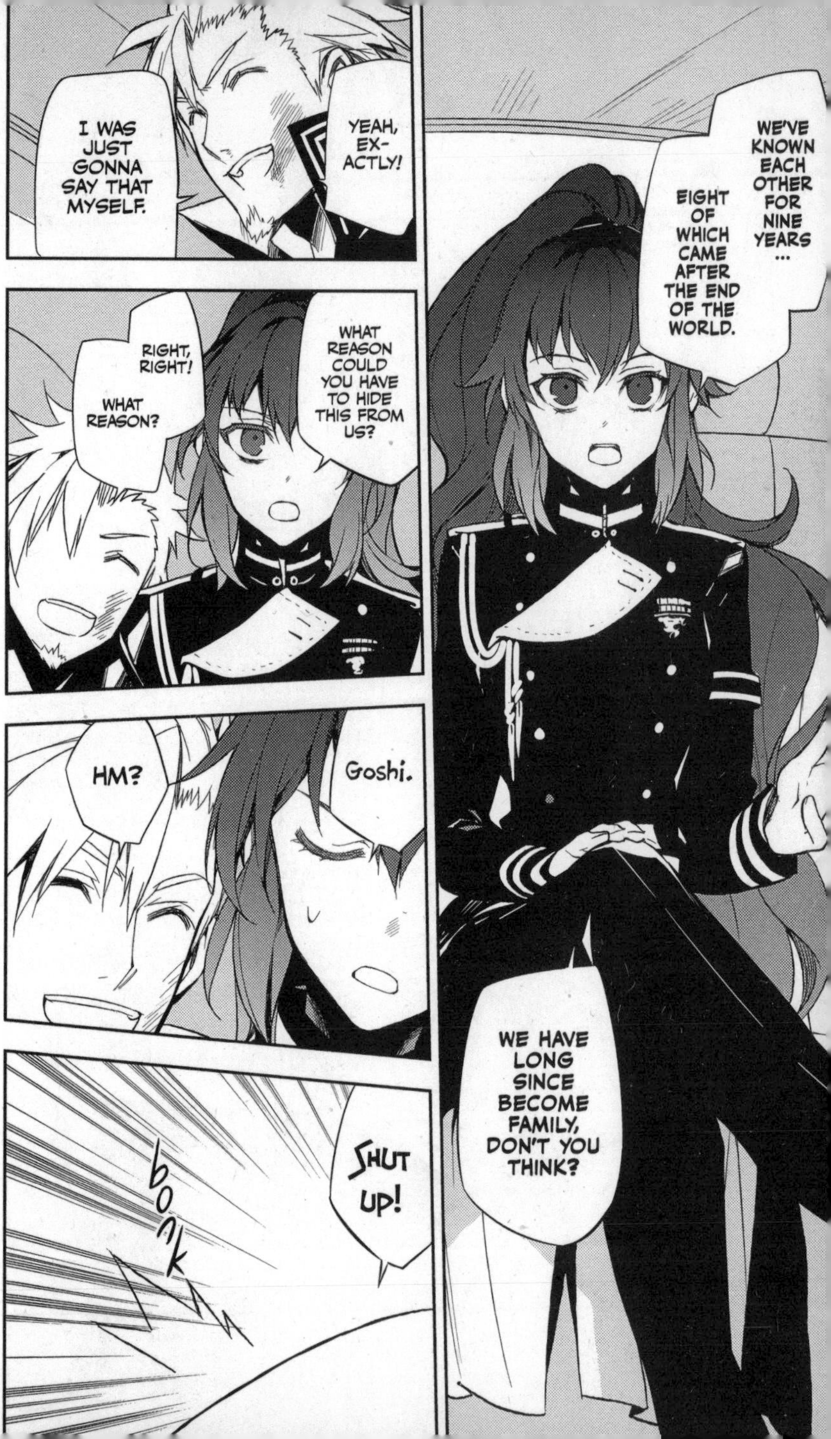
WE'VE KNOWN EACH OTHER FOR NINE YEARS...
EIGHT OF WHICH CAME AFTER THE END OF THE WORLD.
WE HAVE LONG SINCE BECOME FAMILY, DON'T YOU THINK?
YEAH, EX-ACTLY!
I WAS JUST GONNA SAY THAT MYSELF.
WHAT REASON COULD YOU HAVE TO HIDE THIS FROM US?
RIGHT, RIGHT!
WHAT REASON?
Goshi.
HM?
SHUT UP!
bonk

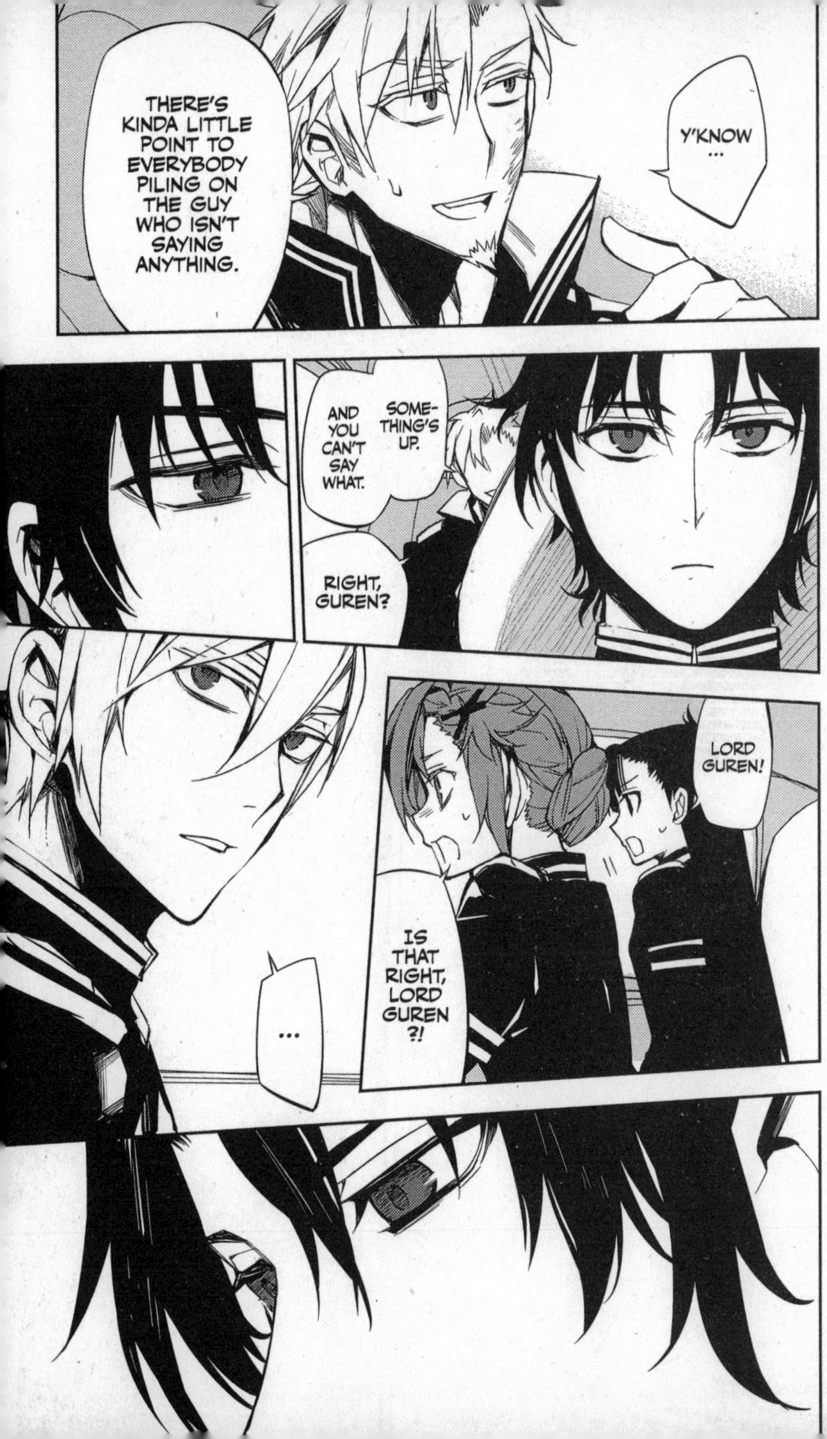
Y'KNOW...
THERE'S KINDA LITTLE POINT TO EVERYBODY PILING ON THE GUY WHO ISN'T SAYING ANYTHING.
SOME-THING'S UP.
AND YOU CAN'T SAY WHAT.
RIGHT, GUREN?
LORD GUREN!
IS THAT RIGHT, LORD GUREN?!
...

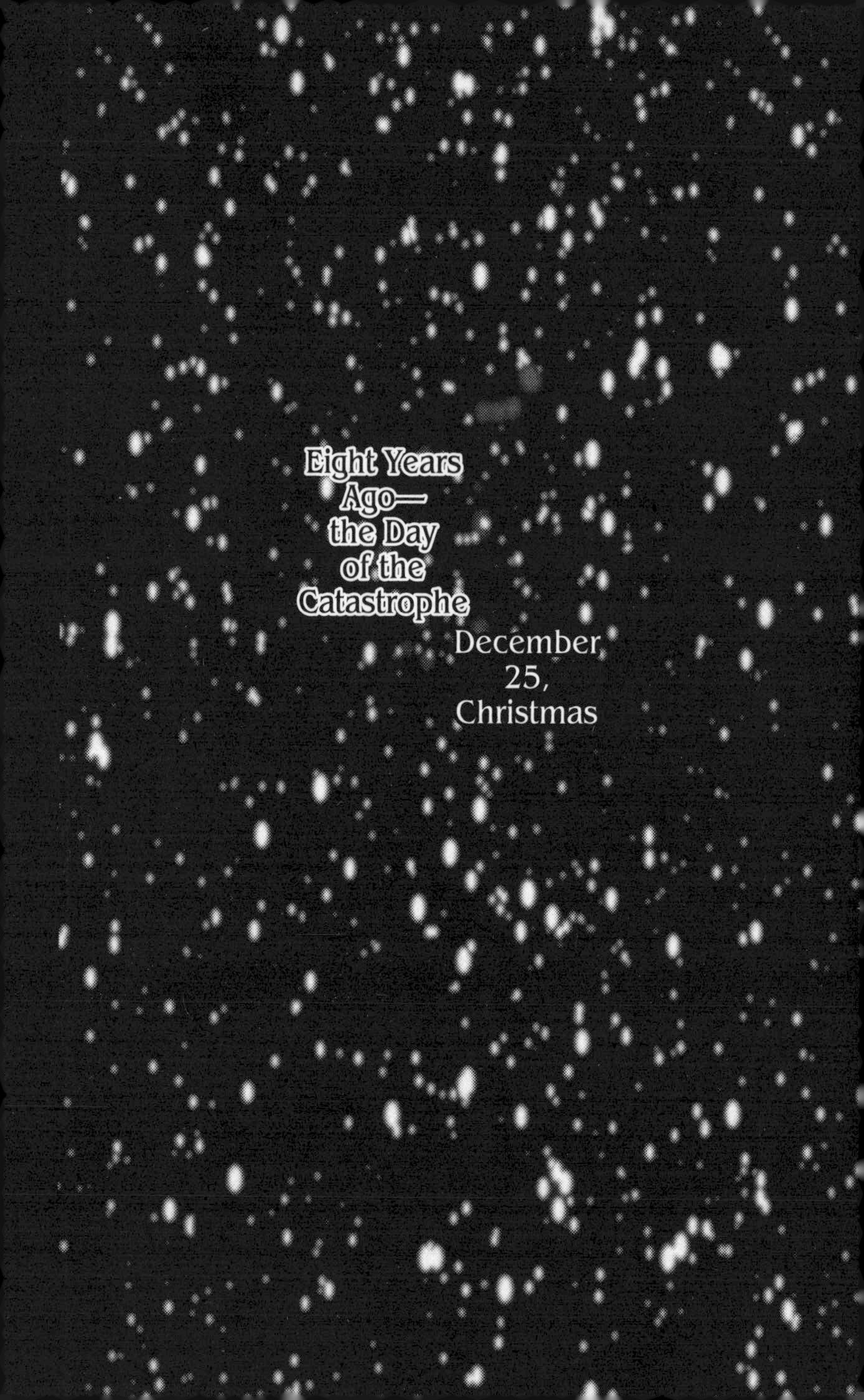
Eight Years Ago—the Day of the Catastrophe
December 25, Christmas

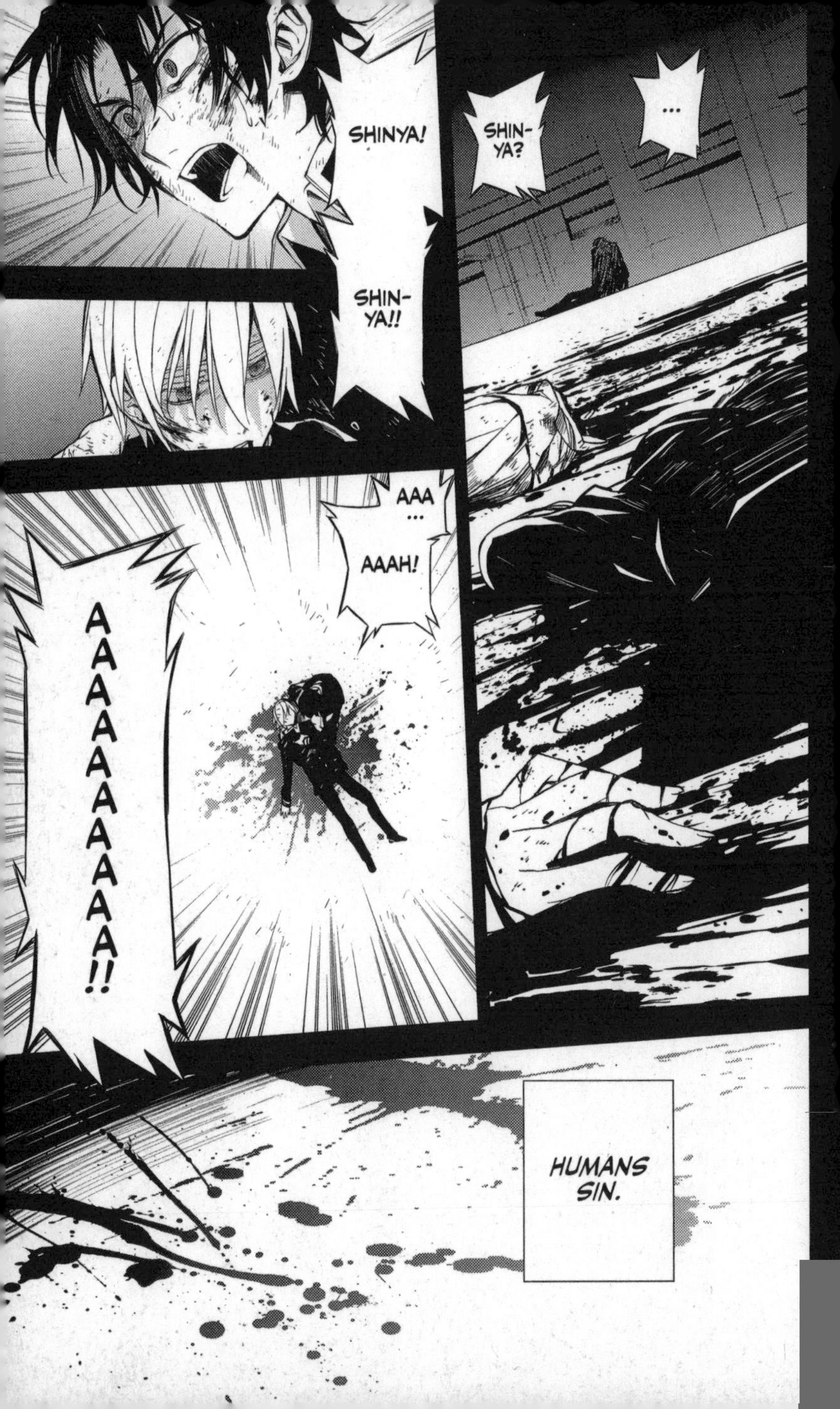
...
SHIN-YA?
SHINYA!
SHIN-YA!!
AAA... AAAH!
AAAAAAAAAA!!
HUMANS SIN.

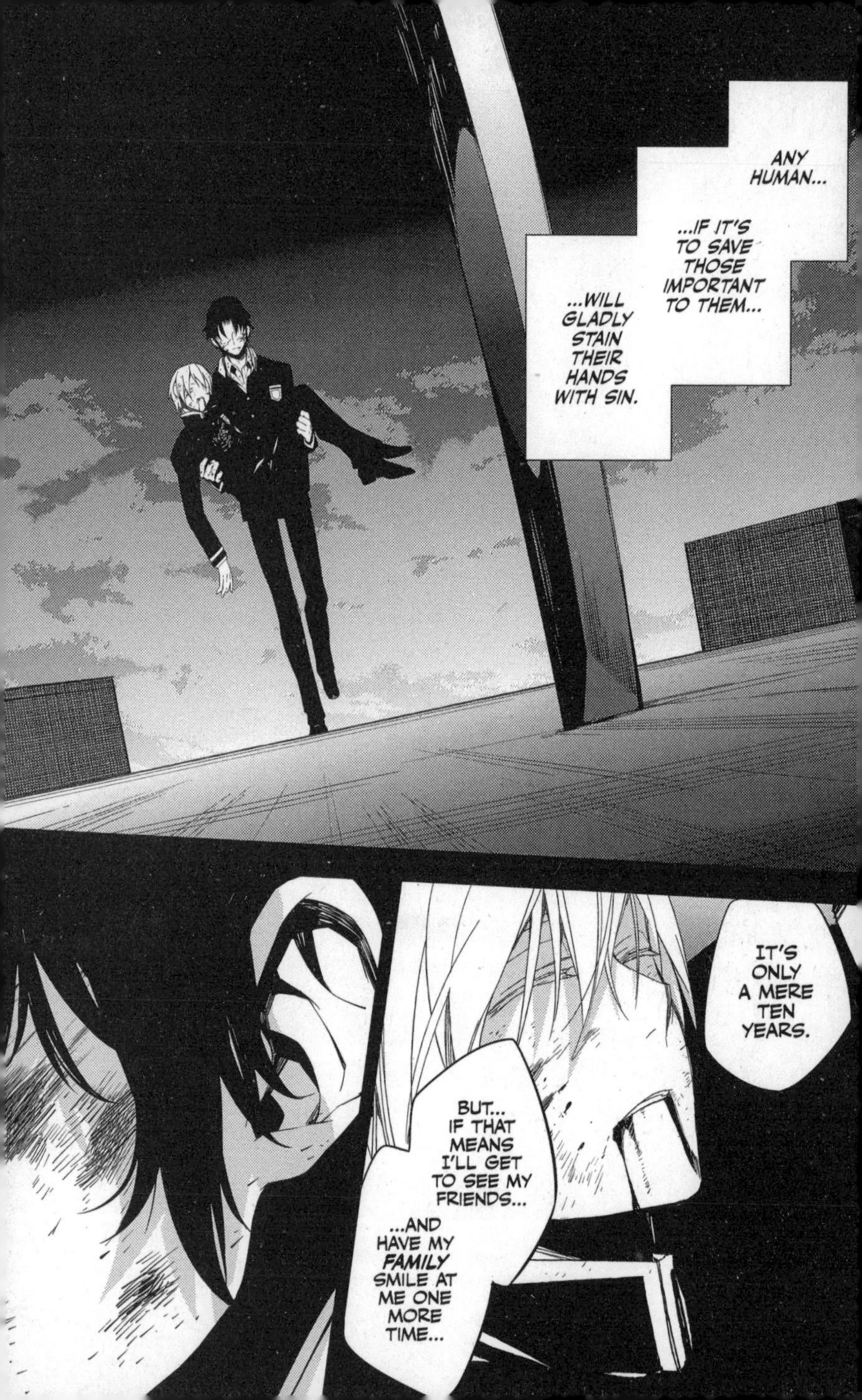
ANY HUMAN...
...IF IT'S TO SAVE THOSE IMPORTANT TO THEM...
...WILL GLADLY STAIN THEIR HANDS WITH SIN.
IT'S ONLY A MERE TEN YEARS.
BUT... IF THAT MEANS I'LL GET TO SEE MY FRIENDS...
...AND HAVE MY *FAMILY* SMILE AT ME ONE MORE TIME...

THE COST OF BRINGING A PERSON BACK FROM THE DEAD...
...IS THE LIFE OF EVERY HUMAN ON THE PLANET.
EVEN THEN, THE ONES REVIVED WILL ONLY LIVE ANOTHER TEN YEARS.
I...
...WILL SHOULDER THIS SIN.
CHK

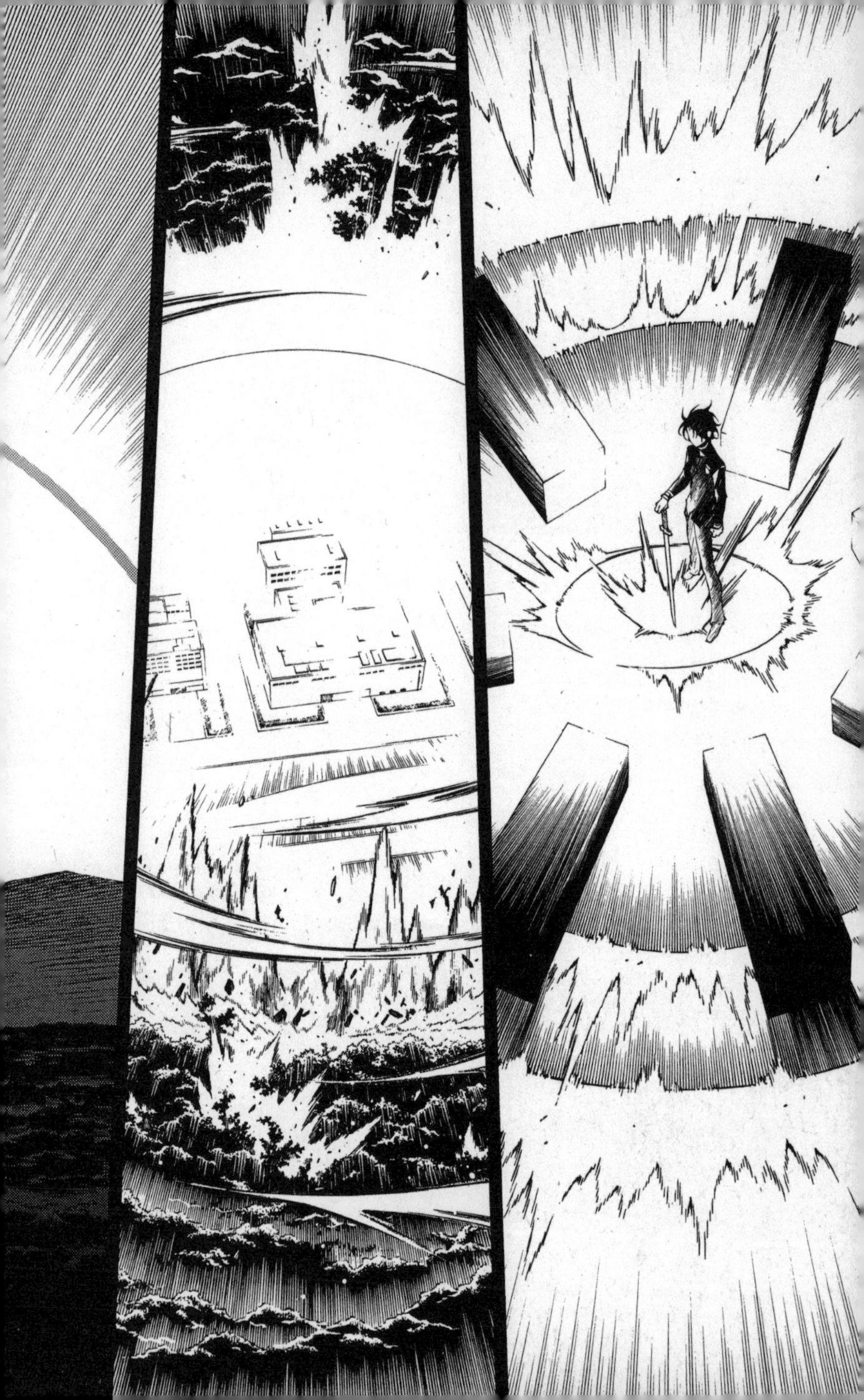

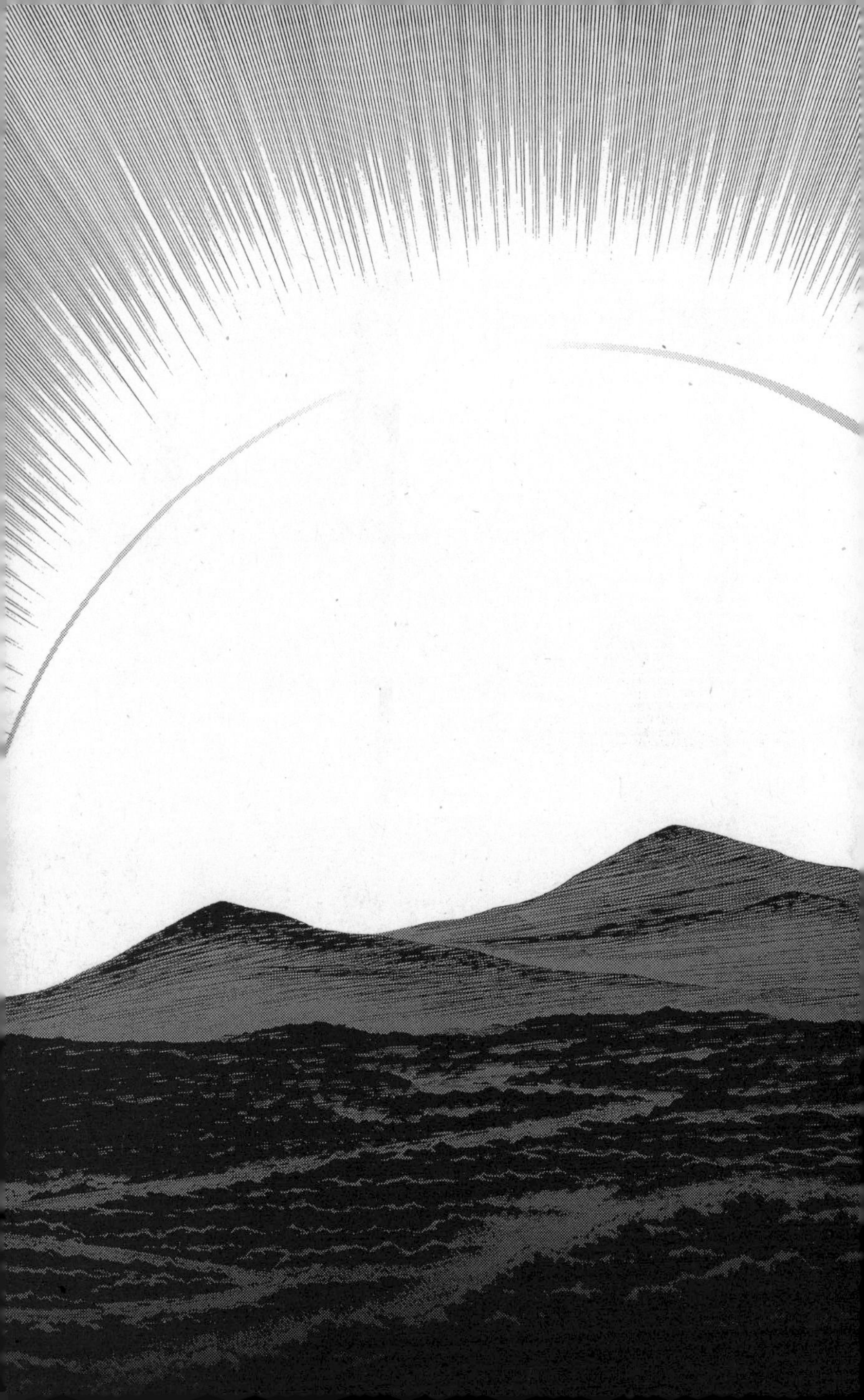

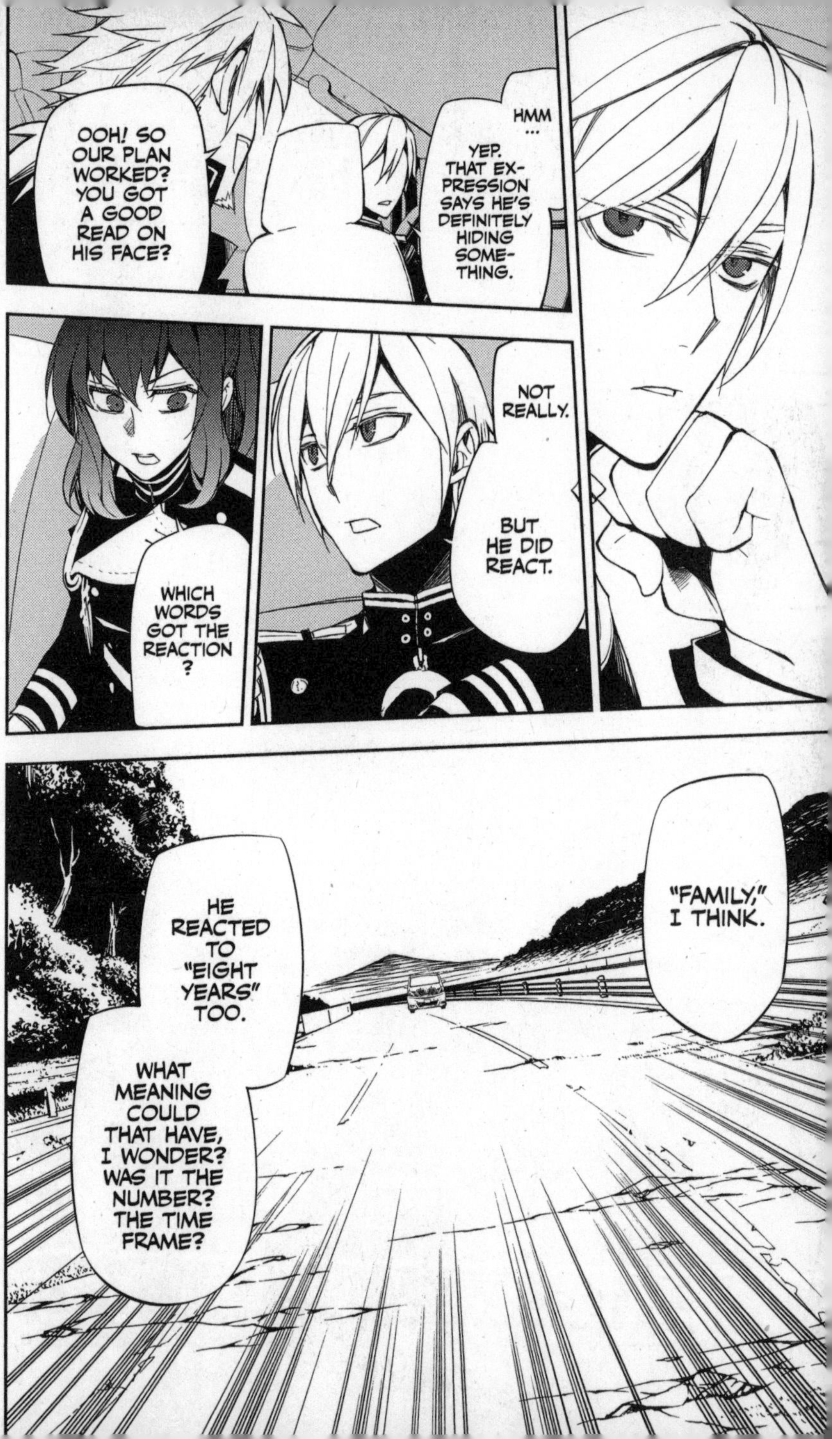
HMM ...
YEP. THAT EXPRESSION SAYS HE'S DEFINITELY HIDING SOMETHING.
OOH! SO OUR PLAN WORKED? YOU GOT A GOOD READ ON HIS FACE?
NOT REALLY.
BUT HE DID REACT.
WHICH WORDS GOT THE REACTION ?
"FAMILY," I THINK.
HE REACTED TO "EIGHT YEARS" TOO.
WHAT MEANING COULD THAT HAVE, I WONDER? WAS IT THE NUMBER? THE TIME FRAME?

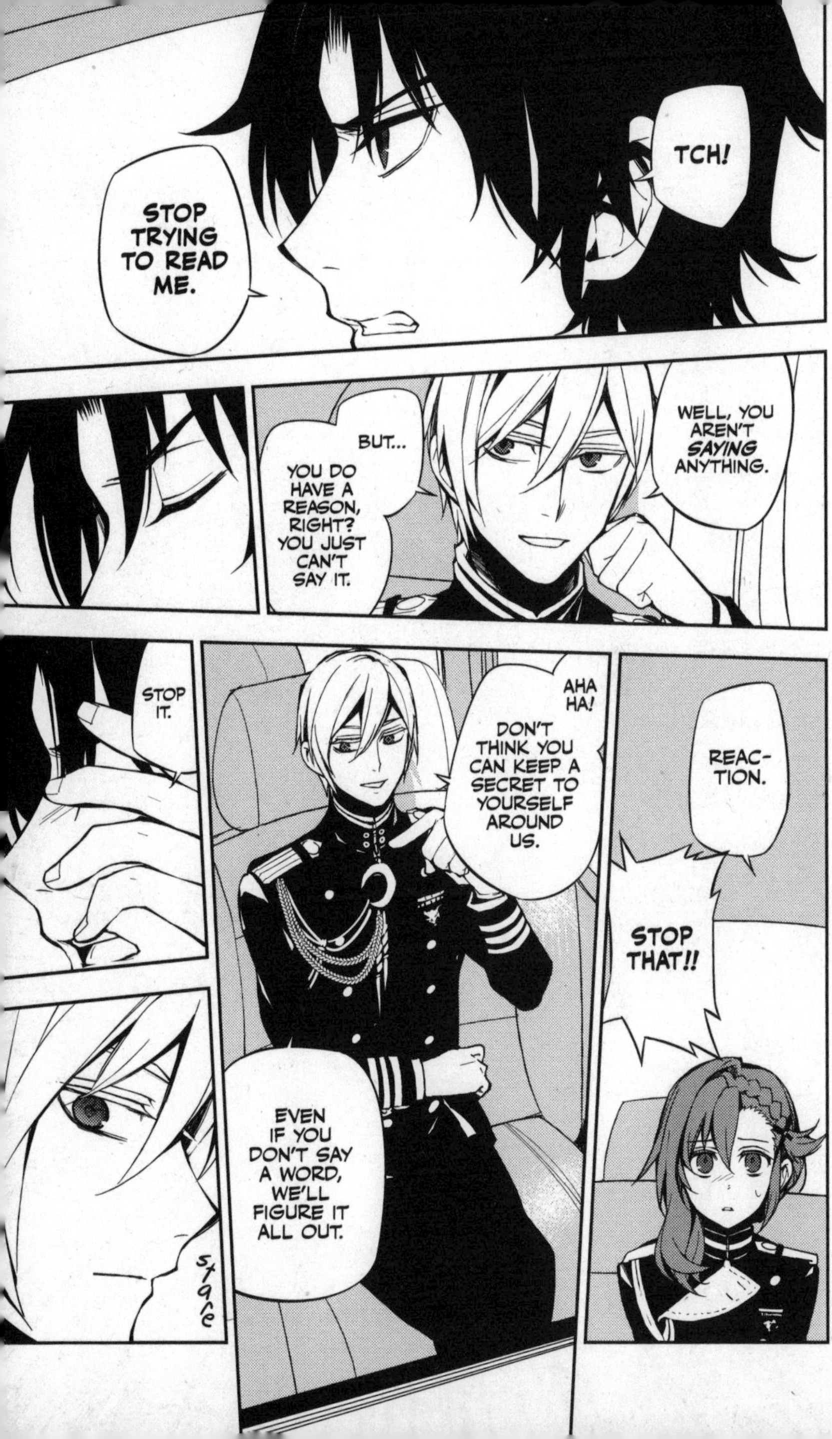
TCH!
STOP TRYING TO READ ME.
WELL, YOU AREN'T *SAYING* ANYTHING.
BUT...
YOU DO HAVE A REASON, RIGHT? YOU JUST CAN'T SAY IT.
REAC-TION.
STOP THAT!!
AHAHA!
DON'T THINK YOU CAN KEEP A SECRET TO YOURSELF AROUND US.
EVEN IF YOU DON'T SAY A WORD, WE'LL FIGURE IT ALL OUT.
STOP IT.
stare

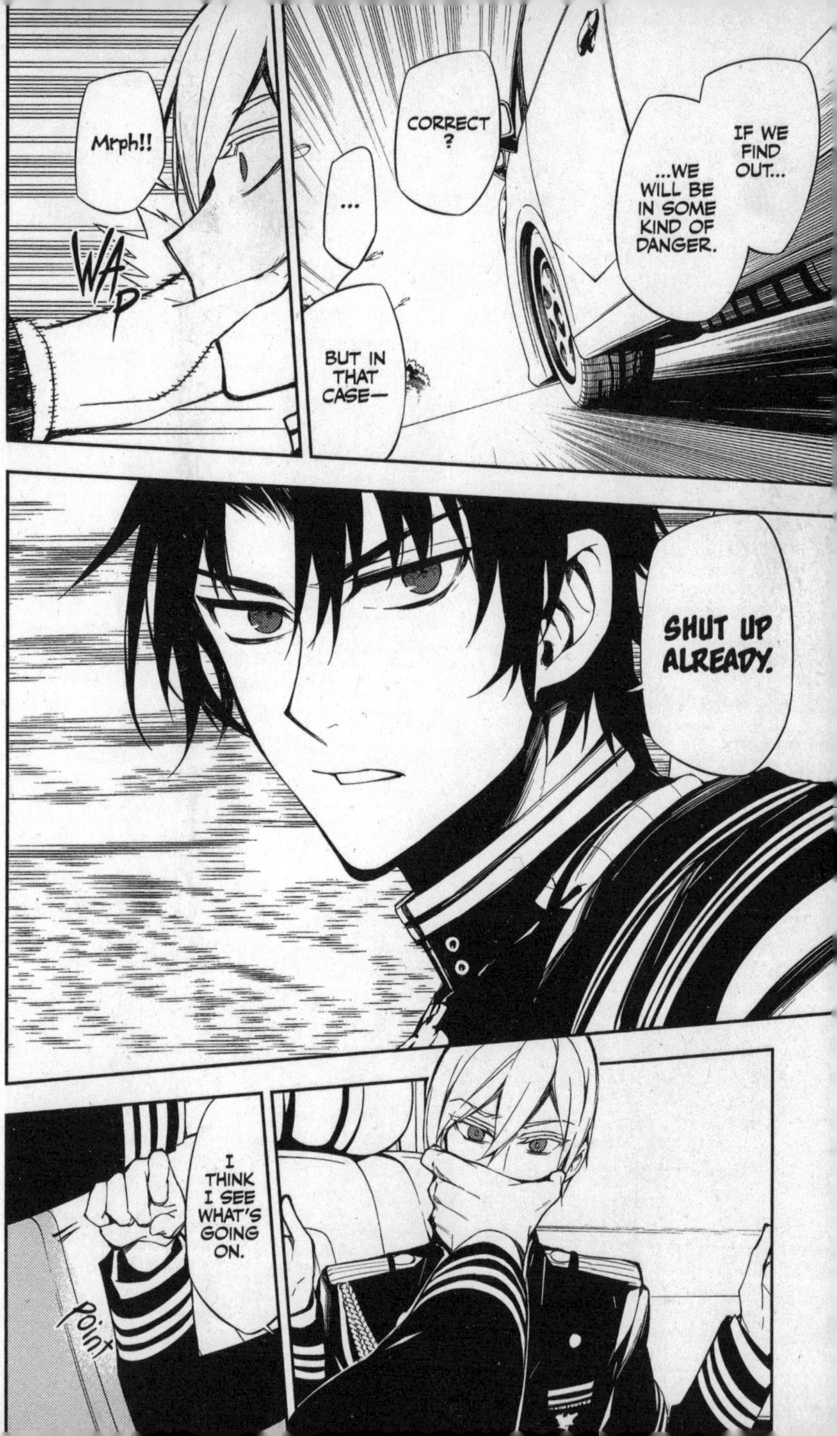
IF WE FIND OUT...
...WE WILL BE IN SOME KIND OF DANGER.
CORRECT?
...
BUT IN THAT CASE—
Mrph!!
WAP
SHUT UP ALREADY.
I THINK I SEE WHAT'S GOING ON.
Point

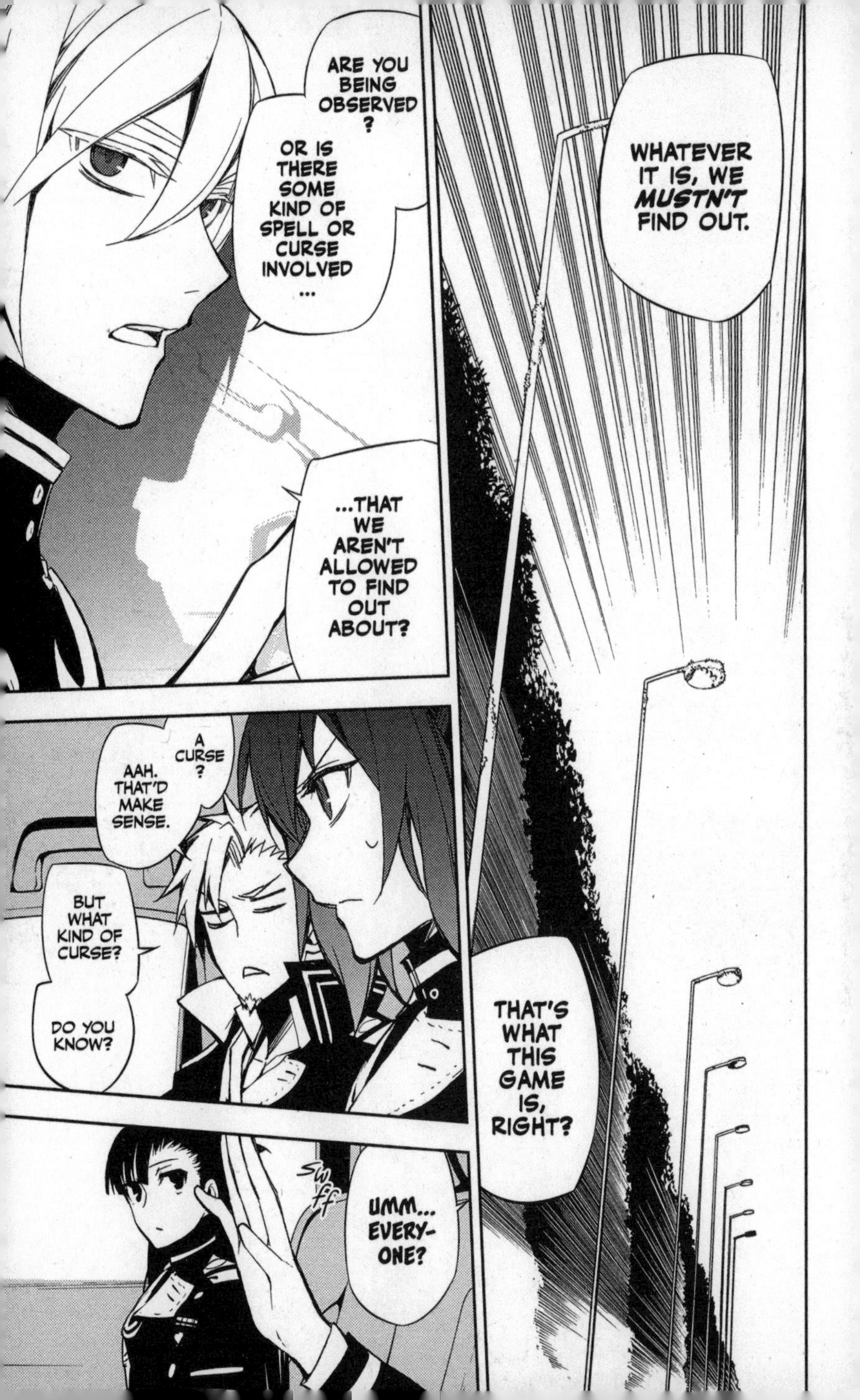
WHATEVER IT IS, WE *MUSTN'T* FIND OUT.
THAT'S WHAT THIS GAME IS, RIGHT?
ARE YOU BEING OBSERVED?
OR IS THERE SOME KIND OF SPELL OR CURSE INVOLVED...
...THAT WE AREN'T ALLOWED TO FIND OUT ABOUT?
A CURSE?
AAH. THAT'D MAKE SENSE.
BUT WHAT KIND OF CURSE?
DO YOU KNOW?
SWFF
UMM... EVERY-ONE?

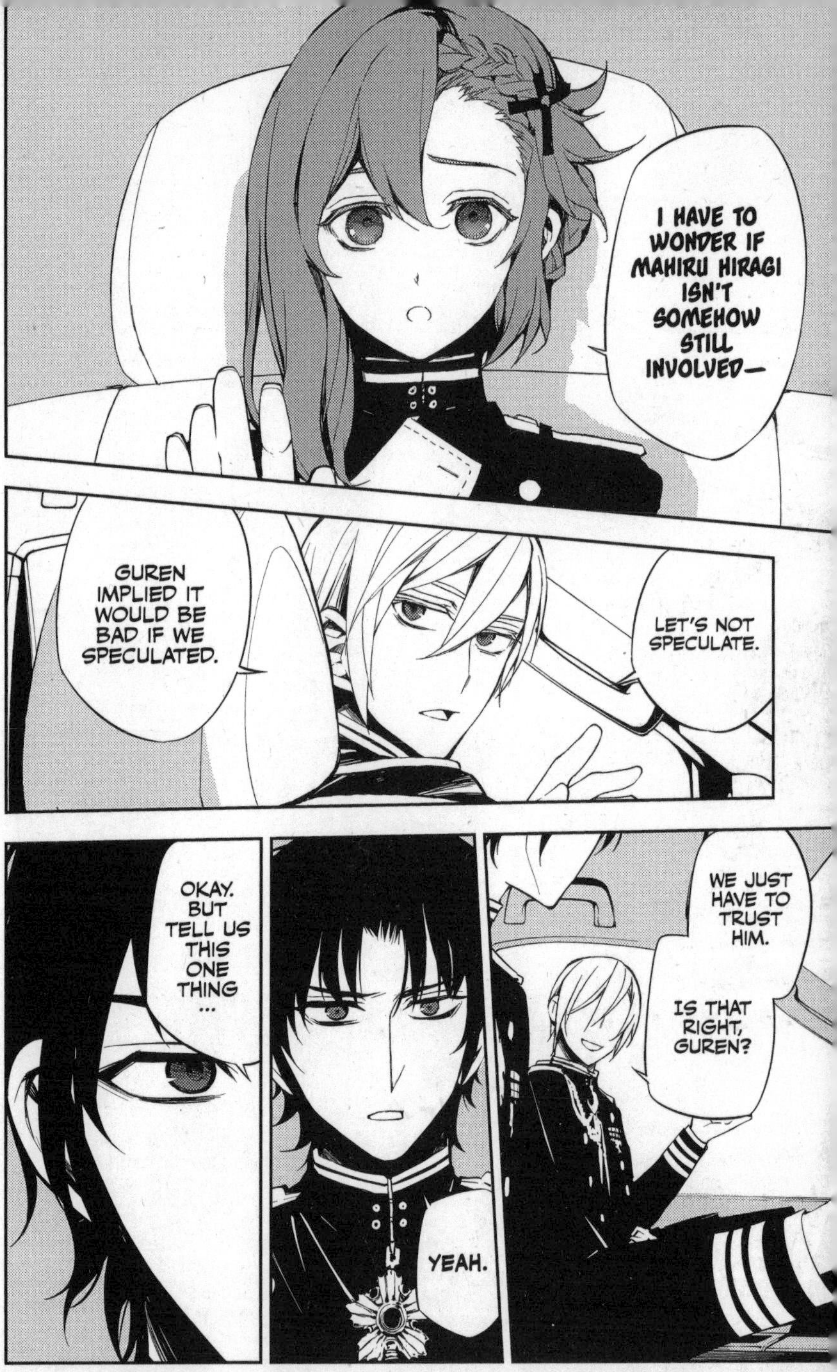
I HAVE TO WONDER IF MAHIRU HIRAGI ISN'T SOMEHOW STILL INVOLVED—
LET'S NOT SPECULATE.
GUREN IMPLIED IT WOULD BE BAD IF WE SPECULATED.
WE JUST HAVE TO TRUST HIM.
IS THAT RIGHT, GUREN?
YEAH.
OKAY. BUT TELL US THIS ONE THING...

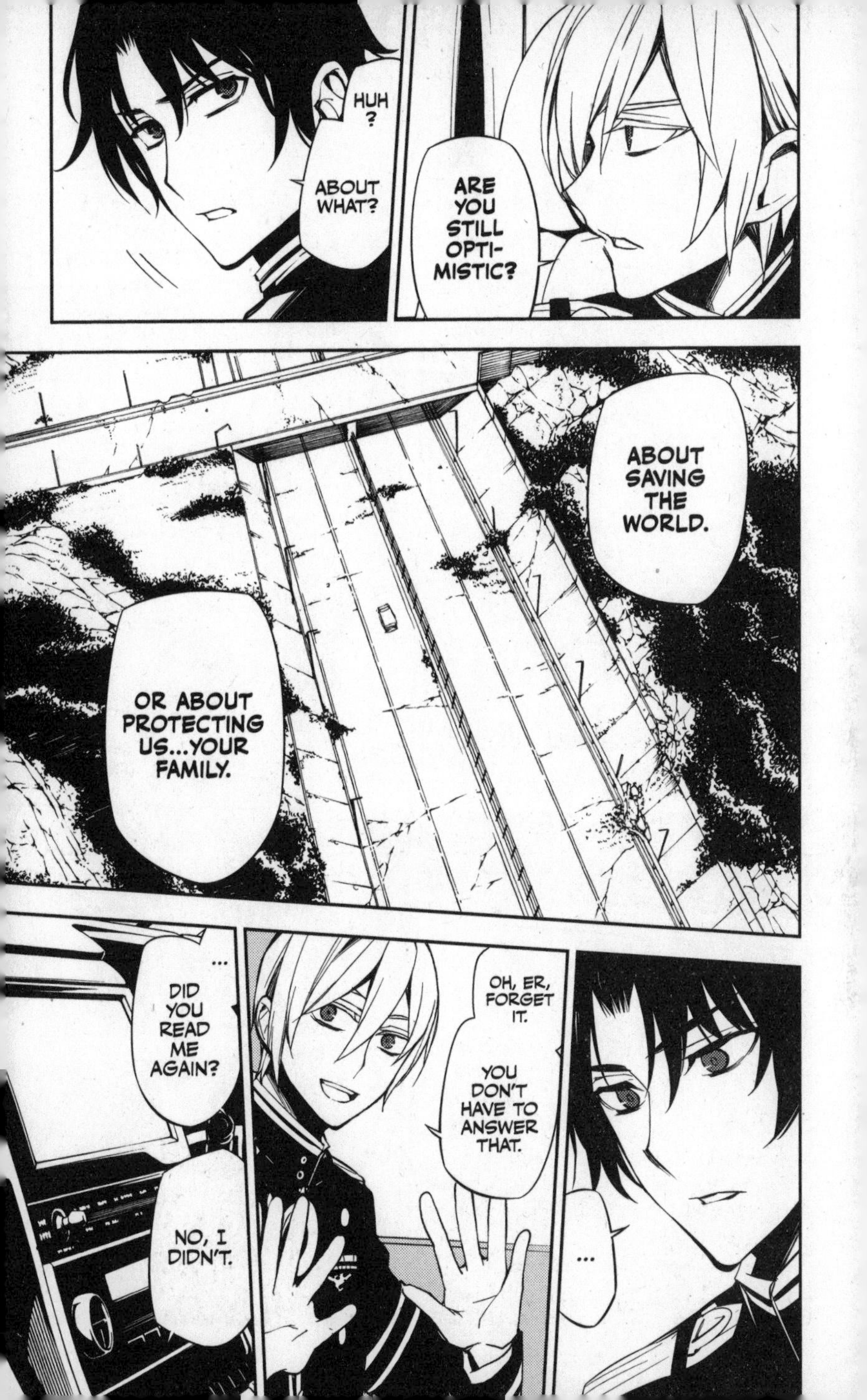
ARE YOU STILL OPTIMISTIC?
HUH?
ABOUT WHAT?
ABOUT SAVING THE WORLD.
OR ABOUT PROTECTING US...YOUR FAMILY.
...
OH, ER, FORGET IT.
YOU DON'T HAVE TO ANSWER THAT.
...
DID YOU READ ME AGAIN?
NO, I DIDN'T.

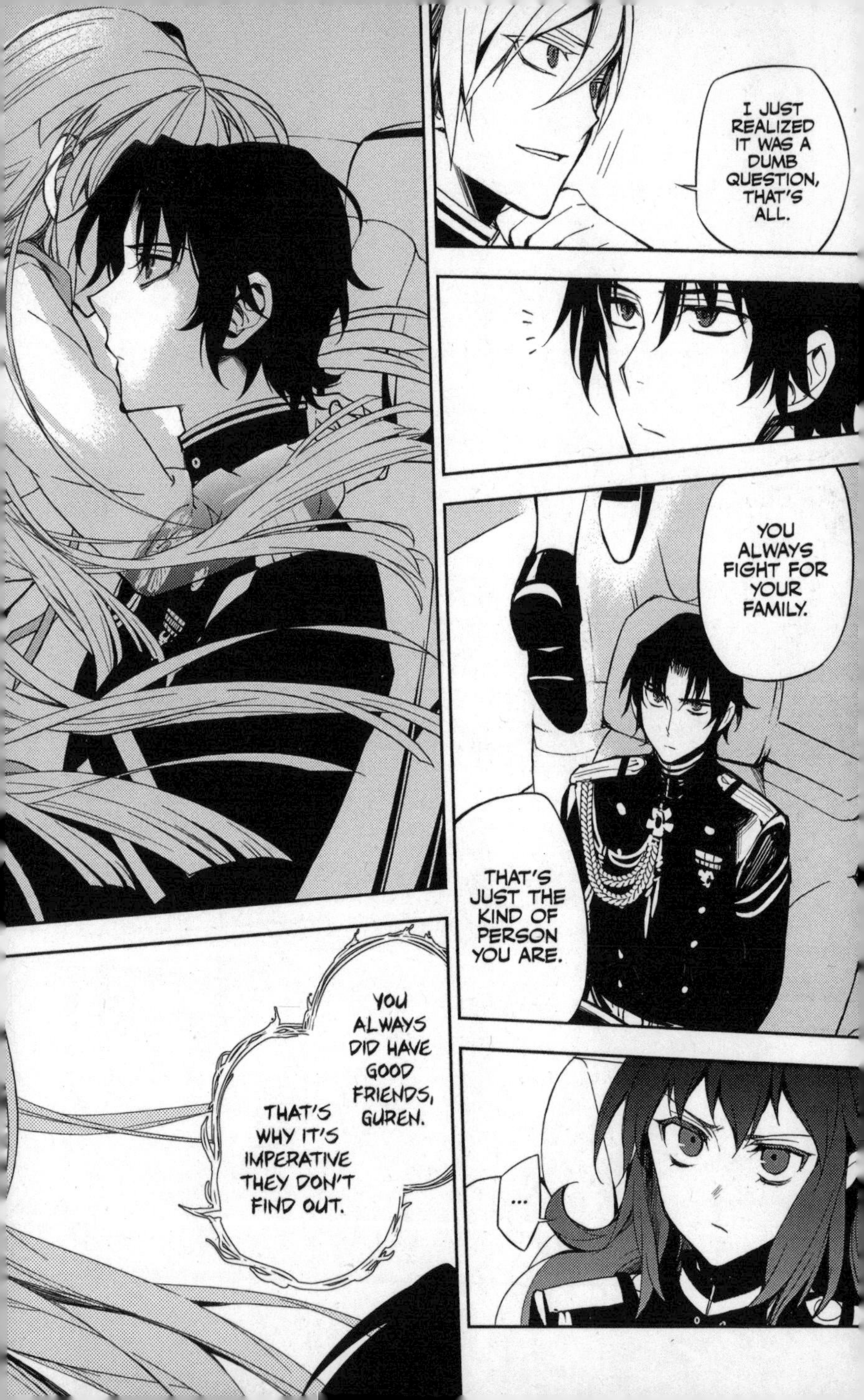
I JUST REALIZED IT WAS A DUMB QUESTION, THAT'S ALL.
YOU ALWAYS FIGHT FOR YOUR FAMILY.
THAT'S JUST THE KIND OF PERSON YOU ARE.
...
YOU ALWAYS DID HAVE GOOD FRIENDS, GUREN.
THAT'S WHY IT'S IMPERATIVE THEY DON'T FIND OUT.

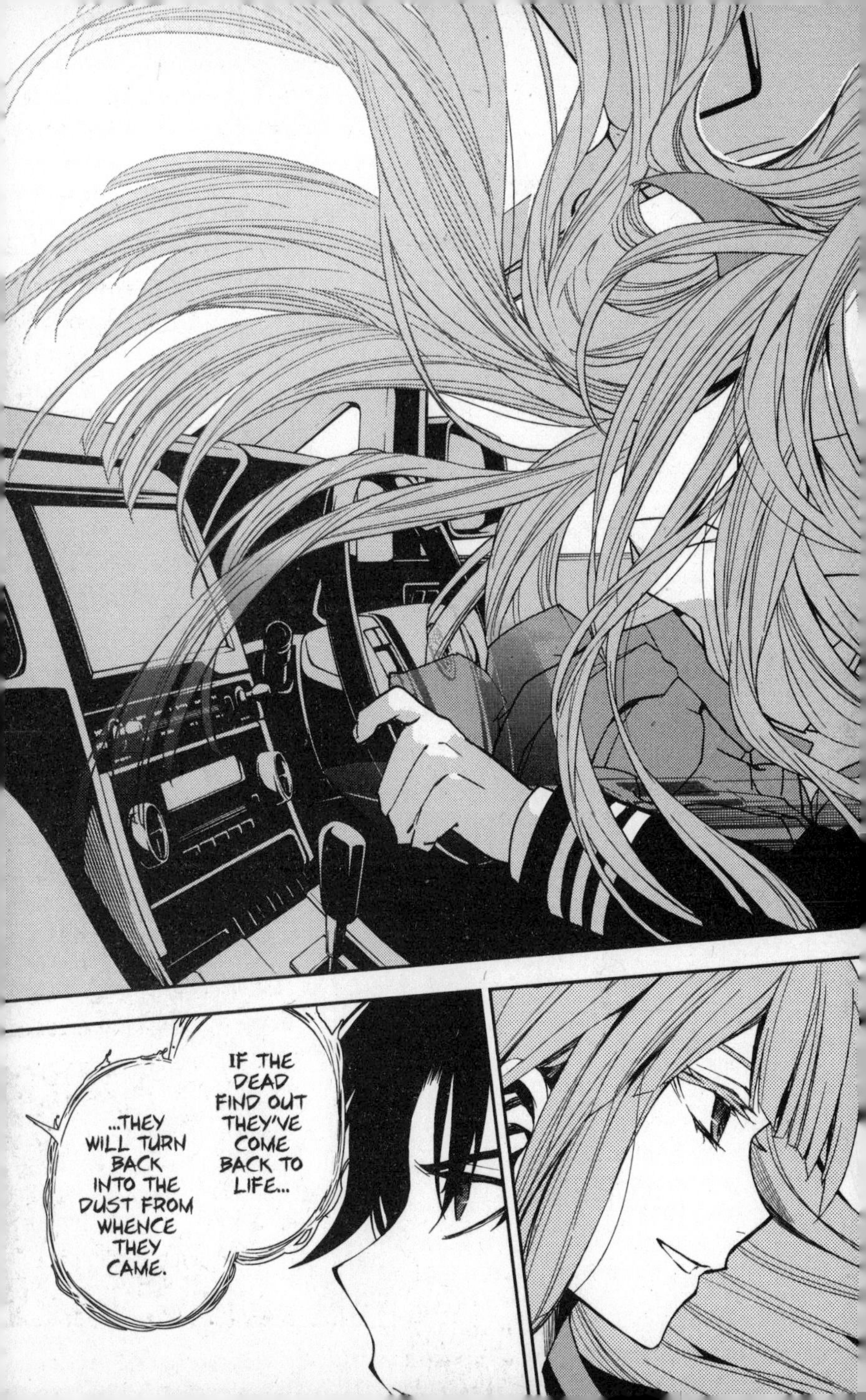
IF THE DEAD FIND OUT THEY'VE COME BACK TO LIFE...
...THEY WILL TURN BACK INTO THE DUST FROM WHENCE THEY CAME.

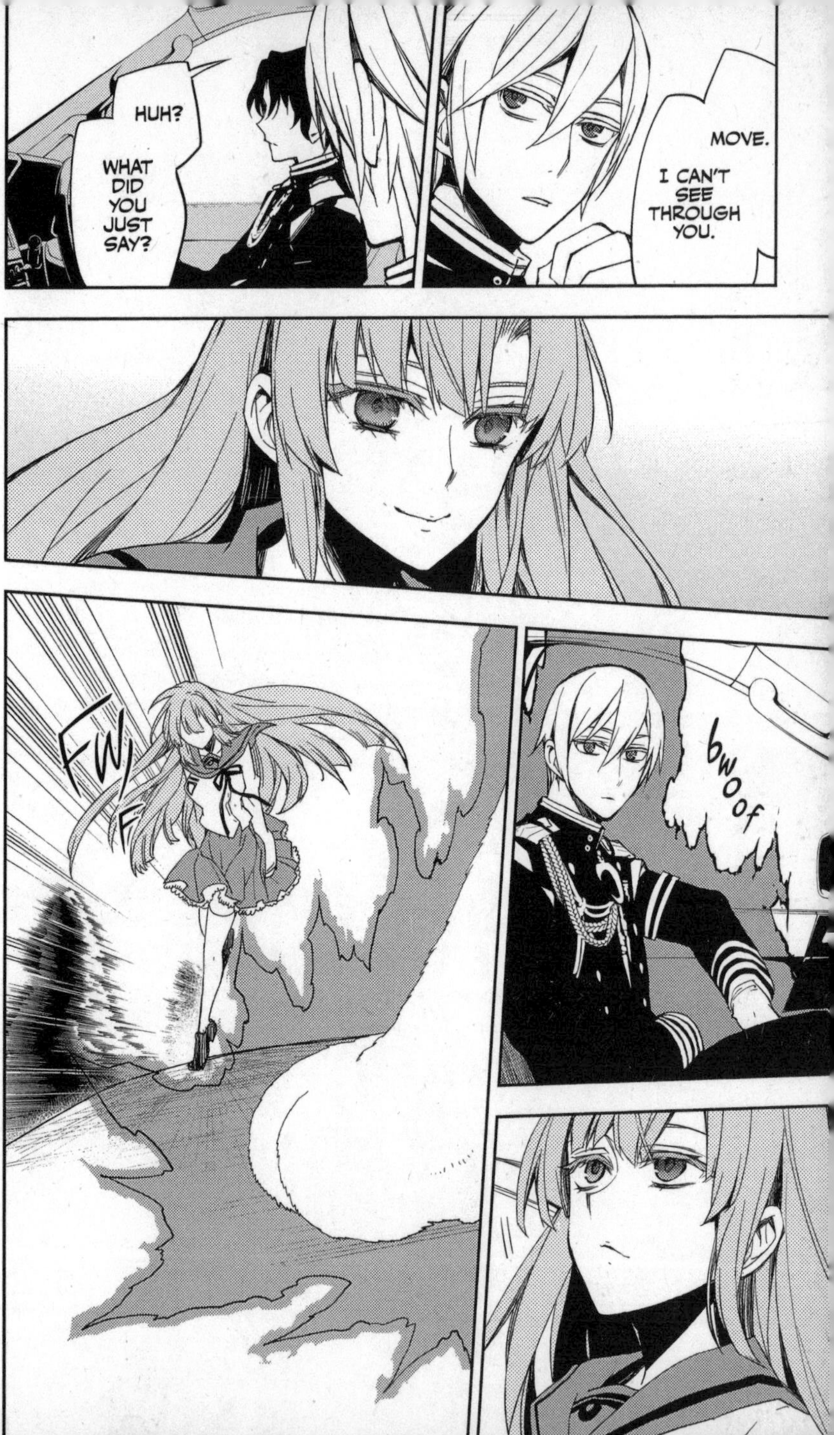
MOVE.
I CAN'T SEE THROUGH YOU.
HUH?
WHAT DID YOU JUST SAY?
bwoof
FWUFF

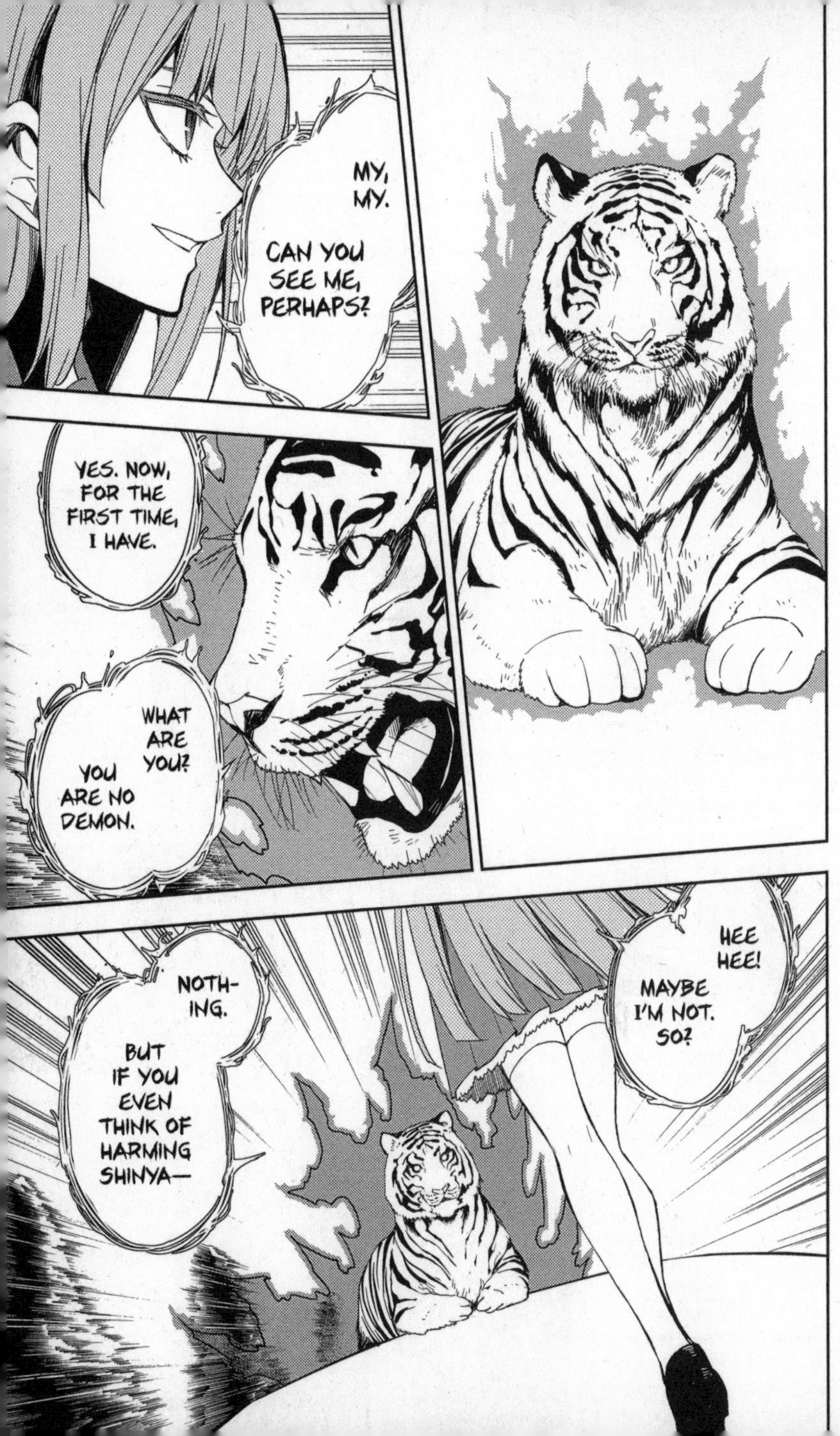
MY, MY.
CAN YOU SEE ME, PERHAPS?
YES. NOW, FOR THE FIRST TIME, I HAVE.
WHAT ARE YOU?
YOU ARE NO DEMON.
HEE HEE!
MAYBE I'M NOT. SO?
NOTH-ING.
BUT IF YOU EVEN THINK OF HARMING SHINYA—

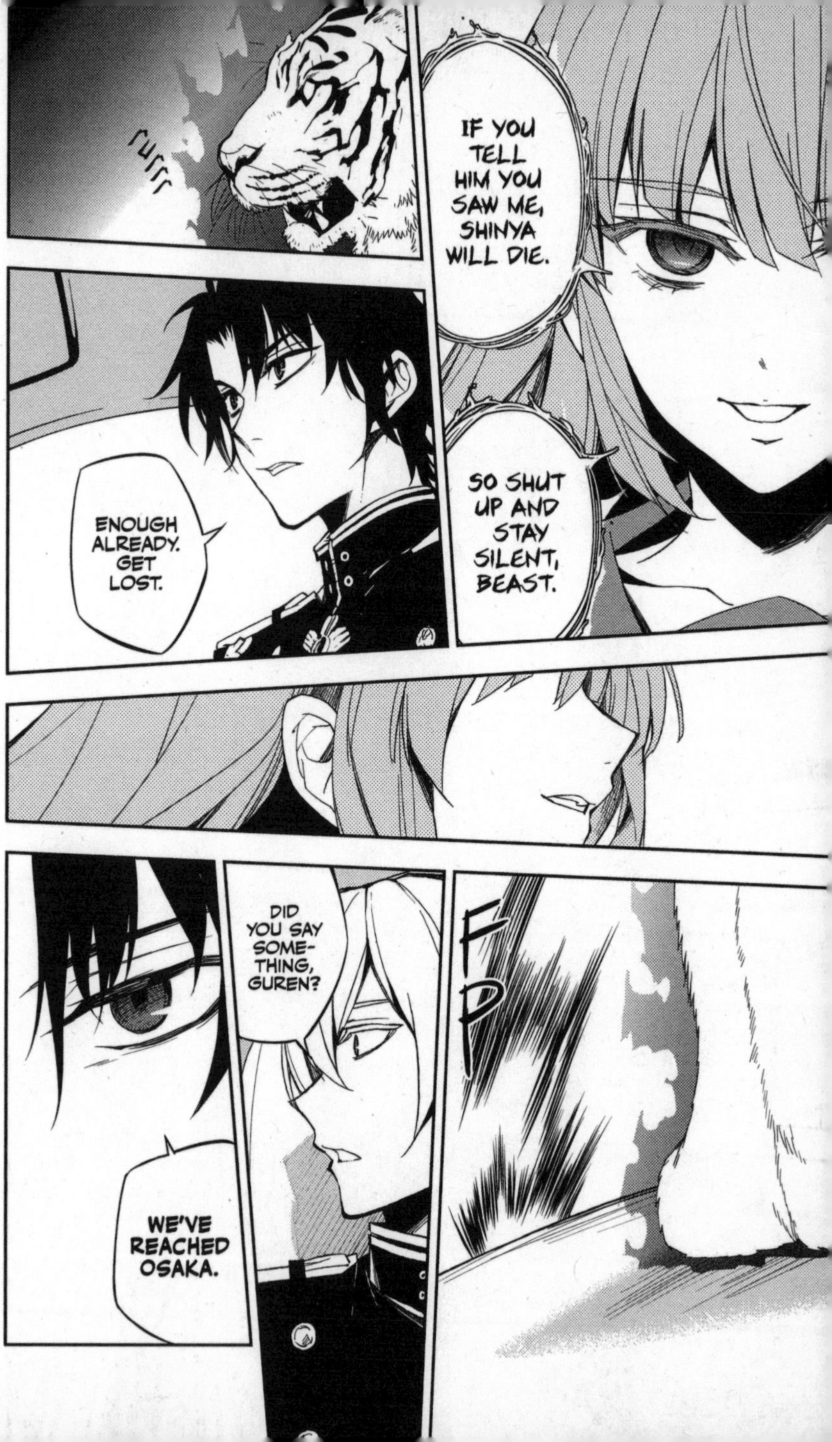
IF YOU TELL HIM YOU SAW ME, SHINYA WILL DIE.
SO SHUT UP AND STAY SILENT, BEAST.
ENOUGH ALREADY. GET LOST.
FP
DID YOU SAY SOME-THING, GUREN?
WE'VE REACHED OSAKA.

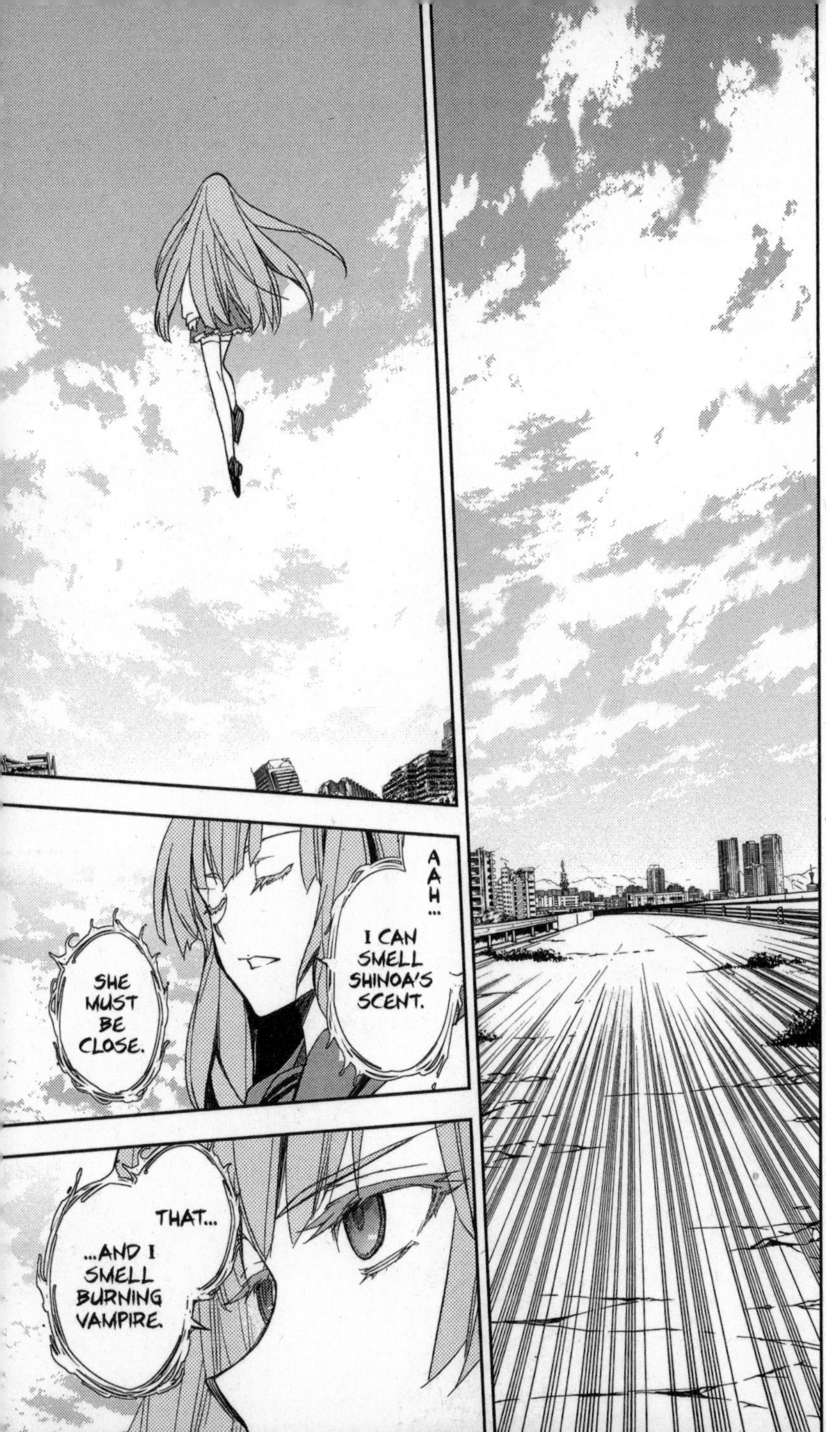
AAH...
I CAN SMELL SHINOA'S SCENT.
SHE MUST BE CLOSE.
THAT...
...AND I SMELL BURNING VAMPIRE.

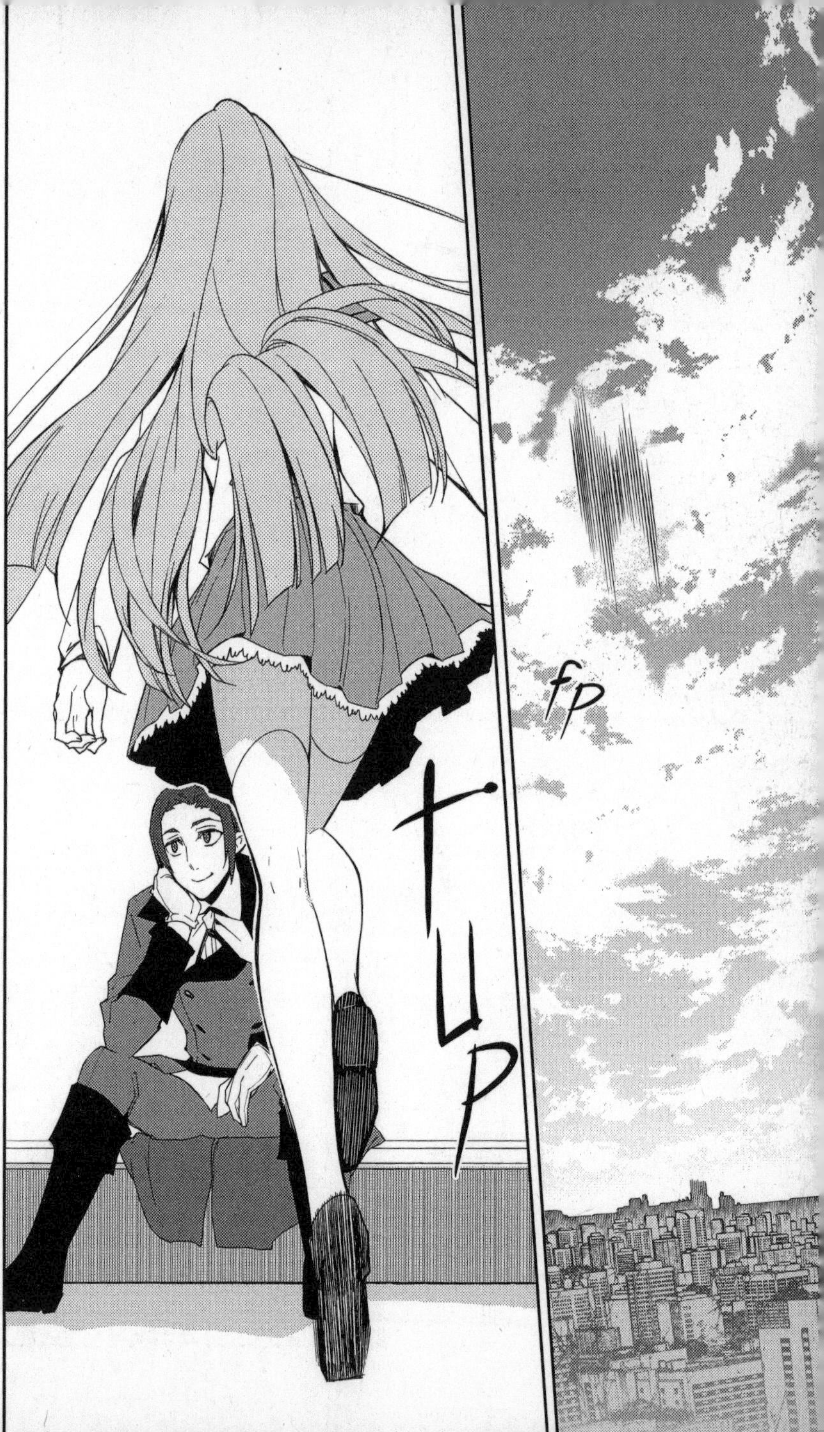
fp
TUP

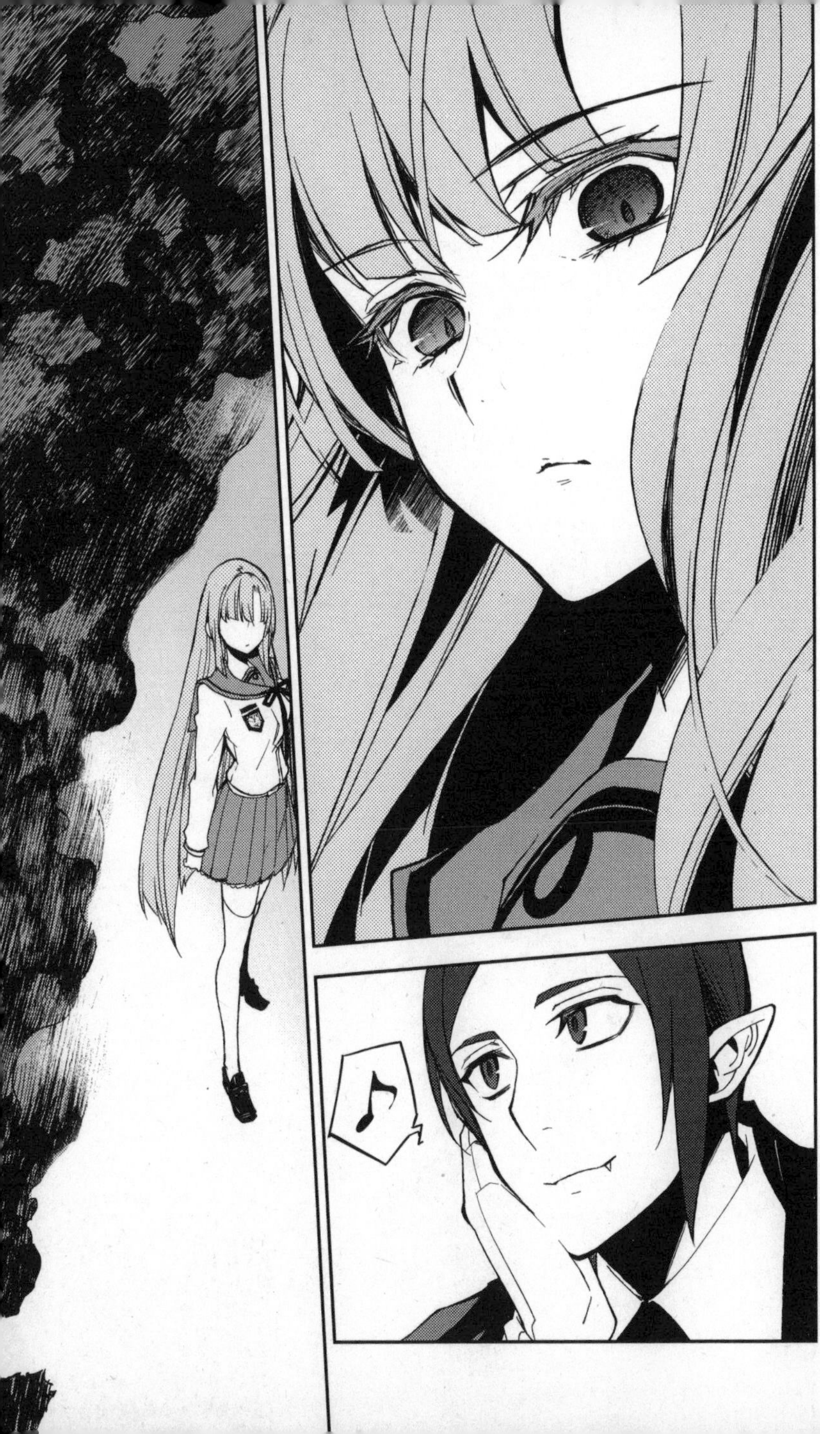
♪

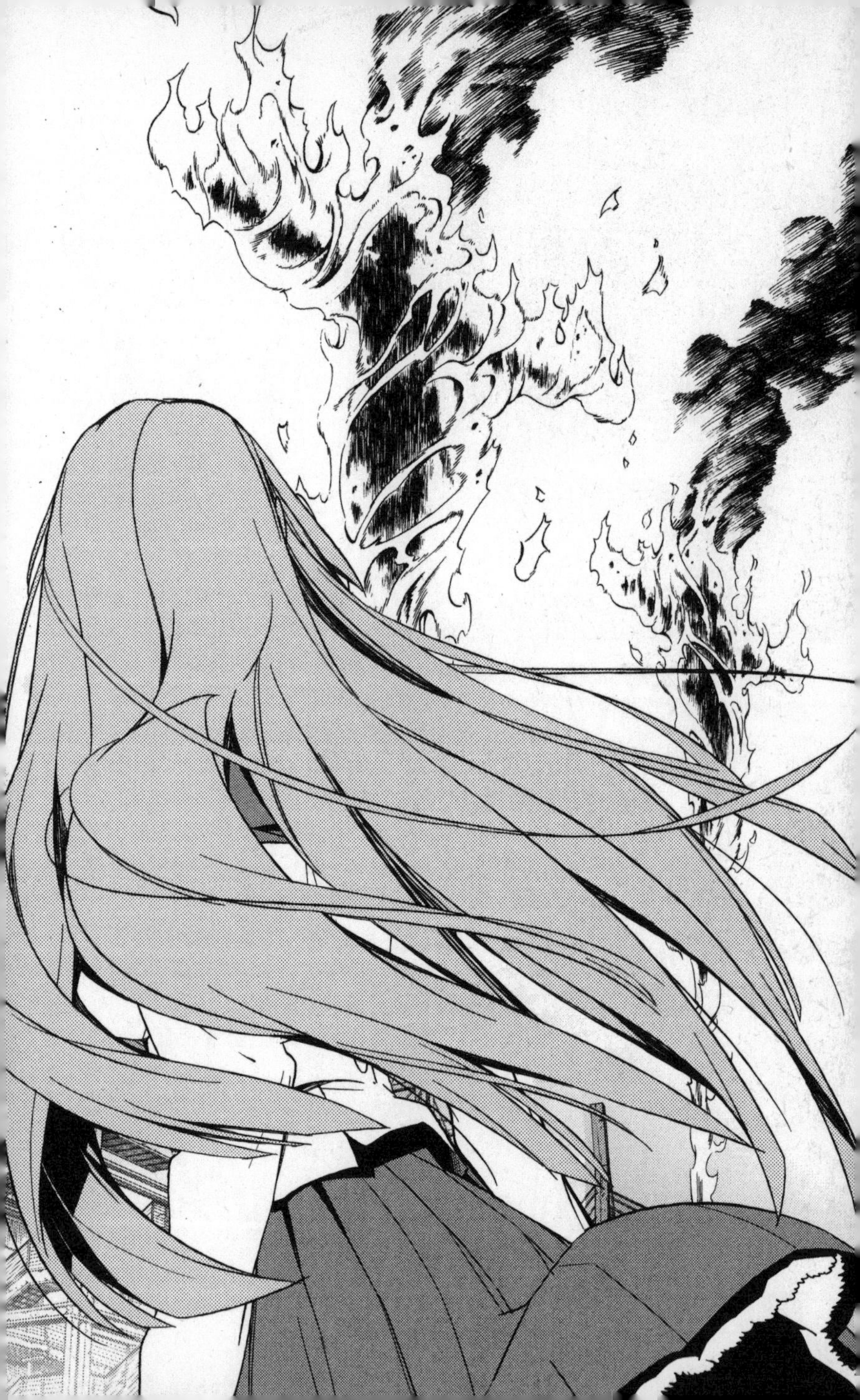

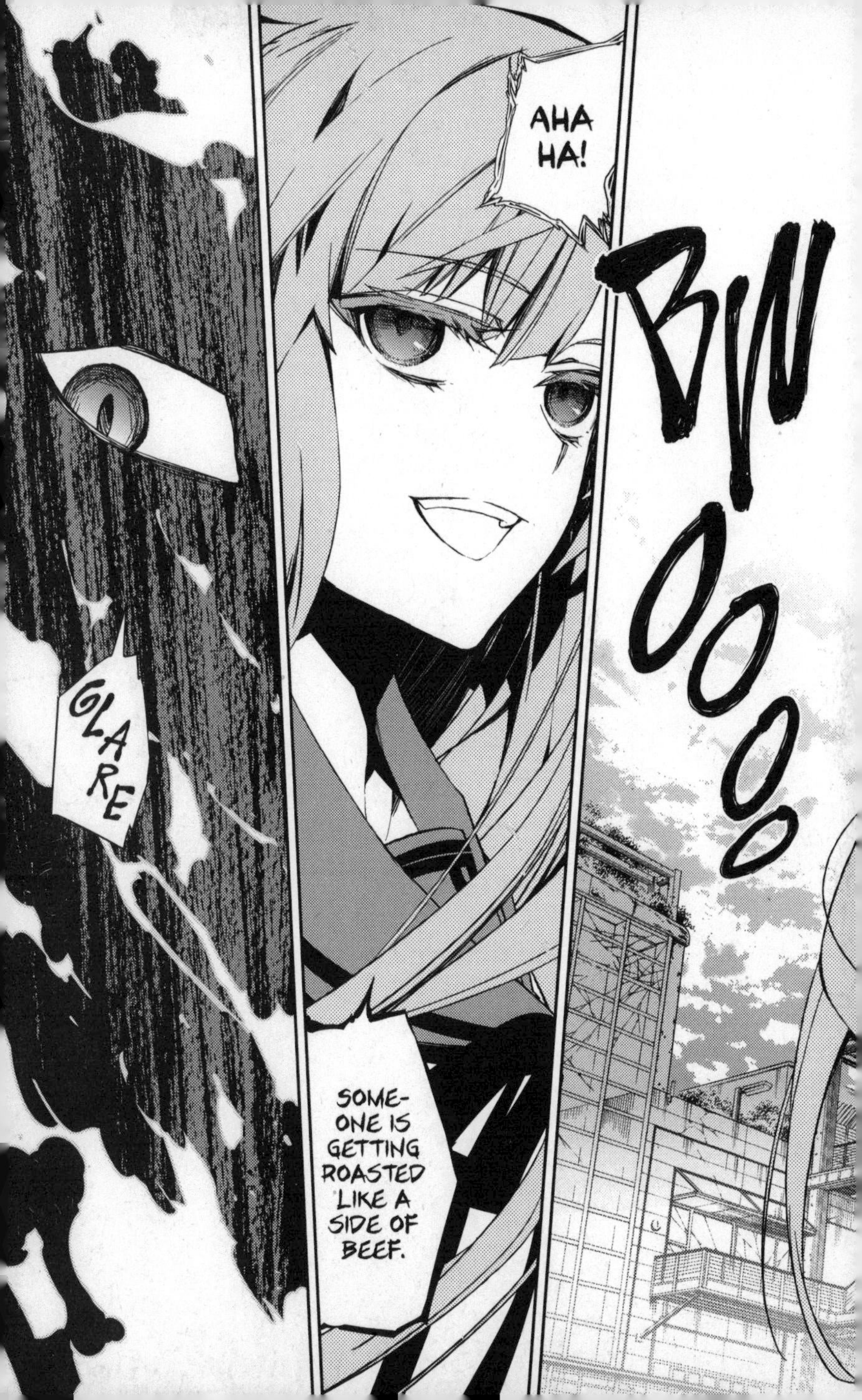
AHA HA!
BWOOOO
SOME-ONE IS GETTING ROASTED LIKE A SIDE OF BEEF.
GLARE

Seraph of the End
—VAMPIRE REIGN—

Chapter 55
Coffins of Obsession

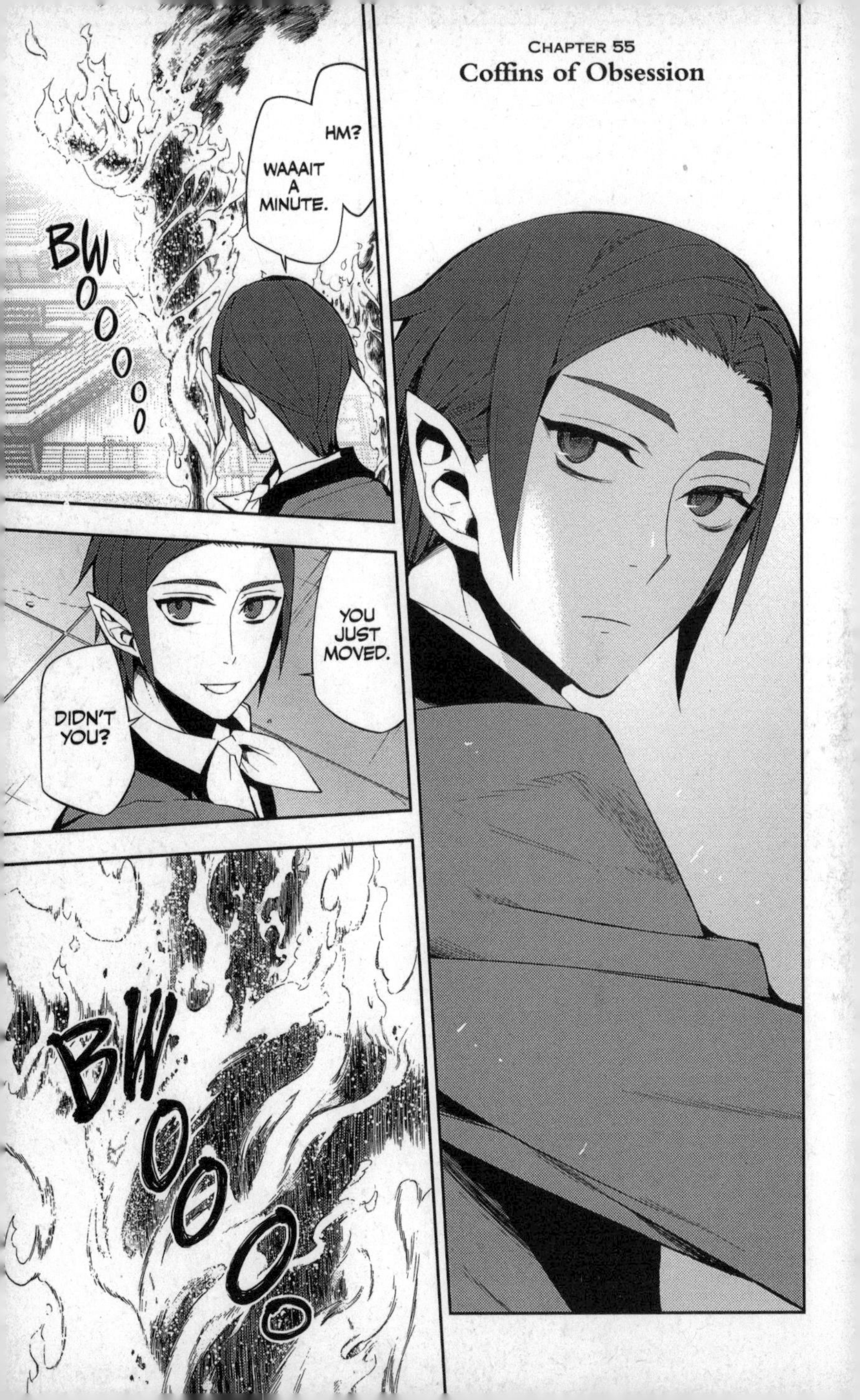
HM?
WAAAIT A MINUTE.
BWOOOOO
YOU JUST MOVED.
DIDN'T YOU?
BWOOOOO

CHAPTER 55
Coffins of Obsession

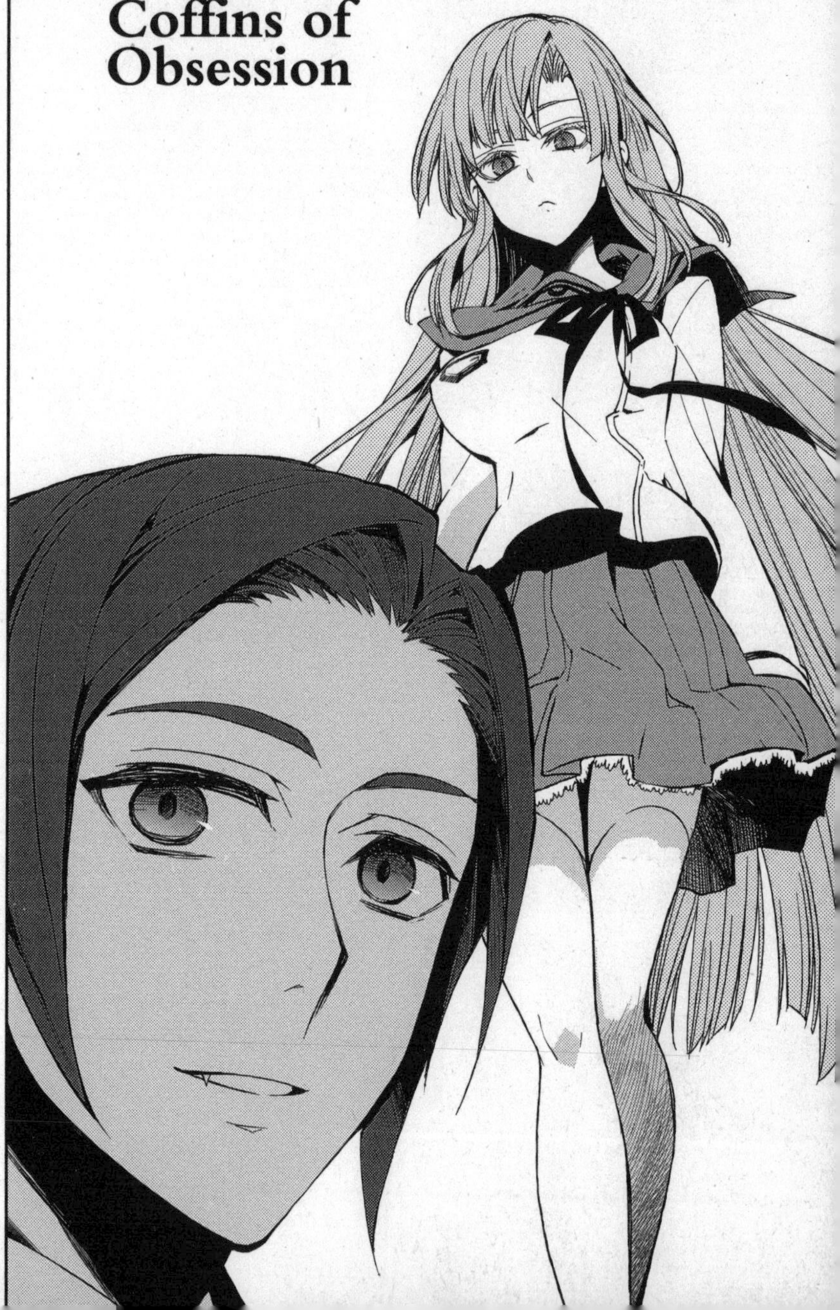

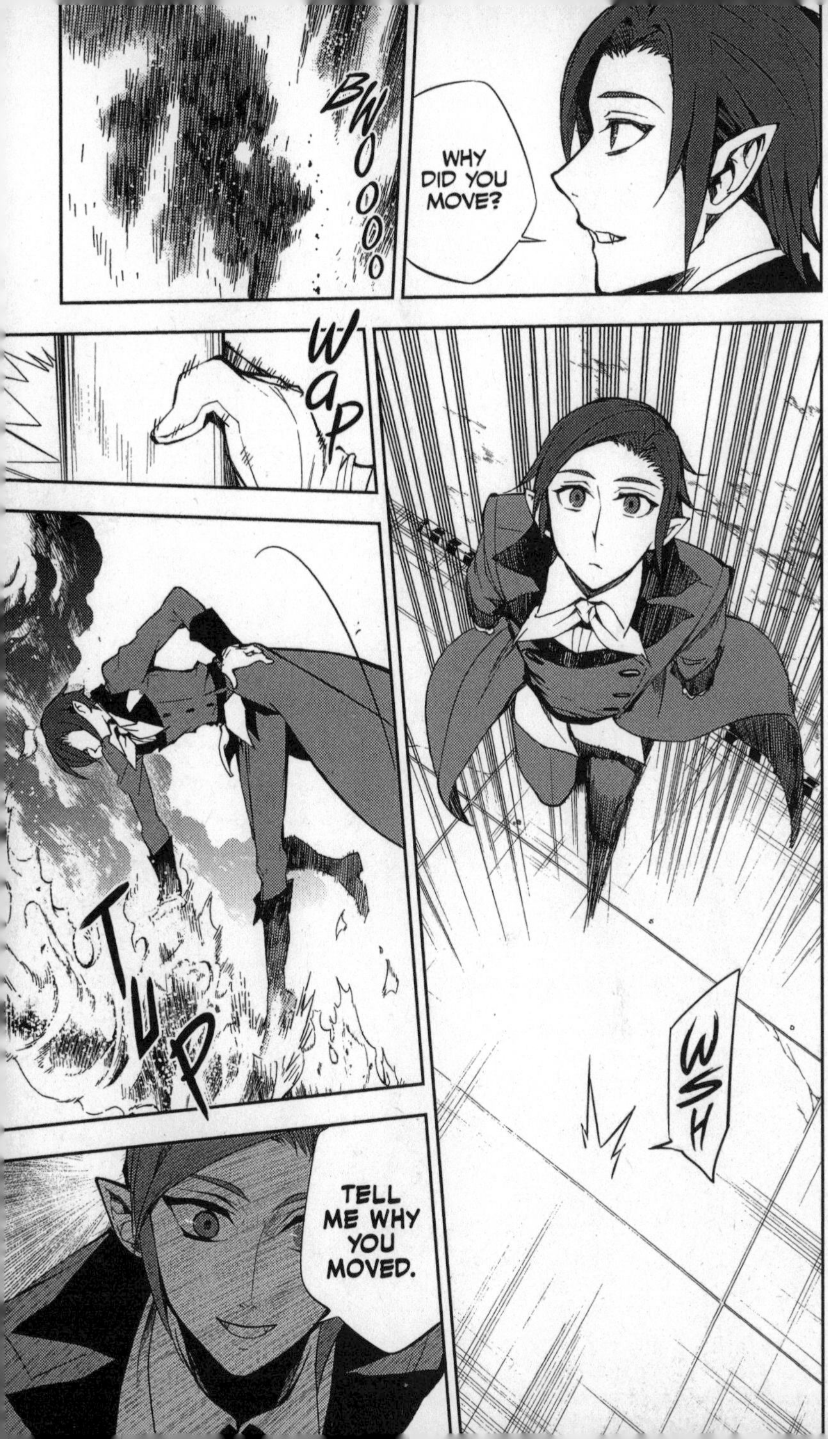
WHY DID YOU MOVE?
BWOOOOOO
WSH
WAP
TUP
TELL ME WHY YOU MOVED.

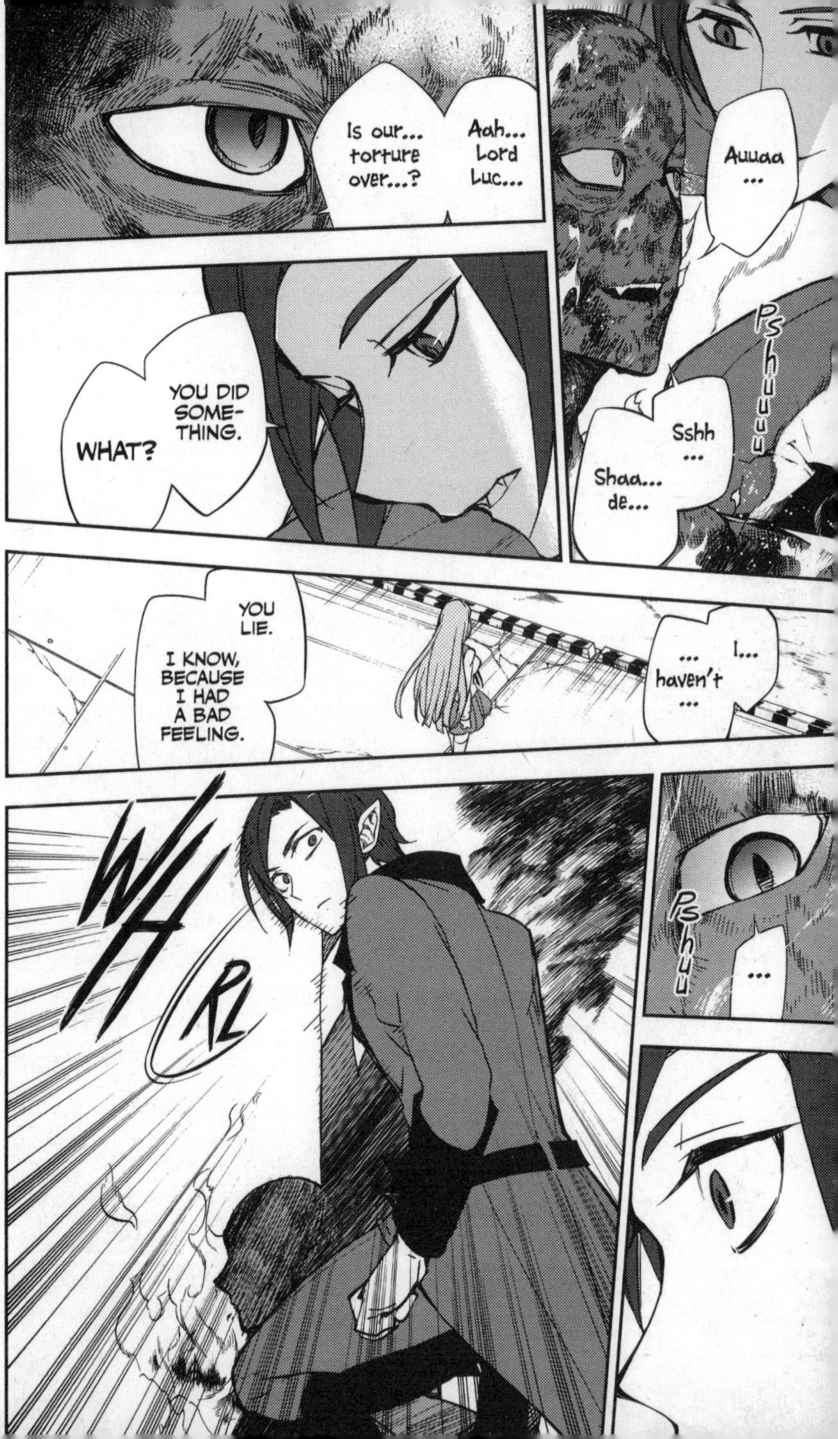

Auuaa ...
Aah... Lord Luc...
Is our... torture over...?
Pshuuuu
Sshh ... Shaa... de...
YOU DID SOMETHING.
WHAT?
I... ...haven't ...
YOU LIE.
I KNOW, BECAUSE I HAD A BAD FEELING.
Pshu
...
WHRL

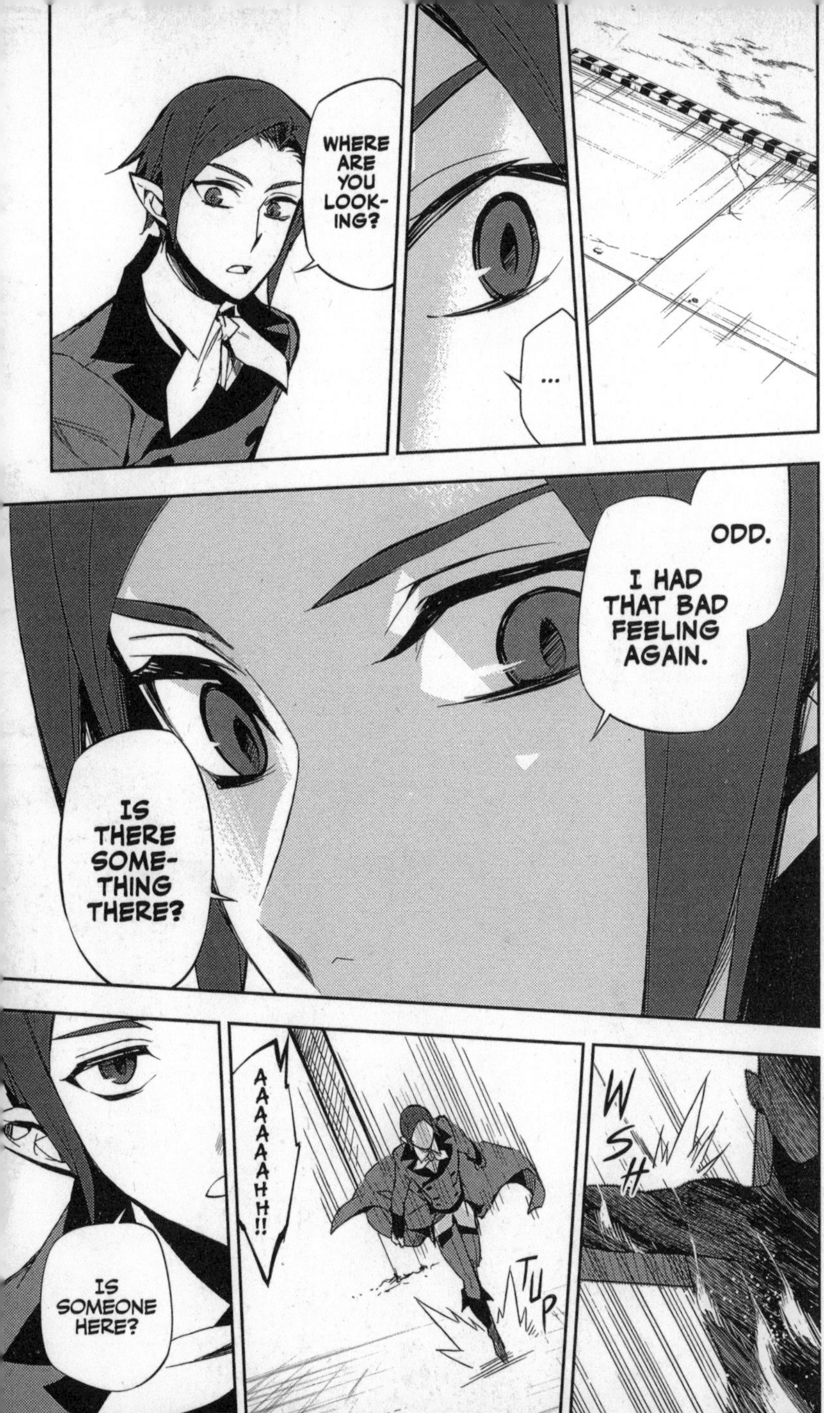
...
WHERE ARE YOU LOOKING?
ODD.
I HAD THAT BAD FEELING AGAIN.
IS THERE SOMETHING THERE?
WSH
AAAAAAAAHH!!
TUP
IS SOMEONE HERE?

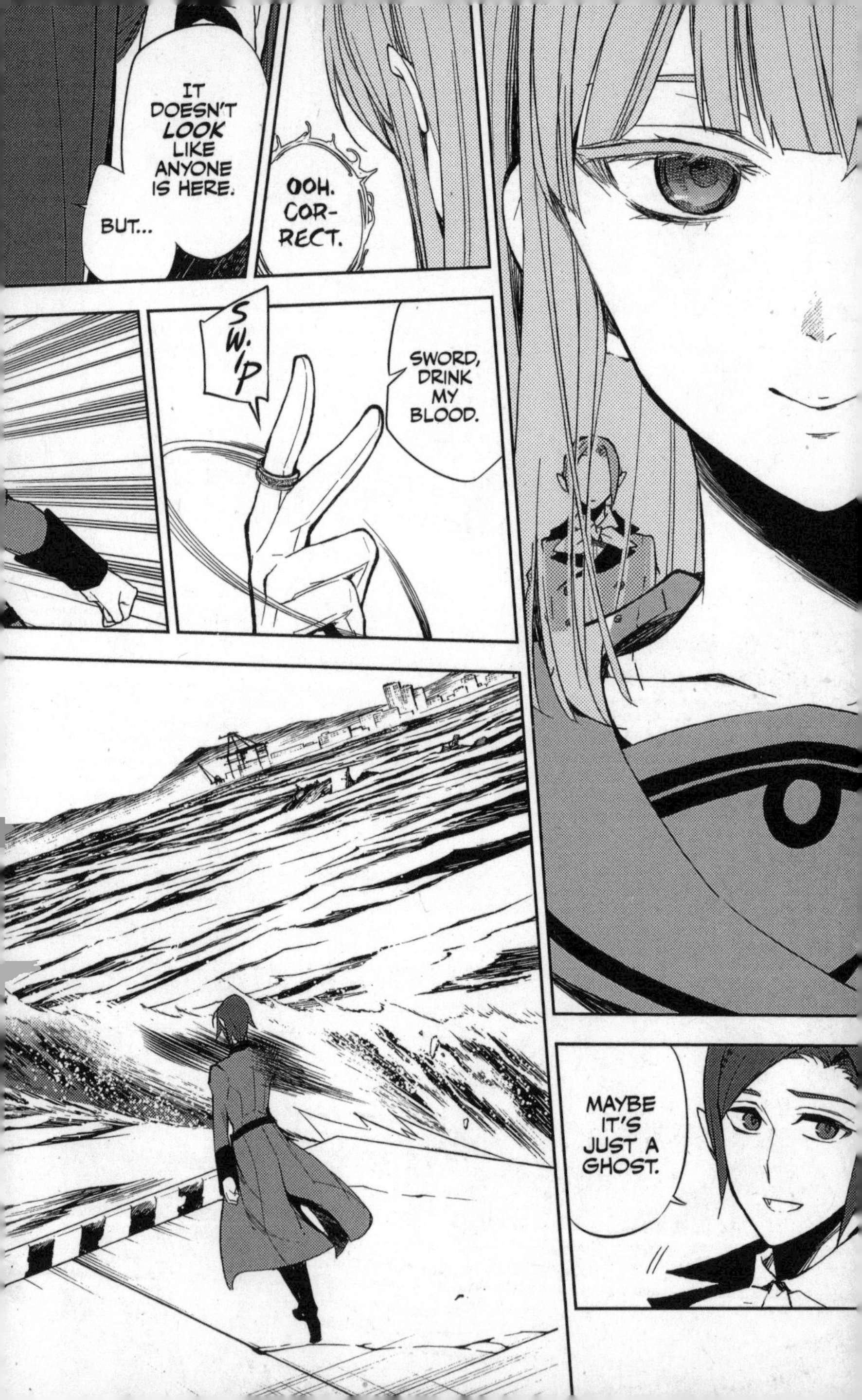
OOH. CORRECT.
IT DOESN'T LOOK LIKE ANYONE IS HERE.
BUT...
SWORD, DRINK MY BLOOD.
SWIP
MAYBE IT'S JUST A GHOST.

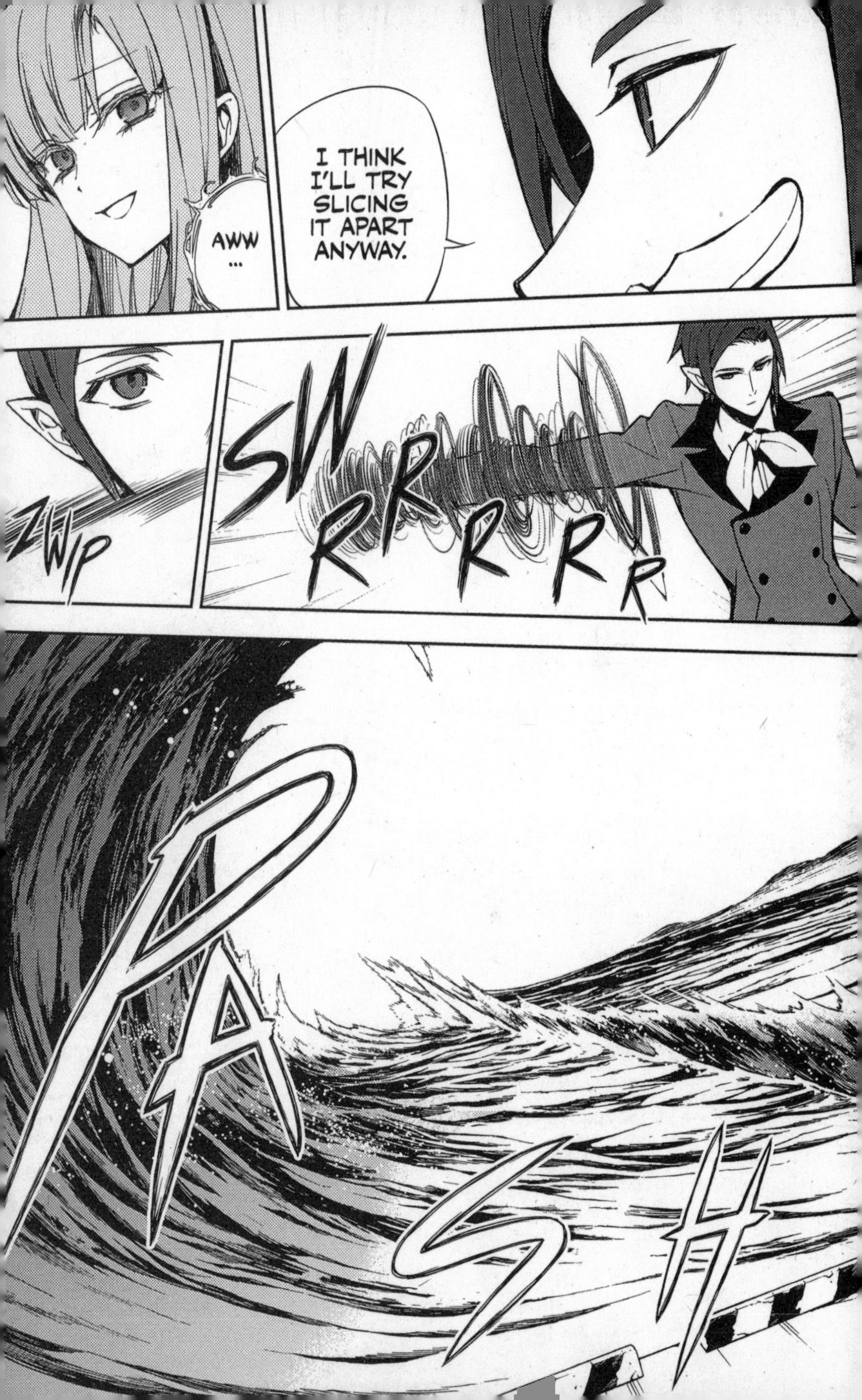
I THINK I'LL TRY SLICING IT APART ANYWAY.
AWW...
SWRRRRR
ZWIP

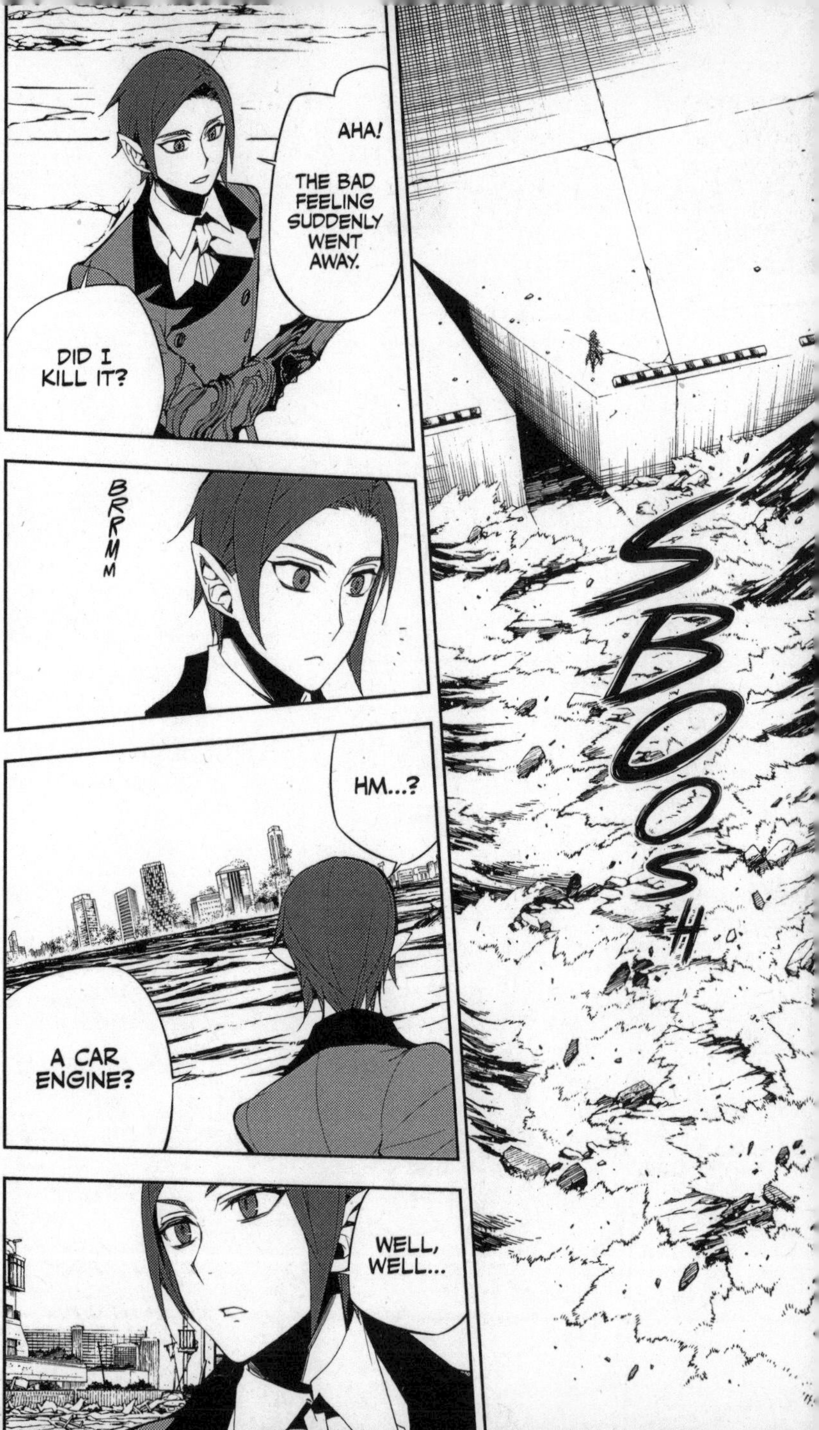
SBOOSH
AHA!
THE BAD FEELING SUDDENLY WENT AWAY.
DID I KILL IT?
BRRMM
HM...?
A CAR ENGINE?
WELL, WELL...

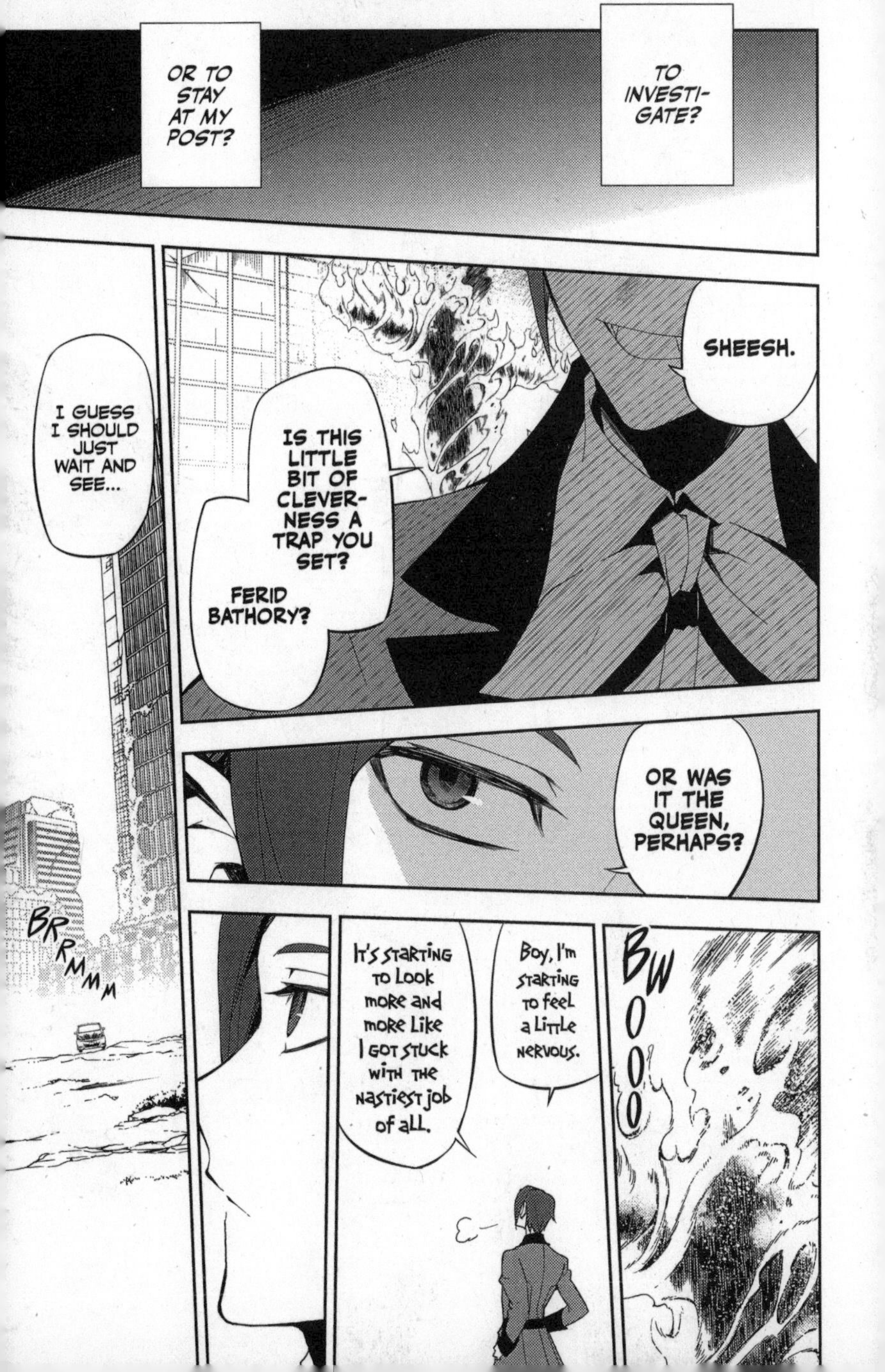
TO INVESTI-GATE?
OR TO STAY AT MY POST?
SHEESH.
IS THIS LITTLE BIT OF CLEVER-NESS A TRAP YOU SET?
FERID BATHORY?
OR WAS IT THE QUEEN, PERHAPS?
BWOOOO
Boy, I'm starting to feel a little nervous.
It's starting to look more and more like I got stuck with the nastiest job of all.
I GUESS I SHOULD JUST WAIT AND SEE...
BRRMMM

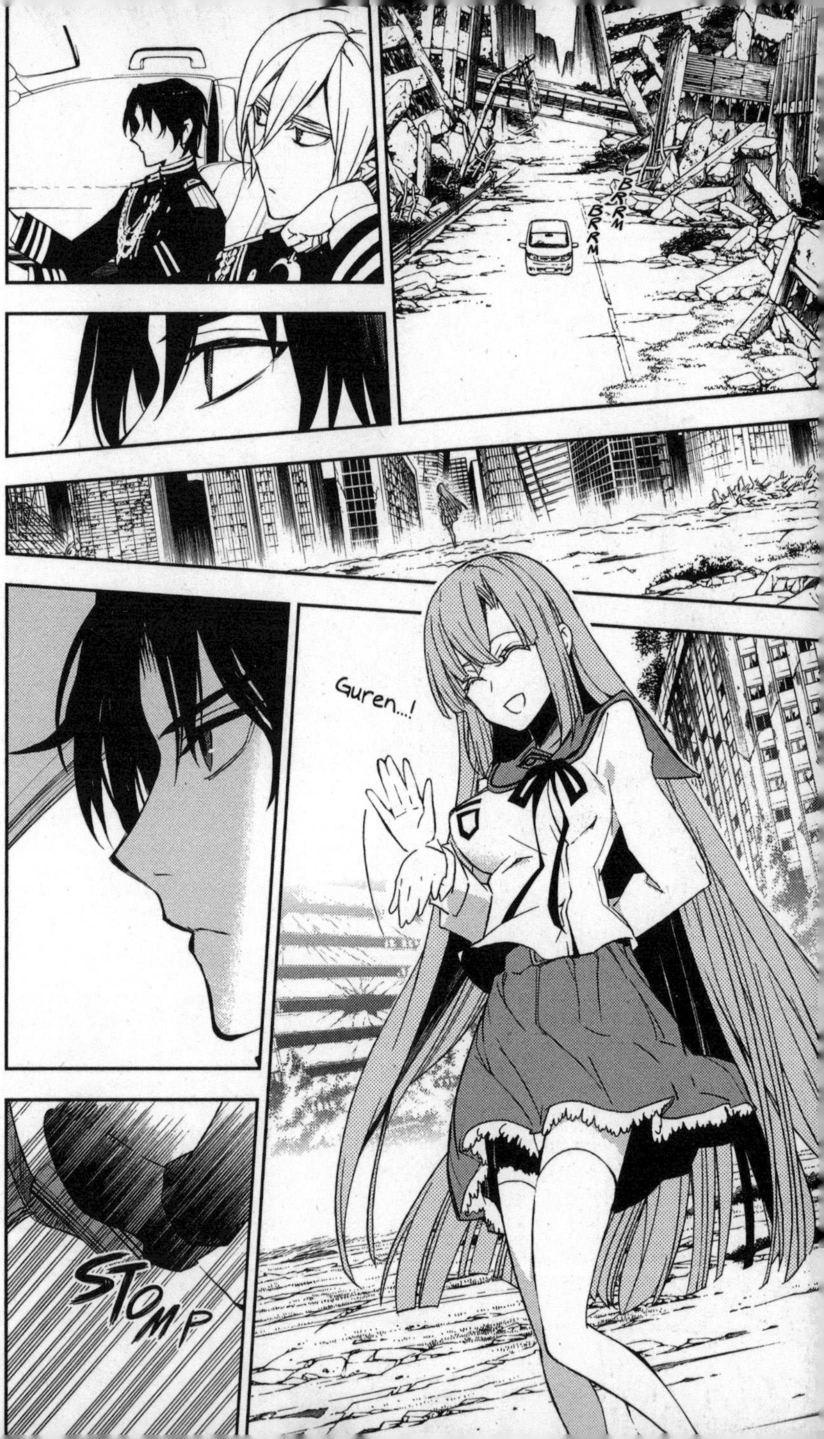
BRRM
BRRM
Guren...!
STOMP

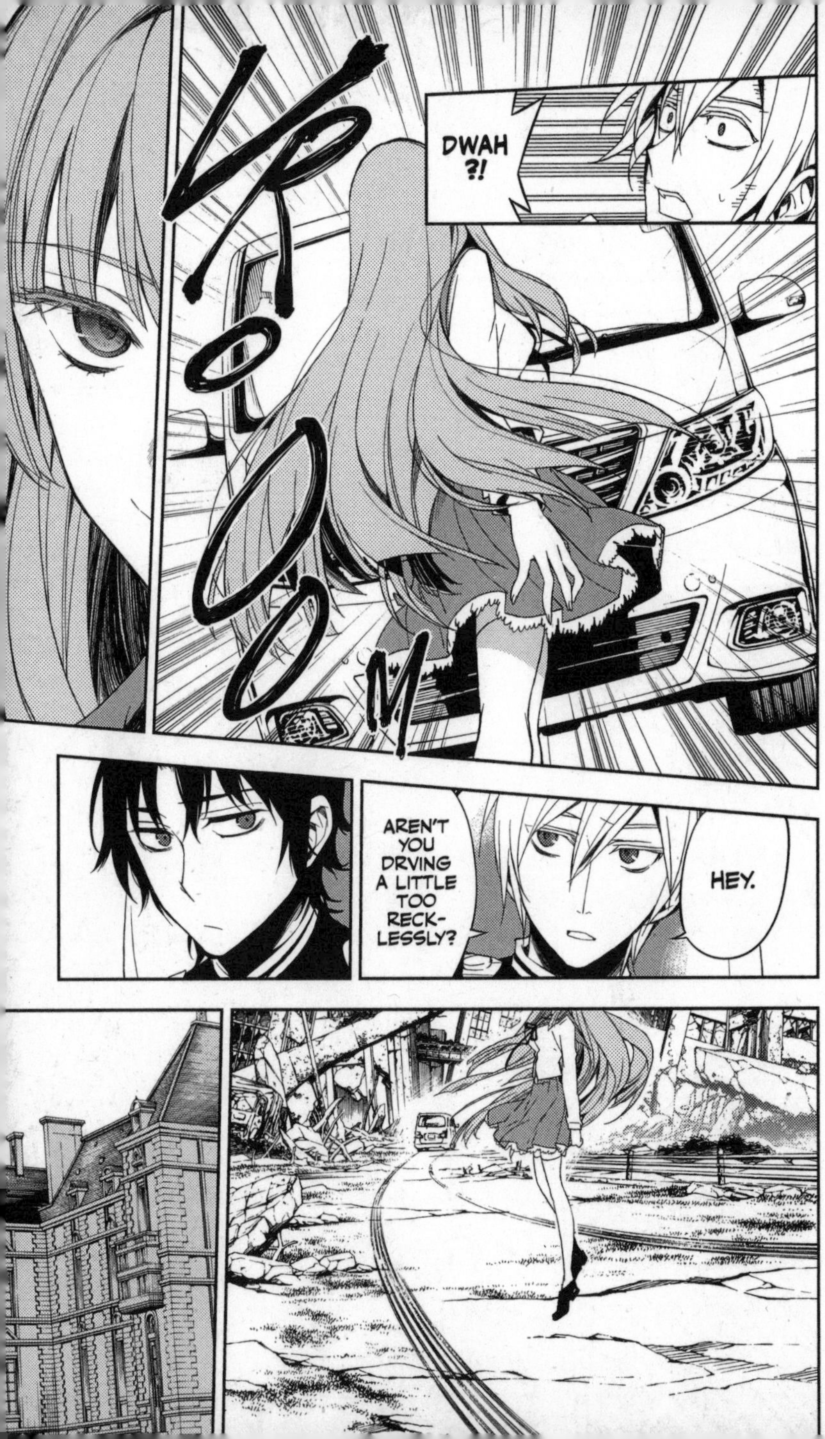
DWAH ?!
VROOOOM
HEY.
AREN'T YOU DRVING A LITTLE TOO RECK-LESSLY?

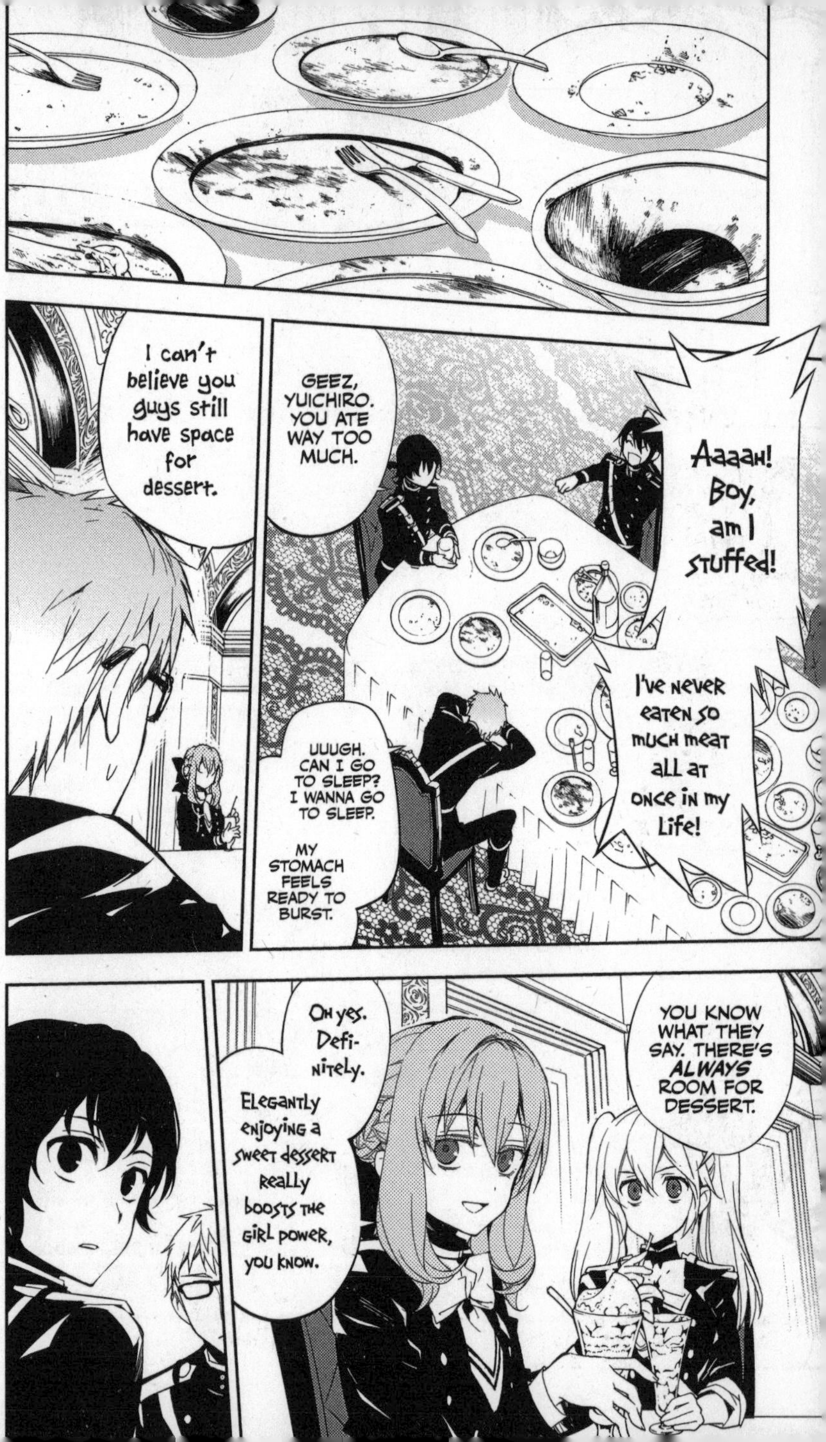
Aaaah! Boy, am I stuffed!
I've never eaten so much meat all at once in my life!
GEEZ, YUICHIRO. YOU ATE WAY TOO MUCH.
UUUGH. CAN I GO TO SLEEP? I WANNA GO TO SLEEP.
MY STOMACH FEELS READY TO BURST.
I can't believe you guys still have space for dessert.
YOU KNOW WHAT THEY SAY. THERE'S ALWAYS ROOM FOR DESSERT.
Oh yes. Defi-nitely.
Elegantly enjoying a sweet dessert really boosts the girl power, you know.

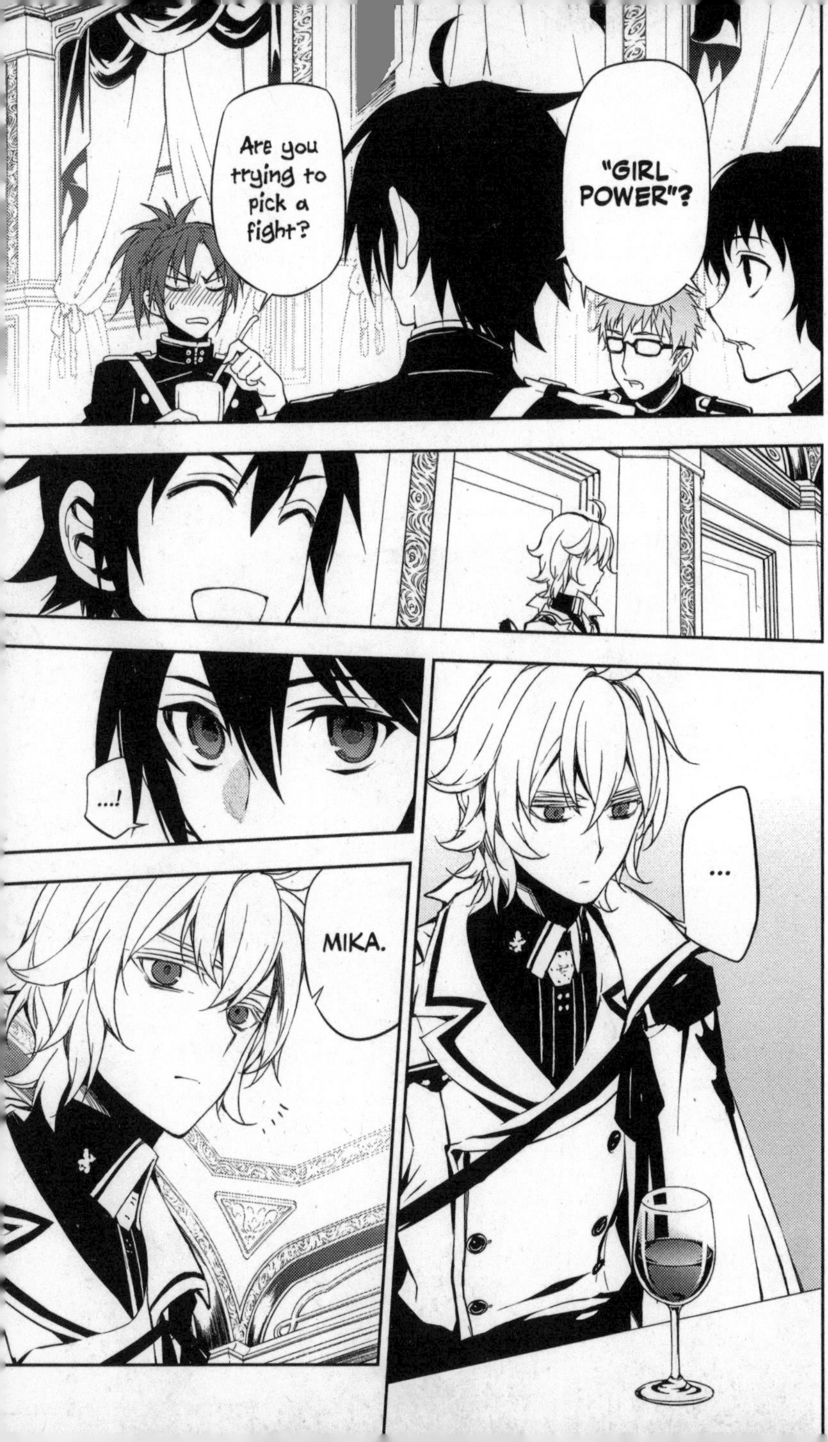
"GIRL POWER"?
Are you trying to pick a fight?
...
...!
MIKA.

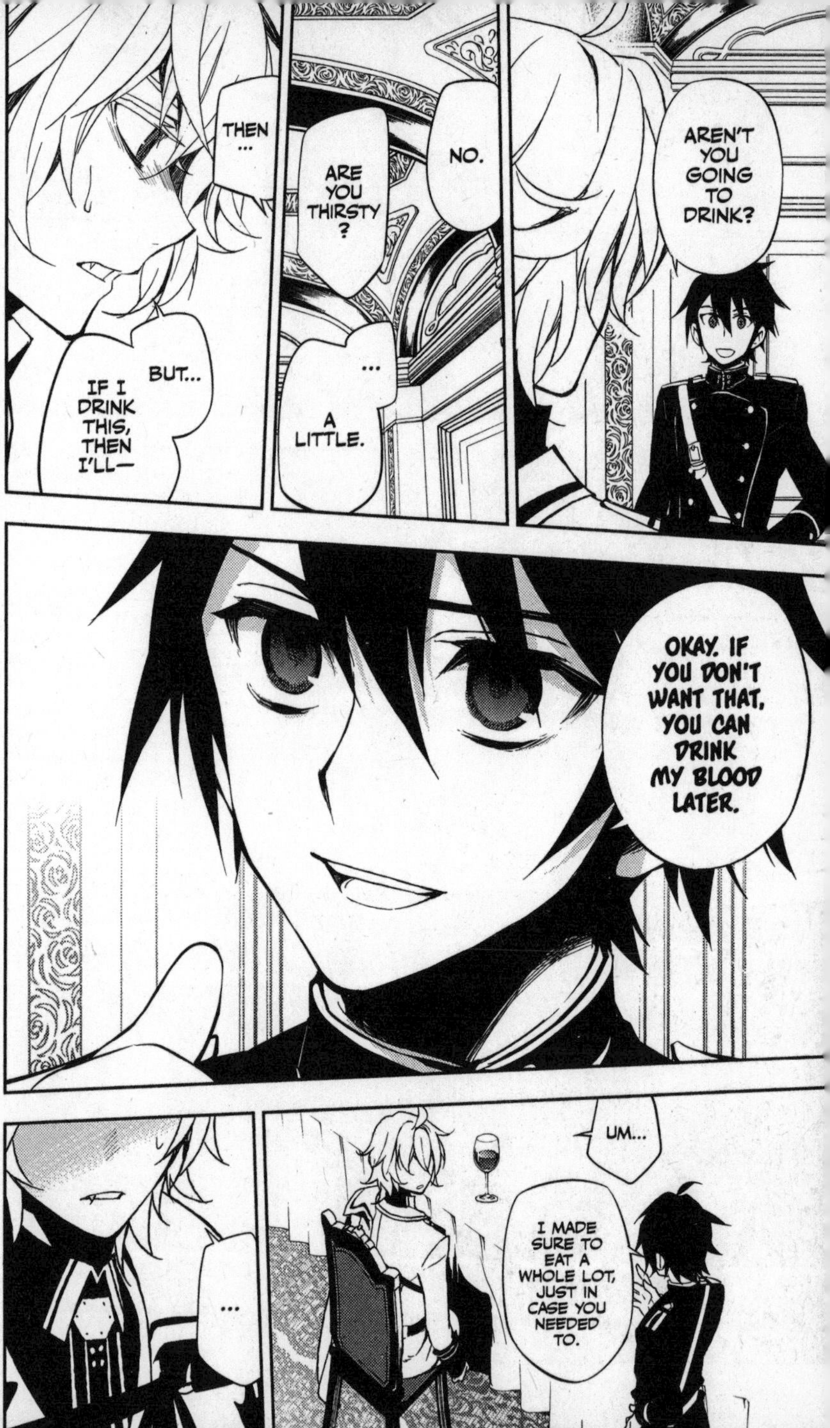
AREN'T YOU GOING TO DRINK?
NO.
ARE YOU THIRSTY?
...
A LITTLE.
THEN...
BUT...
IF I DRINK THIS, THEN I'LL—
OKAY. IF YOU DON'T WANT THAT, YOU CAN DRINK MY BLOOD LATER.
UM...
I MADE SURE TO EAT A WHOLE LOT, JUST IN CASE YOU NEEDED TO.
...

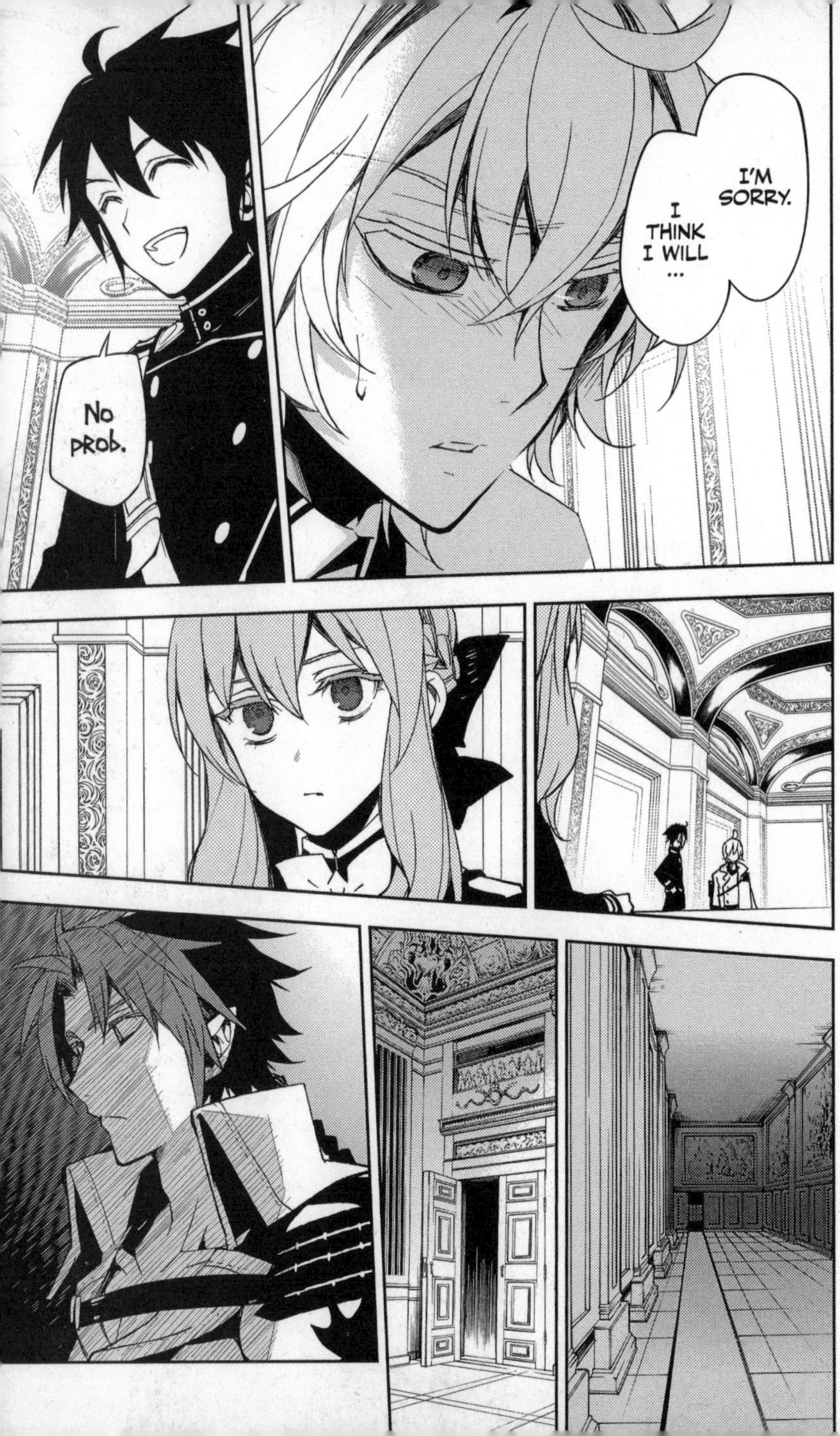
I'M SORRY.
I THINK I WILL ...
No prob.

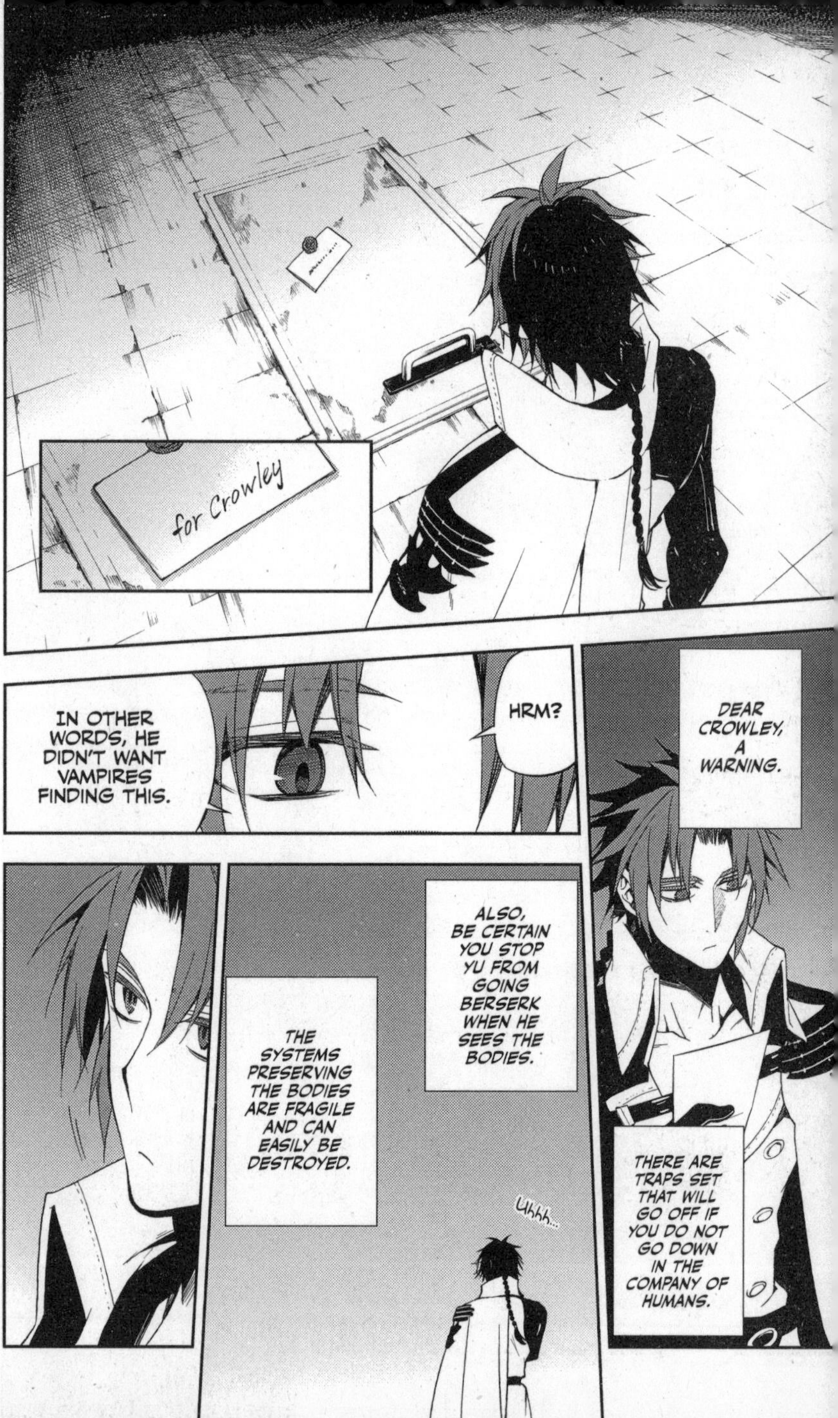
for Crowley
DEAR CROWLEY, A WARNING.
THERE ARE TRAPS SET THAT WILL GO OFF IF YOU DO NOT GO DOWN IN THE COMPANY OF HUMANS.
HRM?
IN OTHER WORDS, HE DIDN'T WANT VAMPIRES FINDING THIS.
ALSO, BE CERTAIN YOU STOP YU FROM GOING BERSERK WHEN HE SEES THE BODIES.
THE SYSTEMS PRESERVING THE BODIES ARE FRAGILE AND CAN EASILY BE DESTROYED.
Uhhh...

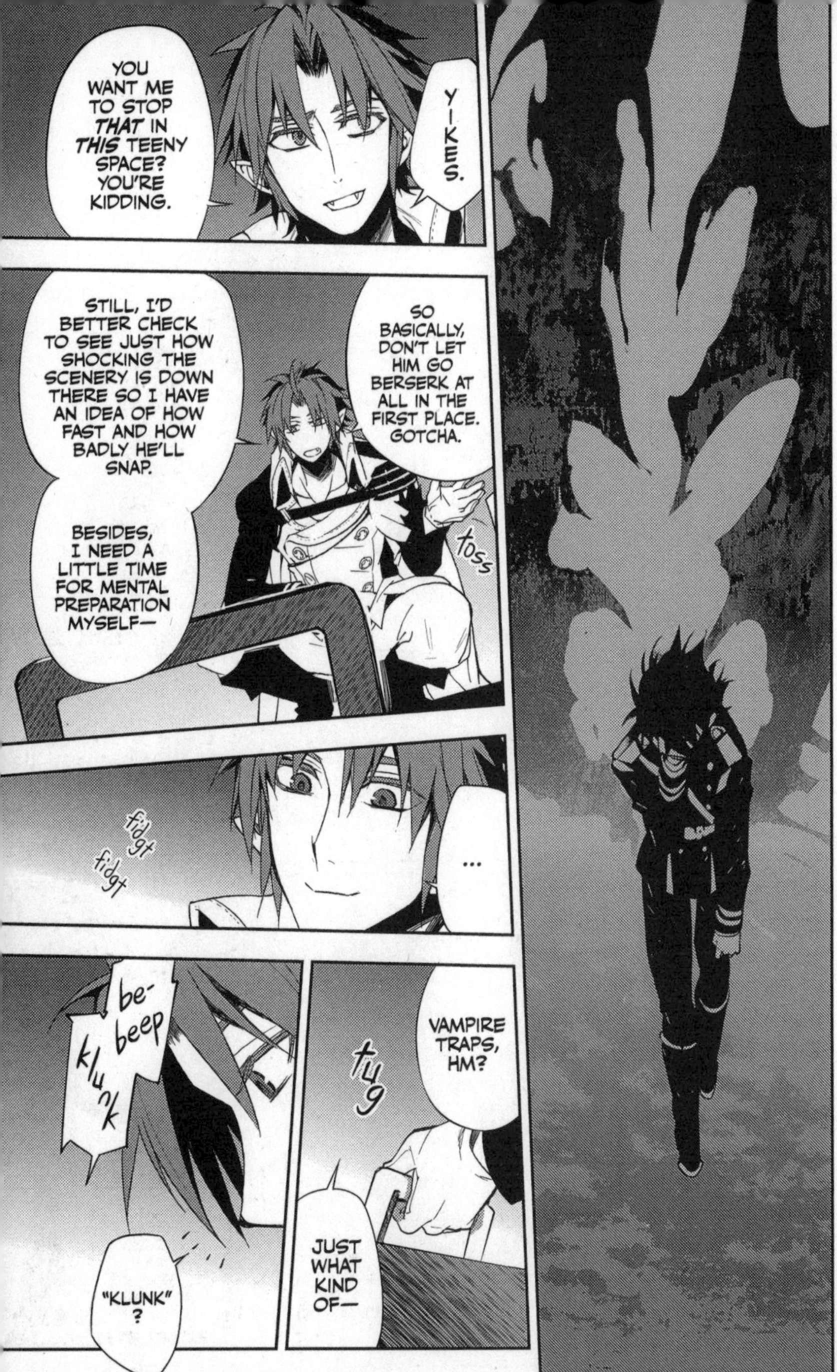
YIKES.
YOU WANT ME TO STOP *THAT* IN *THIS* TEENY SPACE? YOU'RE KIDDING.
SO BASICALLY, DON'T LET HIM GO BERSERK AT ALL IN THE FIRST PLACE. GOTCHA.
STILL, I'D BETTER CHECK TO SEE JUST HOW SHOCKING THE SCENERY IS DOWN THERE SO I HAVE AN IDEA OF HOW FAST AND HOW BADLY HE'LL SNAP.
BESIDES, I NEED A LITTLE TIME FOR MENTAL PREPARATION MYSELF—
toss
...
fidgt fidgt
VAMPIRE TRAPS, HM?
tug
JUST WHAT KIND OF—
be-beep
klunk
"KLUNK"?

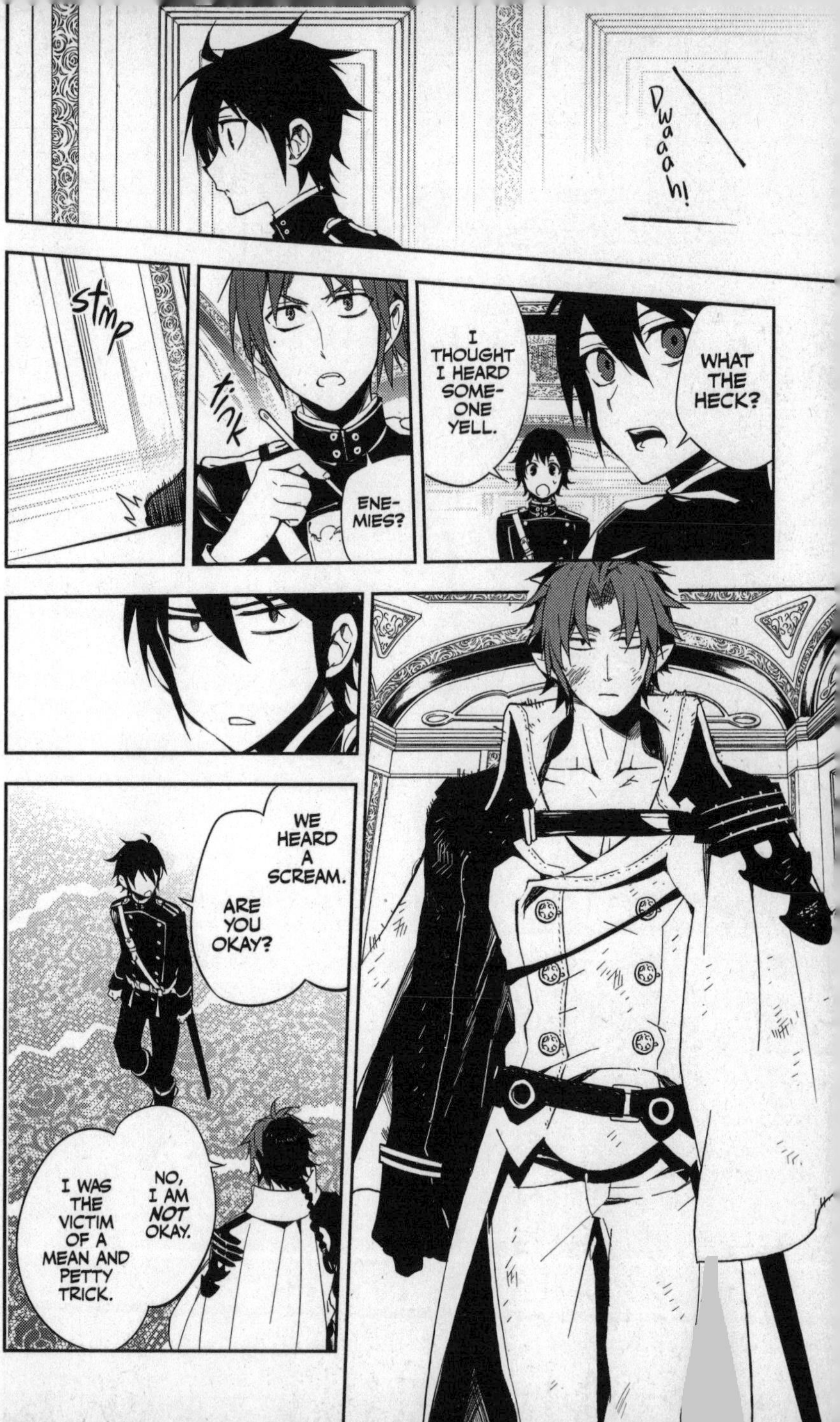
Dwaaaah!
WHAT THE HECK?
I THOUGHT I HEARD SOMEONE YELL.
tink
ENEMIES?
stmp
WE HEARD A SCREAM.
ARE YOU OKAY?
NO, I AM *NOT* OKAY.
I WAS THE VICTIM OF A MEAN AND PETTY TRICK.

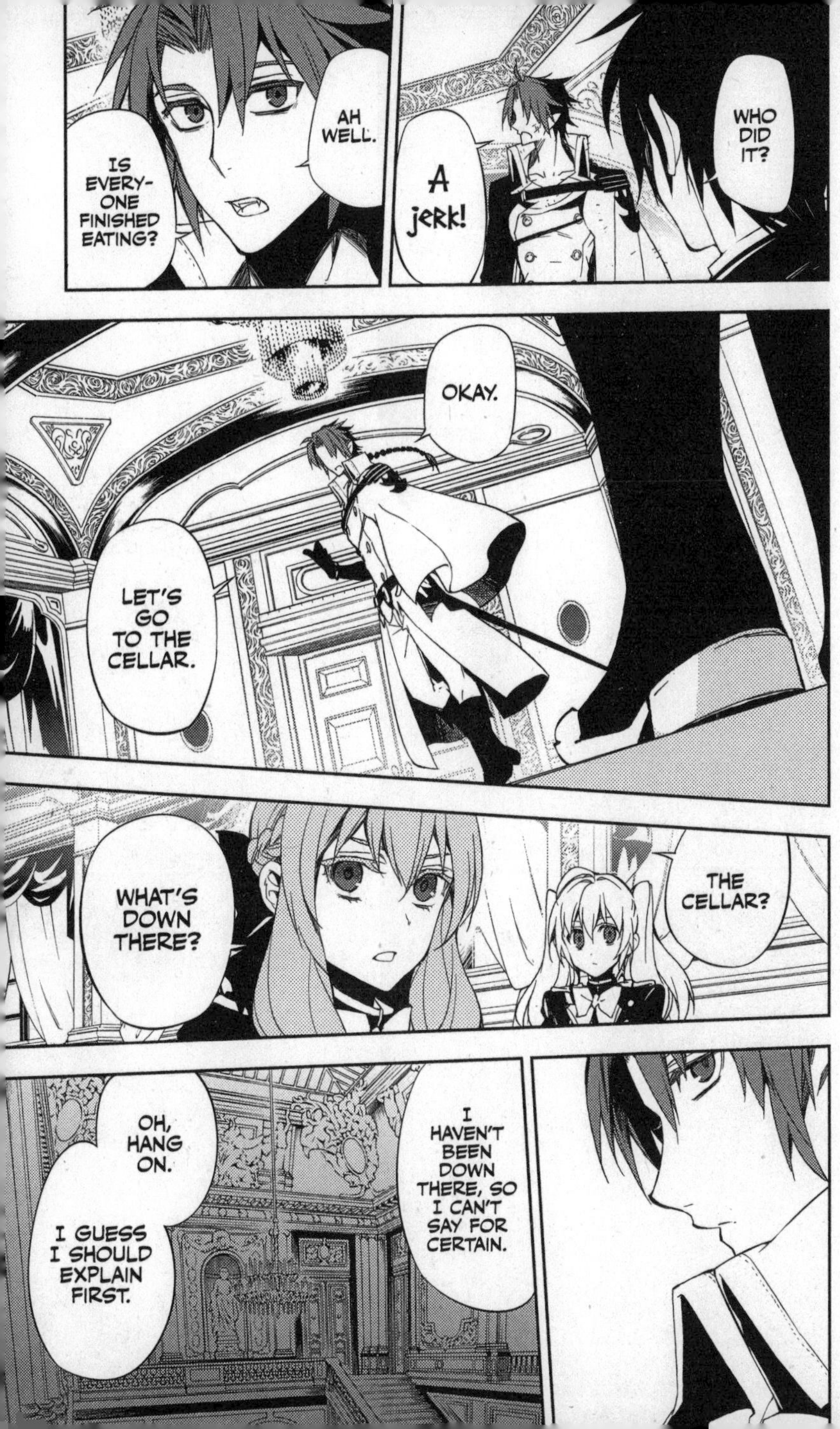
WHO DID IT?
A jerk!
AH WELL.
IS EVERY-ONE FINISHED EATING?
OKAY.
LET'S GO TO THE CELLAR.
THE CELLAR?
WHAT'S DOWN THERE?
I HAVEN'T BEEN DOWN THERE, SO I CAN'T SAY FOR CERTAIN.
OH, HANG ON.
I GUESS I SHOULD EXPLAIN FIRST.

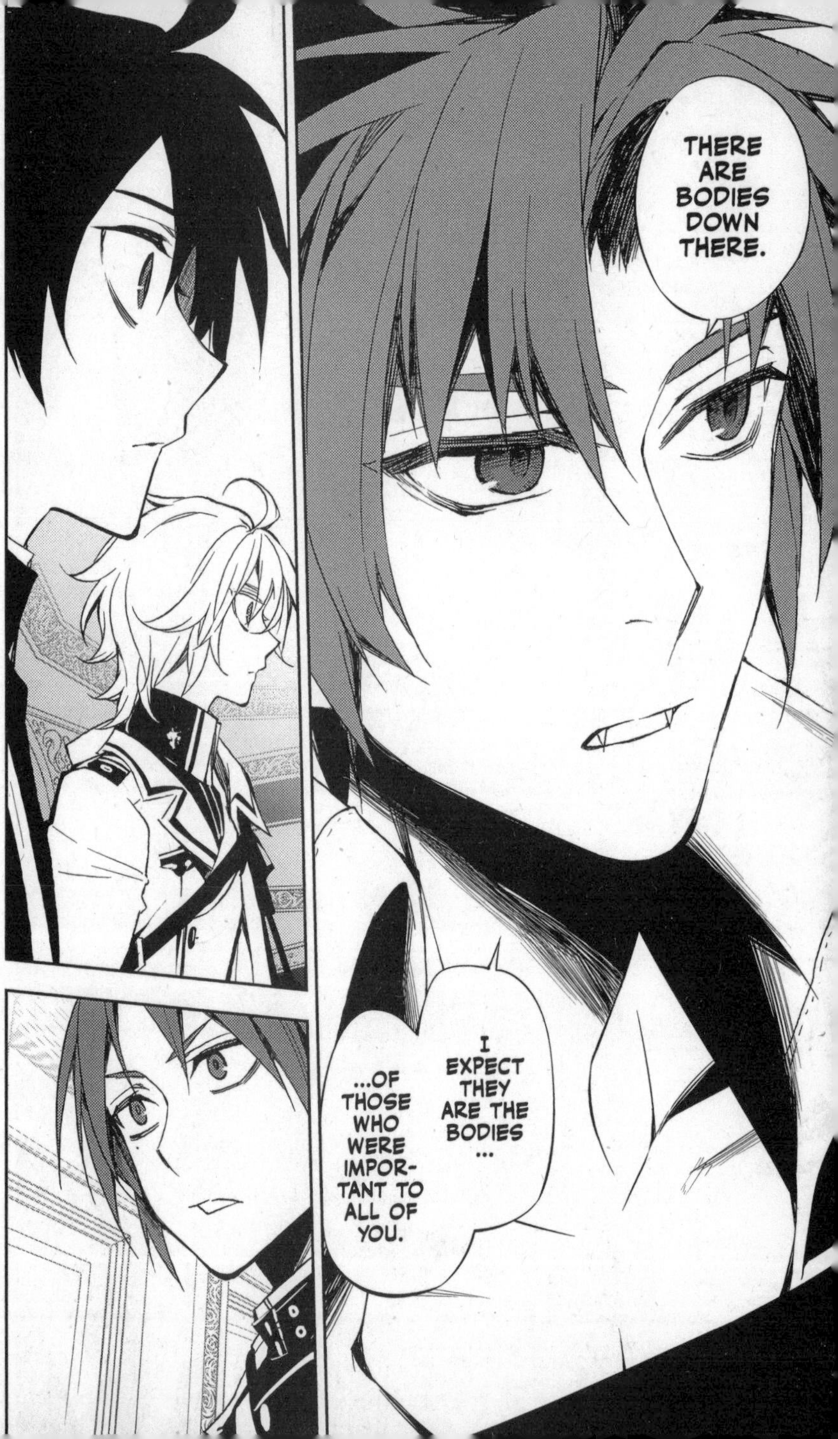
THERE ARE BODIES DOWN THERE.
I EXPECT THEY ARE THE BODIES...
...OF THOSE WHO WERE IMPORTANT TO ALL OF YOU.

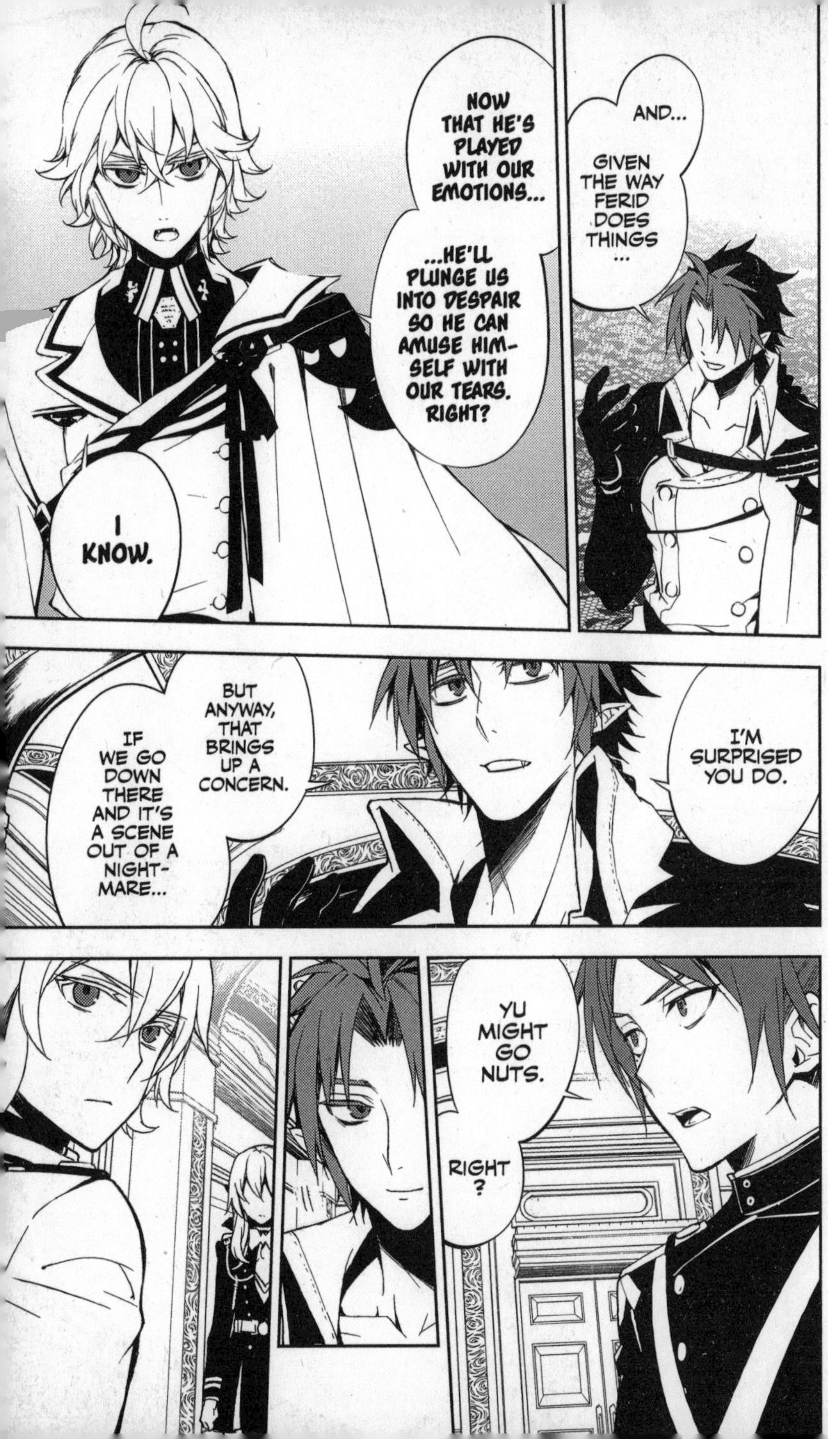
AND...
GIVEN THE WAY FERID DOES THINGS...
NOW THAT HE'S PLAYED WITH OUR EMOTIONS...
...HE'LL PLUNGE US INTO DESPAIR SO HE CAN AMUSE HIM-SELF WITH OUR TEARS. RIGHT?
I KNOW.
I'M SURPRISED YOU DO.
BUT ANYWAY, THAT BRINGS UP A CONCERN.
IF WE GO DOWN THERE AND IT'S A SCENE OUT OF A NIGHT-MARE...
YU MIGHT GO NUTS.
RIGHT?

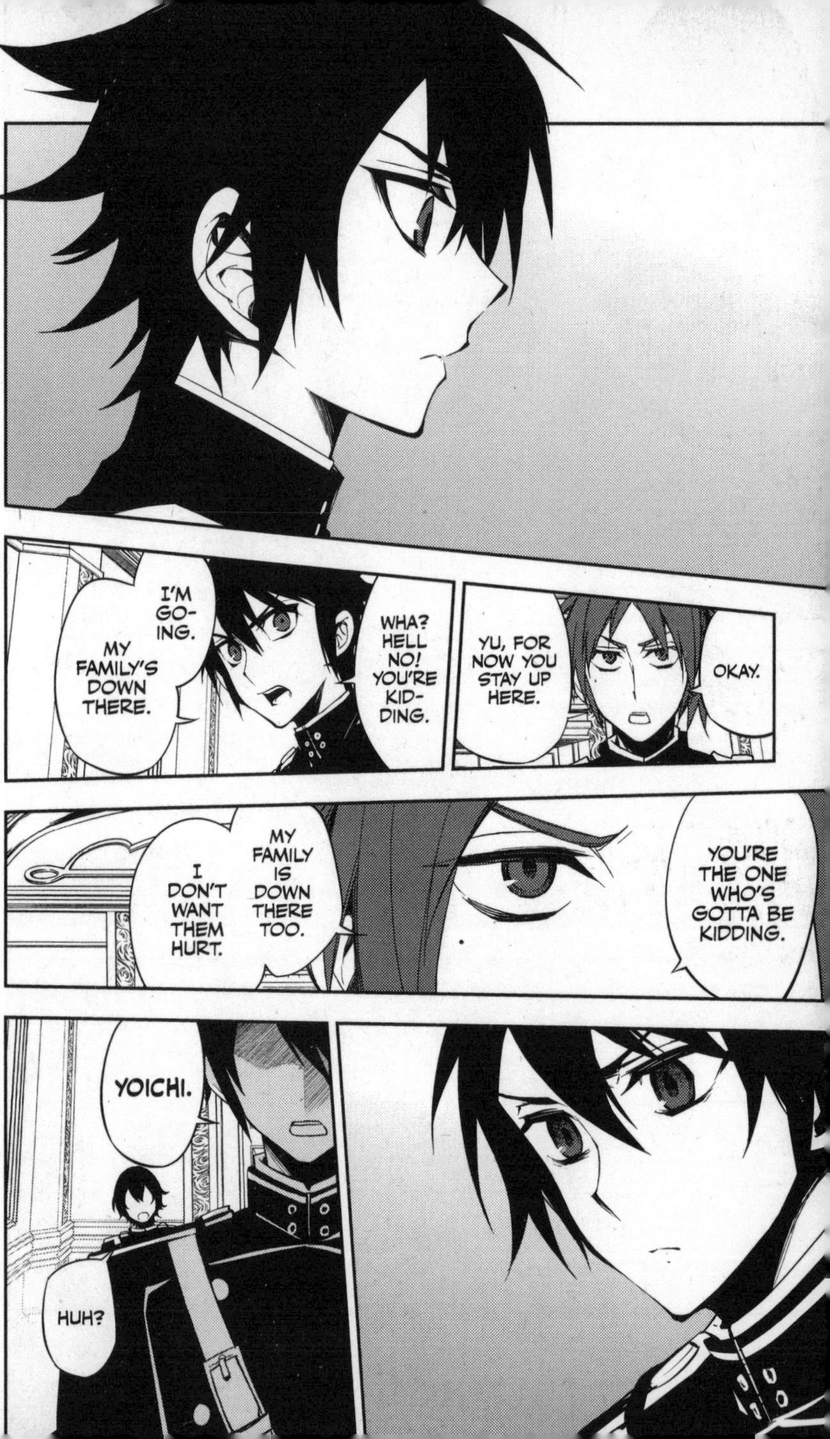
OKAY.
YU, FOR NOW YOU STAY UP HERE.
WHA? HELL NO! YOU'RE KID-DING.
I'M GO-ING.
MY FAMILY'S DOWN THERE.
YOU'RE THE ONE WHO'S GOTTA BE KIDDING.
MY FAMILY IS DOWN THERE TOO.
I DON'T WANT THEM HURT.
YOICHI.
HUH?

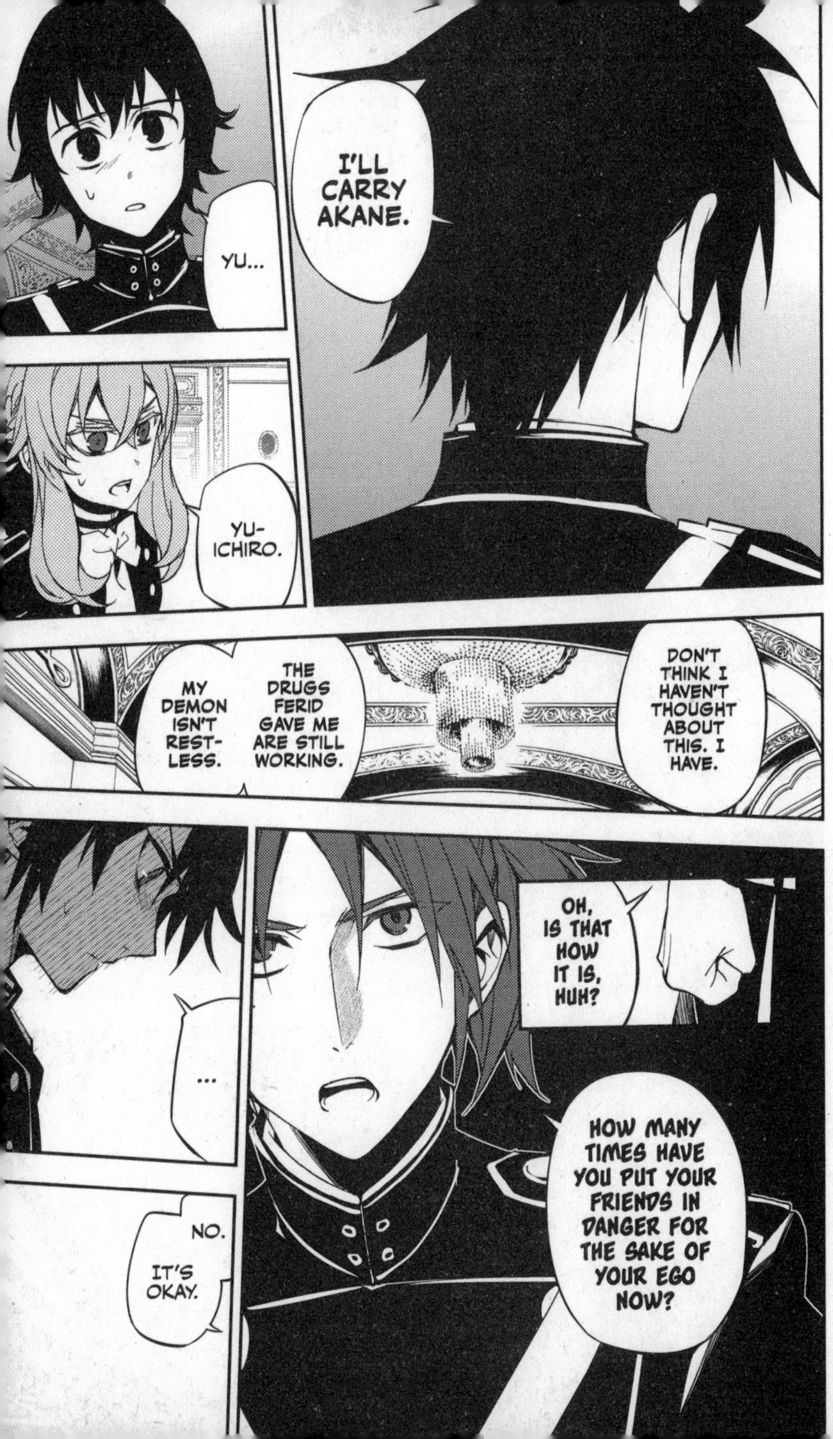
I'LL CARRY AKANE.
YU...
YU-ICHIRO.
DON'T THINK I HAVEN'T THOUGHT ABOUT THIS. I HAVE.
THE DRUGS FERID GAVE ME ARE STILL WORKING.
MY DEMON ISN'T REST-LESS.
OH, IS THAT HOW IT IS, HUH?
HOW MANY TIMES HAVE YOU PUT YOUR FRIENDS IN DANGER FOR THE SAKE OF YOUR EGO NOW?
...
NO.
IT'S OKAY.

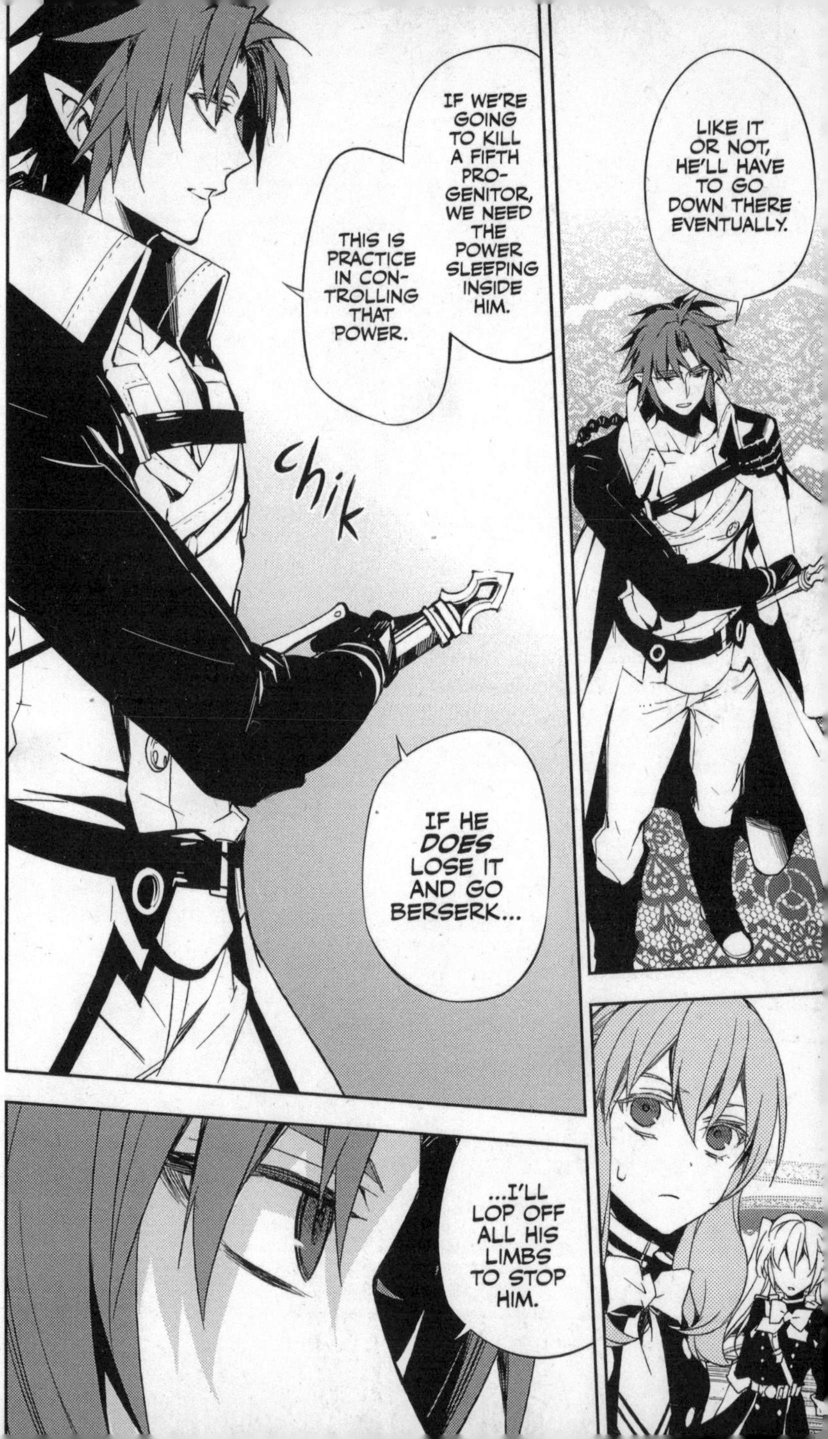
LIKE IT OR NOT, HE'LL HAVE TO GO DOWN THERE EVENTUALLY.
IF WE'RE GOING TO KILL A FIFTH PRO-GENITOR, WE NEED THE POWER SLEEPING INSIDE HIM.
THIS IS PRACTICE IN CON-TROLLING THAT POWER.
chik
IF HE *DOES* LOSE IT AND GO BERSERK...
...I'LL LOP OFF ALL HIS LIMBS TO STOP HIM.

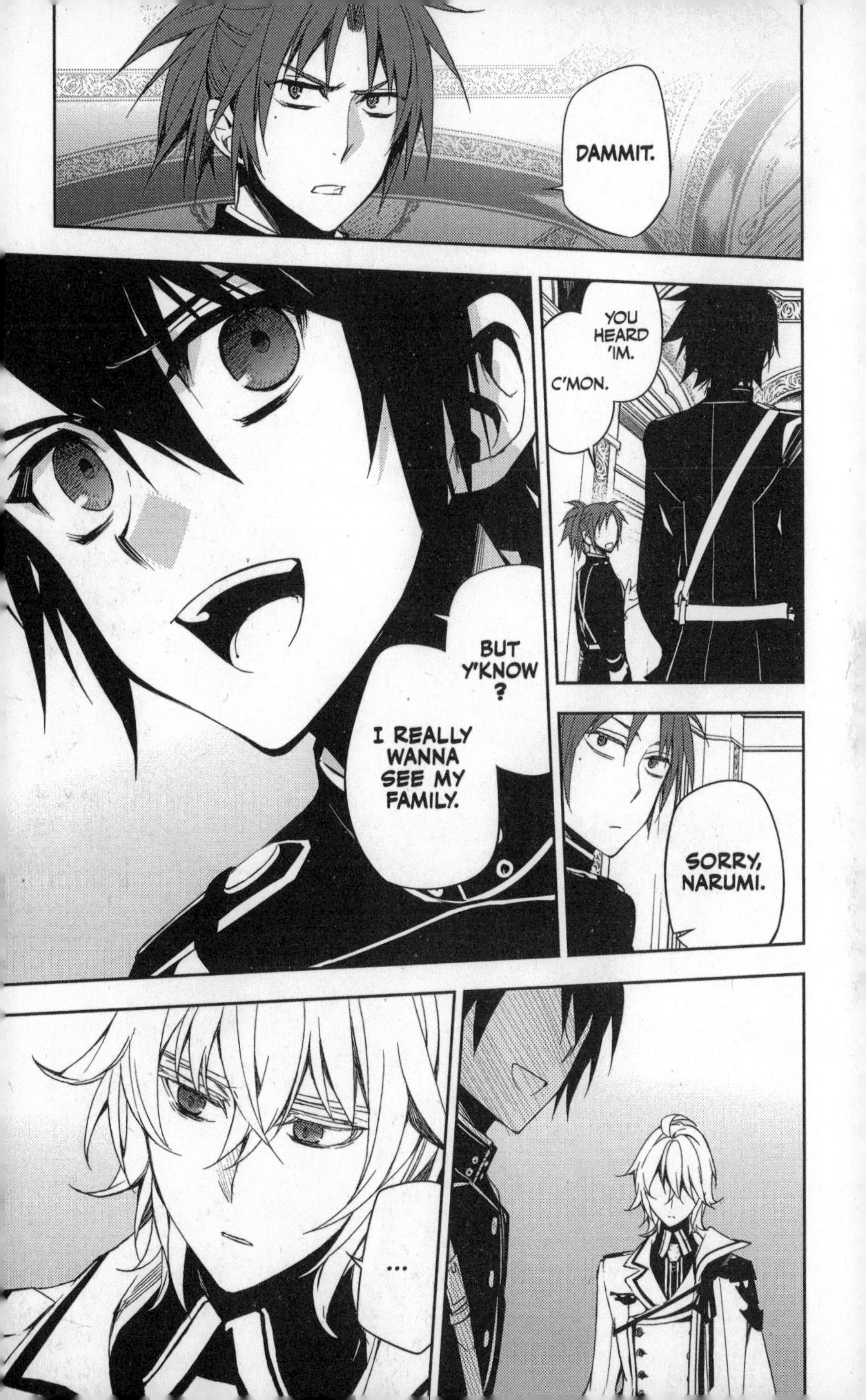
DAMMIT.
YOU HEARD 'IM.
C'MON.
SORRY, NARUMI.
BUT Y'KNOW?
I REALLY WANNA SEE MY FAMILY.
...

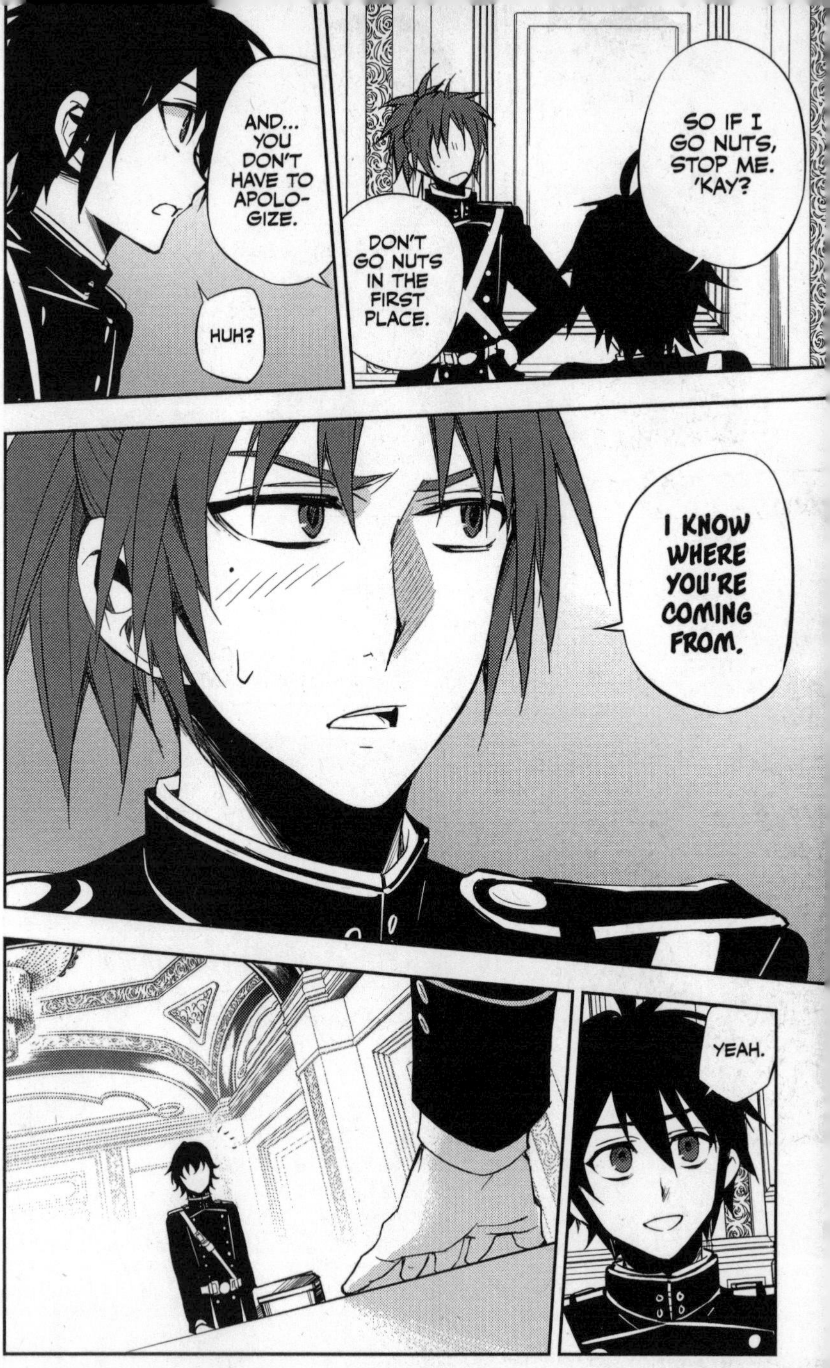
SO IF I GO NUTS, STOP ME. 'KAY?
DON'T GO NUTS IN THE FIRST PLACE.
AND... YOU DON'T HAVE TO APOLOGIZE.
HUH?
I KNOW WHERE YOU'RE COMING FROM.
YEAH.

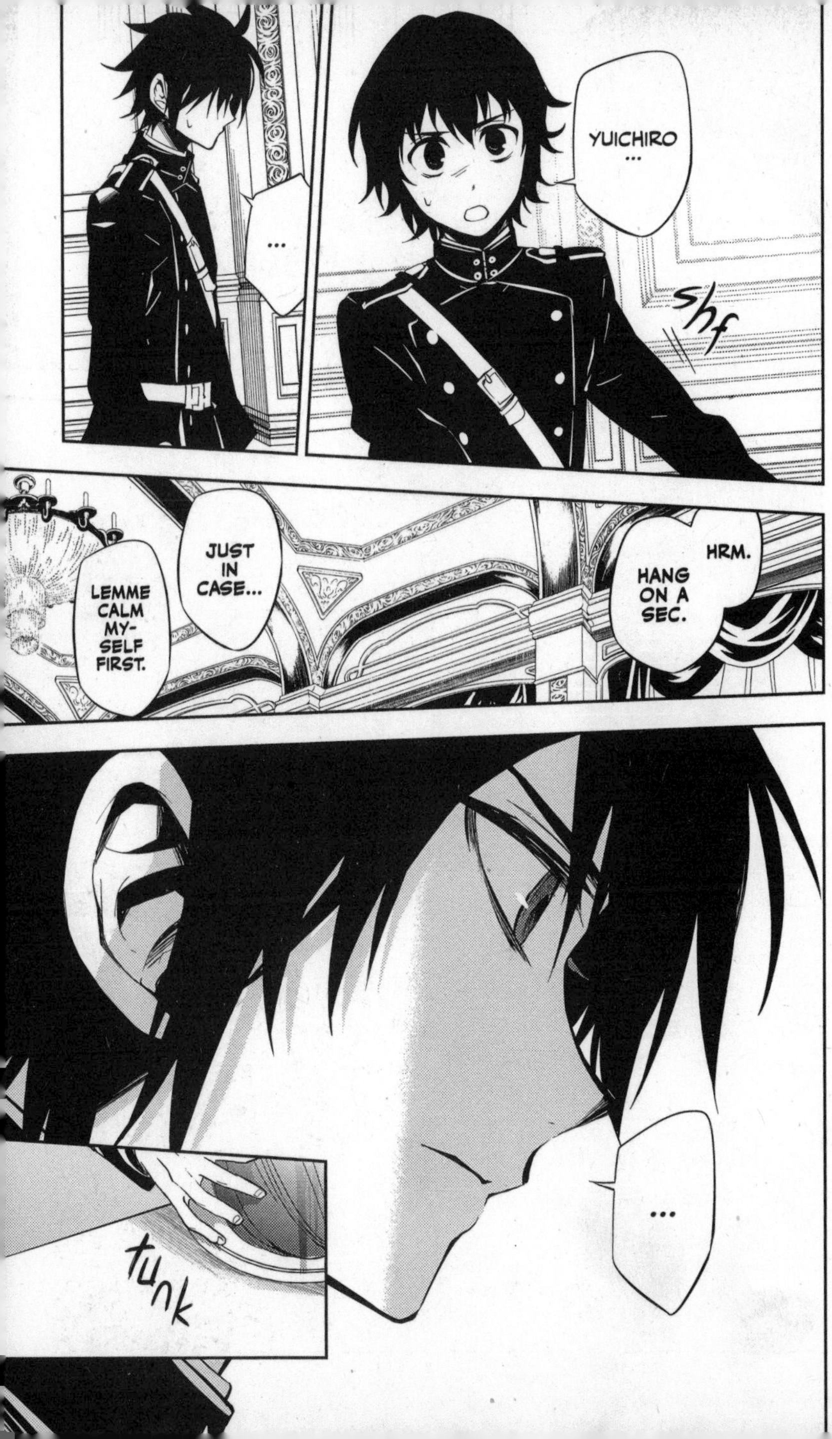
YUICHIRO ...
shf
...
HRM. HANG ON A SEC.
JUST IN CASE...
LEMME CALM MY-SELF FIRST.
...
tunk

tok
swff

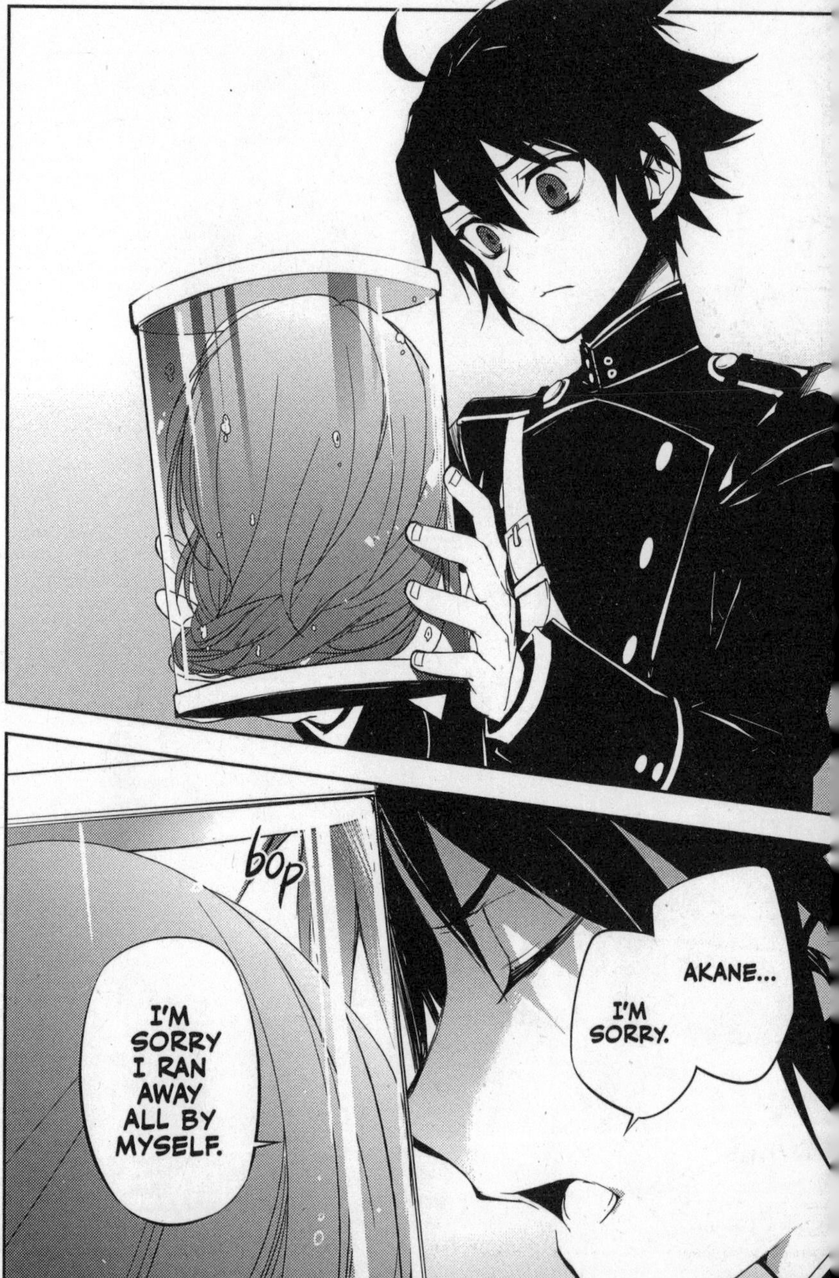
bop
AKANE...
I'M SORRY.
I'M SORRY I RAN AWAY ALL BY MYSELF.

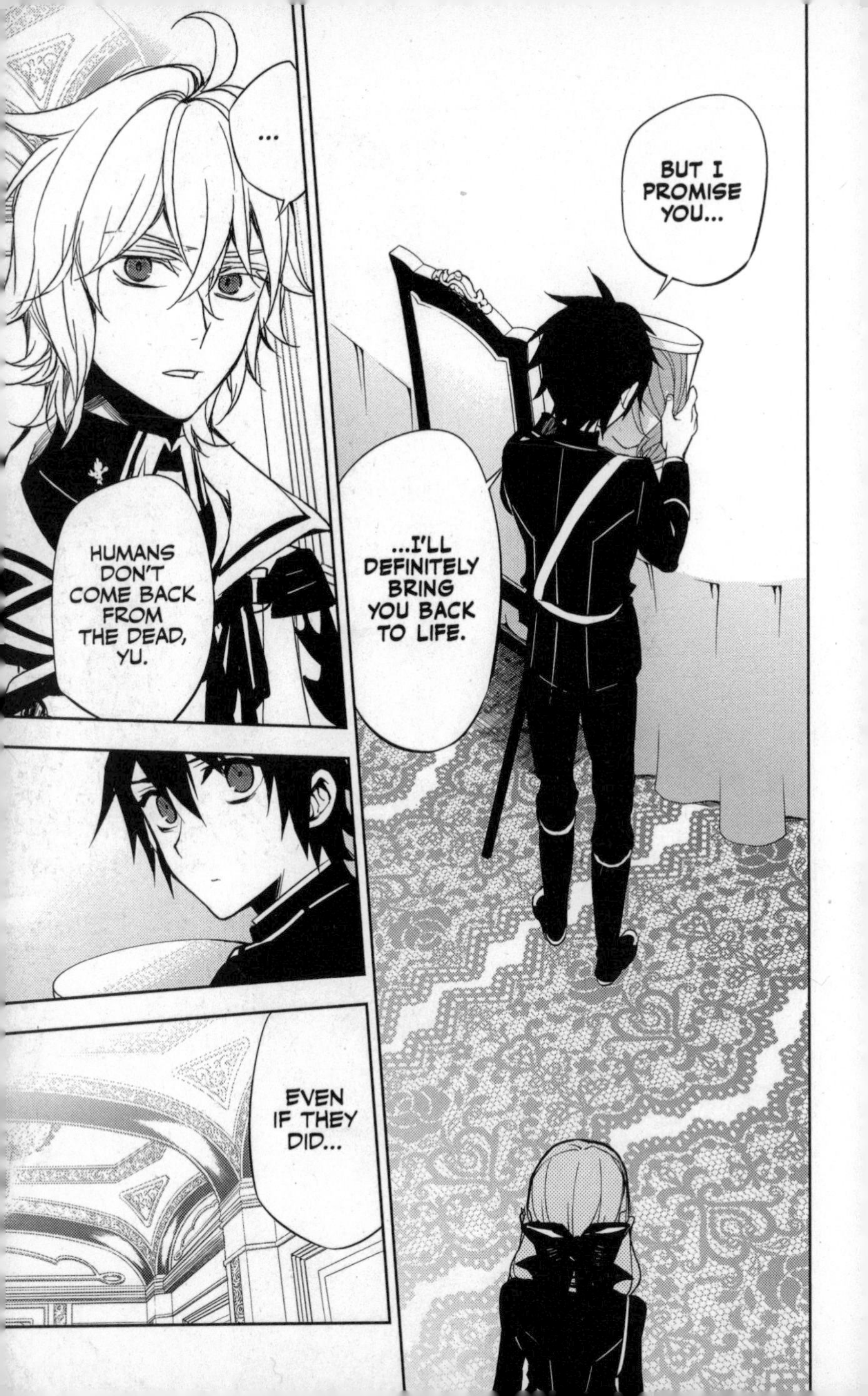
BUT I PROMISE YOU...
...I'LL DEFINITELY BRING YOU BACK TO LIFE.
...
HUMANS DON'T COME BACK FROM THE DEAD, YU.
EVEN IF THEY DID...

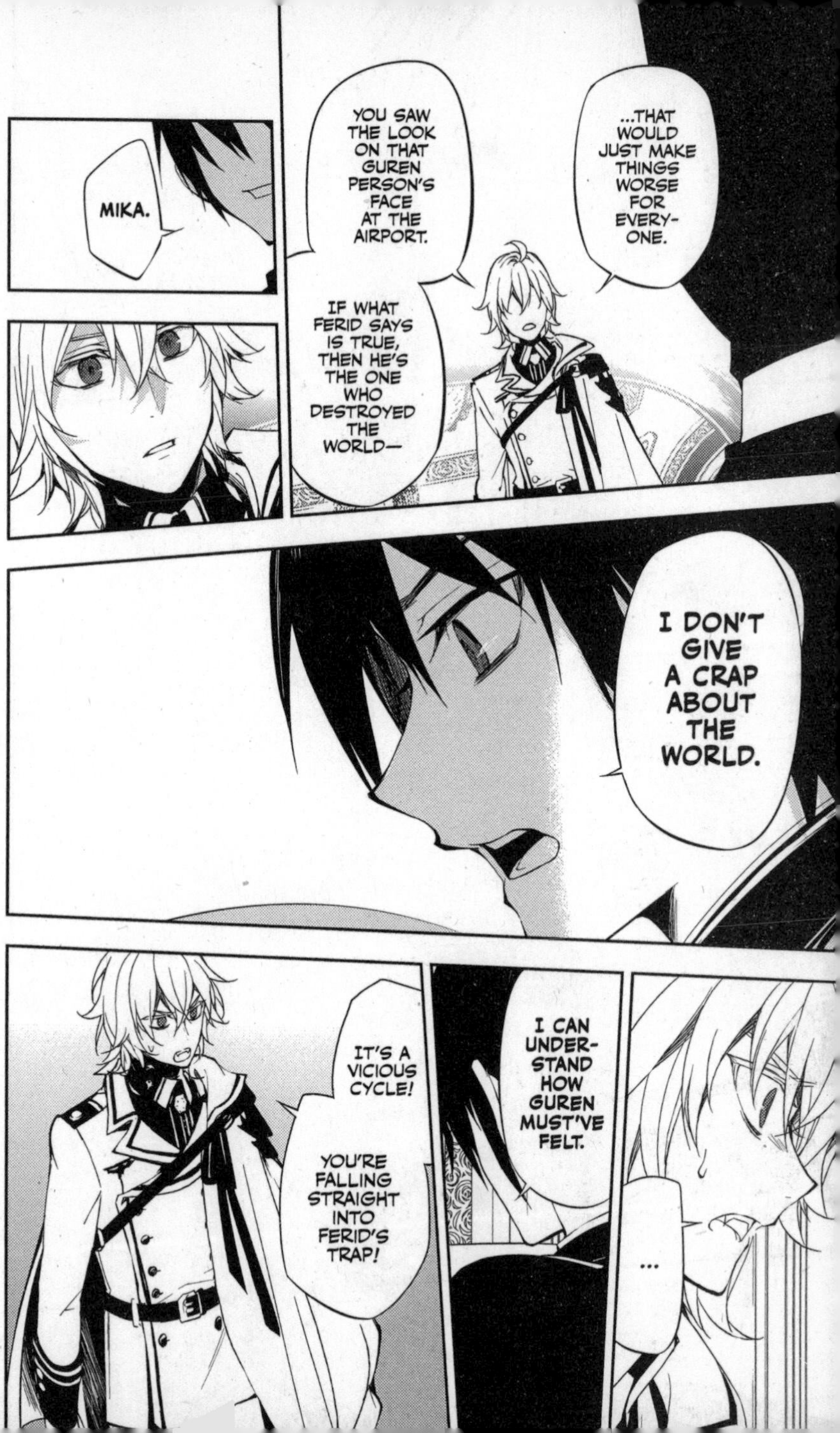

...THAT WOULD JUST MAKE THINGS WORSE FOR EVERY-ONE.
YOU SAW THE LOOK ON THAT GUREN PERSON'S FACE AT THE AIRPORT.
IF WHAT FERID SAYS IS TRUE, THEN HE'S THE ONE WHO DESTROYED THE WORLD—
MIKA.
I DON'T GIVE A CRAP ABOUT THE WORLD.
...
I CAN UNDER-STAND HOW GUREN MUST'VE FELT.
IT'S A VICIOUS CYCLE!
YOU'RE FALLING STRAIGHT INTO FERID'S TRAP!

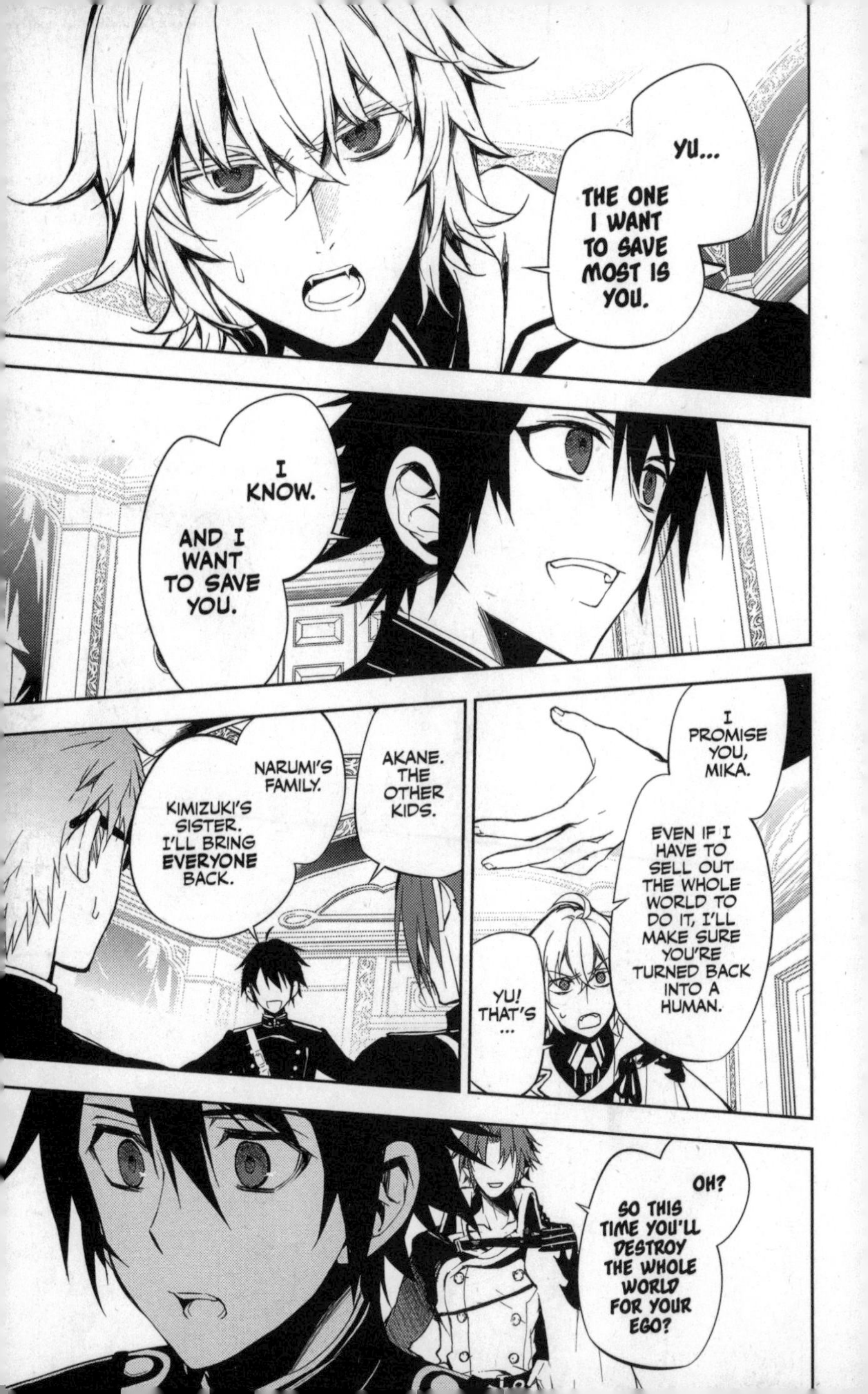
YU...
THE ONE I WANT TO SAVE MOST IS YOU.
I KNOW.
AND I WANT TO SAVE YOU.
I PROMISE YOU, MIKA.
EVEN IF I HAVE TO SELL OUT THE WHOLE WORLD TO DO IT, I'LL MAKE SURE YOU'RE TURNED BACK INTO A HUMAN.
YU! THAT'S ...
AKANE. THE OTHER KIDS.
NARUMI'S FAMILY.
KIMIZUKI'S SISTER. I'LL BRING EVERYONE BACK.
OH?
SO THIS TIME YOU'LL DESTROY THE WHOLE WORLD FOR YOUR EGO?

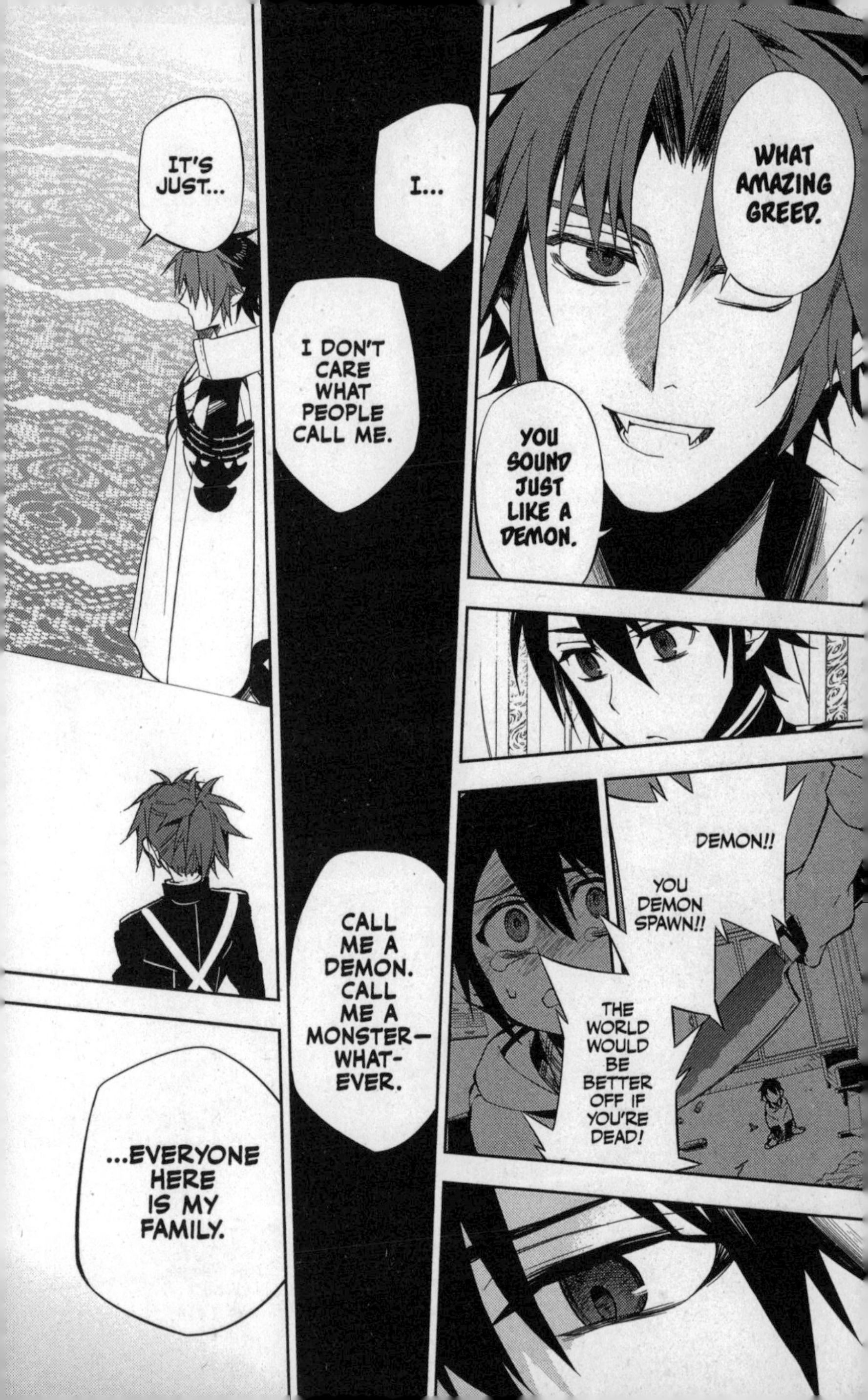
WHAT AMAZING GREED.
YOU SOUND JUST LIKE A DEMON.
DEMON!!
YOU DEMON SPAWN!!
THE WORLD WOULD BE BETTER OFF IF YOU'RE DEAD!
I...
I DON'T CARE WHAT PEOPLE CALL ME.
CALL ME A DEMON. CALL ME A MONSTER—WHATEVER.
IT'S JUST...
...EVERYONE HERE IS MY FAMILY.

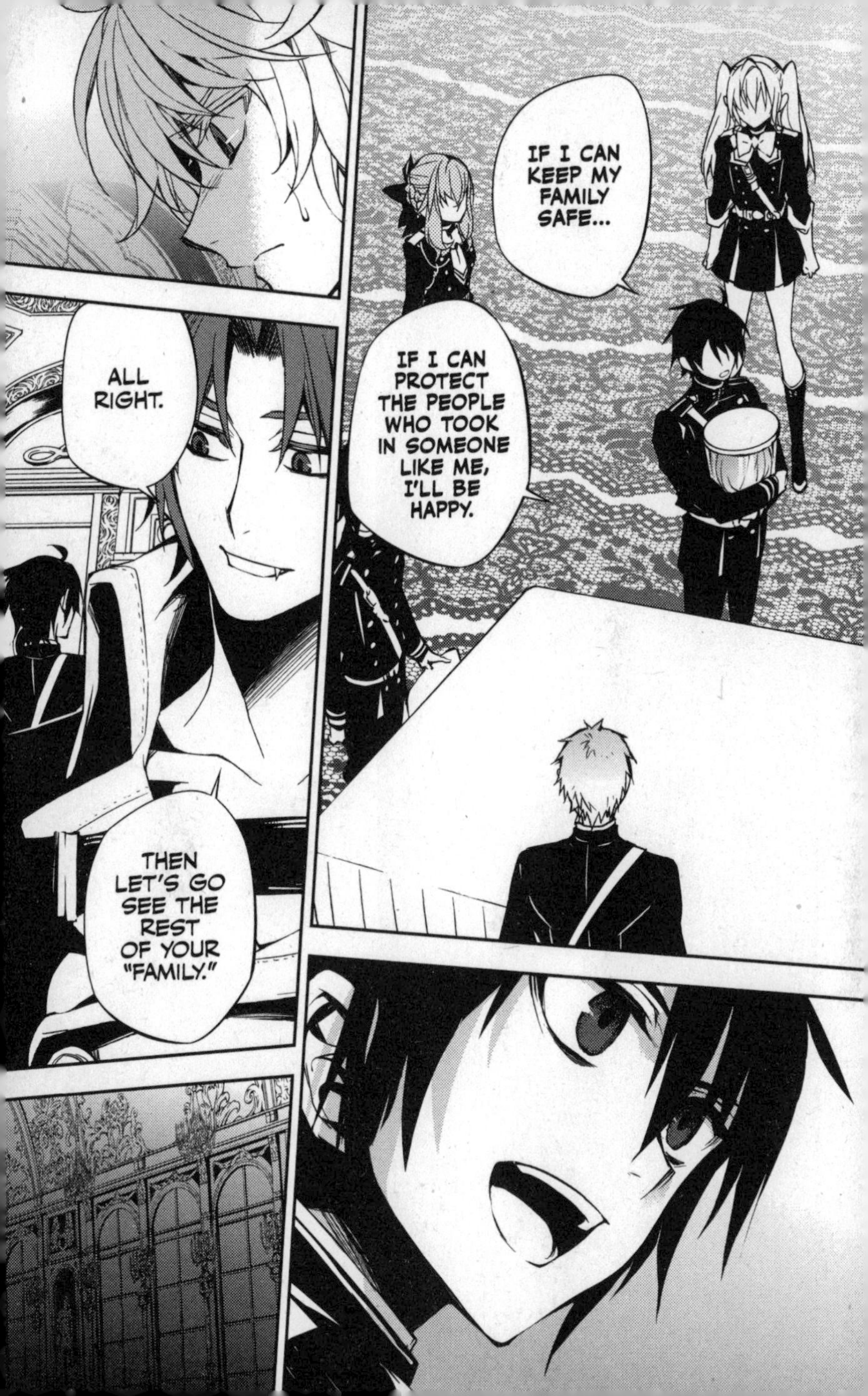
IF I CAN KEEP MY FAMILY SAFE...
IF I CAN PROTECT THE PEOPLE WHO TOOK IN SOMEONE LIKE ME, I'LL BE HAPPY.
ALL RIGHT.
THEN LET'S GO SEE THE REST OF YOUR "FAMILY."

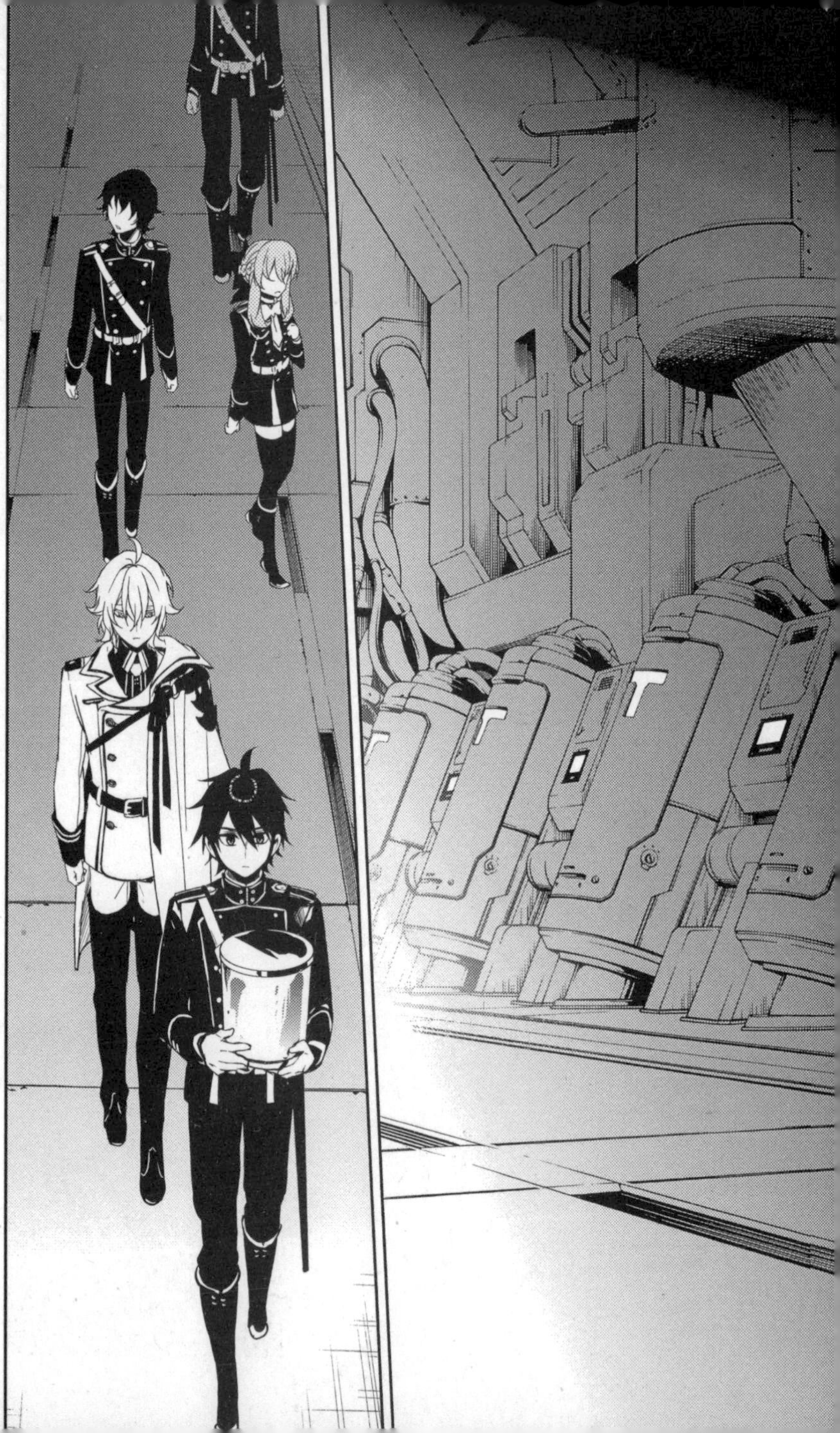

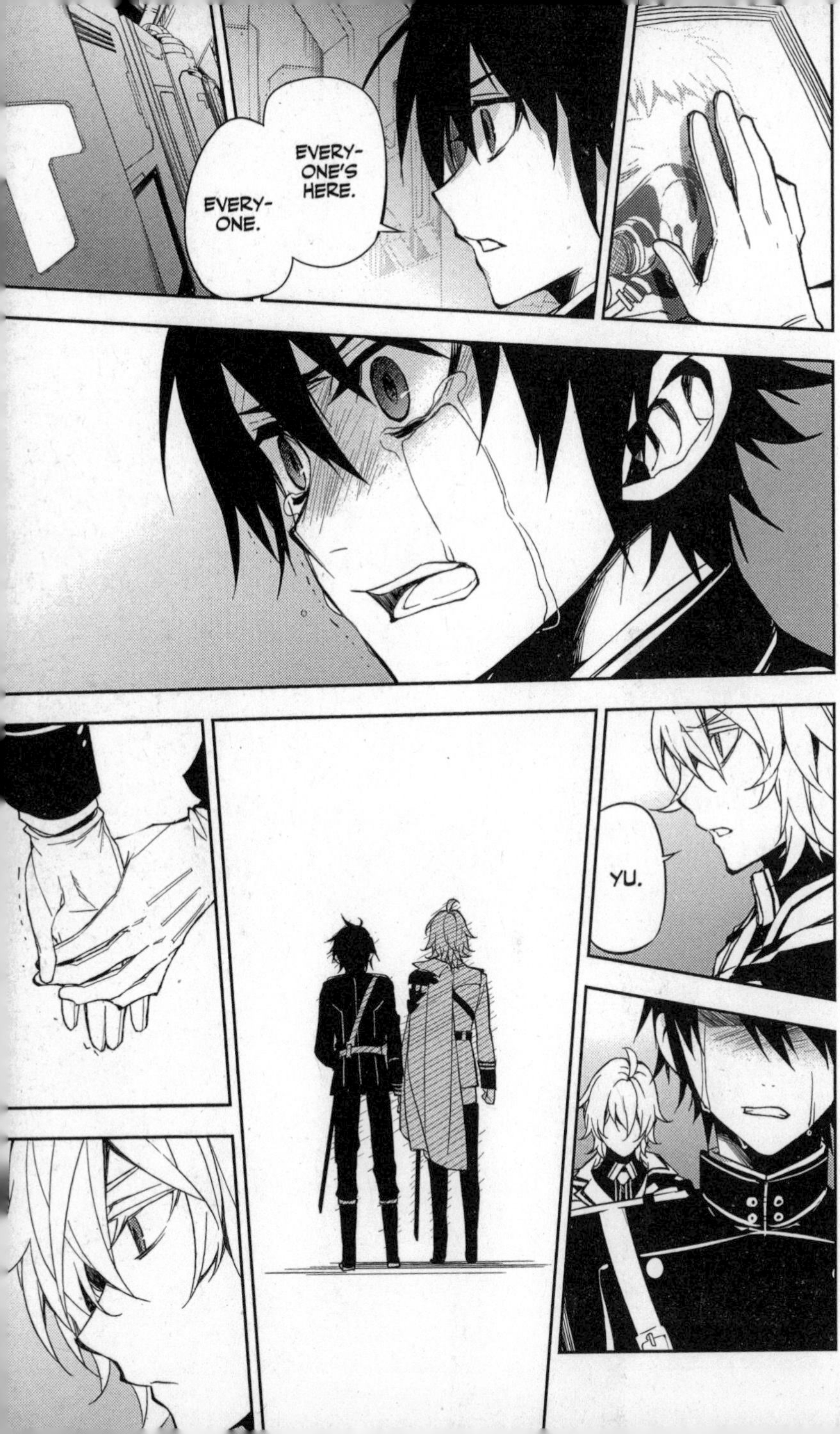
EVERY-ONE'S HERE.
EVERY-ONE.
YU.

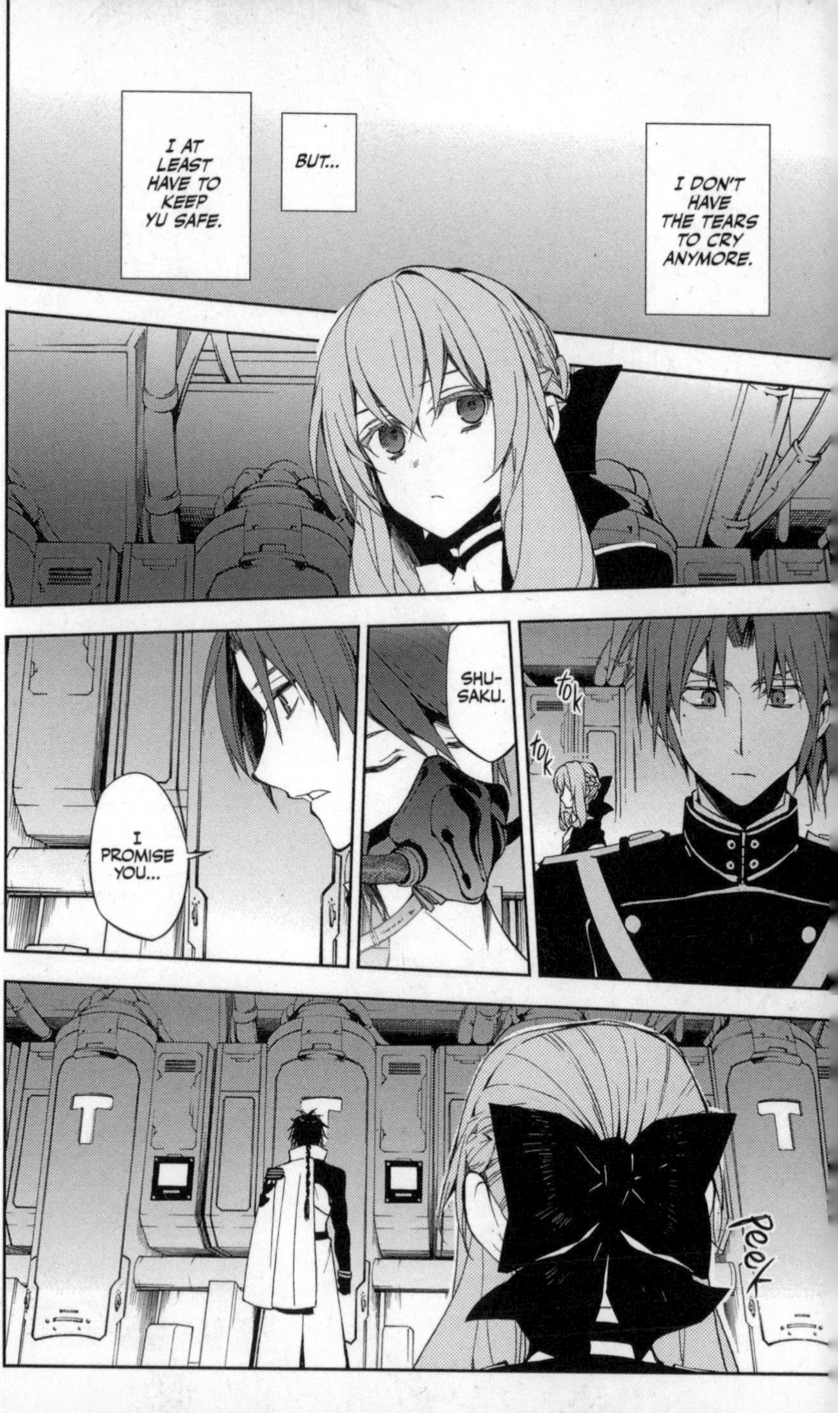
I DON'T HAVE THE TEARS TO CRY ANYMORE.
BUT...
I AT LEAST HAVE TO KEEP YU SAFE.
TOK
TOK
SHU-SAKU.
I PROMISE YOU...
PEEK

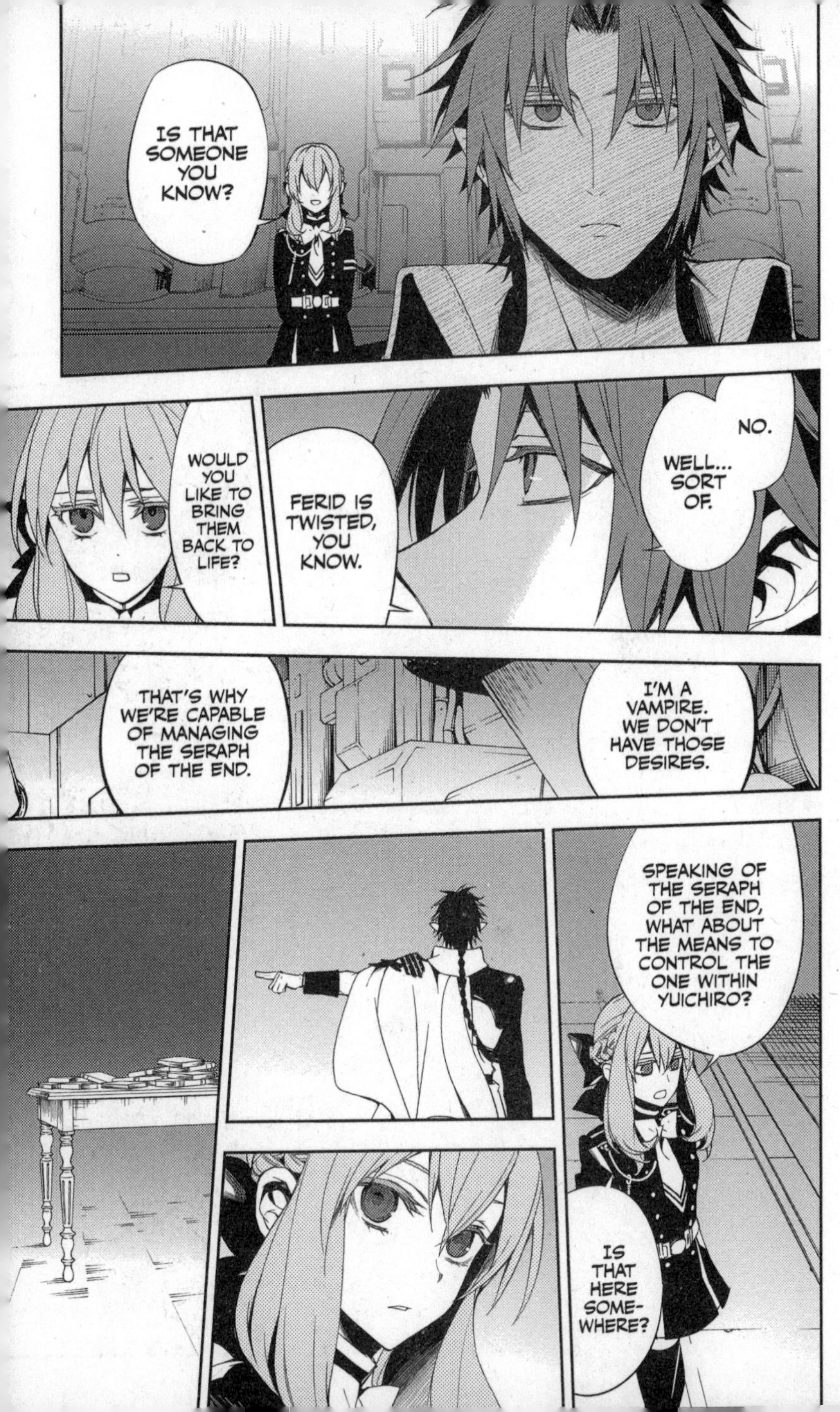
IS THAT SOMEONE YOU KNOW?
NO.
WELL... SORT OF.
FERID IS TWISTED, YOU KNOW.
WOULD YOU LIKE TO BRING THEM BACK TO LIFE?
I'M A VAMPIRE. WE DON'T HAVE THOSE DESIRES.
THAT'S WHY WE'RE CAPABLE OF MANAGING THE SERAPH OF THE END.
SPEAKING OF THE SERAPH OF THE END, WHAT ABOUT THE MEANS TO CONTROL THE ONE WITHIN YUICHIRO?
IS THAT HERE SOME-WHERE?

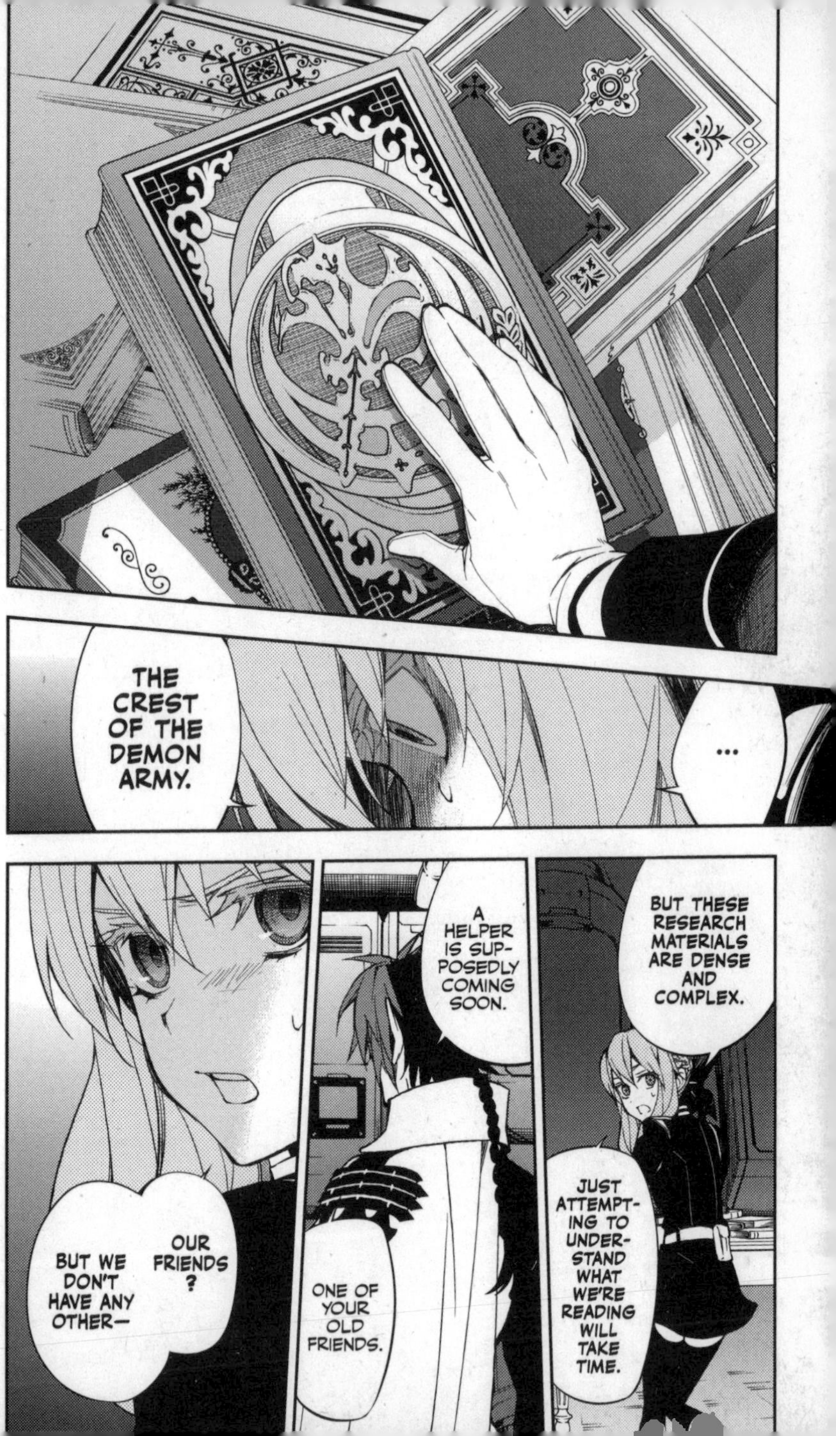
...
THE CREST OF THE DEMON ARMY.
BUT THESE RESEARCH MATERIALS ARE DENSE AND COMPLEX.
JUST ATTEMPTING TO UNDERSTAND WHAT WE'RE READING WILL TAKE TIME.
A HELPER IS SUPPOSEDLY COMING SOON.
ONE OF YOUR OLD FRIENDS.
OUR FRIENDS?
BUT WE DON'T HAVE ANY OTHER—

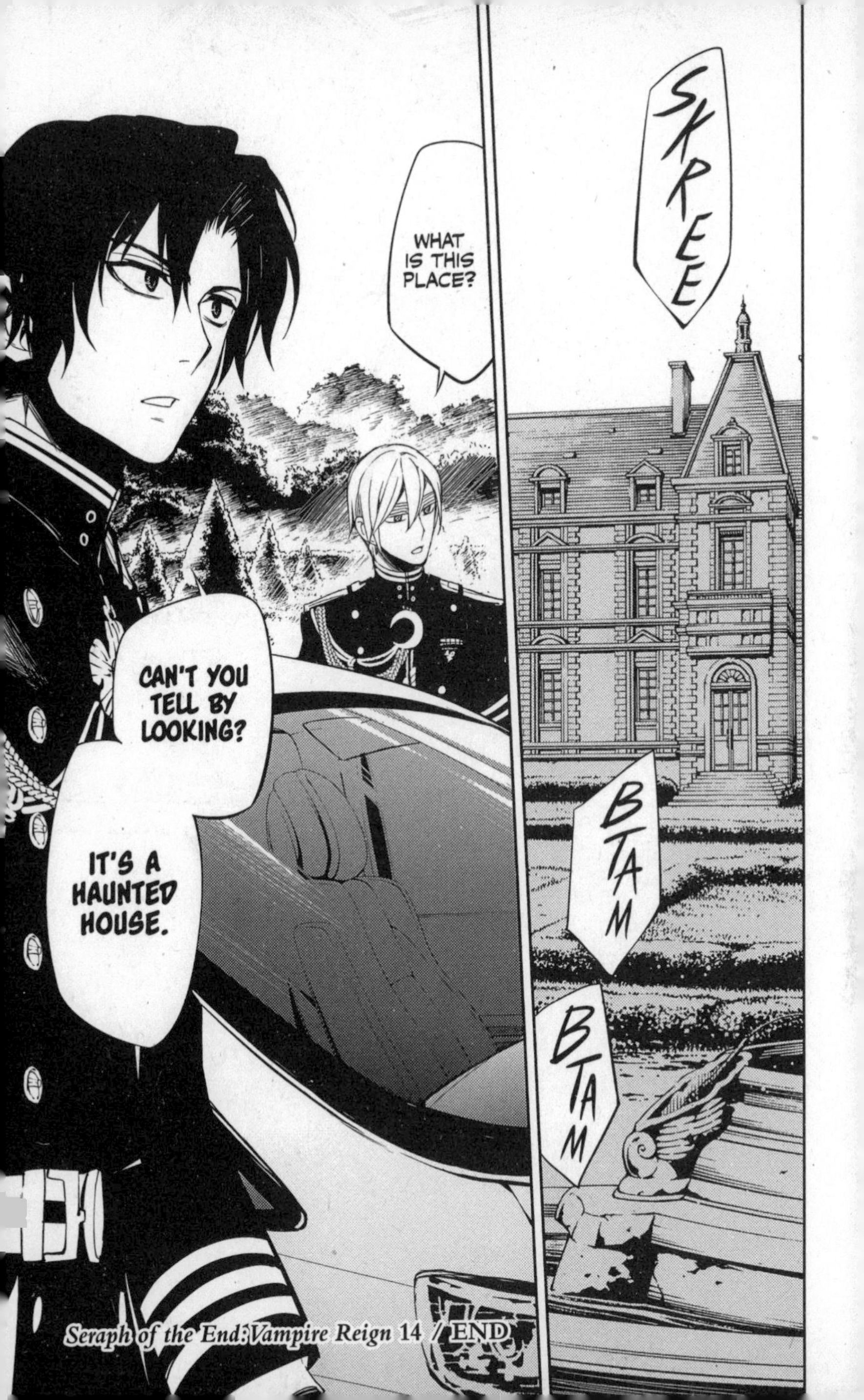
SKREE
BTAM
BTAM
WHAT IS THIS PLACE?
CAN'T YOU TELL BY LOOKING?
IT'S A HAUNTED HOUSE.

Seraph of the End: Vampire Reign 14 / END

Seraph of the End
—VAMPIRE REIGN—

MITO JUJO and NORITO GOSHI

THE JUJO AND GOSHI FAMILIES WERE ONCE TWO OF THE FIVE GREATEST RETAINER FAMILIES WITHIN THE DEMON SECT. BOTH MITO AND GOSHI ARE ELITES WHO WERE RAISED TO SOMEDAY LEAD THEIR FAMILIES. BOTH HAD DETERMINED TO LIVE UP TO THEIR FAMILIES' REPUTATIONS, BUT IN THEIR FIRST YEAR OF HIGH SCHOOL THEY WOUND UP IN THE SAME CLASS AS GUREN ICHINOSE. THEY BECAME FRIENDS AND NOW, EVEN AFTER THE CATASTROPHE, THEY ARE STILL A TEAM.

AS A SIDE NOTE, BEFORE THE CATASTROPHE, MITO CONFESSED HER LOVE TO GUREN AND WAS REJECTED. HOWEVER, EVEN NOW SHE MAY STILL HAVE FEELINGS FOR HIM... OR SHE MAY NOT.

Character Materials Collection and Afterword by Takaya Kagami

---

MITO: "..."

GOSHI: "..."

MITO: "WHAT ARE YOU STARING AT?"

GOSHI: "OH, NOTHING. I WAS JUST, Y'KNOW, WONDERING HOW YOU REACTED TO THAT 'CONFESSED HER LOVE TO GUREN AND WAS REJECTED' SENTENCE UP ABOVE."

MITO: "WHY WOULD THAT BOTHER ME? IT WAS A LONG TIME AGO."

GOSHI: "YEAH, BUT Y'KNOW? WE'RE BOTH 24 NOW, RIGHT? THE PERFECT AGE FOR MARRIAGE, RIGHT? AND YOU KNOW HOW THEY'RE ALL ABOUT HAVING KIDS AND MORE KIDS FOR HUMANITY TO SURVIVE, RIGHT?"

MITO: "AND?"

GOSHI: "REMIND ME...HAVE YOU EVER HAD A BOYFRIEND? LIKE...EVER?"

MITO: "WHY WOULD I BE REQUIRED TO TELL YOU THAT, GOSHI?"

GOSHI: "WELL, WE'RE FRIENDS, RIGHT?"

MITO: "AND THAT'S HOW I KNOW YOU ARE JUST GOING TO SMIRK AND LAUGH AT ME OVER IT."

GOSHI: "WHAT? NO! I'M *CONCERNED* FOR YOU. REALLY. I MEAN IT."

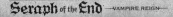

Seraph of the End —VAMPIRE REIGN—

MITO: "..."

GOSHI: "SAY, UH... DO YOU STILL HAVE A THING FOR GUREN? EVEN THOUGH HE, Y'KNOW...REJECTED YOU."

MITO: "SO WHAT IF I DO? IT'S NOT LIKE YOU'RE ALL THAT OR INTERESTING."

GOSHI: "HEY! I'M TOTALLY COOL! AND THERE'S ALSO EVERYONE'S FAVORITE, THE ALWAYS-SUPER-POPULAR-WITH-EVERYONE LORD SHINYA."

MITO: "HE ISN'T COOL EITHER."

GOSHI: "UH-HUH. SO IS GUREN REALLY THAT IMPRESSIVELY AWESOME AND COOL THEN?"

MITO: "NOT...REALLY."

GOSHI: "THEN WHAT THE HECK?!"

MITO: "IT'S JUST HE ALWAYS SEEMS LIKE HE'S TIRED AND...HURTING."

GOSHI: "SO YOU WANNA DO WHAT YOU CAN TO HELP HIM?"

MITO: "YEAH."

GOSHI: "YOU WON'T GET HIM TO FALL FOR YOU THOUGH. THAT'S JUST NOT GONNA HAPPEN."

MITO: "I KNOW..."

GOSHI: "SHEESH. YOU SURE CAN BE DUMB SOMETIMES, Y'KNOW THAT? NO MATTER HOW HARD YOU TRY, YOU'LL ONLY EVER BE A CONVENIENT FRIEND TO HIM."

MITO: "..."

GOSHI: "C'MON. DON'T GIVE ME THAT TEARY LOOK. I MEAN, I TOTALLY UNDER-STAND WHERE YOU'RE COMING FROM. I FEEL THE SAME WAY—I WANNA DO EVERYTHING I CAN TO HELP HIM TOO."

MITO: "YOU KNOW...WHEN IT COMES DOWN TO IT, YOU'RE ALWAYS SO NICE, GOSHI."

GOSHI: "WELL, YEAH. THAT'S BECAUSE I LOVE YOU, MITO."

MITO: "AND WHAT IS THAT SUPPOSED TO MEAN?"

GOSHI: "JUST LIKE I LOVE *ALL* OF HUMANITY. IT'S THAT UNCONDITIONAL STUFF, Y'KNOW?"

MITO: "AHA HA HA...! OH, YOU..."

GOSHI: "OH ME WHAT?"

MITO: "THANKS."

GOSHI: "ANYWAYS! DID YOU HEAR?"

SHINYA: "YEP! I HAVE."

MITO: "EXCUSE ME. WOULD SOMEONE MIND EXPLAINING THIS FOR ME ALREADY?"

SHINYA: "SUPPOSEDLY THIS IS SOMETHING SO INCREDIBLE IT VERGES ON THE IMPOSSIBLE, BUT OUR STORY FROM HIGH SCHOOL, *SERAPH OF THE END: GUREN ICHINOSE: CATASTROPHE AT 16*, IS GOING TO GET A MANGA VERSION SERIALIZED IN KODANSHA'S *MONTHLY SHONEN MAGAZINE* ANTHOLOGY IN JAPAN."

GOSHI: "WHAT?! HOLY CRAP!! THAT'S...! WAIT, IS THAT A BIG THING?"

MITO: "WHAT? REALLY? IS IT?"

SHINYA: "LET'S GET A COMMENT FROM THE MAN HIMSELF—GUREN! A WORD ON THIS DEVELOPMENT, PLEASE..."

GUREN: "NEXT, WE AIM FOR SHOGAKUKAN!"

EVERYONE: "THAT WILL NEVER HAPPEN!!"

AFTERWORD

MITO, GOSHI AND THE OTHERS
MENTIONED IT IN THEIR DISCUS-
SION, BUT STARTING IN THE JULY
2017 ISSUE OF *MONTHLY SHONEN
MAGAZINE* (ON SALE JUNE 6, 2017
IN JAPAN) A MANGA VERSION OF
*SERAPH OF THE END: GUREN ICHI-
NOSE: CATASTROPHE AT 16* WILL
BEGIN SERIALIZATION. THAT'S...
PRETTY AMAZING. I MEAN, NOW
TWO OF THE BIGGEST MONTHLY
SHONEN ANTHOLOGIES ARE RUN-
NING *SERAPH OF THE END!* I HOPE
YOU ALL WILL ENJOY IT! I THINK
EVEN PEOPLE WHO HAVE ALREADY
READ THE NOVEL VERSION OF
THE STORY WILL FIND SOME
SURPRISING THINGS IN THE
MANGA VERSION.

AND NOW, SHIFTING TOPICS OVER
TO THE MAIN STORYLINE...

ALL THE DISPARATE STORY THREADS
ARE STARTING TO TIE TOGETHER
NOW THAT THINGS ARE MOVING
TOWARD THE CLIMAX. STARTING
NEXT VOLUME, WHAT'S TRULY BEEN
GOING ON BEHIND THE SCENES
SHOULD START GETTING CLEARER.
THE REVELATIONS ARE GOING TO
START COMING AT A BREAKNECK
PACE, SO I HOPE YOU WILL ALL
STICK AROUND. BY THE WAY, I AM
WRITING THIS AFTERWORD ON BIG
BROTHER KURETO'S BIRTHDAY!

ANYWAY, *SERAPH OF THE END*
IS ABOUT TO GET EVEN MORE
EXCITING! I HOPE YOU'LL ALL
ENJOY IT!

—TAKAYA KAGAMI

A brilliant sketch of Yuichiro by the author!

TAKAYA KAGAMI is a prolific light novelist whose works include the action and fantasy series *The Legend of the Legendary Heroes*, which has been adapted into manga, anime and a video game. His previous series, *A Dark Rabbit Has Seven Lives*, also spawned a manga and anime series.

❝ Two of the biggest monthly shonen manga anthologies out there— *Jump SQ* and *Monthly Shonen Magazine*—now have *Seraph of the End* in them. I am in awe. Man, strange and unexpected things really can happen in life. This is so exciting! ❞

YAMATO YAMAMOTO, born 1983, is an artist and illustrator whose works include the *Kure-nai* manga and the light novels *Kure-nai*, *9S -Nine S-* and *Denpa Teki na Kanojo*. Both *Denpa Teki na Kanojo* and *Kure-nai* have been adapted into anime.

❝ Rescuing Ferid will be extraordinarily difficult. What will happen next? Expect exciting things. ❞

DAISUKE FURUYA previously assisted Yamato Yamamoto with storyboards for *Kure-nai*.

Seraph of the End
VAMPIRE REIGN

VOLUME 14
SHONEN JUMP ADVANCED MANGA EDITION

STORY BY **TAKAYA KAGAMI**

ART BY **YAMATO YAMAMOTO**

STORYBOARDS BY **DAISUKE FURUYA**

TRANSLATION **Adrienne Beck**
TOUCH-UP ART & LETTERING **Sabrina Heep**
DESIGN **Shawn Carrico**
EDITOR **Marlene First**

OWARI NO SERAPH © 2012 by Takaya Kagami,
Yamato Yamamoto, Daisuke Furuya
All rights reserved. First published in Japan in 2012 by SHUEISHA Inc., Tokyo.
English translation rights arranged by SHUEISHA Inc.

Printed in the U.S.A.

Published by VIZ Media, LLC
P.O. Box 77010
San Francisco, CA 94107

10 9 8 7 6 5 4 3 2 1
First printing, April 2018

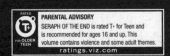

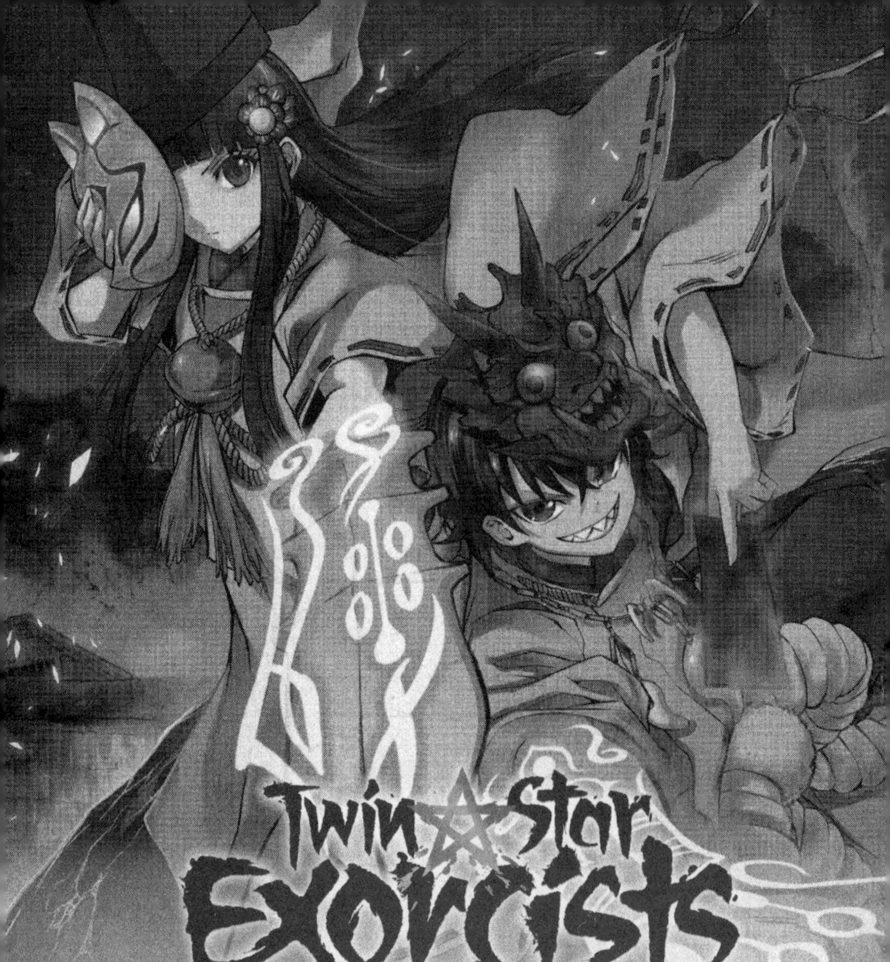
Twin Star
Exorcists
ONMYOJI

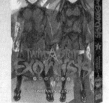

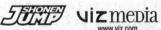

YOU'RE READING THE
WRONG WAY!

SERAPH OF THE END
reads from right to left,
starting in the upper-right
corner. Japanese is read
from right to left, meaning
that action, sound effects,
and word-balloon order are
completely reversed from
English order.

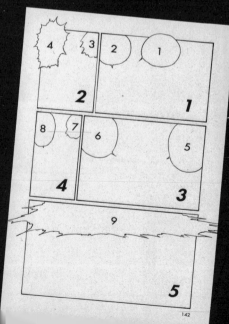

142